THE

CIVIL WAR ERA

VOLUME ONE

A HOUSE DIVIDED

**EDITED BY
HAROLD HOLZER**

**FOREWORD BY
KEN BURNS**

COBBLESTONE PUBLISHING, INC.
7 SCHOOL ST.
PETERBOROUGH, NH 03458

For my daughters, Remy and Meg,
the best examples of family history

Consultant: David Madden, Director, The U.S. Civil War Center
Copyedited by Barbara Jatkola
Design and page layout by C. Porter Designs, Fitzwilliam, New Hampshire
Photo research: Lisa Hill, Melanie Guleserian, Francelle Carapetyan
Interior illustrations by Edith L. Bingham
Printing and binding by D.B. Hess Company

Manufactured in the United States of America
ISBN 0-942389-16-6 (volume 1);
ISBN 0-942389-17-4 (volume 2)

Library of Congress Cataloging-in-Publication Data

The Civil War era / edited by Harold Holzer ; foreword by Ken Burns.
     p.   cm.
    Includes bibliographical references (p.   ) and index.
    Contents: v. 1. A house divided — v. 2. A new nation.
    ISBN 0-942389-16-6 (vol. 1). — ISBN 0-942389-17-4 (vol. 2)
    1. United States—History—Civil War, 1861–1865—Juvenile
literature. 2. United States—History—1849–1877—Juvenile
literature. [1. United States—History—Civil War, 1861–1865.
2. United States—History—1849–1877.] I. Holzer, Harold.
E468.C6244   1996
973.7—dc20
                                 96-26361
                                  CIP
                                  AC

About the Cover
Robert Marshall Root's 1863 painting of the fourth debate between Abraham Lincoln
and Stephen Douglas, which took place on September 18, 1858, in Charleston, Illinois. Courtesy of
the Illinois State Historical Library.

. . . .

PROLOGUE

by Harold Holzer

*By the early nineteenth century,
there were really two different United States of Americas.
One was in the South and the other in the North. Within a
few generations, they were at war with each other.*

The America of the South depended almost totally on agriculture — particularly cotton and tobacco. It relied on a labor force comprising nearly four million human slaves, brought in chains from Africa and then bred here for hard work without pay. By 1860, as many as ten thousand white southerners each owned fifty slaves or more.

The other America, the America of the North, began to turn to manufacturing. More and more people lived in its bustling cities, not just on its farms. New immigrants arrived every week from Europe, bringing new skills and new ideas. Its workers were paid real wages.

Perhaps no one could have prevented these two Americas from one day waging war against each other. As Abraham Lincoln predicted when he ran for the U.S. Senate in 1858, "'A house divided against itself cannot stand.'" The "house" known as the United States was destined to fall.

"Now we are engaged in a great civil war," declared a worried Lincoln, by then president of only half the United States, when he gave his famous address at Gettysburg, Pennsylvania, in 1863. He admitted that he was not even certain that the nation as Americans had known it would "live." But he called for the bloody fight to continue — until America could enjoy "a new birth of freedom."

No war ever fought before or since has cost as many American lives as the Civil War. More than six hundred thousand northerners and southerners died from wounds or disease. And no war more completely changed the country for those men, women, and children who survived.

As one writer put it, before the Civil War people said, "The United States *are*." After the Civil War, people said, "The United States *is*." The war finally made America into one country. The two volumes that make up this set explain how this came to be. They explore every aspect of that terrible but fascinating time in U.S. history — a time that first split America in two, then brought it closer together as one.

Volume 1, "A House Divided," offers a picture of the young country created in the name of freedom — but only for some. Here is a land of opportunity for whites but a land of oppression for African Americans. This volume examines the issues that divided America and the leaders who came forward to speak for both the North and the South.

Volume 2, "A New Nation," recalls the bloodiest conflict our nation ever fought. Here are famous generals and ordinary soldiers alike — the warriors and writers, the politicians and people. Here is death on the battlefield and life on the home front. Here are two peoples fighting for the right to plan America's future, each side convinced that its cause is just. And here is a badly wounded nation, trying to put itself together again.

In the powerful words of Oliver Wendell Holmes, Jr., a young soldier who survived several battles and went on to become a justice of the U.S. Supreme Court, the Civil War was a time when all America was "touched with fire." This is the story of how that fire began, how it burned out of control, and how it was finally extinguished. It is the story of how we lived and died to become what we are today.

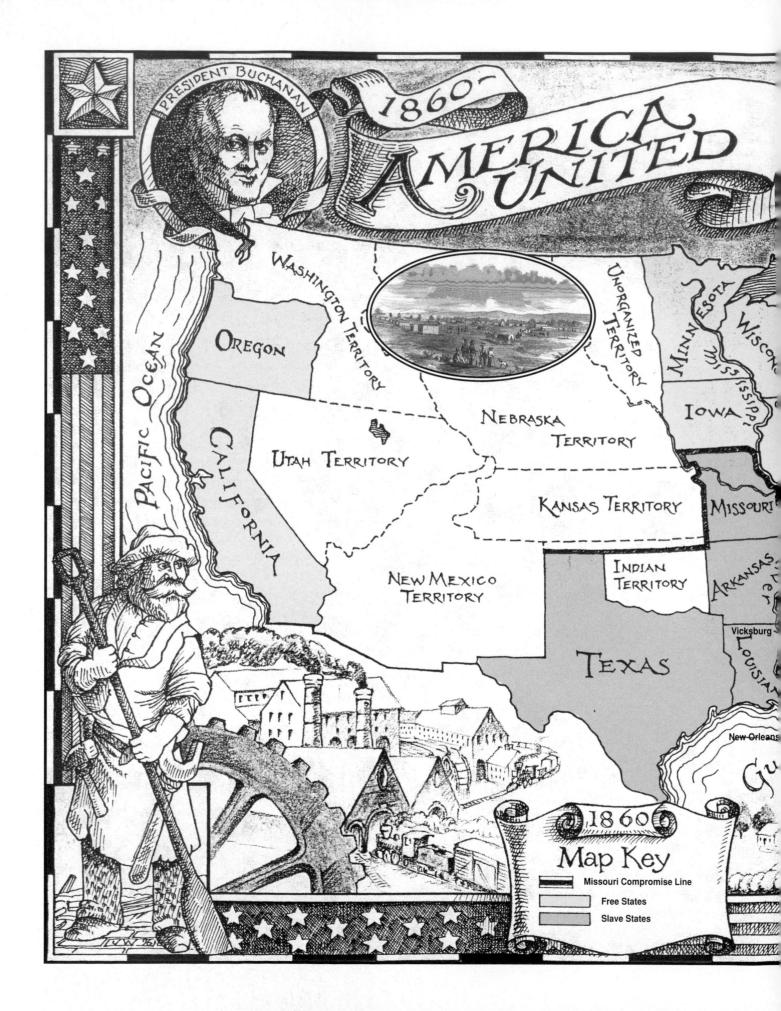

PRESIDENT BUCHANAN

1860

AMERICA UNITED

WASHINGTON TERRITORY

OREGON

PACIFIC OCEAN

CALIFORNIA

UTAH TERRITORY

NEW MEXICO TERRITORY

UNORGANIZED TERRITORY

NEBRASKA TERRITORY

KANSAS TERRITORY

INDIAN TERRITORY

TEXAS

MINNESOTA

WISCONSIN

MISSISSIPPI

IOWA

MISSOURI

ARKANSAS

Arkansas River

Vicksburg

LOUISIANA

New Orleans

Gu

1860

Map Key

Missouri Compromise Line

Free States

Slave States

The United States Before the War

map by Jack Williams

CONTENTS

Foreword

by Ken Burns

We Americans tend to ignore our past.

Perhaps we fear having one and burn it behind us like rocket fuel, always looking forward. And that's a bad thing. The consequences are not just ignorance or stupidity or even repeating. Ignoring our past represents the deepest kind of inattention, and it becomes a tear or gap in who we are.

I think that in each of my films, I have been seized or possessed by one aspect of American history: something that speaks of the aspirations and struggles and motives of people, something that goes to the heart of who we have been to become who we are. And I think that with each film, each story I have struggled with, my sense has sharpened that a thread runs through all the stories, connecting them one to the other.

That thread is the essential American one: the struggle for human freedom. In the Civil War, the issue of human freedom came for this country, for our people, to the most profound and tragic crux. Historian Shelby Foote has called it the crossroads of our being, but somehow when we crossed over, we forgot where we had been: slavery. I think of what James Symington, a former congressman, said in an interview for our film on the Civil War. Slavery, he said, was merely the horrible statutory expression of a deeper rift between peoples based on race, and this rift is what we struggle still

to erase from the hearts and minds of people.

That rift stands at the very center of American history — and at the very center of this book. It is the great challenge to which all our deepest aspirations toward freedom must rise. If we forget that, if we forget the great stain of slavery that stands at the heart of our history, we forget who we are, and we make the rift deeper and wider. And that is what forgetting is: making the human rift wider.

There is a profound connection between remembering and freedom and human attachment. That is what history is to me. Forgetting is the opposite of all that: It is a kind of slavery and the worst kind of human detachment.

Which is why we must remember, even when what memory has to tell us is appalling. It has seemed to me that the meaning of our freedom as Americans is the freedom of memory, which is also a kind of obligation. We must remember that our country was born under the sign that all men are created equal, but we must also remember that that declaration did not include African Americans or women or the poor. We must remember that Abraham Lincoln signed the Emancipation Proclamation, but we must also remember that Lincoln thought of recolonizing African Americans to Panama or Africa as late as April 1861, as the guns opened up at Fort Sumter. We must remember that the Thirteenth and Fourteenth amendments to the U.S. Constitution secured some kind of equality before the law for African Americans. But we must also remember that equality as a human fact did not come at once, has still not come, and if we do not believe that,

...we forget.

"A house divided against itself cannot stand."
I believe this government cannot endure,
permanently half *slave* and half *free*.

Abraham Lincoln, June 16, 1858

INTRODUCTION

by Harold Holzer

The very first African slaves brought to America probably arrived on a Dutch ship in 1619. No white people objected. Few paid attention. And thousands more slaves soon followed. Not for another seventy years or so did the Quakers of New England denounce the idea of slavery and suggest that it be made illegal in the American Colonies. By then, it was already too late. Slavery had taken firm hold in the New World. A debate over whether it was right or wrong, good or bad, would rage for the next two centuries before erupting into war.

Slavery grew rapidly in the Colonies. Slave ships arrived crowded with captured Africans. Slave markets flourished. And, using the strength of slave labor, many southern farms grew into vast plantations. By the time of the American Revolution (1776–1781), one-fifth of all the people living in the Colonies were slaves. In the South, two-fifths were slaves.

The Founding Fathers even included slavery in their otherwise noble Constitution, written in 1787. By then, however, some northern states had begun to outlaw slavery. Vermont had acted first, in 1777. By the early 1800s, slavery had ceased to exist anywhere in the North. It had become limited to one section of the country — the South. There, as one southerner put it, "Cotton is King!" The region's economy depended entirely on cotton, and cotton depended entirely on slave labor.

Many northerners argued that slavery should not be allowed at all in a country founded on the promise that "all men are created equal." Most southerners replied that African Americans were savages who could not be allowed to live free among whites. Some slave owners actually believed that they were providing African Americans a better life by keeping them in chains.

To make matters more complicated, America began expanding. Pioneers were settling the West. New states were seeking to join the original thirteen Colonies. Americans divided bitterly over the question of whether slavery should be allowed to exist in these new lands. That is when slavery first became a heated political issue that threatened to destroy America.

When Missouri Territory requested statehood in 1818, America's leaders began to argue in earnest about slavery. Few people cared much about the slaves themselves. Most northerners worried that if new slave states joined the Union, they would elect new senators and congressmen who would tip the balance of federal power to the South. Southerners wanted very much to add those new senators and congressmen so that they could be certain that the government would protect slavery forever.

The existing Congress decided to postpone a showdown. In 1820, it passed the Missouri Compromise, which allowed Missouri to come into the Union as a slave state but also added Maine as a free state. Neither section would gain in power. The law also drew a dividing line to split the American continent at latitude 36°30´. Below it, slavery would be allowed to flourish. Above it, slavery would be permanently banned.

For more than thirty years, the Missouri Compromise held the nation together in an uneasy peace. Another compromise in 1850 kept a lid on the growing storm, but not for long.

A new generation of northerners deeply opposed to slavery for moral and religious reasons began speaking out for freedom. They were called abolitionists because they demanded that slavery be abolished immediately. Their rise frightened many Americans. In Illinois, a northern state, one editor who urged abolition was murdered and his printing press thrown in the river. Tensions grew.

The storm finally hit in 1854, when Congress passed the Kansas-Nebraska Act. Like the Missouri Compromise years before, it allowed the admission of two new states. But the new law overturned the Missouri Compromise by allowing slavery to move north of the 36°30′ mark for the first time since 1820. The old law that had prevented bloodshed for so long was suddenly thrown away.

Quickly, Kansas erupted. Abolitionists killed slave owners, and slave owners killed abolitionists. The U.S. Supreme Court entered the growing debate when it ruled in the Dred Scott case that African Americans were no better than property anywhere in the nation. The decision cheered the South and outraged the North. Violent emotions even reached the U.S. Capitol itself. A southern congressman nearly beat a northern senator to death with a heavy cane right in the Senate's own chamber.

In 1858, a former Illinois congressman named Abraham Lincoln returned to politics after a nearly ten-year absence, worried that the evil of slavery would be allowed to spread into the territories of the West. Lincoln was chosen by the new Republican party to run for the U.S. Senate against Democratic senator Stephen A. Douglas. Douglas was the author of the Kansas-Nebraska Act so hated by Lincoln and his followers. Lincoln opposed the expansion of slavery. Douglas insisted that no matter where they lived, North or South, citizens of every new territory had the right to vote yes or no on slavery.

Accepting his nomination, Lincoln gave his famous "House Divided" address. "I believe this government cannot endure, permanently half *slave* and half *free*," Lincoln thundered. "...It will become *all* one thing, or *all* the other."

Lincoln went on to challenge Douglas to a series of debates throughout their state. It was the first time candidates for such a high office agreed to argue their beliefs in public. Tens of thousands of Illinois citizens witnessed the debaters' furious arguments over slavery, and hundreds of thousands more followed the debates in newspapers. "The prairies are on fire," wrote one alarmed eastern newspaperman. Douglas went on to win the election, but the debates focused the nation's attention on the increasingly bitter slavery issue.

Just two years later, Lincoln found himself facing Douglas once again — this time for the presidency. Lincoln defeated his old rival in one of the most bitter campaigns in American history. Even before Lincoln reached Washington for his inauguration, seven southern states declared that they could no longer remain part of the Union. The crisis was finally at hand.

At the center of the storm was Lincoln. Although he pledged that he would not touch slavery where it already existed, the frightened South refused to believe him. After he took the oath of office, four more states seceded from the Union. All eleven then formed a government of their own — the Confederate States of America — and demanded their independence from the United States.

Lincoln could have let the South go, but he believed that unhappy voters had no right to break up the country just because they had lost an election. To do so, he argued, would mean the death of democracy itself. And if democracy failed here, he warned, it would never take root anywhere. America had a responsibility to remain a shining example to the rest of the world.

Southerners were just as convinced that they were striking a blow for liberty. They had every right, they argued, to quit a country that threatened their rights and property. They claimed that their cause was every bit as noble as that of the patriots who rose up against the British in the 1770s.

Still left completely out of the argument were the rights of African Americans. They had suffered two hundred fifty years of slavery. They had no rights of any kind. In the South, slaves were still forbidden to learn to read or write. Slave marriages were outlawed, and slave children could be separated from their families. Even in most states where African Americans were free, they could not vote or serve on juries. One northern state had actually voted that free African Americans were no longer allowed inside its borders. Race prejudice had poisoned the American dream.

Some historians argue that America broke apart for many reasons in 1860, not just because of slavery. They insist that northern and southern cultures became so different economically and socially that the sections could no longer live together in peace. The truth is that North and South had grown apart because of slavery. It was the main cause — perhaps even the only cause — of secession and war.

But Lincoln refused at first to embrace the idea that the breakup of the Union gave him the right to destroy slavery. If war came, he insisted, it would be waged to save the old Union as it was. Lincoln could not yet afford to offend the slave-holding border states that remained loyal to his government. Only later did he dare raise the notion that the war could bring, as he put it, both "freedom to the free" and "freedom to the slave." First Lincoln determined to fight to restore the nation.

And so the crisis of the house divided boiled over into open warfare in 1861. Very quickly, the life of each and every American, black and white, male and female, young and old, changed forever. America would never be the same again.

On the following pages, our stories present a picture of a rapidly expanding America, growing richer and more powerful even as the cancer of slavery ate away at the national spirit. How the disease of slavery spread — and then killed the nation as Americans knew it — is just one of the subjects explored in this book. We present a full, fascinating portrait of a young country and its people. Stories explore the lives of whites, African Americans, and Native Americans alike. We hear the voices of people whose words and deeds changed history. And we remember again how our experiment in democracy went wrong.

The Civil War overwhelmed the country, very nearly destroying it. No nation before was ever born with so much hope or came closer to dying more quickly. The following stories help explain how and why. Some are original material I have written especially for this book. A few are reprinted from a series of books by Discovery Enterprises, Ltd. The remaining are reprinted from various Cobblestone publications, especially *COBBLESTONE* magazine.

TIME LINE

HEADING ILLUSTRATION BY JACK WILLIAMS

1619
First African slaves are shipped to the American Colonies.

1700
Twenty thousand Africans a year are sold into slavery.

1776
American independence is declared.

1777
Vermont becomes the first colony to ban slavery.

1787
Founding Fathers draft the Constitution, which officially counts each slave as three-fifths of a human being.

1793
Eli Whitney invents the cotton gin; cotton boom begins.

1808
International slave trade ends.

1820
Missouri Compromise officially divides America in two, allowing slavery in the South but not in the North.

1831
Antislavery leader William Lloyd Garrison starts first abolitionist newspaper, *The Liberator.* In Virginia, slave Nat Turner organizes bloody revolt against local slave owners; he is later captured and executed.

1833
American Anti-Slavery Society is founded.

1841
Escaped slave Frederick Douglass gives speech to the Massachusetts Anti-Slavery Society and becomes leading African American of his age.

1846
Mexican War begins; Americans argue over slavery in newly won land.

1847
Douglass begins the *North Star,* an African American newspaper, in Rochester, New York.

1850
Congress passes the Compromise of 1850, seeking to calm tensions between North and South.

1852
Harriet Beecher Stowe publishes *Uncle Tom's Cabin,* a novel about the evils of slavery; it becomes a bestseller.

1854
Congress passes the Kansas-Nebraska Act, overturning the Missouri Compromise and angering northerners.

1856
Violence erupts in Kansas between proslavery and antislavery groups.

1857
Supreme Court rules in the Dred Scott decision that slaves could never be U.S. citizens and were officially no better than property.

1858
Abraham Lincoln and Stephen Douglas debate slavery throughout Illinois.

1859
John Brown leads a band of followers into Virginia and attacks Harpers Ferry in an effort to free all slaves in the South; he is captured and executed, but his raid infuriates the South.

1860

November 6
Lincoln is elected president of the United States.

December 20
South Carolina secedes from the Union.

1861

January 9
Mississippi secedes.

January 10
Florida secedes.

January 11
Alabama secedes.

January 19
Georgia secedes.

January 26
Louisiana secedes.

February 1
Texas secedes.

February 8
The newly formed Confederate States of America begins drafting a constitution.

February 9
Jefferson Davis is elected president of the Confederate States of America.

February 18
Davis is inaugurated president of the Confederacy at a ceremony in Montgomery, Alabama.

March 4
Lincoln is inaugurated president of the United States in Washington, D.C.

March 6
Davis calls for one hundred thousand troops.

April 12
Secessionists open fire on Fort Sumter in Charleston, South Carolina.

April 14
Fort Sumter is evacuated by federal troops.

April 15
Lincoln calls for seventy-five thousand troops to put down the rebellion.

April 17
Virginia secedes.

April 18
Union abandons arsenal at Harpers Ferry, Virginia, scene of John Brown's raid in 1859.

April 19
Lincoln orders a naval blockade against the Confederate coast.

Mob attacks Massachusetts soldiers as they march through Baltimore, Maryland, en route to defend Washington.

April 20
Robert E. Lee resigns from the U.S. Army to return to Virginia.

May 6
Arkansas secedes.

May 20
North Carolina secedes.

May 24
Lincoln's young friend Colonel E.E. Ellsworth is killed in Alexandria, Virginia, after tearing down the Confederate flag from the Marshall House; first Union officer killed.

June 8
Tennessee secedes.

July 4
Lincoln delivers his "This Is a People's Contest" message to Congress; asks for four hundred thousand more troops.

July 11
General George B. McClellan comes to national attention with a victory at Rich Mountain, Virginia.

July 21
Confederacy defeats Union at the First Battle of Bull Run in Manassas, Virginia.

July 27
Lincoln names McClellan commander of the Union's Army of the Potomac.

August 30
Union general John Charles Frémont "confiscates" all Confederate property in Missouri, including slaves; Lincoln, not ready for emancipation, instructs Frémont to withdraw his order.

October 21
Confederacy defeats Union at Battle of Ball's Bluff, Virginia.

November 1
McClellan is named commander of the entire Union army.

November 7
Union captures Port Royal, South Carolina.

November 8

Union navy seizes Confederate commissioners aboard steamship *Trent;* England threatens to join war against the Union until the Lincoln administration releases the envoys at the end of the year.

1862

January 13

Lincoln names Edwin M. Stanton secretary of war.

February 6

Union, under Admiral Andrew Foote, captures Fort Henry, Tennessee.

February 16

General Ulysses S. Grant demands and wins "unconditional surrender" of Fort Donelson, Tennessee.

February 22

Davis is reinaugurated president of the Confederacy in Richmond, Virginia.

February 25

Union occupies Nashville, Tennessee.

March–August

McClellan launches Peninsular Campaign in Virginia, with the goal of capturing Richmond.

March 8

Worst U.S. naval disaster until Pearl Harbor, as Confederate ironclad *Merrimac* (or *Virginia*) attacks Union's wooden fleet off Hampton Roads, Virginia.

March 9

The *Monitor* battles the *Merrimac* off Hampton Roads, Virginia, beginning the iron age at sea.

March 16

Union abolishes slavery in Washington, D.C., offering to pay compensation to slaveholders.

April 6–7

Union, under General Grant, wins a major victory at Battle of Shiloh (Pittsburgh Landing), Tennessee.

April 16

Davis signs a new law allowing the Confederate government to draft able-bodied men into the army.

April 25

Union admiral David Farragut captures New Orleans.

May 3

Confederates abandon Yorktown, Virginia, after Union siege led by General McClellan.

May 5

Battle of Williamsburg, Virginia.

May 8

Confederates win fight at McDowell, Virginia, under General Stonewall Jackson.

May 15

Confederates win naval battle at Drewry's Bluff on the James River, near Richmond.

May 31

Davis names Robert E. Lee commander of the Army of Northern Virginia.

June 6

Union captures Memphis, Tennessee.

June 12–14

General J.E.B. Stuart leads a daring cavalry raid around McClellan's army.

June 19

U.S. Congress abolishes slavery in all federal territories.

June 25

Seven Days Battles begin near Richmond.

June 26

Battle of Mechanicsville (Beaver Dam Creek),* Virginia.

*The North named battles for the closest waterway, the South for geographic location (for example, the nearest town). When both names are used in this book, the northern comes first with the southern in parentheses.

June 27

Battle of Gaines's Mill (First Cold Harbor), Virginia.

June 29

Battle of Savage's Station, Virginia.

June 30

Battle of White Oak Swamp (Glendale), Virginia.

July 1

Battle of Malvern Hill, Virginia; McClellan's army retreats as his Peninsular Campaign ends in failure.

July 22

Lincoln reads to his cabinet a proposed Emancipation Proclamation; he is advised to postpone it until the Union wins a battle.

August 9

General John Pope and General Lee battle at Cedar Mountain, Virginia.

August 29–30

Lee defeats Pope at the Second Battle of Bull Run, Manassas, Virginia.

September 4

Lee's army moves across the Potomac River in the first Confederate invasion of the North.

September 17

Battle of Antietam (Sharpsburg), Maryland; Union forces under McClellan defeat Lee's Confederate troops in the bloodiest single day of the war.

September 22

Lincoln issues the Emancipation Proclamation, ordering slaves free in all states in rebellion after January 1, 1863.

September 23

Sioux uprising ends with their defeat at the Battle of Wood Lake, Minnesota.

October 3–4

Union wins Battle of Corinth, Mississippi.

October 8

Union wins Battle of Perryville, Kentucky.

November 7

Lincoln removes McClellan, names General Ambrose E. Burnside commander of the Army of the Potomac.

December 1

Lincoln proposes paying slave owners to free slaves in Union slave states.

December 13

Confederates defeat Union at Battle of Fredericksburg, Virginia.

December 31

Battle of Murfreesboro (Stone's River), Tennessee, begins; Union victory assured by January 2.

1863

January 1

"Day of Jubilee" as Lincoln issues final Emancipation Proclamation.

January 19–23

Union army bogs down in "mud march" leaving rain-soaked Fredericksburg, Virginia.

January 26

Lincoln names General Joseph Hooker to replace Burnside as commander of the Army of the Potomac.

March 3

Lincoln signs first Federal Conscription Act, calling for the drafting of able-bodied men into the Union army.

April 2

Hungry citizens of Richmond start bread riots.

April 16

Union fleet under Admiral David D. Porter bursts past Confederate guns at Vicksburg, Mississippi.

May 1

Grant captures Port Gibson, Mississippi.

May 1–4

Confederates win Battle of Chancellorsville, Virginia.

May 10

Stonewall Jackson, shot accidentally by his own men at Chancellorsville, dies.

May 14

Grant captures Jackson, Mississippi.

May 16–17

Confederate defenses outside Vicksburg crumble.

May 18

Grant begins six-week siege of Vicksburg.

May 22

Bureau of Colored Troops is established in U.S. War Department to welcome free African Americans into the Union army.

June 14

Confederate victory at Battle of Winchester, Virginia.

June 27

Lincoln names Major General George G. Meade to replace Hooker as commander of the Army of the Potomac.

July 1–3

Battle of Gettysburg, Pennsylvania, largest battle of war and a victory for Union forces; Lee retreats back across the Potomac as his second and final invasion of the North ends in failure.

July 4

Vicksburg surrenders to Grant.

July 8

Union takes Port Hudson, Louisiana.

July 13–16

Draft riots break out in New York City.

July 18

Union troops driven back at Battery Wagner, South Carolina, but heroism of Fifty-fourth Massachusetts Colored Infantry proves that African Americans are capable of fighting for their own freedom.

August 21

Confederate Quantrill's Raiders slaughter one hundred fifty men, women, and children in Lawrence, Kansas.

September 2

Union army under Burnside captures Knoxville, Tennessee.

September 10

Little Rock, Arkansas, falls to Union.

September 19–20

Battle of Chickamauga; major Confederate victory in Georgia.

November 19

Lincoln delivers Gettysburg Address at the dedication of a new national cemetery for soldiers killed in battle there.

November 23–25

Battles of Chattanooga, Lookout Mountain, and Missionary Ridge, Tennessee, end with Union victories.

1864

February 1

Lincoln issues a call for five hundred thousand troops.

February 27

First Union captives arrive at Andersonville Prison, Georgia.

March 10

Lincoln appoints Grant general in chief of U.S. armies.

April 8

U.S. Senate approves a constitutional amendment outlawing slavery.

April 12

Massacre at Fort Pillow, Tennessee, as Confederates under General Nathan Bedford Forrest murder African American troops after they surrender.

May 3

Union begins Wilderness Campaign in Virginia.

May 5–7

Battle of the Wilderness.

May 7

General William T. Sherman attacks Atlanta, Georgia.

May 8

Battles begin around Spotsylvania Court House, Virginia.

May 12

General J.E.B. Stuart dies from wounds suffered the previous day at Yellow Tavern, Virginia.

Fierce fighting around "Bloody Angle," Spotsylvania, Virginia.

May 13

Influential New York editor Horace Greeley demands that Lincoln be replaced as the Republican candidate for the 1864 election.

June 1–3

Battles of Cold Harbor, Virginia.

June 8

Lincoln is renominated to the presidency by the new National Union party.

June 12

Grant crosses the James River to Petersburg, Virginia.

June 15

U.S. House of Representatives defeats a constitutional amendment ending slavery.

June 19

USS *Kearsarge* destroys Confederate ship *Alabama* off the coast of Cherbourg, France.

June 27

Confederates defeat Sherman at Battle of Kenesaw Mountain, Georgia.

July 4

Lincoln refuses to sign Wade-Davis bill, which would have imposed harsh conditions on defeated Confederate states.

July 11–12

Confederates threaten Washington suburbs; Lincoln witnesses attack at Fort Stevens.

July 17

Battles for Atlanta begin.

July 30

Battle of the Crater, Petersburg, Virginia, ends in Union defeat after Union explodes a huge bomb beneath a Confederate position.

August 5

Admiral Farragut inspires his fleet by crying, "Damn the torpedoes — full speed ahead," and takes Mobile Bay.

September 2

Sherman takes Atlanta.

October 19

General Philip Sheridan defeats General Jubal Early for a Union victory at Winchester, Virginia, after inspiring troops with his famous ride to the front.

Shenandoah Valley Campaign ends with a Confederate loss at Cedar Creek.

November 1

Maryland abolishes slavery.

November 8

Lincoln is reelected president of the United States.

November 16

Sherman begins his march from Atlanta to the sea.

November 22

Sherman's troops capture Milledgeville, Georgia.

November 29

Indian massacre at Sand Creek, Colorado.

November 30

Union wins Battle of Franklin, Tennessee.

December 6

Lincoln names Salmon P. Chase chief justice of the Supreme Court.

December 15–16

Union under General George H. Thomas defeats Confederates at Nashville, ending the war in the West.

December 21

Sherman captures Savannah, Geogia.

1865

January 15

Union captures Fort Fisher, North Carolina.

January 31

House of Representatives finally approves a constitutional amendment abolishing slavery.

February 1

Lincoln's home state, Illinois, becomes the first to ratify the Thirteenth Amendment abolishing slavery.

Sherman begins march through the Carolinas.

February 13

Confederacy approves the recruitment of slaves as soldiers, with the approval of owners.

February 17

Union army captures and destroys Columbia, South Carolina.

February 18

Union army marches into Charleston, South Carolina, the city where the Civil War began.

February 22

Tennessee abolishes slavery.

March 4

Lincoln is reinaugurated; Second Inaugural Address blames war on slavery, proposes charity for enemies.

March 11

Sherman captures Fayetteville, North Carolina.

March 27

Lincoln holds final council of war with Grant, Sherman, and Porter aboard the *River Queen,* City Point, Virginia.

March 29

Grant launches Appomattox Campaign.

April 1

Grant defeats Lee at Battle of Five Forks, Virginia.

April 2

Confederate government flees Richmond.

April 3

Grant captures Petersburg and Richmond, Virginia.

April 4

Lincoln visits Richmond.

April 7

Grant urges Lee to surrender the Army of Northern Virginia.

April 9

Lee surrenders to Grant at Appomattox Court House, Virginia.

April 14

Lincoln is shot at Ford's Theatre by actor John Wilkes Booth.

April 15

Lincoln dies.

April 26

Confederate general Joseph Johnston surrenders to Sherman at Greensboro, North Carolina.

May 10

Jefferson Davis is captured by Union troops at Irwinville, Georgia.

May 22

Davis is imprisoned at Fort Monroe, Virginia.

December 18

The Thirteenth Amendment to the Constitution is ratified, and slavery is finally destroyed forever.

1866

President Andrew Johnson officially declares the rebellion to be over, as new governments are formed in the former Confederate states.

Reconstruction begins; Congress and President Johnson battle over how severely the South should be punished and how many rights African Americans should enjoy.

Congress passes the first civil rights bill over President Johnson's opposition.

Congress passes the Fourteenth Amendment to the Constitution, guaranteeing citizenship and "equal protection of the laws" to freed slaves.

The Ku Klux Klan is organized.

President Johnson pardons Jefferson Davis and gives back his U.S. citizenship.

1868

The Fourteenth Amendment is ratified; Ulysses S. Grant is elected president.

1870

The Fifteenth Amendment to the Constitution is ratified, guaranteeing all Americans, "regardless of race, color, or previous condition of servitude," the right to vote.

1877

The last Republican government still existing in a southern state is defeated, and most rights won by African Americans are lost.

1

AMERICA
BEFORE THE WAR

"Conceived in *Liberty*, and dedicated to the proposition that all men are created equal."

That was how Abraham Lincoln would later describe the birth of the United States of America. But the sad truth was that America's birth offered liberty and equality only to some people and denied it to others.

Native Americans, of course, were excluded from the rights guaranteed to all the citizens of the new nation. And African Americans not only were denied basic rights, but they were denied freedom itself.

Even so, Americans managed to create the purest democracy the world had ever known. But it would take generations before that democracy offered all of its benefits to all of its people.

This is how our national history began.

WESTWARD EXPANSION

by Cheryl Edwards

The indigenous people, often referred to as Indians or Native Americans, have lived throughout North America for thousands of years. American colonists, most of whom arrived on the east coast, have been moving westward ever since the Pilgrims arrived in the early 1600s. America's borders were constantly being pushed farther west as restless settlers looked for new opportunities and adventures on uncharted frontiers. The American colonists were not the only ones interested in the western lands. They had to compete for it with many Native American Nations whose ancestors had lived there for thousands of years before the European settlers arrived. The British, Spanish, and French staked their claims on various pieces of the western wilderness as well. It was not surprising that when all of these parties converged on the West, problems arose and tempers flared. The conflicts were troubling for a new country like the United States, and were to prove even more troubling to the Native Americans.

Before the American Revolution, the British forbade the colonists from set-

From Cheryl Edwards, ed., *Westward Expansion: Exploration and Settlement,* Perspectives on History Series, pp. 5–9. Copyright © 1995 Discovery Enterprises, Ltd., Lowell, Massachusetts.

Daniel
Boone

tling west of the Appalachian Mountains. This artificial border, known as the
Line of Proclamation, kept the British in control of the frontier. Many colonists
ignored the British Proclamation of 1763 and moved westward into the forbidden land to settle. After the American Revolution ended in 1783, the land west
of the Proclamation line, known as Ohio Country, became part of the United
States. Beyond it was the uncharted wilderness, called Louisiana Province,
which belonged to Spain.

Frontier settlement increased, and the idea of "going west" to seek their for-
tunes became the dream of many Americans. The desire for open space, better
soil, cheap land, good hunting, and increased opportunities for trade made the
West very appealing.

Frontiersmen like Daniel Boone and Davy Crockett helped open the Ohio
Country for settlement by clearing trails and making crude roads through the
mountains. Settlers who lived on the frontier used these trails to bring their
families even further west and transport their trade goods to markets in the
East. These trails were a slow, expensive, and inefficient way to travel. Americans needed an easier and cheaper way to transport their goods to market.
Using waterways, like the Mississippi and Ohio Rivers, offered the best
solution. Traders could ship their merchandise directly to the Port of
New Orleans.

When the war between England and the United States ended in
1783, England promised the United States the right to free navigation on the Mississippi River. Spain controlled its mouth, and, at
first, would not permit the Americans to drop off their trade goods at
the Port of New Orleans. A volatile situation brewed.

In 1795, Spain and the United States signed a three-year treaty
which permitted Americans to use the Mississippi River and
deposit trade goods at the Port of New Orleans.
Once that treaty had elapsed, Americans
lost their right of deposit and difficulties
between the two countries resumed.

President Jefferson wanted to avoid a
war. The settlers who sailed the Mississippi
were not going to let a foreign power dictate their
right to use or not use the river. To further com-
plicate matters, Spain gave the Louisiana
Province to France in gratitude for its
help in defeating the British. France
was more powerful than Spain and
presented a more serious threat
to the United States. However,
France's Emperor, Napoleon, was
busy waging battles for the control
of the European continent. He did
not have the time or sufficient

money to defend his North American colonies.

In addition to the problems he faced with France, Jefferson had other concerns. He worried about the Americans who were moving west in great numbers. The settlers needed a system of law enforcement and protection from any potentially hostile Native American nations or foreign governments. Jefferson envisioned the borders of the United States extending across the continent from the Atlantic to the Pacific coasts. He wanted to unify the entire continent to take advantage of the economic possibilities in the West. Most importantly, Jefferson did not want the continued presence of foreign powers on the continent. As a sharp politician and negotiator, he knew what needed to be done to save the United States from going to war again.

In 1803, the United States negotiated the purchase of the western lands known as Louisiana Province from France for 15 million dollars. Jefferson's foresight and courage helped the country avoid a war, double its size, and secure important waterways that would make economic expansion possible. Although critics accused him of buying a useless piece of empty wilderness and wasting money, the President was resolute.

Jefferson had to show the skeptics that the Louisiana Purchase would be a valuable asset. Americans knew very little about their new acquisition. In 1804, Jefferson commissioned two army officers named Meriwether Lewis and William Clark to explore the newly-acquired western land. Jefferson was particularly interested in finding a good water route to the Pacific Ocean. Americans would then be able to trade more easily with countries in Asia.

Lewis and Clark's mission was to explore the Missouri and Columbia Rivers, record data about the flora and fauna, make friends with the Native Americans, and find an intercontinental route to the Pacific Ocean. Their twenty-eight month expedition included a group of men who were called the "Corps of Discovery." These men were specially trained to live in the wilderness. Also included in the expedition were a Shoshone woman named Sacajawea, her baby son Pomp, and her French husband Charbonneau. Clark's slave, named York, also came along. York was popular with the Native Americans, who had never seen a black man before. Through the journals of Lewis and Clark, we know that York had a great sense of humor. He told the Native Americans he met that he was a wild animal who had been tamed by Clark. When the expedition was complete, Clark freed York from slavery, out of respect for him and for his contribution to the success of the journey.

Lewis and Clark's expedition was a model undertaking. Other explorers soon followed, and new western lands were mapped and new trails opened. The rivers became busy with boats filled with goods for trading. Finally, the western lands were ready for settlement. Jefferson had proven his critics wrong: The natural resources and economic opportunities found in the West were magnificent.

Thomas Jefferson

In 1804, Jefferson commissioned two army officers, Meriwether Lewis and William Clark, to explore the newly acquired Louisiana Territory. In the 1811 edition of *Journal of the Voyages and Travels...of Lewis and Clarke* by Patrick Gass, Lewis and Clark are shown holding a council with Indians.

The first Americans belonged to cultures that thrived on this continent for thousands of years before the first Europeans arrived. Native Americans are the forgotten people of the Civil War era, but they were here before it began and remained after it was over.

EARLY NORTH AMERICAN CULTURES

by Randall H. McGuire

There were no "Indians" in North America when Christopher Columbus landed in the Bahamas five hundred years ago, but more than ten million people lived in what is now the United States. Among them were Diné, O'Odhams, Lakotas, Wampanoags, Ganiengehakas, and a host of other nations. They spoke hundreds of different languages. In most of these languages, the name they called themselves means "the people" in English. These people became "Indians" when Columbus called them *una gente en dios,* "a people living in God." In Spanish their name became Indios, or Indians.

The Indians' world was not a new world. According to archaeologists, the first Indians came to North America more than twenty thousand years before Columbus. During the last Ice Age, the great glacial ice sheets took up so much water that the oceans shrank. The Bering Strait, between Siberia and Alaska, dried up. A broad land bridge connected Asia and North America. Asian hunters followed game over the bridge into North America.

Many modern Indian peoples do not accept this theory of migration. They believe that the people were created with the land. The stories they tell explain who they are, where they came from, what the borders of their world are, and how they should live as humans. Each nation has its own Creation story.

Archaeologists call the first peoples in North America Paleo-Indians. *Paleo* is a Greek word meaning "early." These early Indians found a colder climate than the one we know today. Great ice sheets covered much of Canada. The northern United States had an arctic climate. The deserts of the western United States were lush grasslands dappled with large lakes. Paleo-Indian hunters used finely made stone projectile points to hunt large animals such as mammoths (extinct elephants) and bison. By nine thousand years ago, the climate was becoming warmer. The ice sheets melted, and the lakes in the West dried up, leaving the modern deserts.

The lives of Indian peoples changed. Archaeologists call this new way of life the Archaic Phase. Archaic peoples adapted their way of life to the specific environment in which they lived. People hunted smaller game, such as deer and rabbits. They gathered wild grass seeds and ground them into flour. They collected shellfish along the rivers of the eastern United States and along the coasts. They threw the shells in large piles. In the far western United States and in most of Canada, the Archaic Phase lasted until the eighteenth century A.D.

In the eastern and southwestern United States, a new way of life, the Formative Phase, replaced the Archaic. These people lived year-round in one settle-

These shards, or pottery fragments, belonged to the Anasazis, who flourished thousands of years ago in a region where the states of Colorado, Utah, Arizona, and New Mexico now meet.

ment, made pottery, and grew crops. They built great mounds and stone buildings that still dot the landscape.

Archaeologists divide the Formative Phase of the East into the Adena, Hopewell, Late Woodland, and Mississippian periods. Adena people (500–100 B.C.) brought wild sunflowers, amaranth (pigweed), and squash into their gardens. They bred the wild plants to produce larger domestic varieties. They buried their dead in large mounds of earth. They built one mound in present-day Ohio to look like a snake eating an egg. During the Hopewell Period, people continued to build mounds, and they began a trade network that covered most of the eastern United States. This trade network fell apart in about A.D. 400, which marks the start of the Late Woodland Period.

By 800, people based their agriculture on corn, beans, and squash. These crops came from Mexico, where Indian peoples had grown them for thousands of years. The Late Woodland Period continued in much of the East until the Europeans arrived, but in the South, it changed into the Mississippian Period (700–1540). Mississippian societies divided people into nobles, priests, and commoners. The nobles and priests lived on high, flat mounds in great towns of up to twenty thousand people. The modern Cherokee, Creek, Choctaw, Seminole, and Chickasaw Indians are the descendants of Mississippian peoples.

Corn arrived in the Southwest before 1000 B.C., and by A.D. 100, three Formative cultures existed. The Anasazi culture began in the Four Corners region, where the states of Colorado, Utah, Arizona, and New Mexico meet. The Anasazis built large apartment buildings called pueblos and made white pottery with black designs. At the end of the thirteenth century, the Anasazis moved to the Rio Grande, where their descendants live today.

The Mogollon people lived in the mountains and made brown pottery with red designs. Around A.D. 1450, they moved north to become the Hopi and Zuni Indians. In the deserts of southern Arizona, the Hohokams built large canals to water their fields and made buff pottery with red designs. Their descendants, the Pimas, still farm among the ruins of their ancestors.

In 1492, most of the Indian peoples of North America were farmers who lived in villages. European diseases and war destroyed the Mississippian culture and greatly reduced the farmers of the Southwest. Today almost two million Indian people live in the United States. Hundreds of Indian nations survive, and more than two hundred native languages are spoken.

Anasazi ruins of a pueblo — a large "apartment" building — in Chaco Canyon, New Mexico.

The Navajo are the largest Native American group in the United States today. This photo of a Navajo woman was taken in 1996.

A Navajo sand painting of the Lord of Heaven.

DINÉ: THE PEOPLE OF THE NAVAJO NATION

The Navajos cannot say when the first people came to live in the land amid the four sacred mountains. They tell how the mountains were created by First Man and First Woman, who, with other Holy People, made fire, designed the first hogan, and provided day, night, seasons, and harvests. One dawn, First Man and First Woman heard a cry and found a baby girl. They named her Changing Woman, and she taught many things to the animal beings. Before she went west to live with the sun, she created four Navajo clans from the skin of her own body. They lived amid the mountains and followed the teachings of the Holy People.

Archaeologists believe that the Navajos came to live in the American Southwest as a result of migrations over a long time. Their language is one of a group of related languages called Athabascan, centered in northwest Canada. Beginning a thousand years ago, small groups of Athabascan-speaking peoples migrated south. Moving over several hundred years and many generations, the descendants of those people reached the Southwest by the mid-1500s.

The Pueblos already lived in the area where they settled. The people from the north adopted some of the Pueblos' settled ways, learning to live by agriculture as well as their own hunting and food gathering. They built roundish homes called hogans. In the 1500s, when the Spanish came, they called these people Apache de Nabaju, "Apaches of the cultivated fields," and the name Navajo stuck.

They called themselves Diné, "the people." They called their land Dinétah, "land of the people." It is also called the Navajo Nation.

The Navajo Nation was hard won. The Diné were not one tribe but scattered related groups. They were united in their shared history and beliefs and their feelings that Dinétah is a sacred land. White people nearly drove them from that land in the 1800s, but today the Navajos are united under an eighty-eight-member tribal council and elected tribal chairman. Their 25,000-square-mile nation has been governed by the council since the 1920s from an immense hogan-shaped building in Window Rock, Arizona.

In this century, income from oil, coal, minerals, and timber sales has led many Navajos to change from their traditional occupations as farmers, sheepherders, and craftsmen. The Navajo Nation now includes industries, schools, hospitals, and museums, but it is not a wealthy land. Although the Navajos are the largest and most prosperous Native American group, many people live in poverty, have a hard time finding work, and experience the same social problems related to alcohol and drugs as other Americans. Many Navajos now live in modern homes and go to college in faraway places; others still live in hogans and follow traditional ways.

THE IROQUOIS: MEN LEAD, WOMEN CHOOSE

by Trudie Lamb Richmond

The Six Nations of the Iroquois are eastern woodland Indians whose territory at one time stretched from the Great Lakes through New York State and over large portions of land on the Canadian side of the St. Lawrence River. For centuries,

Left: American artist George Catlin (1796–1872), who painted many portraits and scenes of American Indian life, painted three Iroquois Indians in the 1860s.

Below: Besides raising children, Iroquois women choose who will lead each of the six nations. As the center of the family, they also are the heartbeat of the nation. This Iroquois woman and child lived in Sharon Springs, New York, in the 1800s.

they lived in longhouses, each shared by several related families, and they still call themselves Haudenosaunee, "people of the longhouse."

The land of the Iroquois was rich and fertile, and the people depended mostly on farming for their food. As with many societies, men did the hunting and fishing and provided protection. In turn, women maintained the village, tended the crops, prepared and preserved the food, and raised the children.

Long ago, five nations, or tribes — the Oneidas, Mohawks, Cayugas, Onondagas, and Senecas — formed the League of the Iroquois to protect their trade routes to the west and to keep peace among themselves. Later, a sixth nation, the Tuscaroras, joined the league.

The idea of the league originated with Dekanawida many generations ago. He had been searching for a way to bring peace and unity to his people, whose warring and quarreling were dividing them at a frightening pace. Dekanawida's league and the Great Law of Peace still unite the Six Nations of the Iroquois and have enabled them to preserve their identity and culture. There are many unique factors of the Great Law. One of these is the political power of Iroquois women. Not only do the women decide who will be the leaders of each nation, but if a leader fails in his duties, only the women have the power to remove him.

In Iroquois society, the woman is the center of the family and the heartbeat of the nation. The Creation story explains how Sky Woman fell from the Sky World, landing on the back of Turtle. As she began to dance and sing their ceremonial songs, Turtle's back grew larger, creating our great continent — Turtle Island (North America). When she died, she became part of the earth. Almost from that moment, the role of women, the Givers of Life, was clear. That is why Indian people say, "The earth is our mother; treat her with great respect."

Indian people describe all natural forces in kinship terms, as they believe that they are related to all living things. For example, they call the moon Grandmother and the sun Elder Brother. All within the animal kingdom are relatives. This belief creates a sense of unity not only in a spiritual sense but also in the sense of managing society. And it is with this outlook that the Iroquois link themselves in a series of circles. At the center is the family. The next circle is made up of clans, the next of tribes, and the largest of nation. These circles explain how groups are related and define their responsibilities to one another. For example, the people within a clan are all descended from a common ancestor, and each clan is named for an animal relative, such as the turtle, bear, wolf, deer, or snipe (a bird).

Women are the heads of clans as well as households. They are called clan mothers. Children belong to their mother's clan rather than their father's (people within the same clan do not marry each other). When a young man marries, he goes to live with his wife's family.

The women within each clan appoint the male chiefs, who in turn speak for their clans in tribal councils. Consulting with the other women within their clan, the clan mothers decide on issues and questions to be debated and acted upon in the council. They recommend to their male spokesmen what view to express and push for. The clan mothers look for certain qualities and strengths in their leaders. Besides loyalty and trustworthiness, a leader must be a skilled speaker.

The women have great political power. Not only do they have authority over their homes, the land, and the children, but they also determine a person's name, which does not belong to the person but to his or her mother's clan. Each clan keeps a record of names, maintained by the women. When a child is born, he or she receives a name not in use; when the person dies, that name goes back in the record and becomes available again.

When a man is selected as chief, he is given a chief's name. Each clan has a long list of chief's names, which, like the chief's position, must be treated with respect. Among these are Shononses, meaning "his house is long"; Skanaawadi, meaning "across the swamp"; and Dayohronyonkah, meaning "it reaches or pierces the sky."*

As with U.S. Supreme Court justices, a council position is for life. But if a leader fails to carry out his responsibilities or considers himself more important than his people, the women can use their power to remove him from his posi-

Captain Cold

Captain Cold, or Ut-ha-wah, an Onondaga, was keeper of the Iroquois League council fire in the late eighteenth century. Like all fire keepers, he called grand councils of the League, kept the League's wampum records, and protected Iroquois traditions and practices.

*The names were obtained from Elizabeth Tooker, *Handbook of North American Indians,* volume 15, 1975.

tion. He is given three warnings. If there is no change, the leader is stripped of his right to rule in a "dehorning" ceremony.

And so it has been for many generations that the voices of Iroquois women are not only heard but also listened to with great respect. What is even more remarkable is the fact that the democratic principles of the Iroquois were of great importance in the founding of the U.S. government. The U.S. Constitution was modeled after their oral constitution, the Great Law of Peace. The founders of the United States ignored one very important aspect of the Iroquois League, however. American women did not win the right to vote until 1920, more than 125 years after the Constitution was adopted.

INDIAN CULTURES OF THE SOUTHEAST

by E. Barrie Kavasch

Southern Indian cultures flourished in the warm, temperate regions of our country for thousands of years. In these diverse areas, various chiefdoms ruled complex native societies. Many had capital towns, often located on surrounding massive mounds and other notable earthworks, which supported temples and council lodges.

More than ten thousand eastern Cherokees live on the Qualla Boundary Reservation in North Carolina. This artisan demonstrates finger weaving at Oconaluftee Indian Village on the reservation.

The first recorded European encounter occurred in 1513, when Juan Ponce de León encountered a hostile reception from the native people of southern Florida. Hernando de Soto's disastrous, meandering intrusion among southeastern peoples in the years 1539 to 1543 ended his life but was even more devastating to the native tribes, many members of which were killed, kidnapped, enslaved, and raped. Countless others later died of European diseases, to which native populations possessed almost no resistance. The English established the colony of Jamestown in 1607, the first permanent English settlement in North America. They encountered the powerful Indian chief Wahunsonacock. Because they could not pronounce his name, they called him Chief Powhatan, the name of his tribe and confederacy of about thirty different bands inhabiting possibly as many as two hundred villages in the tidewater region that came to be called Virginia.

The Cherokee people originally lived in the regions that are now parts of Georgia, Alabama, Tennessee, Kentucky, North and South Carolina, Virginia, and West Virginia. Noted farmers and hunters, they worked the fertile bottomlands along the rivers, where they cultivated corn, squash, beans, sunflowers, gourds, sunchokes, tobacco, and cotton. Southeastern forests were full of deer, bears, mountain lions, bobcats, beavers, raccoons, opossum, wild turkeys, quail, grouse, ducks, pigeons, and countless other animals and birds, as well as valuable medicinal plants.

The Cherokee, Creek, Choctaw, Chickasaw, and Seminole Indians of the Southeast have shared very similar ways of life, political restrictions, and conflicts. Other southeastern tribes include the Catawbas of South Carolina; the Alabamas, Chitimachas, and Koasatis of Mississippi; the Mikasukis (Miccosukees) of Georgia and Florida; the Tunica-Biloxis of Louisiana; and the Yuchis of the Appalachian highlands.

Most of these native peoples were pushed beyond their ancestral homelands by American settlers. Many chose to live among other tribes and confederacies in Texas, Mexico, and Canada. Many others, primarily the so-called Five Civilized Tribes, walked the Trail of Tears during the U.S. government's shameful forced removal of the southeastern tribes to Indian Territory, now Oklahoma, in 1838–39. Still others remained in the Southeast; hid out; intermarried with other tribes, African slaves, and white Americans; and tried to "live white" where they could. Many native people of the Southeast are now biracial or triracial and proud of their mixed heritage, although early laws forbidding interracial marriage prevented many of our ancestors from talking about their cultural histories.

Since removal, the Five Civilized Tribes of Oklahoma have increased in population and economic development, while maintaining their cultural bases. The 180,000-member Cherokee Nation, the second-largest tribe in the United States, is headquartered in Tahlequah, Oklahoma, while 10,000 members of the Eastern Band of Cherokees continue to live on the Qualla Boundary Reservation, the capital of which is Cherokee, North Carolina. The capital of the Choctaw Nation is Durant, Oklahoma, while the Mississippi Band of Choctaws live on lands surrounding their capital of Philadelphia, Mississippi. Wewoka is the capital of the Seminole Nation of Oklahoma; the capital of the Seminole Nation of Florida is Hollywood, Florida. The Muscogee (Creek) Nation is headquartered in Okmulgee, Oklahoma, and the Chickasaw Nation is headquartered in Ada, Oklahoma.

THE SIOUX

The Sioux once occupied the vast plains region of the United States, from Minnesota west to Montana and from Canada south to Oklahoma. For food, they hunted buffalo, elk, deer, and small animals and birds. They also gathered nuts, root vegetables, fruits, and berries. Sometimes they had to fight to protect their hunting grounds from rival Indians, but they fostered friendships and formed strong alliances with other neighboring tribes. Their beliefs focused on the natural world, and their god, Wakan Tanka, the Great Mystery, tied all living things together. Humans, they believed, were related to the earth, plants and animals, and other natural phenomena.

The nineteenth century brought traumatic changes to the Sioux and other Native Americans. White

Perhaps the most widely known event in Sioux history happened in June 1876 when Crazy Horse and Sitting Bull led the Sioux in their victory over Lieutenant Colonel George Armstrong Custer and his troops. As many as two thousand Indian warriors rode out to meet George Armstrong Custer at the Little Bighorn. "The smoke was like a great cloud, and everywhere the Sioux went the dust rose up like smoke," recalled Cheyenne chief Two Moons, who fought in the battle. "We circled all around him [Custer] — swirling like water around a stone. We shoot, we ride fast, we shoot again. Soldiers drop, and horses fall on them." Custer's entire command was wiped out.

settlers moved west with an appetite for land and little regard for the Indians' way of life. Sioux chiefs tried to establish boundaries for their people, to protect their hunting grounds and sacred places. Treaties were made, in white men's terms, but as the demand for land increased among whites, many of these treaties were broken. In the course of a few decades, the Sioux were confined to a few reservations, a fraction of the land they had previously called home.

Perhaps the most unfortunate thing about America's westward expansion was the lack of interest on the part of so many white soldiers, settlers, and government officials in finding out who the Sioux were and how they had lived in balance with nature for hundreds of years. A century later, the Sioux still must fight to protect their way of life. However, more and more people are learning the wisdom of Sioux beliefs and recognizing the need to carry on their traditions. In learning from the Sioux and helping them to preserve their culture, we can make our own lives richer.

'GO WEST, YOUNG MAN!'

by Carol J. Flatt

Hundreds of families, encouraged by Horace Greeley and others, took these words to heart. They packed their belongings, sold their homes, and with hope and a great deal of courage, headed west to begin a new life in the vast open spaces of the prairie.

They left large, crowded cities with tall buildings, busy streets, and modern conveniences to cross miles of land very different from anything they had seen before. What was this land called the prairie? What did these early settlers see as they traveled across territory with no mountains or fences and few trees as landmarks?

A model of a covered wagon.

Cowboys sang, "Oh, bury me not on the lone prairie,...where the rattlers hiss, and the crow flies free." Newcomers compared traveling across the prairie to sailing the open seas. They could travel for days with nothing to mark their progress. It was a sea of grass, some as tall as a man, which moved in the wind like the waves on the ocean. Covering one-fifth of the earth's surface, the prairie stretched from Canada in the north to the state of Texas in the south. From the eastern forests to the western steppes, only an occasional hill broke the monotony.

The prairie was not as dry as the desert, but it did not have an abundance of moisture. Chilling winters sent temperatures to thirty degrees below zero. During the hot summers, temperatures climbed to more than one hundred degrees. This was the time of year when the winds blew fiercely, adding to the ever-present danger of a prairie fire. These fires could be ignited by the slightest touch of lightning from a summer storm, sending walls of flame over the land at great speeds.

The prairies were called the grasslands and with good reason. Grasses grew in

PRAIRIE SCHOONERS

by Jane Barrett

Many settlers to the unknown lands of the American West traveled in a covered wagon, or "prairie schooner." For months, they lived in this mobile home, carrying everything necessary to stay alive. It was called a prairie schooner because of its boatlike shape, with a flat bottom and sides that sloped outward. This shape helped it stay afloat during the many river crossings pioneers encountered. The double-thick white canvas used to cover its top also resembled a sail, especially as it billowed and waved in strong prairie winds.

Prairie schooners, which functioned daily during America's land rush of the 1870s and 1880s, were developed from the earlier Conestoga wagon. Used throughout the 1800s, these wagons were heavier than schooners, required large teams of animals to pull them, and were used mostly for freight, transporting several thousand pounds at a time. Prairie schooners required only two to six horses or oxen to pull them. Because of their lighter design, they were easier and cheaper to construct, making them affordable for families. Because of the rugged travel, extra supplies for wagon repair were strapped to the sides or underneath. The travelers needed extra bows for the top, spokes and grease for the wheels, tar to seal slats tight before entering water, and heavy rope for emergencies.

varying heights and kinds. They could endure heat and cold and withstand the winds. These grasses, with their tangles of roots, helped form some of the richest soil and toughest sod in the world.

The short-grass plains received little rainfall, experienced harsh winters, and produced shallow-rooted grasses no more than sixteen inches high. Buffalo grass and bluegrass were found in abundance. Where the land was drier, short grasses were frequently mixed with cacti and other desertlike plants.

Mid-grasses tended to grow in bunches and reached a height of two to four feet. Little bluestem, western ragweed, and June grass could grow in places with less moisture.

Where rainfall was heavier, the tall grasses flourished. Tall bluestem often grew eight feet tall and had roots six feet deep. Indian grass and switch grass mixed with tall bluestem to cover thousands of acres.

This was not a land lacking in color. With spring came the wildflowers, which polka-dotted the new green and aging yellow grasses with other colors. Hundreds of species of flowers, such as prairie clover, sunflowers, asters, and brown-eyed Susans, all grew on their own schedules.

Nor was the prairie treeless. Needing more moisture than grasses, trees grew near water sources such as rivers or marshes. The sturdy burr oak grew along the edge of the prairie. Its thick bark protected it from the ravages of fire. Cottonwood, willow, elm, and box elder trees were scattered along stream edges.

With an abundance of grass, it is natural that the prairie supported a wealth of grass-eating animals. Because of a lack of protective cover, the smaller animals tended to live underground in burrows. They were expert diggers and speedy runners. The burrowers included ground squirrels and prairie dogs, whose "towns" once numbered millions of inhabitants. The many varieties of mice and rats were a mixture of vegetarians and meat eaters. Some preferred seeds, roots, and other plant material, while others, such as the grasshopper mouse, consumed insects and lizards.

Grass-nesting animals included the cottontail and the jackrabbit. Early white settlers gave the jackrabbit its name because its ears reminded them of those of a jackass (donkey). Many varieties of birds built their nests in tangles of grass.

Prairie chickens gathered to perform their noisy courtship dance on a "booming ground." The sage grouse likewise had his colorful dance, in which he inflated huge air sacs that nearly touched the ground. Other birds included long-legged waders such as the marbled godwit and enthusiastic singers such as the meadowlark.

Black-footed ferrets, skunks, and a variety of wolves hunted other animals for food. Wolves hunted in packs, following the great buffalo herds that once inhabited the plains. Another herd animal was the pronghorn antelope. It was well adapted to the full sun and color pattern of its surroundings, and it relied on great speed, which could reach forty-five to sixty miles per hour, for protection.

Today the prairie is different than it was when the pioneers were crossing it. Waves of settlers changed it forever, but its rich color and variety remain the same.

MANIFEST DESTINY: WHITE MAN'S DREAM, RED MAN'S NIGHTMARE

by Nancy Barton

In the early nineteenth century, America was a young nation eager to prove to the world that its new constitutional government would work. The U.S. government and much of the country's white population believed it was America's manifest destiny (or inevitable mission) to settle all the land between the Atlantic and Pacific oceans. It would be a test of the country's ability to govern itself and to protect its entire territory from European takeover.

So the great westward migration became the American dream. But the white man's dream was the red man's nightmare. The manifest destiny vision of America's future included no place for the Indians, America's original inhabitants, and their cultures. It soon became apparent that if the red man was to survive, he must either get out of the white man's way or become like him. As the white man struggled to settle the continent, the red man struggled to survive.

In the 1800s, America was intent upon "winning the West" from the foreign powers that held the land west of the Mississippi River. Spain occupied California and much of the Southwest, and Britain claimed Oregon Territory. Both Spain and France had alternately laid claim to Louisiana Territory until 1803, when it was purchased by America. The fact that Indians had always occupied these lands meant little. If the Indians resisted the progress of the white man, the nation would solve the problem by moving the Indians.

And that is exactly what it did. The Indian Removal Act of 1830 autho-

Jackson was the seventh president of the United States (1829–1837). During his presidency, the Indian Removal Act of 1830 was passed, forcing eastern Indians to move west against their will.

Andrew Jackson

rized President Andrew Jackson to grant the eastern tribes perpetual title to certain lands west of the Mississippi River. By 1840, nearly the entire eastern Indian population of one hundred thousand had moved west — against its will.

But this did not end the matter. By 1840, the western territories were no longer as remote as they had once seemed. Rumors of gold, unlimited land grants, and promises of easy fortune had brought many easterners to the West. Technological advances speeded up the process. First, the steamboat took settlers to California by traveling around South America. Later, the transcontinental railroad replaced the earlier wagon trains. And as eastern and foreign markets increased their demands for the western products of cattle, grain, and minerals, new settlers flooded into the West to help meet those demands.

Many treaties were made as the white man sought rights of free passage across the continent. But the Indians objected to the white man's progress because, as an old Wintu Indian explained, unlike the Indians, the white man "never cared for land or deer or bear." The white man shocked the Indians with his careless destruction of their food supply, which the great Sioux chief Black Elk described: "I can remember when the bison were so many that they could not be counted, but more and more white men came to kill them.... (They) did not kill them to eat;...they took only their hides to sell. Sometimes they did not even take their hides, only their tongues."

Although the Indians fought to keep the white man from their homeland, the settlers became more firmly entrenched in the West. Overcoming the hardships of disease, starvation, and Indian harassment, families established successful farms and ranches on the plains. Many of the fortune seekers who crossed the continent in search of gold and silver remained to build large cities in the West. Immigrants, with hopes of trading the repression and poverty of the Old World

Chief Joseph

Chief Joseph (c. 1840–1904), or Hinmaton-Yalaktit ("Thunder-in-the-Mountains"), was a chief of one of the major bands of the Nez Perce tribe. He is shown here with his family.

for the freedom and prosperity of the New World, swarmed to the frontier to labor on the railroads, in the mines, and at the slaughterhouses.

By mid-century, armed forts were built to protect the white man's progress, and as the Shawnee chief Tecumseh foresaw, "No treaty will keep whites out of our lands." In fact, between 1850 and 1880, most treaties were abandoned as the land was developed by white men. Despite the efforts of eastern abolitionists and religious leaders to safeguard the rights of the Indians, one tribe after another was herded onto reservations. To Indians, who did not believe in the idea of "buying" or "owning" the land, the white man's actions were bewildering. As Chief Joseph of the Nez Perce explained, "I never said the land was mine to do with as I chose.... I claim a right to live on my land, and accord you the privilege to live on yours."

By the end of the nineteenth century, the continent had been settled. America could claim all the land between the Atlantic and Pacific oceans and the Great Lakes and Rio Grande. The true frontier was a thing of the past. America's government had proven itself. But not all people were permitted to enjoy all the individual liberties promised by the Constitution. Among those who still lacked certain rights were women, African Americans, and Indians.

Chief Joseph had been ignored when he had admonished the white man to treat all people alike. He said, "Let me be a free man, — free to travel, to work, to trade where I choose, to choose my own teachers, to follow the religion of my fathers, free to think and act for myself."

But liberty and self-government belonged only to the white man until after the West was won. Then, burdened by the costs of running the reservations, the government cut off much of its financial support, saying that the Indian should now become independent and self-sufficient like the white man.

Today about eight hundred thousand Indians live on or near reservations. For the most part, they govern themselves. The U.S. government's relationship with the reservations is a complex one. Among other things, it involves providing aid in various forms and, in some cases, repaying the Indians for wrongs done them in the past.

STRUGGLE FOR A HOMELAND

by Kathleen Burke

In 1796, Benjamin Hawkins, the principal agent for the southern Indians under President George Washington, visited Cherokee country. Hawkins later recalled how generously the Indians welcomed him: "They gave me good bread, pork and potatoes for supper, and ground peanuts and dried peaches. I had corn for my horses. The hut in which I lodged was clean and neat. In the morning, I breakfasted on corn cake and pork. They had a number of fowls, hogs, and some cattle, the field of 4 acres for corn and half an acre for potatoes."

The orchards, well-tended crops, herds of cattle, and comfortable cabins that Hawkins saw were not unusual. By the 1790s, the Cherokees were the most

> **I never said the land was mine to do with as I chose.... I claim a right to live on my land, and accord you the privilege to live on yours.**
>
> *Chief Joseph*

In the 1800s, white hunters nearly destroyed the bison herds by over-hunting, producing a profound effect on the Indians. Today bison roam the meadows of Wood Buffalo National Park that straddles the border of Alberta and the Northwest Territories in Canada. There are many domestic bison herds across Canada.

prosperous of the eastern Indians. Nevertheless, Hawkins was witnessing an amazing scene. Only fifty years before, the Cherokees were the most feared of all the Mississippi Valley tribes. "We cannot live without war," they had declared. "War is our beloved occupation."

The Cherokees' first contact with whites came almost three hundred years before the Hawkins visit. Spanish explorer Hernando de Soto met the Cherokees in 1540. But it was not until 1673 that the tribe started to have regular contact with whites. In that year, two traders from Virginia came into Cherokee country. They exchanged guns, beads, and ribbons for dressed deerskins and pelts that would be exported to England.

Even then, the Cherokees were intensely curious about the white man's world. In 1730, several Cherokees visited England, where they were presented to King George II. One observer wrote that as a gesture of peace, the Cherokees "laid at his Majesty's feet the crown of the Cherokee people, with five eagle tails."

These Cherokee warriors made a pact with the English king. "Although we are red and you are white," they swore, "yet our hands and hearts are joined together. In war, we shall always be with you."

The Cherokees lived up to their word. When the French and Indian War broke out in 1754, the Cherokees helped the English fight the French and their Indian allies. Lieutenant Colonel George Washington was one of those who witnessed the Cherokees in combat, and he never forgot their courage as warriors.

After America established its independence, the Cherokees signed a treaty with the new nation in 1785. But conflicts continued, as whites seized Cherokee land.

Finally, in 1791, the tribe gave up large amounts of territory. In return, they secured a promise from the government that their remaining land would be theirs forever. The result was the prosperous scene Hawkins found in the 1790s.

Nevertheless, more and more whites continued to look enviously at the fertile Cherokee fields. By 1806, government officials persuaded two Cherokee chiefs to sign away more land. With the approval of President Thomas Jefferson, these officials bribed two Cherokees — Doublehead and Tahlonteskee — to give up large tracts of land in Tennessee, southern Kentucky, and Alabama. In return, Doublehead and Tahlonteskee received land in the territory they had given away.

The other Cherokees were enraged when they learned of this. They executed Doublehead for treason. Tahlonteskee and a band of his followers fled for their lives. Following secret paths, they crossed the Mississippi River. Eventually, they settled in Oklahoma Territory. These Cherokees called themselves the "Old Settlers" or the "Cherokee West," and their colony was the beginning of the Cherokee Nation in the West.

Although this experience angered the eastern Cherokees, they continued to try to get along with the whites. In 1814, Cherokee warriors helped American soldiers defeat the Creek Indians, who had terrorized and killed white settlers. In fact, Cherokee fighters won the decisive battle at Alabama's Horseshoe Bend when General Andrew Jackson's own troops failed against the Creeks.

John Ross

Ross was chief of the Cherokee Nation from 1828 until his death in 1866. In 1838, the Cherokees were forced from their homeland to begin their terrible journey west, known as the Trail of Tears.

The Trail of Tears — 1838

Jackson was a bitter enemy of the Indians. He wanted all the eastern tribes removed to the West, and after the Battle of Horseshoe Bend, he took action. With President James Monroe's permission, he bribed twelve Cherokees to sign a treaty giving away thirty-five hundred acres of land.

A few years later, Jackson convinced a few Cherokees that they could make a better life in the West. In 1818, seven hundred Cherokees set out down the Tennessee River in flatboats. They eventually settled near where the "Old Settlers" had and began to clear land for farming.

Life in the West was hard. The new settlers found themselves fighting other hostile Indian tribes and making a living from less productive land. Eventually, they returned to the old tribal land in the East.

Although most Cherokees were dismayed at the idea of leaving their land, by 1818 the Cherokees had given up one-half of their territory (twenty thousand acres), hoping to satisfy the whites. The next ten years were a time of increasing trials for the Cherokees. Their farms were attacked, and others repeatedly tried to establish claims to their territory.

In 1829, gold was discovered on Cherokee land. White men seeking gold poured into the territory and became even bolder in their attempts to seize the land. Also in 1829, the Cherokees' old enemy Andrew Jackson became president.

John Ross was the Cherokee leader at the time. On several occasions, he trav-

When the four southeastern Indian nations — the Choctaws, Chickasaws, Creeks, and Cherokees — were forced to walk the Trail of Tears, they took little with them.

eled to Washington to ask Congress to help the Cherokees. He believed, as did his people, that the United States would honor its treaties and protect the Cherokees. He counseled his people to wait patiently for the help that was sure to come.

But time was running out. By 1836, attacks on the Cherokees had grown almost intolerable. The Georgia state government, insisting that Georgia was owner of the Cherokees' land, allowed whites to beat and murder the Indians.

That year, a handful of the tribe gave up hope. They signed a treaty that called for the Cherokees to be exiled from their land and removed to the West. In return for their signatures, these Cherokees were given special payments and provisions for traveling.

Most of the Cherokees still clung to the hope that the government would not desert them. But whites began taking over their farms. Many Cherokee families had to live in the forests and hunt animals on their own land.

In 1838, American troops enforced the treaty signed in 1836. The troops herded the tribe away, forcing members to begin the terrible journey that became known as the Trail of Tears. Several thousand died on this journey.

The Cherokees who did survive the Trail of Tears arrived at their new home in a state of destitution. "We had no shoes," remembered one Cherokee girl. "Many went bare-headed, but when it was cold they made things of hides to cover their heads." They had no tools. Even simple items such as spoons had to be hand-crafted of wood.

Many of the newly arrived Cherokees suffered terrible hardships. They grieved for their homeland and their dead. And they bitterly resented those tribesmen who had signed the treaty allowing the removal.

In that first year, 1839, grief erupted into violence. The leaders of the Treaty Party (the Cherokees who had signed the removal treaty) were murdered by unknown assailants. For the next seven years, the Cherokees were on the verge of civil war. Members of the Treaty Party and the Old Settlers joined together in fighting against the other Cherokees.

The warring factions signed a peace agreement in 1846. It looked as if the Cherokees might be able to achieve unity at last. But another war changed all that. When the Civil War broke out in 1861, the Cherokees faced divisions again. Some of the tribe sided with the North, some with the South. They fought on different sides throughout the four-year conflict.

Finally, in 1907, the old ways and hatreds gave way to a new order. The western territory that included Cherokee land was admitted to the Union as the state of Oklahoma. The Cherokee Nation discontinued its tribal form of government. Instead of land being held by the entire tribe, it was held by individual Cherokee citizens.

The Cherokee Nation as it had existed in the East was no more. But the proud Cherokee heritage remained. Today Americans of Cherokee descent still gather on special holidays to celebrate the richness of their ancient tribal culture.

Cherokee Nation principal chief Joe Byrd (right rear) and deputy principal chief James Garland Eagle (left rear) present awards to tribal youths.

THE INDIAN AND THE BUFFALO

by Otis Hays, Jr.

At the time Christopher Columbus arrived in America, about sixty million buffalo roamed this unsettled country from the eastern woodlands across the Great Plains to the West. The Indian tribes of the plains, from the Comanches and Utes in the south to the Dakotas, Crows, and Cheyennes in the north, all had one thing in common: They depended on the buffalo for food, clothing, and shelter. Some tribes were nomadic and spent the entire year following the slow migrations of the buffalo herds. Other tribes, such as the Pawnees, lived in established villages but sent out large hunting parties to bring back buffalo meat and skins at least twice a year. The great shaggy buffalo, which wandered in herds that sometimes covered fifty square miles of prairie, had poor eyesight and an awkward gait, and they were fairly easy prey for Indian hunters.

Before the Spanish explorers brought horses to the New World, Indians hunted on foot, often herding buffalo toward a cliff, where the animals would fall over the edge and be killed. Two of these buffalo jumps used by Shoshone Indians in Montana are still visible. The larger of the two has a huge pile of buffalo bones at the base. In the winter, Indians would try to herd the buffalo into deep snow, where they would be helpless and could not avoid the Indians' arrows.

Once dead, a buffalo was carefully butchered with stone knives. The back fat and tongue were the choice cuts. Spanish explorer Francisco Vásquez de Coronado, whose soldiers were the first white men to see the buffalo on the plains, admired the way in which the Indians used not merely the meat but the whole animal. "With the skins," Coronado wrote, "they build their tents, clothe themselves, make ropes and get wool." He also noted that the Indians used buffalo horns, hoofs, and bladders to make tools and containers. The Indians even collected dried buffalo dung, or "chips," for fuel because firewood was so scarce on the plains. Indians did not believe in killing animals for sport and used the entire carcass.

After about 1650, when Spanish horses had begun to spread among the Plains Indians, the tribes quickly realized the advantages of hunting buffalo on horseback. Many tribes became totally nomadic, moving wherever the buffalo went. Others kept their villages and tended their crops but sent out mounted hunting parties that could bring buffalo meat back from a great distance.

A "surround" became the Indians' favorite way to hunt buffalo. In a surround, two groups of hunters on horseback rode toward a herd, one group on one side of the herd, the second group on the other side. Naturally, the herd began to run. Then the Indians raced their horses in front of the leading buffalo and screamed and waved their arms. The confused buffalo usually turned back into the herd, causing the frightened animals to mill in circles. Despite the dan-

John Mix Stanley painted *Buffalo Hunt on the Southwestern Prairies* in 1845.

ger to both hunter and horse, the Indians rode among the buffalo, killing them with arrows and lances.

When the hunters returned to their camp, their packhorses were loaded with buffalo hides and meat. Behind them, where the buffalo had been killed, the Indians often left the hunting ground littered with pink buffalo hearts. Many Indians believed that, through magic power, the hearts were seeds for new buffalo.

Until 1800, the only white men seen by the Indians north of the Spanish settlements were a few French fur traders. These traders were anxious to get beaver pelts because the fashionable men and women of Europe demanded them. When the first American explorers crossed the plains, they saw vast herds of buffalo, but the buffalo hides did not interest them. After 1830, however, the supply of beaver pelts began to decline. Suddenly, there was a rising market for buffalo hides. White traders wanted more and more. By 1840, the Indians were trading at least one hundred thousand hides every year.

At this same time, the westward movement of American settlers had begun. The movement was continued after the Civil War by more settlers and cattlemen. Too late, the Indians became alarmed. They said that the unplowed, unfenced buffalo country was theirs. White Americans did not heed the Indians' words. Soon after the Civil War, Congress began creating reservations to which the tribes would be forced to move. The Indians did not want to live on reservations because they would not be able to follow the buffalo herds. To the Indians, hunting buffalo meant life, and a world without buffalo meant death. The wars between the Indians and white Americans lasted for years, but the Indians were doomed from the start.

The buffalo also was doomed. A new high-powered Sharps rifle was being used. With it, a white hunter could kill a buffalo that was nearly half a mile away, and one hunter could kill as many as two hundred buffalo every day. In addition, a new tanning process that made buffalo hides soft and useful for many leather products was invented.

Shot at the rate of one million a year, the buffalo rapidly began to vanish from the plains. The hunters, who wanted only the hides, left each skinned buffalo on the ground where it had been killed. The smell of rotting meat carried for miles. Years later, buffalo bones were gathered and shipped by the railroad carload to processing plants for products such as fertilizer and bone china.

Some members of the U.S. Army were pleased with the work of the hunters. General Philip Sheridan, a Civil War hero who was one of the Army commanders in the Indian wars, wanted all the buffalo dead. "For the sake of lasting peace," he wrote, "let the hunters kill, skin and sell until they have exterminated the buffalo." Without the buffalo to hunt and eat, the Indians would be forced to accept reservation life.

The hunters did their job well. The sixty million buffalo that had roamed the plains in 1492 were reduced to fewer than a thousand by 1886. The animal that

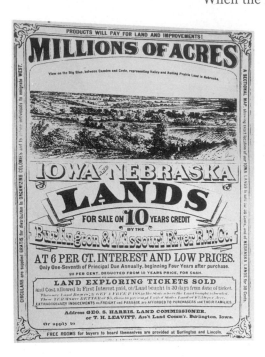

In 1873, the Burlington and Missouri River Railroad Company encouraged people to settle the millions of acres available in Iowa and Nebraska.

had been the mighty king of the plains was nearly extinct.

In 1913, Congress decided to make the buffalo nickel, a new five-cent coin that once again brought the animal and the Indian together. On one side of the coin was the buffalo, and on the other side was the face of an Indian chief. More than a billion of the coins were minted during a twenty-five-year period. Once plentiful, the coin can now be found only in private collections and museums.

The surviving buffalo have fared better than the coin. In the early 1980s, more than fifty thousand bison thrive in zoos, parks, ranches, and wildlife refuges. The numbers are increasing so rapidly that herds must be reduced to maintain a balance between numbers and rangeland.

One proposal for the use of surplus bison from America's national parks includes distribution to Indians who live on reservations. Canadian Indians of Cree and Chippewa descent continue to hunt bison that roam outside Wood Buffalo National Park in Alberta and the Northwest Territories, and some Indian tribes have herds of their own. The relationship between the Indian and the buffalo continues, although their way of life on the Great Plains has passed.

A CLOSED ROAD

by Walton Duryea

Explorer Zebulon Pike thought Santa Fe looked like a "fleet of flat-bottomed boats" when he first glimpsed the town from the crest of the low red hills that guard the eastern approach. It was March 1807, and Pike and his party had been exploring the southwestern reaches of the new Louisiana Purchase for the U.S. government. They arrived in Santa Fe as prisoners of the Spanish, however, as Americans were not welcome in New Mexico, still part of the Spanish colony of Mexico. Spain feared U.S. expansion into its territory and wished to keep Americans out.

The capital of New Mexico, Santa Fe was narrow, long, and unimpressive. At its center was a large dirt plaza shaded by a few ragged cottonwood trees. Tan adobe one-story buildings — government offices, an inn, a few stores, and some homes — surrounded the plaza. Their windows were small and their doors low. Their fronts were shaded by wooden awnings from which hung dried meat and chilies.

Zebulon Pike

Before he explored the southwestern reaches of the new Louisiana Purchase for the U.S. government in 1807, Pike searched for the source of the Mississippi River in 1805. He is shown here at Leech Lake in Minnesota in February 1806.

A few narrow streets stretched from the plaza toward outlying homes, where small fields of grain surrounded clusters of buildings.

To Pike the town appeared primitive and the people poor. The only vehicles he saw were *carretas* (two-wheeled carts) pulled by oxen. The carts were roughly made, with sides of woven sticks and wheels of round slabs cut from the ends of tree trunks. A few important citizens rode horses, but most people rode donkeys. Other donkeys carried huge loads of cornhusks or bundles of firewood brought down from the mountains. Beside the donkeys walked their masters, wrapped in colorful blankets and wearing tall hats. The women pulled shawls tightly around their heads and shoulders to keep out the cold mountain air.

Theodore R. Davis sketched Santa Fe's East San Francisco Street for *Harper's Weekly* magazine in 1866.

Spanish officials escorted Pike and his men to a long, low building on the plaza. This was the Palace of the Governors. A rough adobe building with a roof made of sod laid over poles and a floor of hard-packed earth, it was office and home to the Spanish governor. The plaza in front of the palace was the town's center and marketplace.

After questioning Pike, the governor, who suspected that Pike was a spy, sent him and his men five hundred fifty miles south to Chihuahua for further questioning by Mexican officials. It was up this trail to Chihuahua, Pike noted, that all goods and supplies for people in Santa Fe had to travel, since the town was closed to contact from the north.

Everything a family needed had to be hauled hundreds of miles across desert and through Indian territory, a five-month roundtrip by mule train. By the time goods reached Santa Fe, their prices were incredibly high. After seeing Santa Fe, Pike was sure that American traders would be welcome and could make a good profit if only they would be allowed to trade there.

Mexican officials questioned Pike closely in Chihuahua. He continued to insist that he was just an ordinary explorer, and finally, fearing trouble with the U.S. government, they released him. When Pike and his men returned to Missouri, his tale of Santa Fe and its need for reasonably priced supplies caught people's attention.

In the following years, several parties ventured west in hopes of opening up a trade route. Some wound up in Spanish prisons; others were tried and sent out of the territory. It was not until 1821, when William Becknell arrived just after Mexico's successful revolt against Spanish rule, that the gates on the road to Santa Fe were finally opened.

FATHER OF THE SANTA FE TRAIL

by Marjorie Loester

The men did not attract much attention as they rode in one late January day in 1822 — just two traders back from an unsuccessful trip. But as they began to unload their bags, the story goes, one of the bags opened, and a shower of Spanish coins fell on the main street of Franklin, Missouri, a town with little hard currency of its own at the time. Whether or not William Becknell's coins actually spilled onto Franklin's street, questions about where the traders had obtained their wealth began to fly. Where had they been? What kind of coins were they? Were there more?

A wagon train pulls into Santa Fe's Elsberg-Amberg Plaza in October 1861.

William Becknell, leader of the little group that had set out on September 1, 1821, with seventeen packhorses, had an exciting story to tell. He had decided to go west to trade with the Indians, and historians today believe that he also may have intended to go to New Mexico. His friend Zeke Williams may have warned him to steer clear of Santa Fe: "The Spanish don't want you to trade there. The last American trader that went into Mexican country landed in jail." But Williams also told him how to reach the New Mexico settlements.

They had not seen many Indians and had been traveling for some time when they reached Raton Pass in the Rocky Mountains, where they spent hours clearing rocks before their horses could get through. As they rode out of the mountains, they saw riders on the horizon — riders in uniform. They must have wondered whether they would soon be going to jail.

To their surprise, they were greeted by Mexican, not Spanish, soldiers. Mexico had won its independence from Spain in 1821, and the Spaniards had left Mexico in September. Encouraged by this news, Becknell's party headed for Santa Fe, arriving on November 16, 1821. The people of Santa Fe, with access only to expensive goods in faraway Chihuahua, rushed to buy the cheaper American goods. Becknell's group made a huge profit, and leaving all but one of his men behind, he hurried back to Missouri with the news that trade and settlers were welcome.

Little is known about Becknell before about 1810, when he married and settled in St. Louis, Missouri. He was born in 1787 or 1788 in Amherst County, Virginia, probably lived in a log cabin, and did not receive much formal education. He fought in the War of 1812 as a paid mounted ranger in one of several companies authorized by Congress to defend Missouri. Under the command of Daniel Boone's son Daniel Morgan Boone, Becknell became famous as an Indian fighter. Discharged in 1815, he probably entered the salt trade in central Missouri. In 1820, he ran unsuccessfully for the Missouri House of Representatives. A stack of bad debts prompted him on a trading and trapping trip in the West — a trip that would earn him the title "Father of the Santa Fe Trail."

Becknell did not "discover" the route; others had traveled to Santa Fe before him. But he was the first to enter the city after the Mexicans had defeated the

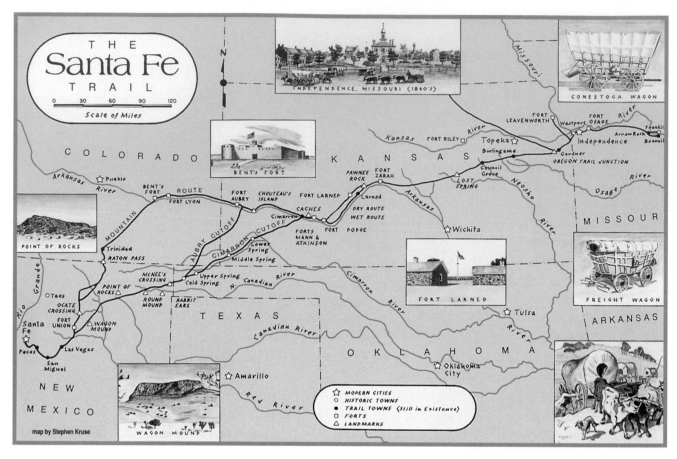

Spanish. He made his second trip with wagons so that he could carry more goods. Some historians consider this his first trading expedition because numerous traders followed the route he took with his wagons.

The second expedition left Missouri in May 1822 with twenty-one men, three wagons, and only a pocket compass and the stars to guide them. Besides the hardships of the trail, they had other problems. One night their horses were frightened off by buffalo, and eight men went after them. Two of the men were overtaken by hostile Indians, whipped, and robbed of their horses, guns, and clothes. A dangerous situation was avoided by the intervention of another trader named Auguste Chouteau, who was at the Indians' camp. Becknell and his men were allowed to continue on their way.

Knowing that he could not cross the Raton Pass with wagons, as he had done with horses on his first trip, he decided to go southwest across the Cimarron Desert, not knowing they would have to cross a sixty-mile stretch between the Arkansas and Cimarron rivers without firewood or water. If they lost their way, it would mean death.

They did reach the Cimarron River and, in New Mexico, crossed the Canadian River. Just twenty-two days after leaving the Arkansas River in Kansas, they arrived at the first settlement in New Mexico, the village of San Miguel, announcing their arrival with three rounds of rifle fire. Amazed Mexicans watched as the first American wagons ever rolled into town.

Becknell's second trip proved that wagons could cross the plains, and it did not take Missourians long to catch on. In 1824, one of the first well-organized caravans to make the trip after Becknell consisted of twenty-three wagons and eighty-one men carrying $35,000 in trade goods. They also made sure they carried water barrels. The caravan returned with $180,000 in Spanish dollars, some gold and silver bullion, and trade goods.

Becknell made a third trip through the Rockies in 1824. When he returned to Missouri in 1825, he worked with a congressional commission to map out an official route for a road that would eventually be a carrier of not only foreign goods but also foreign culture. The trail that Becknell blazed in 1822 had an enormous impact on New Mexico until 1880, when the railroad silenced the crack of the teamster's whip and the familiar cry as the wagons began to roll: "Stretch out! Stretch out!"

Wagon ruts are still visible on the Santa Fe Trail, shown here near Fort Union, New Mexico, around 1905. (Also see the map on page 38.)

NO FRILLS OR FEATHERS

by Nancy Norton Mattila

Many people died traveling west on the Santa Fe Trail. Yet you would not be exaggerating if you said the trail saved Josiah Gregg's life. Not only did it cure an apparently fatal illness, but it also gave him a consuming interest in life. Gregg spent nine years traveling the trail, then wrote a book, *Commerce of the Prairies.* This book is our most reliable account of the land, its people, and the

To this caravan, Santa Fe lies far in the distance.

life of a Santa Fe trader.

Josiah was born in Tennessee on July 19, 1806, the youngest of seven children. His parents, Harmon and Suzannah Smelser Gregg, moved first to Illinois, then to Missouri. There, they eventually established their permanent farm near present-day Independence.

Josiah was a maverick, a sensitive, delicate boy in the midst of robust frontiersmen. Yet the roughest boys could not help being impressed when, at age twelve, he built his own quadrant to measure the height of trees. Curious about everything, Josiah attended a log schoolhouse briefly but was mainly self-educated, encouraged by his mother. He taught himself mathematics and surveying, read classical literature, and worked on languages. Later his brother wrote that even as a young child, Josiah never heard a question without puzzling over an answer. Early on, he formed the habit of noting down things that interested him.

Choosing a career was difficult for this versatile young man. At eighteen, he opened his own school, then decided he did not like teaching. After his application to apprentice with a doctor was rejected, he tried reading law but found it was the most difficult subject he had ever tackled. In truth, Josiah's health was failing. His doctor tried remedy after remedy, but nothing worked. Finally, at his wit's end, he prescribed a trip down the Santa Fe Trail.

In May 1831, twenty-four-year-old Josiah Gregg left Independence, Missouri, with a caravan, lying down in a wagon. His pony trotted along behind without its saddle. Gregg ate only the fruit, rice, crackers, and tea he had brought with him. Soon, however, the open spaces and clean air improved his digestion. He slept well and awoke excited by new sights. Within a week, he had saddled his pony; within two weeks, he had abandoned the special diet. By the time the caravan reached the buffalo range, Gregg joined the hunt and relished his first buffalo meat. He now felt so well that he got himself a job as bookkeeper for a caravan merchant and studied Spanish so he could communicate in Santa Fe. And he began to record observations about this fascinating prairie experience: the sky, weather, plants, birds, animals, mirages, traders, and Indians he encountered.

During a total of eight crossings to Santa Fe and back, Gregg continued to take careful notes. He always carried a small writing desk, paper bound into little notebooks, pens, ink, and a few books and instruments. He became a merchant himself, trading American cotton goods for Mexican silver and mules. Until 1840, Gregg relished life on the open plains, free from the irksome rules of polite American society. Plagued by bouts of sickness throughout his life, he never felt better than when on the Santa Fe Trail.

Gregg began organizing his travel notes in 1842. The next year, he went to Philadelphia to complete his editing and find a publisher. When the task proved more difficult than expected, he hired an editorial assistant to work on his manuscript. Gregg wanted no frills or feathers in his book — only what he had seen, heard, or learned from reliable experience. With editorial help from John Bigelow, a young New York lawyer and writer, *Commerce of the Prairies* was published in July 1844. Gregg's maps were long considered the most accurate available.

Fifty years later, some claimed that Bigelow should have been listed as coauthor. But Bigelow wrote, "My laundry work added no more value to the washing of it than the washing and ironing adds to the value of a new garment."

Gregg had made himself an expert on the Santa Fe trade and life on the southern plains in the 1830s. His book and maps became a guide for later merchants. *Commerce of the Prairies* not only provided useful information, but it also has helped those who have come after see, hear, and feel the strangeness and mystery of the vast, empty plains.

Although wagons were too small to allow pioneers to move much furniture to their new homes, the wagons did contain bedding on which to sleep, clothing, and ammunition. If the family was lucky, they might have had room for some special possession, such as a favorite clock or a set of china, among all the necessities.

THE ROLE OF THE SUPREME COURT

by Ray Michaels

How is it that the Constitution — a document that is nearly two hundred years old and less than four thousand words long — still manages to be up-to-date and to provide the basic laws for our nation? Part of the answer has to do with the amendments. But there are still specific cases brought to court every year that are different from any that have come before, and somehow it must be decided how the laws apply to these special cases. This job of interpreting the Constitution and its twenty-six amendments is the responsibility of the Supreme Court.

THE CONSTITUTION OF THE UNITED STATES

by Frances Nankin

After the outbreak of the American Revolution in 1776, the Continental Congress, which was the assembly of people governing the United States, had to find a way to keep the thirteen states united. The document that they came up with in 1777 was called the Articles of Confederation and Perpetual Union.

The Articles gave the states the powers of taxing their citizens and regulating trade. The central government, which was made up of a Congress consisting of ambassadors from each state, had almost no power. It was supposed to handle foreign and Indian affairs, borrow money when necessary, and settle disputes between the states. But there was no way for Congress to enforce any of its decisions, because the individual states had the final say.

By 1786, almost every state was facing a crisis caused by debts, high prices, and worthless currency. The new nation was in danger of failing. In September 1786, five states attended a meeting where the larger problem of trade between all the states could be discussed. This meeting was called the Annapolis Convention. Alexander Hamilton of New York and James Madison of Virginia attended, and these two men suggested that a convention to revise the Articles of Confederation was needed. They believed that the country needed to overhaul its government.

The delegates at the Annapolis Convention invited all the states to send representatives to a meeting to be held in Philadelphia. The states appointed seventy-four delegates in all, but only fifty-five actually attended. Rhode Island sent no delegates because its government saw the convention as a conspiracy to overthrow the existing government. Other Americans also were suspicious. Patrick Henry, well-known for his leadership during the Revolution and for his speeches, refused to attend the convention because he believed it would result in the creation of a strong central government. Henry felt that state governments needed to be stronger than the central government so that citizens' individual liberties could be protected.

The delegates chose General George Washington to preside over the convention. Benjamin Franklin, who was eighty-one years old and crippled with gout, also attended. Most of the delegates had studied law, served in Colonial or state legislatures, or been in Congress. Many, especially Madison, knew a great deal about philosophical theories of government. The debates that took place both during the convention and during the period of ratification are among the most famous debates over theories of government in history.

On May 25, 1787, the Constitutional Convention officially began. The first plan put forth was the Virginia Plan, sometimes called the Large-State Plan. Presented by Edmund Randolph of Virginia, it proposed a strong central government with leadership and representation based on wealth and population. The larger states, with their greater number of people, would have a greater voice in the government.

The New Jersey Plan, also called the Small-State Plan, was presented in opposition to the Virginia Plan. Under the New

The Supreme Court is not a court in the usual sense. There is no jury. Instead, the Supreme Court has judges, called justices. The Court is made up of one chief justice and eight associate justices. The nine members of the Court are considered experts in matters of law, and they are expected to rule justly. Once on the Court, a justice remains there for life, unless he or she resigns, breaks the law, or otherwise proves untrustworthy. In addition, a justice's salary may not be cut for as long as he or she is on the Court. These two policies help to ensure that the justices need not worry about being punished for making unpopular rulings.

During its early years, the Court was not as important or as respected as the legislative

Opposite: George Washington (right) presides over the signing of the U.S. Constitution, while an ailing Benjamin Franklin (seated center) looks on.

Jersey Plan, all states, regardless of wealth or population, would have equal representation in the central government.

The basic ideas in both plans were later combined into what became known as the Great Compromise or the Connecticut Compromise. This plan, presented by Oliver Ellsworth of Connecticut, proposed two houses of Congress instead of the one house then in use under the Articles. The lower house, or House of Representatives, would have members elected according to the population of each state; the upper house, or Senate, would have members elected according to equal representation from each state regardless of its size. Once the Great Compromise was accepted, the worst disagreements were settled. The Constitution was on its way to completion.

The Constitution of the United States, adopted by the convention on September 17, 1787, is the world's oldest written constitution. It provides the rules for a central government, while still allowing some matters to be decided by the state governments. It includes provisions for separation of powers among the executive (president), legislative (Congress), and judicial (Supreme Court) branches of government, and it provides a system of checks and balances so that no one branch can dominate.

The Constitution as it was adopted in September 1787 does not include guarantees of individual liberties. These were provided for in the Bill of Rights, the first ten amendments to the Constitution added in 1791.

On September 28, 1787, Congress, still operating under the Articles of Confederation, sent copies of the newly written Constitution to each state. Nine of the thirteen states had to approve the Constitution. On the first day of summer the following year, after months of heated debate throughout the states, the ninth state gave its approval. The Constitution of the United States had been ratified. George Washington took office as the first president of the United States in 1789.

More than two centuries have passed. The Constitution has endured and continues to inspire the thousands of people who view the original document at the National Archives every year.

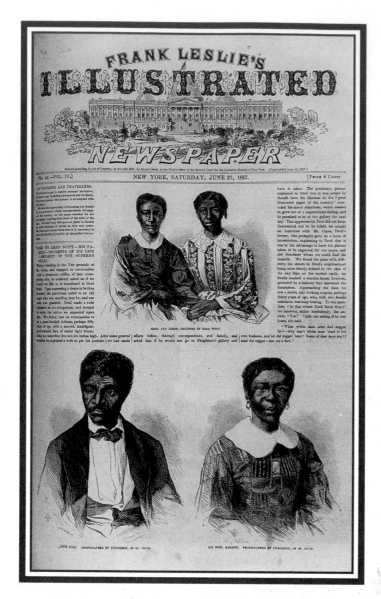

One of the most important Supreme Court cases of all time involved Dred Scott, a slave from Missouri who sued for his freedom. The front page of *Frank Leslie's Illustrated Newspaper* featured the Scott family — his children top center and Dred and his wife below — on June 27, 1857.

(Congress) and executive (president) branches of government. But in 1801, when John Marshall became the fourth chief justice of the Court, the role of the Supreme Court began to change. Under Marshall's leadership, the Court took on the power to rule on laws passed by the president and Congress. The Court could rule that these laws were "unconstitutional," or illegal. This gave the court a greater authority than it had held previously, and it is a power that is still very important in the Court's activities today.

Supreme Court justices are expected to base their decisions on the arguments they hear and on legal principles. They should not be swayed by popular opinion or their personal attitudes. But justices cannot help but be aware of the attitudes of their fellow citizens, and in some cases they share these attitudes. Through the years, the justices of the Supreme Court have made a number of rulings that seem unfair to us today when we look back on them. But because the rulings reflected attitudes popular at the time, many people agreed with them.

Many Supreme Court cases in our history show our Constitution at work, using a built-in system of checks and balances. They also show how popular opinion can influence the justices' decisions and how only the passage of time makes that influence apparent.

The following case is considered by many to be the Court's most famous. The year was 1857. A slave from Missouri named Dred Scott had taken his owner to court to demand his freedom. Scott said he had a right to his freedom because he had traveled with his owner through Illinois and Wisconsin Territory, where slavery had been made illegal by an act of Congress known as the Missouri Compromise. But the Court ruled that it was unconstitutional for Congress to pass laws affecting territories that had not yet become states. It also ruled that Congress could not pass laws affecting African Americans, since African Americans were not considered citizens under the Constitution. Thus Dred Scott could not claim his freedom. Scott's owner set him free not

long after the ruling anyway, but a great many people were outraged by the Court's ruling. Many Americans at the time wanted to bring an end to slavery, and they considered the Missouri Compromise to be an important step toward that goal.

In the years after the Civil War, many states passed laws to prevent newly freed African Americans from taking part in government and society. States passed laws that forced African Americans to use separate facilities from whites. There were separate waiting areas in train depots, separate schools, and so on. In 1896, the Supreme Court ruled that such "separate but equal" laws were acceptable. At the time, many people agreed with the decision.

THE SELLING OF A PRESIDENT IN 1840

by Andrew Baker, Old Sturbridge Village

Economic depression. A threat of war. Disputes over the powers of the president and the federal government. An unpopular Democratic president finishing up a difficult four-year term. These were some of the circumstances surrounding the presidential campaign of 1840. The Whigs, with a very good chance to elect a president for the first time, passed over well-known politicians like Henry Clay and Daniel Webster. Instead, they nominated William Henry Harrison, an aging ex-general from Ohio. He had little political experience and few enemies.

The campaign of 1840 paid little attention to issues and a great deal of attention to personalities, images, and hoopla. It established, in the words of one historian, "a new pattern in American politics. It inaugurated the circus-carnival atmosphere that would mark presidential elections for years in the future and that would awe or amuse European beholders. It was the start of vast meetings, shouting parades, party badges...and campaign songs."

The Whig campaign very quickly took on the character of a well-organized media event. "Tippecanoe and Tyler, too!" became the widely used slogan. The slogan had more rhyme than reason to it, as one Whig delegate admitted. Harrison's greatest claim to fame was a somewhat questionable victory over an Indian alliance at Tippecanoe, Indiana. Harrison was governor of Indiana Territory at the time.

The Democrats had many unkind words for Harrison, but one of their criticisms was that he was suited for little more than life in a log cabin with plenty of hard cider to drink. The Whigs, however, turned this criticism around and made the log cabin and hard cider symbols for Harrison's campaign. The symbols gave Harrison popular appeal and helped get him elected president.

Ignoring many of the important issues of the day, Whig politicians traveled the nation addressing conventions, meetings, and demonstrations. These get-togethers were organized to recruit and persuade many citizens who were undecided to vote for Harrison. Biographies and portraits of Harrison appeared in newspapers. Songs were composed. Whig storekeepers sold merchandise

William Henry Harrison

Before Harrison became president in 1841, he was commander of the troops in the Northwest Territory and defeated the Shawnee chief Tecumseh at the Battles of Tippecanoe and the Thames River.

labeled with Harrison's likeness and pictures of log cabins.

Women took part in the festivities, even though they could not vote. They occasionally joined in the parades and held their own celebrations, complete with banners, dinner, and toasting. One company of Whig women wore uniforms of dark dresses and palm-leaf hats decorated with sprigs of wheat.

Most Whig meetings were incomplete without the usual music and singing. Refreshments consisted of cider, cheese and crackers, and even a meal of "plain log cabin fare": cold beef, ham, bread, cider, and nut cakes. Local and sometimes national politicians spoke at the gatherings.

The Democrats tried in vain to keep up with this new type of campaign strategy. Unfortunately, they were forced to spend most of their time trying to correct the lies and half-truths printed in Whig newspapers. They spread a few rumors of their own but had little time to discuss the issues.

Because of their campaigning, the Whigs were able to attract many new voters. In Massachusetts, they won by a margin of fifteen thousand votes. It made no difference that the Democrats again voted for their candidate, Martin Van Buren. With the help of the new Whig voters, William Henry Harrison won the election.

Several things happened during the campaign and election of 1840 that set a new trend for elections in later years.

Martin Van Buren

President Van Buren (1837–1841) lost the 1840 presidential race to Harrison. He ran again in 1848 as a Free-Soil candidate and lost to Zachary Taylor.

- Harrison was the first presidential candidate to campaign actively for himself. Before 1840, candidates had allowed others to do the campaigning for them.

- The Democrats, in an attempt to get the public to focus on the issues, published the first national party platform. Before 1840, no official party platform had been released.

- The Whigs used campaign gimmicks — buttons, songs, slogans — more than any campaigning political party had done before. Presidential elections would never be the same.

- A political party addressed the question of slavery in the United States. The Liberty party, founded by abolitionists, campaigned for the abolition of slavery. Even though the Liberty party had little effect on the election, the party initiated many changes that were to take place over the next twenty years.

The 1840 election also was full of ironies. The greatest of these was that Harrison died only one month after taking office. John Tyler, who had only recently joined the Whig party (he had been a Jeffersonian Democrat), became president. It was also ironic that Harrison, who was in fact the son of a wealthy aristocrat, was featured as a log cabin farmer in his campaign. His opponent, Van Buren, the son of a poor tavern keeper, was cast by the Whigs as an aristocrat and a monarchist.

One town historian wrote in 1856, "The log cabin had its day and will not probably again exert its magic influence in making presidents." Perhaps not, but electioneering techniques pioneered in 1840 still help to make presidents today.

THE MEXICAN WAR

by Howard Mansfield

Early in April 1846, two armies were perched along the banks of the Rio Grande. On the north bank of the muddy river, General Zachary Taylor's Army of Observation drilled under the Texas sun. Across the river sat the Mexican army. At sundown, the regimental band of each played its showiest music. The Americans played "Yankee Doodle," one officer said, "because it made a loud noise." Then they gathered on the riverbank to hear the Mexican music, which, the same officer said, "surpassed anything ever heard from a military band."

The next month, when the Mexican army advanced across the river and attacked Taylor's troops, President James Polk called on Congress to declare war. "Mexico," Polk said, "has shed American blood upon the American soil.... War exists...by the act of Mexico herself."

But whose land was it? Mexico regarded the land north of the Rio Grande as its own. The United States claimed that land for the new state of Texas. Mexico had broken off relations with the United States when the Texas Republic had been granted statehood the previous year, and since that time, the two countries had been at a standstill.

The dispute along the Rio Grande was the last in a long line of disagreements that touched off the Mexican War of 1846 to 1848. Historians say the war was avoidable, needless, and yet bound to happen. The United States and Mexico had many conflicting interests, and attempts to settle them peacefully had failed.

Prior to the war, American settlers had been flowing into the disputed territory. Many Americans believed that the country had a "manifest destiny," a God-given mission, to occupy the continent from the Atlantic to the Pacific. Polk had been elected on the promise of adding Oregon and Texas to the Union. He also wanted California, which was part of Mexico. More radical elements called for annexing all of Mexico. Added to this were unsettled claims Americans had against the Mexican government for losses during Mexico's war for independence, which had taken place in the early 1800s. Attempts to settle the claims had dragged on for twenty years.

At the request of the Mexican government, Polk had sent a diplomat to Mexico to settle the claims. Polk also had instructed him to suggest that the United States buy California and New Mexico. The Mexicans, who wanted to discuss only the claims, were angered that the two issues had been combined. They sent the diplo-

Zachary Taylor

The Mexican War made Taylor (1784–1850) a hero and paved the way for him to become president in 1849.

General Winfield Scott and his troops entered Mexico City on September 14, 1847, ending the war.

mat home, and Polk sent U.S. troops to the Rio Grande, setting the stage for war.

In a crowded and tense session, Congress approved Polk's call for war even though there were strong opponents. One young congressman, Abraham Lincoln, accused the president of stationing troops on what was clearly foreign territory. Antislavery forces opposed the war because they feared that any new territory would enter the Union as a slave state. And in Concord, Massachusetts, far from the disputed border, Henry David Thoreau went to jail for refusing to pay his poll tax in protest of slavery and ultimately the war.

The Mexicans expected an easy victory. They were encouraged by past victories over Texans at the Alamo and by their observations of Taylor's army across the river. Military experts in Europe also thought the Mexicans would win. But despite these predictions and their superior numbers, the Mexican army did not win one battle. After the war, American success was attributed in part to their use of light artillery and to political upheaval in Mexico.

The war was fought in four areas (northern Mexico, California, New Mexico, and central Mexico) in a stop-and-go fashion, with months between some battles. From the Rio Grande, Taylor advanced south, winning victories in the first days of the war at Palo Alto and just across the river at Matamoros. He then sat still for four months, awaiting recruits and transport. In September, his troops advanced farther south, taking the city of Monterrey after a four-day siege. Taylor then agreed to an eight-week armistice but cut it short after being criticized by President Polk.

Taylor's last and most famous battle occurred five months later at Buena Vista. Many of Taylor's soldiers had been sent south for an attack on Mexico City. The orders for the troop movement were intercepted by Mexican president and general Antonio López de Santa Anna, who marched on Taylor's diminished army, expecting to rout him. Outnumbered three to one, Taylor's troops held off the attack. There were no further battles in northern Mexico, and Taylor returned home to a hero's welcome.

Meanwhile, other action was taking place in California and New Mexico. Just prior to the war, American settlers in California had revolted against Mexican rule and had declared that territory the Bear Flag Republic. Captain John Frémont led several campaigns against Mexicans in California and helped secure the territory for the United States. In New Mexico, General Stephen Kearny and the Army of the West took Santa Fe without firing a shot. The army then marched on to California.

By the end of 1846, eight months after declaring war, Polk had control of all the territory he sought, but Mexico remained unconquered. The spotlight fell on General Winfield Scott, who led the last campaign of the war. Landing at Veracruz, Scott surrounded and shelled that city and then marched on to Mexico City. In five months, Scott's army won a number of fierce battles, and on September 14, 1847, General Scott and his troops entered the central square of Mexico City, ending the war.

The following February, the Treaty of Guadalupe Hidalgo settled the terms of peace. Mexico ceded half of its territory to the United States, including land that now comprises California, Arizona, Utah, Nevada, and parts of Colorado, New Mexico, and Texas, making up about one-sixth of the continental United States. In return, the United States paid Mexico fifteen million dollars and released its citizens from all claims.

The war produced many heroes in the United States. Zachary Taylor became the next president, and Winfield Scott and John Frémont later made unsuccessful runs for the presidency. It also provided a training ground for many soldiers, including Ulysses S. Grant, Robert E. Lee, William T. Sherman, and "Stonewall" Jackson, who later fought in the Civil War.

In Mexico, General Santa Anna resigned the presidency, but he would return several times in the coming years as Mexico continued to face political turmoil.

James Gadsden

THE GADSDEN PURCHASE
by Howard Mansfield

A few years after the Mexican War ended, the United States bought more land from Mexico. The Treaty of Guadalupe Hidalgo had been vague about the boundary at the Gila River, which is located in what are now Arizona and New Mexico. The governor of New Mexico threatened to send troops to occupy the area in question, but Mexico quickly sent in troops instead.

For several years, proponents of a transcontinental railroad wanted the land south of the Gila River for a southern rail route. In 1853, President Franklin Pierce appointed James Gadsden, a railroad builder, to negotiate a purchase. Pierce also wanted Gadsden to purchase lower California, known as the Baja Peninsula. General Santa Anna was once again in power, and his government needed money. But Gadsden's attitude insulted Mexican nationalists, so Santa Anna agreed to sell only the narrow strip of land that was needed for the proposed rail route. The United States paid ten million dollars for the 29,670 square miles of land, which made construction of the Southern Pacific Railroad possible.

The Gadsden Purchase set the final boundaries of what would become the forty-eight states. No more land would be added to the continental United States.

NUGGETS, HALOES, AND SWEET CHARIOTS: HITCHING WAGONS TO OTHER STARS

Gold was discovered in the Sacramento Valley the same year the United States gained California from Mexico. The largest single group of Americans set off, most of the time less interested in settling than in getting rich quick and returning to families in the East. They were less careful in making preparations, and many risked unknown short-cuts when they left the Oregon Trail west of the Rockies. Those who travelled in 1849 encountered the worst summer weather of any year.

The Donner party split off through the Sierra Mountains, ignoring the advice of Indian guides. A few survived only because they lived off the flesh of mules and humans who perished in an early autumn storm. A twelve-year-old girl in the group summed up the trip with a warning: "Never take no cut-offs and hury [sic] along as fast as you can."

The spring of '49 was uncommonly cold. At Independence, one man slept forty nights in his wagon, waiting for the grass to sprout enough to feed his mules along the way. Leaving too late meant risking blizzards at the other end. Chilling winds and bitter nights continued across the plains all summer. Flour and sugar were ruined by rain, wheels sunk to their hubs in mud, and cattle ran for miles during hailstorms and a Nebraskan tornado in May. Many people died of cholera. Teamsters had to wear kerchiefs over their faces to avoid the pain of whirling sand and gravel. The Forty-Niners had the roughest experience of any along the trail. Some chose to reach the California goldfields by steamer. It was more expensive but safer and faster. At times they had to burn the furniture to keep the engines moving, and those who went overland through the isthmus of Panama risked yellow fever and malaria for the promise of instant wealth.

Relations between miners and Indians worsened. Isolated skirmishes made headlines, and myths of racial superiority became policies of extermination. When the Federal Government spent $80,000 to open a shorter route from Sioux City to the mines of Virginia City, local Crow warriors retaliated at the destruction of their homelands. By a treaty in 1865 they gave up the 300,000 square miles promised them in a treaty signed fourteen years earlier. The Crow were "removed" to the north, and soon the Northern Cheyenne and Nez Perce were forced from their ancestral homes because of gold discoveries there. Unfortunately, the Chinese who found employment in the mines were also mistreated.

Former slaves, emancipated after the Civil War, looked to the West to live out

Panning for gold in the Colorado River in the 1890s.

From Katharine Emsden, *Voices From the West: Life Along the Trail,* Perspectives on History Series, pp. 38–42. Copyright © 1992 Discovery Enterprises, Ltd., Lowell, Massachusetts.

50

Although Bent's Fort was in the middle of the plains, something was always going on. Indian tribes camped near its walls, traded, held dances, and waited for the payments promised to them in peace treaties. The fort also served as a ransom center for Mexicans and Americans captured by Indians.

Many famous people in frontier history spent time at the fort. Long before Kit Carson gained fame as a military scout and soldier, he was a frequent visitor to Bent's Fort. His friendship with the Bents began in 1829, when he and about ninety trappers helped rescue them and their Santa Fe–bound caravan from a prolonged Indian attack. In the 1830s, Carson brought his Arapaho wife, Singing Wind, to live at Bent's Fort, and later he worked there as a hunter.

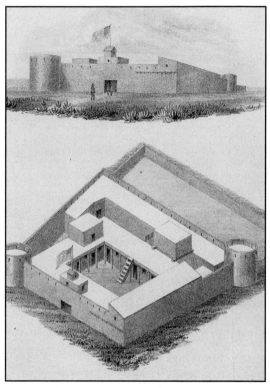

An 1845 lithograph of Bent's Fort.

Some tourists traveled the trail, stopped by the fort, and spread its fame in newspaper articles, books, and diaries. Susan Shelby Magoffin honeymooned on the trail with her prominent trader husband, Samuel, in 1846. She kept a diary of her adventures, including her twelve-day stay at Bent's Fort.

Few white women had traveled the trail, and Magoffin's visit created quite a stir. Everyone was anxious to get a peek at her and to pay their respects to "Madam." Susan described the fort as "an ancient castle." She was delighted by the ice water served there, fascinated by the Mexican and Indian women, and critical of the billiard table and the gambling that went with it.

At the time of Magoffin's visit, Bent's Fort had another guest — Stephen Watts Kearny — along with his sixteen-hundred-man Army of the West. As William Bent scouted the way, Colonel Kearny launched the invasion of New Mexico in the Mexican War. Kearny peacefully captured Santa Fe, and New Mexico became U.S. territory.

The war and its aftermath brought changes to the trail and to Bent's Fort. Government supply wagons, troops, and land-seeking emigrants soon outnumbered traders, scattered the buffalo herds, and doomed the Indians' way of life. The fur trade was no longer prosperous.

Charles Bent was killed in 1847 in an uprising of Mexicans and Indians in Taos, New Mexico, where he served as governor. In the late 1840s, Ceran St. Vrain dissolved the partnership. The huge fort was costly and filled with painful memories. William Bent stripped it and moved his family and crew downriver. Then he blew up the fort, probably because the U.S. Army, which had offered to buy it, would not pay him the price he wanted.

He built a smaller stone trading post, Bent's New Fort, in 1852–53. It was on the Santa Fe Trail, too, and also buzzed with activity. He rented it to the government in 1860 and spent his last years on a ranch at the mouth of the Purgatoire River in Colorado, trading, distributing government payments to the Indians, and doing all he could to help the Cheyennes adapt to the new world coming down the Santa Fe Trail. Bent died at his ranch in 1869 after taking one last caravan over the Raton Pass section of the trail.

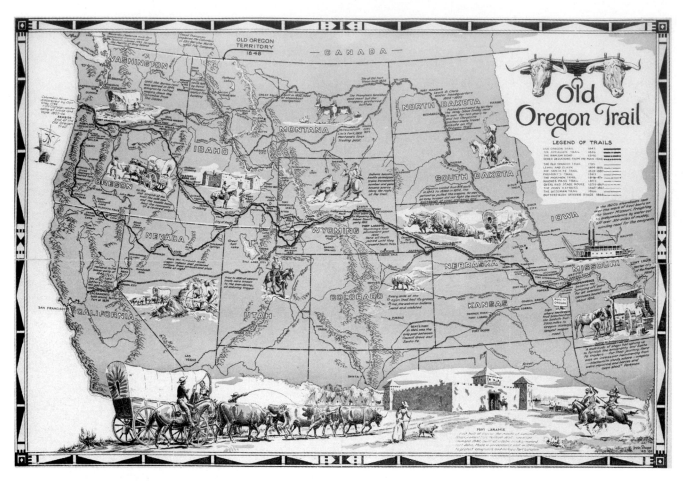

The Old Oregon Trail "was issued by the American Pioneer Trails Association in connection with the 1948 Old Oregon Centennial commemorating the admission in 1848 of Oregon into our union — a vast, rich realm out of which has been carved not only present Oregon, but Washington, Idaho, and parts of Montana and Wyoming."

THE OREGON TRAIL

Americans have long been thought of as a restless people. They seem to have always been on the move, searching for a better place to live. From America's first colonies, small groups of people uprooted themselves, migrating west to look for better farmland. They built pioneer roads, or trails, such as the Cumberland Road that led into the Ohio Valley and the Genesee Road that led across New York to the shores of Lake Erie. Many of these roads and trails have disappeared. Others can still be traced, revealing artifacts along the way that help us to re-create their story.

The Oregon Trail is one of these trails. Even today, you can retrace its path, walking beside wagon ruts that were gouged almost a century and a half ago. The Oregon Trail was different from the earlier trails and roads that had crossed the Appalachian Mountains in the East. It was longer and more difficult than most pioneers had experienced. Unlike the eastern trails, the Oregon Trail crossed nearly two thousand miles of unfamiliar prairies, deserts, and mountainous regions. There were no settlements along the way that could offer friendly hospitality, and emigrants could not scout out their new homeland before they moved there. Oregon Country was so far away that it took four to six months to get there. When people moved there, they moved to stay.

The story of the Oregon Trail and the people who used it begins when the trail was an ancient Indian footpath used by explorers and fur traders. Independence, Missouri, was the frontier town that served as the starting place. The trail wound westward, following the banks of the Platte, North Platte, and Snake rivers. It crossed the Rockies through the South Pass, crossed the Blue Mountains farther north, and ended in Oregon Country at a place called The Dalles. From The Dalles, anyone continuing on to the Willamette Valley floated down the Columbia River. Up until the mid-1830s, no wagon or white woman had ever made the trip.

It is difficult for us to imagine Oregon Country as it was a century and a half ago. A vast wilderness that stretched from the crest of the Rockies to the Pacific coast, it included the present states of Oregon, Washington, and Idaho. The area was inhabited by several Indian tribes, including the Cayuse, Umatilla, and Nez Perce tribes. There were some trappers and traders in the region, but to most white Americans, the area was too far away and too strange for them to consider settling there.

Americans have long been thought of as a restless people. They seem to have always been on the move, searching for a better place to live.

President Thomas Jefferson was the first to encourage exploration of Oregon Country. After the Louisiana Purchase of 1803, he sent Meriwether Lewis and William Clark into the area to seek a trade route to the Pacific. Jefferson knew that their explorations would help the United States strengthen its claim to the Pacific Northwest.

It is important to remember that for the first half of the nineteenth century, both Great Britain and the United States occupied the Pacific Northwest. Great Britain already had a strong claim to the land that was to become Canada, and the Hudson's Bay Company had many fur-trading posts in the Pacific Northwest. There were American fur-trading posts as well, such as the American Fur Company organized by John Jacob Astor in 1808.

In 1818, Great Britain and the United States signed a treaty that allowed both countries to occupy the area, but it was not until the 1830s that Americans began moving in. Missionaries such as Marcus and Narcissa Whitman were among the first settlers. When people learned that the Whitmans had journeyed successfully over the Oregon Trail in 1836, they began to think differently about Oregon Country. The facts that a woman had made the journey safely and that

Felix Octavius Carr Darley (1822–1888), widely known for his pen-and-ink sketches, produced this illustration of emigrants crossing the plains.

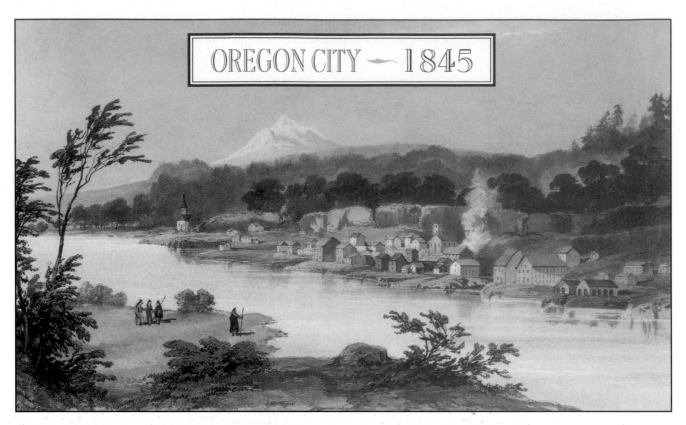

OREGON CITY ～ 1845

the Whitmans had traveled with a wagon encouraged others to think that they could make the journey, too.

When Marcus Whitman returned to the East in 1842 to help promote his missionary work, he found many people eager to travel to Oregon Country. In 1843, some one thousand people and two thousand animals joined Whitman and a surveyor named Jesse Applegate as they led a wagon train over the Oregon Trail. The "great migration" — one of the greatest migrations in recorded history — had begun.

Why were so many people going to Oregon Country? Some said they had Oregon fever, a "disease" that made them restless, hungry for new land, and eager for adventure. But why were they going all the way to Oregon Country? One very important reason was that the U.S. government was encouraging them to do so. Since Thomas Jefferson's presidency, the government had come a long way toward believing that the United States should stretch from coast to coast. If Americans were to settle Oregon Country in large numbers, the United States' claim to the land would be strengthened.

One man in particular wrote reports about Oregon Country that were designed to make people want to go there. His name was John Charles Frémont. He was a soldier who, in 1838, was asked to be the chief assistant in mapping the upper waters of the Mississippi and Missouri rivers. He wrote very detailed descriptions of his explorations, and his reports were reprinted and read by many people. It was Frémont who wrote guidebooks for emigrants who were encouraged to settle in Oregon Country and help wrest it from British control.

As Americans began pouring into the Willamette River valley in the 1840s, a dispute between Great Britain and the United States almost caused a war. The biggest disagreement was over the northern boundary of Oregon Country. The British wanted the boundary to be on the north bank of the Columbia River. The Americans wanted it farther north on the fifty-fourth parallel. After careful negotiations, war was prevented when the two countries signed the Oregon Treaty of 1846. They agreed to compromise, placing the boundary on the forty-ninth parallel.

The Oregon Treaty gave the United States undisputed claim to the Pacific Northwest, encouraging even more emigrants to move west. By the 1850s, the Oregon Trail had become a series of parallel wagon ruts that could be seen even in solid rock. Oregon Country officially became Oregon Territory in 1848. In 1859, the state of Oregon was created and admitted to the Union as the thirty-third state. Twenty years earlier, the area had been an unknown wilderness.

What was it like to travel on the Oregon Trail in the 1840s and 1850s? Fortunately, many accounts have survived, written by people who used the trail and who wanted to preserve their experiences for later generations. When we read these accounts, we can easily imagine the hardships, anxiety, and excitement the emigrants must have experienced.

According to several historians, at least thirty thousand emigrants died on the Oregon Trail between 1843 and 1859. You might say that there is an average of one grave for every one hundred yards of trail from the Missouri River to the Willamette River. Why did so many people die? Cholera, a disease that spreads in filthy conditions caused by garbage and sewage, claimed thousands of lives. Emigrants passed through, and sometimes camped near, the refuse left by earlier wagon trains. Other diseases caused people to die, but cholera was probably the most common.

Accidents were another common cause of death. Children often hurt themselves as the wagons rolled along. Doctors were not always available, and even when they were, they often lacked necessary supplies. Most of the emigrants were simply not prepared for the difficult journey ahead, and they were careless.

Indians created some problems as the emigrants passed through Indian territory. Indian attacks usually took the form of raids on livestock, but few people were killed. The Indians officially owned much of the land on both sides of the Oregon Trail, and the emigrants were trespassing. Some tribal leaders demanded payment as the wagon trains rolled through, and if the emigrants cooperated, there was no further trouble. In other instances, the Indians made a surprise attack, took livestock, and left the wagons unharmed.

It would be several years before the Indians would realize that their homelands had been lost forever. Tribal chiefs such as Red Cloud and Crazy Horse, both of the Oglala Sioux, devoted their lives to trying to save their homelands and peoples. But the idea that the United States should stretch from coast to coast had already taken hold. The Oregon Trail, no longer just a footpath, had opened the way to the West.

John Charles Frémont

Frémont's reports of his travels in Nevada, the Rocky Mountains, Oregon, and California urged many people to go west. It is not surprising that he was known as the "Pathfinder."

LEGENDS
OF THE GRAND CANYON

Once, a very long time ago, there was a curious young man named Tiyo. Tiyo was an ancestor of the Hopi Indians. He lived near the rim of the Grand Canyon and would often sit on the cliffs, looking down at the mysterious river far below. Tiyo's people did not know where the river went, and Tiyo wanted very much to find out. He thought about how he could do this and one day sealed himself up inside a hollowed-out log. He set himself adrift on the river and journeyed for days without knowing where he was going. Finally, he arrived in the underworld of the Hopi gods. There he met the snake people, who took him in and taught him many things.

Tiyo fell in love with a young snake girl and married her. He returned to the land of his people with his bride, and she bore him many children. But Tiyo's people were afraid of the snake children, and they drove them and their mother from the village.

When the Hopi gods learned of this, they grew very angry. They caused a drought. The people suffered and knew they must bring the snake children and their mother back so that the drought would end. So they welcomed the snake people into their village. To this day, the Hopis make snakes a part of the ceremony they perform to bring rain.

There are other legends told by Native Americans living in the region of the Grand Canyon. The Hualapai Indians have a tale that tells how the Canyon came into being. They say that ages ago, a flood covered the earth. Water was everywhere, and there was no place for it to drain away. So Packithaawi, a legendary hero, "struck his knife deep into the water-covered ground, and there the great canyon was soon formed."

The Havasupai Indians, who live inside the Grand Canyon today, have a legend that tells how they came to settle there. The story centers on two pillarlike rocks perched on the cliffs just above their village. They call these rocks the Wigeleeva. The Havasupais believed that the Wigeleeva were protective spirits, and they settled beneath them to ensure a good harvest each year. The legend warns that if the Wigeleeva should ever fall, the Havasupais will no longer exist.

These legends were passed down from generation to generation, and they helped to make the Grand Canyon seem less mysterious to the people who lived in and around it. Today there are more scientific explanations about the Canyon and its beginnings. There are also many mysteries still waiting to be solved.

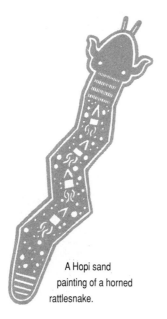

A Hopi sand painting of a horned rattlesnake.

The Grand Canyon of the Colorado River

The Grand Canyon is the major chasm of the Colorado River and its tributaries. Located in the northwest corner of Arizona, the Canyon is about one mile deep in its central section and about ten miles across from rim to rim. One of the greatest geological exhibits on earth, it is listed with the Nile River as one of the seven natural wonders of the world. No one has ever looked at it without wondering how it came to be.

Over a period of about ten million years, the Colorado River and its tributaries have been cutting downward through the slowly lifting plateaus of northwestern Arizona. The rocky cliffs exposed by the erosion have origins dating as far back as two billion years. Many people earn their living by studying the geological history of the Canyon's walls. Archaeologists have explored limestone caves in the walls and found figures of animals made from twigs that are four thousand years old. They dug into the layers of rock and found the bones of an extinct mountain goat and a giant vulture. As they dug deeper, they found driftwood dating back thirty-seven thousand years! No one is sure how the driftwood got there, because the entrance to the cave in which it was found is one hundred forty feet above the river. This is only one of the Canyon's mysteries still to be solved.

Native Americans Settle in the Region

About four thousand years ago, Native Americans lived in the region of the Grand Canyon and probably used the Canyon as their hunting grounds. About one thousand years ago, the Pueblo Indians actually made the Canyon their home, building their houses in the cliffs and farming on the Canyon floor. More than five hundred Pueblo ruins have been found in the Grand Canyon area. However, by the year A.D. 1200, the Pueblos had abandoned their villages and never returned. No one knows why they left the area.

At the same time that the Pueblo people were leaving the region, the Havasupai Indians were settling beneath the Wigeleeva in Havasu Canyon. They have been hunting, farming, and living in the Canyon ever since. Their story begins hundreds of years before the story of the white man in this country.

Today the Grand Canyon is in the heart of the Hualapai, Havasupai, and Navajo reservations. These Native Americans and others living nearby have played an important part in the history of the region.

Spanish Conquistadors Explore the Region

In 1540, eighty years before the Pilgrims landed at Plymouth Rock, a small band of Spanish conquistadors, led by the Hopi Indians, arrived at the Canyon's rim. They went in search of riches and wealthy cities that they could claim for Spain. The Grand Canyon was disappointing to them. It seemed to be a barren,

In the years 1871 to 1879, photographer John K. Hillers captured the Colorado River, which flows through Arizona's Grand Canyon.

69

empty land that served no purpose. Looking down at the river far below, they estimated that the river was only six feet wide and that the way to the bottom was a few hours' walk. But after trying several times to get to the bottom, they gave up and went back the way they had come.

The Hopis must have thought the Spaniards were very strange. To the Hopis, the Canyon was an old friend. They knew the way to the bottom and knew that the river was much wider than six feet. But they said nothing, hoping their visitors would go away, which they did.

Two hundred years passed before the Canyon had another Spanish visitor. This time, a missionary searching for new Indian tribes climbed down into the Canyon. He traveled down a very steep trail and entered a canyon whose walls were so high that the sun did not rise until ten o'clock. He came to a place with trees, grass, and rich crops. There was a good system of irrigation ditches, and horses and cattle were grazing. The year was 1776, and he had found the Havasupai people in their home. The Havasupais were very polite to him, treating him to a feast that lasted five days, but they did not ask him to stay any longer, and he left.

John Wesley Powell led the first expedition down the Green and Colorado rivers through the Grand Canyon in 1869. His studies were largely responsible for unlocking the mysteries of the West for the American public.

The American Frontier Arrives

It is important to remember that the Grand Canyon was part of Mexico until 1848, when the war between the United States and Mexico ended. Until that time, white men visiting the Grand Canyon from the east were traveling in Mexico. They were mostly trappers and fur traders. To them, the Grand Canyon was a barrier. It made it very difficult to get to the other side of the Colorado River. For the most part, they avoided the region.

However, when the Civil War ended and railroads extended into the area, people became interested in exploring this part of the American frontier. In 1869, the same year the first transcontinental railroad was completed, Major John Wesley Powell, a Civil War veteran, made the first scientific expedition down the Colorado River. At that time, maps usually left the Canyon area blank, but Powell's studies helped to change that.

Unfortunately, the arrival of white men to the region brought changes to the lives of the Native Americans living there. Prospectors in search of precious metals invaded the Canyon with burros used to carry their equipment. Some of the burros were set free and made the Canyon their home. It was not long before there were more burros than the land could feed. The Canyon was grazed until there was not enough food for the bighorn sheep and deer already living there. Many animals starved. Because these animals were food for the Havasupai and Hualapai Indians, and for other reasons as well, the Native Americans were angered by this invasion of their homelands. Trouble soon broke out, and by the end of the 1800s, the Native Americans were under strict government control.

Mining in the Canyon was never really successful. Few people struck it rich. But as more and more people came to the Canyon to marvel at its incredible beauty, some of the prospectors discovered that they could earn a better living as guides. They built tourist camps and organized Canyon tours. By the early 1900s, tourism had become the way to make money. To protect the environment in and around the Canyon, rules were drawn up for its use. Finally, in 1919 an act of Congress created Grand Canyon National Park.

There are still many problems to be solved in the preservation of the Grand Canyon. About five million people visit the Canyon every year. Nearly one-third of them hike and/or camp there. The National Park Service works very hard to protect the land and the wildlife from the pollution and destruction caused by so many people.

Why do so many people visit the Grand Canyon? Probably every visitor has a different reason, but people come from all over the world to stand on its rim and look down. In 1964, American astronauts trained for their first landing on the moon in the Grand Canyon. Because the Canyon is one of the best places in the world to study geology, Russian astronauts have been invited to train there, too. The Canyon is a place to be shared by everyone, and if we are careful, it can be shared by all kinds of visitors for years to come.

Bighorn sheep

A stagecoach travels on Big Oak Flat Road in Yosemite Park, California. The Yosemite Park Act of 1864 set aside forty square miles in the Yosemite Valley and another four square miles in the Mariposa Grove as public parks under California state protection.

PRESERVING THE AMERICAN WILDERNESS

by Karen H. Dusek

More than thirty years ago, wilderness lands were formally recognized as an important part of the American landscape with the passage of the Wilderness Act of 1964. This act, which took eight years, nine congressional hearings, and sixty-six revisions before finally being passed, guaranteed that there would be wilderness areas for future generations of Americans to explore and enjoy.

Americans have not always

Henry David Thoreau's most famous work, *Walden,* details his two-year stay in a cabin on Walden Pond in Concord, Massachusetts. While living there, Thoreau learned to exist in harmony with his natural surroundings and developed his transcendental views. (Also see pages 155–156.)

been so eager to protect their wilderness. The early settlers probably would have laughed at the idea. For them, the wilderness was a dark and frightening place filled with strange and fearsome creatures — a place where one could easily become lost. It was a place to be conquered and tamed into farms and cities.

Because of this belief, settlers cut down trees, dammed rivers, built roads, and expanded the civilized world whenever and wherever possible. As Americans began to rely more on machines and less on the land to survive, it became easier to conquer wild lands. Trains carried thousands of emigrants westward to escape the increasingly crowded conditions of cities in the East, and even the most remote settlements could be reached by telegraph. As civilization spread, the amount of remaining wilderness shrank.

By the mid-1800s, a few people had begun to realize that there was something very special about the American wilderness. Such vast expanses of open space could no longer be found in Europe. The wilderness set the United States apart from the rest of the Western world. It became a popular topic for writers, poets, and artists.

One of the best writers on the subject was Henry David Thoreau of Massachusetts. He believed that the wilderness was the "raw material of life," that wilderness experiences helped people to think clearly, and that people should spend time in both the civilized world and the wilderness. To make it easier for people in Massachusetts to do that, he proposed creating parks of "primitive forest" in towns throughout the state. Although Thoreau's own wilderness adventures were never very far removed from civilization, he urged that wilderness areas be preserved.

This new awareness of wilderness values led to the passage of the Yosemite Park Act of 1864, which set aside forty square miles in the Yosemite Valley and another four square miles in the Mariposa Grove as public parks under California state protection. The act allowed the valley to be developed for recreational use. It was not until 1872, when two million acres of land in present-day Wyoming were designated by Congress as Yellowstone National Park, that a large area of wild land was preserved as wilderness. Even then, the area was protected not for its wilderness qualities, but for its geysers, hot springs, waterfalls, and other tourist attractions.

As open space continued to be used up by a rapidly expanding population, Americans grew more concerned about preserving what remained. One of the men most responsible for promoting the preservation of wilderness areas was John Muir. Muir believed that all living things, no matter how small, are equally important. He thought people should go to the wilderness to learn how they are connected with the earth and other living creatures. His eloquent writing greatly influenced public attitudes toward conservation. Muir helped found the Sierra Club in 1892. Its fight to save the Hetch Hetchy Valley in Yosemite created more widespread support of wilderness preservation.

Until the 1920s, the beauty of the wilderness, as well as its positive effects on mental and physical health, were the conservationists' main arguments in favor of preservation. Then a young forester with the U.S. Forest Service named Aldo

Leopold began to write about the ecological importance of the wilderness. Because people depended so much on modern technology, he believed, they no longer felt connected to the land, and so they no longer took care of it. In his book *A Sand County Almanac,* published in 1949 after his death, he stressed the necessity for all people to develop a "land ethic," or respect for the earth. As a professor at the University of Wisconsin and a leader in the conservation movement, Leopold shared his ideas with many people. Those ideas are still popular today among environmentalists.

One of Leopold's ambitions was to create wilderness areas in national forests. As a result of his efforts, the Gila Wilderness Area was established in the Gila

As open space continued to be used up by a rapidly expanding population, Americans grew more concerned about preserving what remained.

National Forest of New Mexico in 1924. A little later, another forester, Robert Marshall, worked toward the same goal. An extraordinarily energetic man, Marshall helped to preserve fourteen million acres of Forest Service land as wilderness before his death in 1939.

Marshall believed that the only way wilderness areas stood a chance against the expansion of civilization was for people to unite in some sort of conservation organization. With this in mind, in 1934 he joined with Benton MacKaye, a regional planner; Harvey Broome, a Knoxville lawyer; and Bernard Frank, a forester, to form an organization dedicated to the preservation of wilderness areas. The following year, The Wilderness Society formally began operation. Members were kept informed of wilderness issues through the society's magazine, *Living Wilderness.*

Yosemite Valley, in Yosemite National Park, is surrounded by cliffs and peaks. Half Dome is one of the highest peaks, rising about 4,800 feet above sea level.

E.O. Beaman's *The Heart of Lodore, Green River*, 1871. The Green River flows through many deep canyons, including the Canyon of the Lodore in Dinosaur National Monument.

One of the more important battles in which The Wilderness Society participated was the struggle during the 1950s to prevent the construction of a dam on the Green River in Utah. That would have flooded much of Dinosaur National Monument. David Brower, executive director of the Sierra Club, and Howard C. Zahniser, executive director of The Wilderness Society, helped arouse public opinion about the dam. Opponents staged a nationwide campaign with pamphlets, magazine and newspaper articles, a movie, and other forms of publicity. Their persistence paid off in 1956, when Congress decided "that no dam or reservoir constructed under the authorization of the Act shall be within any National Park or monument."

To environmentalists, the victory meant that the tide was turning in favor of wilderness protection. Zahniser decided that the time was right to publicize an idea he had had for a long time — legislation that would permanently protect the United States' wilderness. His determination resulted in the Wilderness Act of 1964.

Today the original 9 million acres designated as wilderness by the act have been increased to more than 103 million. But The Wilderness Society and other environmental organizations continue to work toward their goal of protecting approximately 100 million more acres of wilderness.

THE VISION OF FREDERICK LAW OLMSTED

by Marnie Laird

One hundred twenty-five years ago, the proposed site for Central Park in New York City presented a dismal picture. The 843 acres were swampy and brush-filled, with poor soil. Squatters' tumbledown shacks were eyesores, and debris littered the ground. Thousands of wild dogs and goats infested the area. The air stank from nearby slaughterhouses and hog farms.

Thanks to the vision of Frederick Law Olmsted, Central Park today ranks as one of the most beautiful and famous city parks in the world. Born in 1822 in Hartford, Connecticut, this strange and brilliant man came into a world where there were no public parks. But during his lifetime, he built many beautiful parks, because he believed that people needed green places to keep them healthy in both body and spirit.

By the time Olmsted was thirty-five years old, he was a jack-of-all-trades and master of none. As a writer and journalist, he spoke out against slavery. Appointed by Abraham Lincoln to the Sanitary Commission during the Civil War, he laid the foundation for the American branch of the Red Cross. One hundred years before conservation became a worldwide issue, Olmsted was dedicated to preserving our environment. As a farmer, he combined gardening and engineering to create a new profession called "landscape architecture." It was through his use of landscape architecture that he changed the face of this country. The most attractive features of many cities across the United States today are the parks that he designed.

Olmsted's work began in 1857. The Central Park commissioners declared a competition for a new plan for the future park. Calvert Vaux, a noted architect, asked Olmsted to join him in designing a plan for the competition. They were the perfect team: Vaux designed the buildings and bridges, and Olmsted concentrated on the landscape design. To ensure as much open space and rural atmosphere as possible, Olmsted conceived a brilliant plan for sinking the cross-town roads below ground into open cuts and tunnels, so that traffic would not intrude on the scenery. He designed lakes, nature walks, and recreation areas. The plan, named Greensward, won first prize.

Vaux considered the park a work of art, but Olmsted saw the park in terms of people. The city was rapidly swelling with immigrants. Living in crowded, unhealthy tenements, these poor people had little access to green grass and fresh air. At a time when much of New York City was still undeveloped, Olmsted foresaw the vast metropolis it would someday become. He recognized the need for open space for its residents. He believed that natural surroundings were essential to the well-being of all people — an outlook shared by today's mental health experts.

Olmsted saw the park as a way to bring the rural countryside into the bustling city. With startling accuracy, Olmsted predicted, in a speech delivered in 1858, "No longer an open suburb, Central Park will have around it a continuous high wall of brick, stone, and marble. The adjoining shore will be lined with commercial docks and warehouses. Steamboat and ferry landings, railroad stations, hotels, theaters, and factories will be on all sides of it, and above it, all of which our park must be made to fit."

The transformation of the existing swampland into the great park we know today was a monumental job. Olmsted was appointed supervisor of the entire park and commanded a crew of twenty-five hundred men. Sixty miles of pipe were laid to drain the swampland. Two hundred sixty tons of gunpowder were used for blasting rock and making reservoirs. Almost five million trees and shrubs were planted in a space stretching two and a half miles north and south and half a mile across.

Olmsted's vision of the city's growth and the walls of brick and stone came true. Today the more than seven million people living in New York love their park, and thousands use it every day.

Central Park made Olmsted world famous. He proceeded to design Brooklyn and Prospect parks in Brooklyn, as well as Morningside and Riverside drives in Manhattan, Mont Royal Park in Montreal, and Jackson Park in Chicago. In Boston, he planned a regional park system that became a necklace of green

Frederick Law Olmsted

. . . .

Before becoming a designer and developer of public parks, Olmsted (1822–1903) wrote travel accounts of southern life in the 1850s. Among these were *A Journey in the Seaboard Slave States* (1856), *Journey Through Texas* (1857), *A Journey in the Back Country* (1860), and *Journeys and Explorations in the Cotton Kingdom* (1861).

New York City bought the land that is now Central Park in 1856. Landscape architect Frederick Law Olmsted and architect Calvert Vaux took about fifteen years to finish their work on the park. This photograph, taken in 1894, shows the park's Old Boathouse.

space surrounding the city.

Olmsted also designed the grounds of the U.S. Capitol in Washington, D.C. He created open spaces, shaded walkways, and vistas on one side and planned an impressive marble terrace to surround the rest of the huge building. Foreseeing the "suburban commuter towns" of today, where many city workers live, he created plans for communities to protect the beauty of the existing landscape.

When asked by the City of San Francisco to submit a plan for a great park, Olmsted designed a remarkable plan that would reduce damage caused by earthquakes and fires. He proposed a sunken parkway that also would serve as a firebreak. Had the city adopted his plan, the parkway would have helped to control the city's terrible fire caused by the 1906 earthquake. Ironically, the fire was finally checked by dynamiting houses along the very site of his proposed parkway.

Olmsted's vision of parks for people spread across the United States. He encouraged the federal government to involve itself in the creation of national recreation areas. The seeds of environmental awareness he was planting would one day bear fruit as the National Park System.

Olmsted remained active in landscape design until his death in 1903 at age eighty-one. Even though he had left school at age fourteen, both Harvard and Yale awarded him honorary degrees. By the end of his life, Olmsted's dream to preserve open space for future Americans had been realized in projects throughout the country and in Canada.

HOW AMERICA BUILT THE WASHINGTON MONUMENT

by Harold Holzer

George Washington himself approved the site — a graceful little hill midway between where the Capitol Building and the White House would be built. Congress obliged by voting to place there a statue of Washington riding his horse.

The year was 1783. No American was ever more beloved than George Washington, but by the time a tribute to our first president was finally built on this spot, more than a hundred years had passed.

Actually, it took only twelve years of work to erect the now-famous obelisk. But fifty years went by before work even started. And it took thirty-six years to raise money to build it, choose a design, and even fight religious prejudice.

Well before the Washington Monument became a national symbol, it was a national embarrassment.

For twenty-two years, it remained only one-third completed. Cattle and pigs grazed and Civil War soldiers camped there. At one time, a slaughterhouse operated on the site.

When Mark Twain saw the eyesore, he compared it to "a factory chimney with the top broken off." For a while, no one thought the monument would ever be completed.

Congress was to blame for the original delay. It wanted to bury Washington beneath the Capitol and for fifty years campaigned unsuccessfully to get his body moved there, forgetting about the monument. Finally, in 1833, private citizens started the Washington National Monument Society to build on the very spot Washington had approved in 1783. The group launched a fundraising drive, limiting contributions to one dollar per person. In three years, the group collected a mere $28,000. A decade later, the total in hand was just $87,000. It was not enough to complete the monument, but organizers decided to start building anyway.

On July 4, 1848, twenty thousand people joined President James Polk for the

By 1876, only the lower third of the Washington Monument had been built (above). By 1884, all but the cap was finished (left). The monument was dedicated on February 21, 1885, and opened to the public in 1888.

groundbreaking. In the huge crowd were three future presidents: James Buchanan, Abraham Lincoln, and Andrew Johnson.

The committee had chosen a complex design: a tall marble column surrounded by an ornate building at the base. A statue of Washington driving a Roman chariot would grace the top. Thankfully, all that would ever be built was the simple but beautiful column.

The Washington Monument as seen from the Lincoln Memorial (see page 282), located at the other end of Potomac Park and the Reflecting Pool.

Work moved quickly. By 1854, the obelisk rose about 150 feet. Then the money ran out. In desperation, organizers begged the states to send blocks of stone. Before long, thirty-nine states and seven foreign countries had responded. Unfortunately, when an anti-Catholic group learned that the pope had sent a slab, members broke into the site and rolled it downhill into the river.

What was worse, just as Congress decided to approve $200,000 to finish the monument, this same anti-Catholic group took control of the Washington Monument Society. Horrified, Congress canceled funding. For the next three years, the new organizers raised only $285, and all the marble they bought proved so cheap that it had to be removed. Americans stopped contributing altogether. Then came the Civil War. One observer sadly admitted that the ugly, unfinished stump became an "emblem of a divided and ruined country."

Not until 1876 — the Centennial of American independence — did Congress finally vote $200,000 to finish the Washington Monument. To cut costs, the original design was altered. Only the obelisk would be built.

Work proceeded rapidly. The column rose 20 feet in 1880, 74 feet in 1881, 90 feet in 1882, 70 feet in 1883, and the final 125 feet in 1884. The monument topped off at more than 555 feet. No structure in the world stood taller. None in Washington, D.C., ever would. Visible then, as now, was the spot one-third of the way up where work stopped in the 1850s. The marble is a different color above that line.

On February 21, 1885, thousands of spectators arrived for the dedication. It was a day of "national rejoicing," one of the speakers declared. President Chester Arthur gratefully accepted the monument on behalf of all Americans.

Ever since, Americans have made the Washington Monument their own. Nearly seventy million people have ridden its elevators or climbed its nine hundred stairs to enjoy the spectacular view. The capital's "exclamation point" has remained what President Herbert Hoover called it during the Depression: "a thing of the spirit."

Now forgotten is the century-long struggle to build the Washington Monument. But if visitors could read the inscription on the aluminum pyramid at the very top, they would understand both the pride and the relief that greeted its completion. It says *Laus Deo*, Latin for "Praise be to God."

HOMES FOR OUR NATION'S HISTORY

by Billie Kay Tye

Have you ever wondered what happened to the original copies of famous documents such as the Declaration of Independence and the Bill of Rights? Did someone remember to save them, or were they lost in the confusion and excitement of founding a new nation? Did the early presidents' important papers survive, or were they tossed into wastebaskets in succeeding generations?

The United States is the only major nation whose entire history has taken place since the invention of the printing press. Happily, a great deal of that written history has been saved. There are countless repositories (places where things are put for safekeeping) of historic documents all over the United States — from the records found in family Bibles to those housed in historical and genealogical societies. Two of the largest repositories for these papers and documents — the Library of Congress and the National Archives — are found in our nation's capital.

Visitors to the National Archives Rotunda can view the Charters of Freedom — the Declaration of Independence, the Constitution, and the Bill of Rights — as well as rotating exhibitions.

The National Archives Rotunda

George Washington's inaugural address, the first page of which is shown here, is housed at the Library of Congress.

George Washington

The Library of Congress is almost as old as the United States itself. When the national capital was moved from Philadelphia to Washington in 1800. Congress appropriated five thousand dollars over five years for the foundation of a library to be used by members of Congress. This collection of books and maps was housed in the Capitol Building. Some three thousand books in this first library were destroyed when the British burned the Capitol during the War of 1812.

Shortly after this tragedy, Thomas Jefferson offered to sell his personal library of more than six thousand books to the United States as the basis for a new congressional library. Congress bought Jefferson's books for $23,950 in 1815. Since that time, the Library of Congress has expanded to fill three enormous buildings that are connected by underground tunnels and contain eighty-four million items. The library still serves members of Congress, but it is also our national library. As such, it is open to all who wish to use its vast resources.

The Library of Congress collection is a treasure-trove of books, pamphlets, charts, engravings, manuscripts, maps, motion pictures, music, photographs, and recordings. The forty-million-piece manuscript collection contains the papers of almost every president who served before 1930. Here scholars can view an original copy of George Washington's first inaugural address (another is in the National Archives) and read Calvin Coolidge's terse note to reporters: "I do not choose to run for President in 1928."

Also housed here are the records of the National Association for the Advancement of Colored People (NAACP) from 1909 on. This is a rich source of information for those interested in African American history.

The library's Rare Book Room includes one of eleven known copies of the *Bay Psalm Book,* the earliest surviving example of printing in the American Colonies. It also owns escape artist Harry Houdini's extensive collection of books on magic and the occult.

The Folk Archives Division of the Library of Congress houses the stories, songs, and history that make up this country's oral tradition. Since 1928, Library of Congress employees have been traveling to remote regions of the United States to collect samples of folk music and stories before they are lost forever.

The National Archives, established by Congress in 1934, is devoted to preserving the documents most precious to our nation's history and has been the legal custodian of the records of our federal government since 1774. On permanent display are the original Declaration of Independence, the Constitution, and the Bill of Rights. In addition, the Archives is home to three billion letters, reports, and other official written government records; ninety-one million feet of documentary films and newsreels; five million photos; and twelve million maps, charts, and aerial photos created by or for the federal government. The collection also includes seventy thousand sound recordings of congressional hearings, Supreme Court arguments, and the Nuremberg trials (during which German officials were tried for war crimes following World War II).

The Archives also administers ten presidential libraries, which consist of museums and archives. Each library is devoted to a particular president and located in his home state. The individual collections include official papers from the president's time in office, diaries, letters and papers of the president's associates, and related materials.

The Archives is an important resource for anyone researching the history of his or her family. U.S. Census records from 1790 through 1910 can be found here, as can passenger lists of ships bringing immigrants to the United States from 1820 to 1945 and military service records. Anyone sixteen years or older may use the records.

Both the Library of Congress and the National Archives wage a constant battle against the effects of time on their documents. Surprisingly, the older documents age more slowly than do those of the past century. This is because early paper was made from linen rags and had a very low acid content. When paper made of highly acidic wood pulp came into common use in the late nineteenth century, documents became literally self-destructing, with the acid slowly eating away at the wood pulp until there was nothing left but a pile of crumbs. To make matters worse, many precious documents were stored in celluloid envelopes, which also contained an acid that hastened deterioration.

Both the Library of Congress and the National Archives have an entire division devoted to preservation and restoration. Here materials are microfilmed to preserve their contents. The most valuable documents are put through an expensive deacidifying process. Manuscripts are fumigated to kill any present or future mold or insect.

Proper storage is another important part of preservation. At the National Archives, the Declaration of Independence, the Bill of Rights, and the Constitution are kept in helium-filled glass and bronze cases that keep out moisture and pollutants. Yellow filters protect the documents from harmful light rays. Each evening, the documents are lowered twenty feet into a fifty-five-ton steel and reinforced concrete vault. The temperature and humidity of the entire building are carefully controlled.

The Library of Congress stores its film collection in vaults kept at only a few degrees above freezing. Rare books are stored in steel and concrete vaults kept at a constant 68°F and fifty percent humidity.

Another problem in preserving history for future generations is that of space limitations. The Library of Congress has added two buildings to its original structure in the past two centuries. Every day, more books are written and more history is made and documented. Although the National Archives saves only one to two percent of all government papers, it still houses three billion documents and opened a new building in Maryland in 1994.

The Great Hall of the Thomas Jefferson Building at the Library of Congress includes this bust of our third president.

3

SLAVERY AND THE AFRICAN AMERICAN EXPERIENCE

No one *knows for sure how many Africans and their descendants lived and died in slavery from the beginning of American history.*

All we know is that nearly four million African Americans were living in slavery in the South when the Civil War began. Millions more had labored in chains before them.

Slavery is often referred to as the cause of the Civil War. And so it was. But it should not be forgotten that slavery was much more than the reason for the wartime deaths of white people. It also was a tragic condition of life for black people. In the eyes of many foreign nations at the time, it was America's great national shame.

In this chapter, we learn how slavery first arrived in a nation "dedicated to the proposition that all men are created equal," as Abraham Lincoln insisted in his Gettysburg Address of 1863. We also learn how black slavery grew, expanded, and thrived, while the overwhelming majority of white people either approved or looked the other way.

Even before the Civil War began, America in fact made war on African Americans by buying and selling them and by forcing them to work without pay — in short, by keeping them in slavery.

$150 REWARD.

RANAWAY from the subscriber, on the night of Monday the 11th July, a negro man named

TOM,

about 30 years of age, 5 feet 6 or 7 inches high; of dark color; heavy in the chest; several of his jaw teeth out; and upon his body are several old marks of the whip, one of them straight down the back. He took with him a quantity of clothing, and several hats.

A reward of $150 will be paid for his apprehension and security, if taken out of the State of Kentucky; $100 if taken in any county bordering on the Ohio river; $50 if taken in any of the interior counties except Fayette; or $20 if taken in the latter county.

July 12-84-tf
B. L. BOSTON.

CHRONOLOGY OF SLAVERY

From Ellen Hansen, ed., *The Underground Railroad: Life on the Road to Freedom,* Perspectives on History Series, pp. 16–19. Copyright© 1993 Discovery Enterprises, Ltd., Lowell, Massachusetts.

1619

The first African laborers are shipped to Virginia.

1641

Massachusetts colony legalizes slavery.

1642

Virginia colony passes law to fine anyone harboring or assisting runaway slaves.

1660

Virginia colony legalizes slavery.

1775

The first Quaker anti-slavery society, the Society for the Relief of Free Negroes Unlawfully Held in Bondage, is organized in Philadelphia.

1776

North American colonies declare independence from Great Britain.

1777–1804

Northern states abolish slavery through state constitutions and gradual abolition laws.

1787

The Northwest Ordinance bans slavery in the Northwest Territory.

1793

Fugitive Slave Act becomes a federal law, providing for the return of slaves escaped across state boundaries.

1794

The first national anti-slavery society, The American Convention for Promoting the Abolition of Slavery, is founded.

1807

Congress passes a law prohibiting the importation of slaves into the U.S. after January 1, 1808.

1818

As a response to the Fugitive Slave Act of 1793, abolitionists use the "underground" to assist slaves to escape into Ohio and Canada.

1820

The Missouri Compromise admits Missouri as a slave state; Maine as a free state; and establishes the 36°30′ parallel of latitude as the dividing line between free and slave areas of the territories.

1821

Benjamin Lundy, a Quaker, starts publishing his anti-slavery paper, the *Genius of Universal Emancipation.*

1822

Former slave Denmark Vesey leads a slave uprising in Charleston, South Carolina.

1829

Black abolitionist David Walker issues *Walker's Appeal.* Afterwards, several slave revolts occurred throughout the South.

1830

Levi Coffin leaves North Carolina, settles in Indiana and continues abolitionist activities.

1831

William Lloyd Garrison prints first issues of his anti-slavery newspaper, *The Liberator.*

1831–1832

Virginia constitutional convention narrowly defeats emancipation. The Nat Turner Rebellion takes place in Virginia.

1832

Louisiana presents resolution requesting federal government to arrange with Mexico to permit runaway slaves from Louisiana to be reclaimed when found on foreign soil.

In Boston, Garrison founds the New England Anti-Slavery Society, urging immediate emancipation.

1833

Slavery ends in the British Empire.

The American Anti-Slavery Society is founded in Philadelphia.

THE RUNAWAY.

1834

The moderate and church-oriented American Union for the Relief and Improvement of the Colored Race is founded by Massachusetts Congregational ministers.

1837

Elijah Lovejoy's press is destroyed, and Lovejoy is killed in Alton, Illinois.

1838

Underground Railroad is "formally organized." Black abolitionist Robert Purvis becomes chairman of the General Vigilance Committee and "president" of the Underground Railroad.

1839

American Slavery As It Is: Testimony of a Thousand Witnesses, edited by Sarah and Angelina Grimké and Theodore D. Weld, is published. It exposes atrocities and outrageous conditions under slavery.

1840

The World Anti-Slavery Convention is held in London. Women are denied seats on the floor.

1842

Supreme Court rules in *Prigg v. Pennsylvania* that state officials are not required to assist in the return of fugitive slaves.

1845

Frederick Douglass prints *Narrative of the Life of Frederick Douglass,* an account of his slave experience and escape to freedom.

1847

Douglass begins publishing his anti-slavery newspaper, the *North Star.*

1849

Harriet Tubman makes her escape from Maryland.

1850

Compromise of 1850 attempts to settle slavery issue. As part of the Compromise, a new Fugitive Slave Act is added to enforce the 1793 law and allows slaveholders to retrieve slaves in northern states and free territories.

1852

Harriet Beecher Stowe's *Uncle Tom's Cabin* is published. It broadens and popularizes the anti-slavery debate.

1854

The Kansas-Nebraska Bill is passed, stirring up civil war in Kansas Territory over the slavery issue. The fugitive slave Anthony Burns is returned from Boston to Virginia. Over 2,000 federal troops are called out to ensure his return.

1857

In the *Dred Scott* case, the Supreme Court declares that blacks are not U.S. citizens, and that slaveholders have the right to take slaves in free areas of the country.

1858

Abraham Lincoln condemns slavery in his "House Divided" speech.

1859

John Brown's failed raid on federal arsenal and armory in Harpers Ferry, which was aimed at starting a general slave insurrection.

1860

Republican candidate Abraham Lincoln is elected President of the United States.

1861

Civil War begins.

1863

President Lincoln issues the Emancipation Proclamation which declares "all persons held as slaves within any state…in rebellion against the United States shall be then…forever free."

1865

Civil War ends.

The Thirteenth Amendment to the U.S. Constitution is ratified, abolishing slavery permanently.

A is an Abolitionist—
A man who wants to free
The wretched slave—and give to all
An equal liberty.

B is a Brother with a skin
Of somewhat darker hue,
But in our Heavenly Father's sight,
He is as dear as you.

THE SLAVERY YEARS

by Laurel Sherman

As early as the 1500s, the slave trade was big business in the New World. Different historians believe that between fifteen million and one hundred million Africans were brought to the New World between the 1500s and the 1800s, and this figure does not include the thousands who died or committed suicide during the long, brutal sea voyages, or those who died trying to escape capture in their West African homeland.

The first African slaves in the New World were brought to South America in the 1500s by Portuguese and Spanish *conquistadores.* They worked in mines and on plantations. African workers were first brought to the English colony at Jamestown, Virginia, in 1619. But these Africans were not considered slaves; they were indentured servants. This meant that they were required to work for a specific length of time — usually from five to seven years — and then they were supposed to be set free. African indentured servants often worked alongside white bondsmen, people who were given their passage to the Colonies in exchange for work they did as indentured servants.

But the two groups were not equal. African servants did not come to the Colonies voluntarily, as did nearly all white bondsmen. And Africans were much more likely to be harshly punished if they protested or attempted to run away before completing their term as servants.

Under the indentured servant system, some Africans did gain their freedom at the end of their work periods. By the mid-1600s, however, laws had been passed that made Africans servants for life — slaves.

The growing Colonies suffered from a severe labor shortage, and many colonists considered Africans — whom they viewed as heathens — as the best solution to the shortage.

During the 1600s and afterward, major portions of the southern colonies became farm areas, where slaves were used to do the difficult work of caring for and harvesting large crops. Slaves in the North usually served as house servants or laborers. Some northern slaves learned skills that enabled them to earn enough money to buy their freedom.

Top: A Warrenton, North Carolina, handbill announces "Negroes for Sale" on October 28, 1859.
Above: The New Orleans slave market, one of the busiest in the South, often sent traders to other cities to buy new slaves.

By the time of the Constitutional Convention in 1787, there were widely differing views about what this new country — founded on the principles of liberty and
justice for all — should do about slavery. The South needed the cheap labor its
slaves provided to make money on its crops. The North did not depend on slaves
for its survival, and some northerners wanted slavery abolished. But northerners
also wanted to form a country made up of "united" states, and northerners were
willing to compromise to persuade southerners to join them.

Slaves at work on Pope's Plantation,
near Hilton Head, South Carolina.

The Constitution of the United States, written in 1787, upheld the legality of
slavery. Southerners wanted their slaves to be counted as part of the population
— even though slaves were officially regarded as property, not citizens — so that
the South could have greater representation in Congress. Northerners, who held
fewer slaves than southerners, did not go along with this idea. In the end, it was
agreed that three-fifths of the slaves would be counted in determining each
state's population and how many representatives it would have in Congress. In
addition, the Constitution said that states could continue to import slaves for
another twenty years after the Constitution became law and that slaves who
escaped into free states must be returned to their owners.

But it was an invention, not a law, that was probably most responsible for
sealing tight the bonds of slavery. In 1793, Eli Whitney invented the cotton gin,
a machine that speeded up the difficult job of seeding and cleaning cotton. The
invention made cotton a tremendously valuable crop, and southern farmers
began to grow huge amounts of it. To meet their growing labor needs, southerners imported thousands of African slaves to plant, raise, pick, and help process
cotton. As the South grew more and more dependent on cotton as a means of

A slave girl carries a tub on her head at a plantation near Charleston, South Carolina. Perhaps she is helping the woman on the right with the washing.

making money, slave labor and the slave trade grew tremendously.

Still, holding people against their will posed a serious problem. A successful slave revolt in 1791 in Haiti, an island in the West Indies, had convinced southerners that they would have to be constantly on guard against rebellion. Some northerners worried that in the event of a national emergency, the South would not be able to help because southerners would have to stay at home to watch their slaves. Also in the North, where slavery was eventually abolished, many citizens resented the fact that they would have to support troops that might be required to protect southerners against their slaves.

There were numerous small slave rebellions during the 1800s, until slavery ended after the Civil War. None was completely successful. Many new local laws were passed to limit the travel of free African Americans in the South, who were blamed for causing these revolts, and the federal government passed laws raising a militia to deal with slave revolts. But the possibility — and the fear — of a revolution remained.

As cotton became a bigger and bigger crop and Americans pushed westward, slavery spread into new states, including Alabama and Mississippi. When the areas that had been bought in the Louisiana Purchase of 1803 began to come up for statehood, a new conflict arose. The North wanted to stop the spread of slavery, while the South wanted to allow slavery. The agreement finally reached in 1820 was called the Missouri Compromise. Under the compromise, the new state of Missouri would enter the Union as a slave state, while Maine would enter as a free state. This meant that there would be a total of twelve free and twelve slave states in the country. The compromise also stated that slavery would not be allowed in any new states north of Missouri's southern border, or the 36°30′ line of latitude.

At the end of the Mexican War in 1848, the borders of the United States extended to the Pacific Ocean. The first effort to organize these far western territories was the Wilmot Proviso, which tried to exclude slavery from the new territories. This effort was defeated in Congress.

Finally, in 1850, a shaky compromise was reached. The Compromise of 1850 stated the following: (1) California would enter the Union as a free state; (2) the federal government would not interfere with the slave trade between states;
(3) slavery, but not the slave trade, would continue in Washington, D.C.; (4) the law concerning the return of runaway slaves would be made harsher.

A slave village on Drayton's Plantation, Hilton Head, South Carolina.

In fact, the Compromise of 1850 served only to agitate matters. Abolitionists in the North were outraged by it because it threatened their efforts to aid slaves who had escaped to the North. In addition, the compromise did little, if anything, to end slavery itself. Later laws, such as the Kansas-Nebraska Act of 1854 — which said that states, not Congress, could decide whether to allow slavery — further aggravated the issue and helped to make slavery one of the major factors that led to the outbreak of the Civil War.

COTTON: THE KING OF CLOTH

by Deborah H. DeFord

Joe wakes up and stretches between the cotton sheets on his bed. He gets out of bed, tosses off cotton pajamas, and heads for the bathroom to wash up with a cotton washcloth and towel. Back in his room, he pulls on cotton jeans, T-shirt, sweat socks, and canvas high-tops. He grabs a cotton sweat suit for soccer practice later and takes his jean jacket from the hook on the back of his closet door. Then he dashes for the school bus, a walking advertisement for the use of cotton.

Joe is not unusual. He is just one of millions of people, young and old, all over the world, who wear and use cotton cloth in a dozen ways every day. But the popularity of cotton did not begin with the first pair of designer jeans. Thousands of years ago, people in ancient Egypt and Asia grew cotton plants and used the fiber to spin and weave cloth. Long before European explorers sailed to the New World, Native Americans in North and South America grew cotton and knew how to turn it into woven cloth.

The type of cotton that came to be grown in America is a shrubby plant called upland cotton. It grows best in the American South, where the weather stays hot and humid at least half the year. It has divided leaves and changing blossoms that start out white, then turn pink, blue, and finally purple before

they wither. The withered blossoms are replaced on the plant by a pod called a boll. When it is fully grown, the boll looks like a green golf ball with a point at the top. The boll splits open to show the cotton fibers containing the plant's seeds. Those fibers are the raw material for cotton cloth.

When Joe wants a new jean jacket, he goes to a store and buys it. But for most of human history, people could not buy ready-made cotton cloth or clothing from a store. Cotton grew wild, or people grew it on small farm plots. The cloth was made by the same people who grew the cotton. All the work was done by hand — planting, picking, separating the cotton fibers from the seeds, and combing the fibers. The fibers, which are less than two inches long, would then be spun into the long threads used to weave cloth.

The English colonists in the New World were familiar with cotton, as they had used cotton cloth in their homeland. Although England imported most of its cotton from East India, colonists in the American South discovered that they could grow their own cotton and use it to hand-spin rough cloth for their own uses.

By the end of the American Revolution (1781), cotton cloth production had become the most important source of jobs and international trade in England, due principally to the invention of amazing new machines for making cloth. Because of this, England had to import more and more of the raw cotton fiber needed to make the cloth. A logical source of this cotton was the American South.

Southern farmers jumped at the opportunity. Since the time of early settlement, southerners had used an additional source of labor: African slaves. These slaves had been captured in their native Africa and forced onto boats to be shipped to the New World. Many of them died on the boats, and the rest were bought like property by farmers who wanted to make their farms more profitable.

Following the Revolution, farmers could no longer support their investment in slaves with what they produced on their farms. Rather than free the slaves and lose money, they were looking for a new crop to put their slaves to work. England's growing demand for raw cotton seemed to be the answer to their troubles.

Southern cotton growers had to solve one problem before they could produce enough cotton to supply England. Even with slave labor, removing the seeds from the cotton fibers by hand took too long, and the planters could not deliver enough raw cotton to England. Eli Whitney, an American inventor, came to the rescue with his cotton gin, a machine that could remove the seeds and separate the cot-

Top: A slave girl photographed in New York.
Above: Fannie Virginia Casseopia Lawrence, a five-year-old slave girl redeemed in Virginia by Catharine S. Lawrence and baptized in 1863 in Brooklyn, New York, by Henry Ward Beecher, brother of Harriet Beecher Stowe.

ton fibers with the speed the growers needed. With the cotton gin, the American South became the biggest cotton producer in the world, and the United States became an important part of the world economic market.

The success of the southern cotton planters had another side, though. Without cotton, the use of slaves had been dying out because they cost more money to keep than they made in free labor. With the huge success of cotton, the cotton farms (called plantations) needed more slaves than ever before. Thus, slavery became a central part of the South's prosperity.

Many people in other parts of the United States were strongly opposed to slavery. They said that owning another human being was evil and demanded that slavery be outlawed. Slave owners refused to give up their slaves, as they knew they could not make a profit without them. While cotton was becoming the most important item in foreign trade, slavery was becoming the central issue in a growing division between the North and South. That division eventually led to the Civil War.

Although slavery was abolished after the war and the production of cotton today no longer depends on slave labor, we still feel the effects of this institution more than one hundred years later. "King Cotton," the salvation of the southern farmer and the source of so much of our cloth, also left a lasting scar on race relations in the United States. The continuing tension between African Americans and white Americans is a high price to pay for the success of cotton in this country.

Top: A Currier & Ives print from 1883 shows a cotton plantation on the Mississippi River.
Above: Cotton was king, as seen in this plantation scene from Georgia in 1895.

An estate sale in New Orleans includes slaves.

THE TRIALS OF SLAVES

by David M. Rosen

Before the Civil War in the United States, slavery was legal in all the southern states. White slave owners could buy and sell African slaves as they could cattle or horses, land, or any other property. Slaves could be given as gifts or loans, they could be rented out for up to a year, and they could be inherited after death.

Many people in the United States, both slave and free, looked for ways to end slavery. Some of these people broke the laws that enforced slavery and were dealt with very harshly. The story of slavery and the resistance to it show that laws can be unjust and unfair and that sometimes it is necessary to break such laws in order to change them.

Before the American Revolution (1776–1781), most southern states prohibited a slave owner from emancipating, or freeing, his or her slaves. But after the Revolution, many of these states passed laws that allowed slaves to be freed. George Washington, Thomas Jefferson, and many other Americans freed some or all of their slaves in what is sometimes called the First Emancipation. In fact, so many

NAT TURNER
by Peter Roop

Nat Turner was born in 1800. His father fled north to be free when Turner was still young. Turner grew up under the care of his mother and grandmother. The two women taught him that he was not meant to be only a slave and that his ability to read was an indication that he had a special mission in life.

What the mission was remained unknown until 1825, when Turner felt he had a vision from God. The vision convinced Turner that there would be an uprising of African slaves against their white masters. "I saw white spirits and black spirits engaged in battle," Turner recalled. Three years later, he had an even more powerful vision. "I heard a loud voice in the heavens, and the Spirit instantly appeared to me and said...I should arise and prepare myself, and slay my enemies with their own weapons...for the time was fast approaching when the first should be the last and the last should be first."

Turner's rebellion began on August 22, 1831. Armed with hatchets and axes, Turner and his companions entered his master's house, where they killed all the inhabitants. Turner then moved on, gathering more men to his cause. At one point, Turner's freedom fighters included more than sixty slaves and free men, and they killed a total of sixty white people.

Within a day, the rebellion had been put down. Some of the rebels had been captured. Others, along with a number of African Americans not involved in the uprising, were killed. Turner alone escaped capture. He lived in hiding for about two months before being caught, put on trial, and hanged. He went bravely to his death, still believing his actions had been proper.

As a result of Nat Turner's rebellion in August 1831, southern states passed more restrictive slave laws.

slaves were freed that many people assumed that slavery would die out in America. That did not happen, however. At the beginning of the nineteenth century, politicians in many southern states began to rethink their emancipation laws. Fearing that they would lose all their slaves, some states reinstituted harsh laws that prohibited the freeing of slaves.

The fact that many slaves had been freed meant that by the time of the Civil War, the African American population in the Old South was composed of both slave and free persons. Free African Americans had some of the same rights as white Americans: They were allowed to marry (a right denied to slaves), own property, farm their own land, and work as craftsmen, laborers, and traders. By 1800, about one hundred thousand free African Americans lived in the South.

Most slave owners feared that this growing population of free African Americans would encourage those still enslaved to revolt so as to gain their freedom. White Americans made life as difficult as possible for free African Americans. Laws required them to pay high taxes and sometimes to wear special badges on their clothing. Most important, southern states tried to stop the growth of the free African American population by making it impossible for slave owners to free any more slaves.

Some slave owners and other people resisted these laws. They were called abolitionists. The abolitionists wanted to abolish, or end, slavery and tried to find ways around the laws. For example, in 1830 a North Carolina slave owner named Letitia Gardner wanted to free her slaves, an African American woman and her children. But it was against the law there to free a slave if the slave remained in the state. Newly freed slaves had to leave the state, or they could be enslaved again. They faced a choice between freedom and staying close to their family and friends.

Gardner tried to solve this problem by allowing her slaves to live as semifree persons — that is, by granting them personal liberty even though they were still legally her slaves. But she could not guarantee that after her death her slaves would continue to be treated as free persons. In her will, she tried to give the slaves to another abolitionist, but after she died, her relatives went to court to reclaim the slaves. The court decided to give the slaves to Gardner's relatives. After many years of freedom, they became slaves once again.

Most slaves were not content to wait for their owners to free them. Many tried to run away to the North or to blend in with the free African American population in the South. Others engaged in open rebellion against the slave system. Throughout the history of slavery in America, there were at least two hundred fifty slave revolts or attempted revolts in which slaves sought to gain their freedom. As the slave owners feared, free African Americans were sometimes the leaders of these rebellions. Two famous revolt attempts were the Denmark Vesey conspiracy in South Carolina in 1822 and the Nat Turner revolt in Virginia in 1831.

Denmark Vesey was an African-born slave who had purchased his freedom. A religious man who often read from the Bible, he was especially struck by the story of how the children of Israel were led out of slavery in Egypt. He, too, wished to free the slaves, this time in the United States. He planned a revolt for June 16, 1822, but the revolt was betrayed by spies and informants. Although the revolt never took place, 131 conspirators (planners) were arrested. At the trial, 49 of the conspirators, including Vesey, were sentenced to death. Thirty-one, including Vesey, were hanged between June and August of 1822. The other 18 had their sentences reduced.

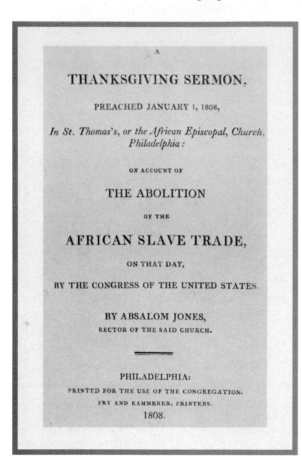

This title page from a sermon delivered in Philadelphia in 1808 praises an 1807 law prohibiting the importation of slaves. African American churches in the North celebrated the end of the slave trade.

Nat Turner was a slave who taught himself to read. Like Vesey, he was strongly influenced by the Bible. The Nat Turner revolt began in August 1831 with Turner and a handful of slaves. Turner began the revolt by killing his owner. Joined by more than sixty rebels, he went to a neighboring town to acquire arms and ammunition. But the band soon encountered hundreds of soldiers and volunteer militia, who killed many of the rebels. Turner was not captured until October 1831. He was tried and sentenced to hang.

During the Civil War, on January 1, 1863, President Abraham Lincoln's Emancipation Proclamation freed the slaves in those parts of the South that came under the control of the North during the war. After the war, the U.S. Constitution was amended to make slavery illegal.

THE STORY OF
THE AMISTAD AFRICANS

by Mary Ann Limauro

Locked in a crowded Connecticut jail cell with thirty-two fellow West Africans, a world away from his village in Sierra Leone, eleven-year-old Kali longed for the familiar surroundings of his homeland. He missed the wide blue sky and tall palm trees of Mendeland. He missed running and playing with his friends. He wished he could be back home with them, fishing in the river again. A tear glistened in Kali's dark eyes as he thought about his family — his sister and brother, his mother and father. So much time had passed since he had seen them.

The date was January 4, 1841. Kali and the other prisoners, all of whom had been kidnapped in Africa and sold into slavery, had been fighting for their freedom for almost two years. Their fierce determination to return home, coupled with the efforts of a group of supporters who believed in the right of freedom for all, would soon make them the first slaves ever to gain their freedom through the U.S. courts.

The Amistad Africans, as Kali and his group were known, first came together in the spring of 1839 at an illegal slave market in Havana, Cuba. There, two Spanish slave traders had purchased the original group of fifty-three, planning to bring them to a sugar cane plantation on the other side of the island.

Once aboard the *Amistad,* the Africans revolted against their captors. After an ill-fated attempt to sail back to Africa, both ship and Africans were taken into U.S. custody in Long Island Sound. The group was charged with murder and mutiny and jailed in New Haven, Connecticut.

Kali, though only nine, was kept with the men. The three girls in the group — Teme, age twelve; Kagne, age ten; and Margru, age seven — were sent to live with the jailer and his wife. Criminal charges were soon dropped because of a lack of jurisdiction, but the ship's owners then claimed that the Africans should be returned to them as "cargo."

Finally, after two trials and several months' imprisonment, the court ruled that the group be freed and returned to their home-

land. The U.S. attorney, acting on the orders of President Martin Van Buren, appealed that decision, and the case was now pending before the Supreme Court.

Looking around at his companions gathered in the damp cell, Kali, a small, dark-skinned boy with a stout build, felt a deep love for these brave men. Cinque, who had led the revolt aboard the *Amistad,* was acknowledged as the group's leader. A strong, powerfully built man in his mid-twenties, Cinque also was kind and gentle and showed much concern for Kali and the others. He, like the small, wiry Grabeau, had been a rice planter at home. Several of the others were blacksmiths. Almost all were married and had been snatched away from their families. Young Kali, who had been taken while walking along a road in his village, shared their pain of separation from loved ones.

The past two years, though difficult, had held some moments of happiness, thought Kali. Many of the townspeople in New Haven had befriended the captives, visiting them and bringing them food and clothing. Professors and students from Yale University had come regularly to instruct the captives in religion and English, bringing them Bibles and books to read. And several local clergymen who strongly disapproved of slavery had banded together with other abolitionists from around the United States to raise funds for the Africans' defense.

These supporters, who called themselves the Amistad Committee, had hired several of the best local attorneys for the captives' earlier trials. Now that the case was going before the Supreme Court, the committee members felt that an attorney with a national reputation was needed. They decided on former president John Quincy Adams.

Though not an abolitionist, Adams was a strong foe of slavery, and even though he was seventy-three years old and had not appeared before the Supreme Court in thirty years, "Old Man Eloquent" agreed to take the case. Now Kali, a bright boy who had quickly learned English, was chosen by Cinque and the others to write a letter to Adams.

"Dear Friend Mr. Adams," he began. "I want to write a letter to you because you love Mendi people, and you talk to the grand court." Speaking for all the captives, Kali poured out his heart, ending with a plea to "make us free."

The next month, Adams successfully argued the Africans' case. On March 9, 1841, the Supreme Court justices ruled that the Amistad Africans were free men and should be returned to their homeland. Six months later, Kali and his countrymen returned to Sierra Leone.

James Forten

....

Forten gained recognition in 1813 when he published a booklet of five essays called *Series of Letters by a Man of Color.* He later became friends with William Lloyd Garrison and served for many years on the American Anti-Slavery Society's Board of Managers.

*The goal of the American Colonization Society was to send African Americans back to Africa. In its first twenty years, the society sent four thousand African Americans to the west coast of Africa, to a settlement that was named Liberia in 1824.

JAMES FORTEN:
SAIL MAKER AND FREEDOM FIGHTER

by Pam Deyell Gingold

"I would rather remain as James Forten, sail-maker of Philadelphia, than enjoy the highest office in the gift of your society." Head held high and shaking with outrage, Forten would not even consider the offer from the newly formed American Colonization Society to make him ruler of what would be called Liberia.* A fourth-generation African American and tireless crusader against slavery, Forten was offended by the very idea of colonization.

In 1817, most white antislavery advocates believed that American slaves should be set free and returned to Africa. The American Colonization Society made use of this sentiment to coerce free African Americans to return "home to their people" because they were not welcome in white society. Forten launched a campaign to inform African Americans about the society's scheme to "exile us from the land of our nativity."

He warned that colonization would cripple all efforts to free their fellow African Americans from slavery.

In response to an appeal by Forten, three thousand people gathered in Philadelphia in August 1817. The largest meeting held by free African Americans to date, the assembly put the African American community on record against colonization.

Born in 1766, Forten fought in the American Revolution at age fourteen, inspired by the Declaration of Independence's proclamation that "all men are created equal." As a young sail maker, he invented a sail-handling device that made him a fortune. By age thirty-two, he owned a sail-making establishment employing forty African American and white workers.

A self-made man and wealthy business owner, Forten was active in free African American churches and educational societies and had great influence in the African American community. His political efforts began as early as 1800, when he circulated a petition to Congress calling for changes in the 1793 Fugitive Slave Act and a gradual ending of slavery. When Congress sternly rejected the petition, Forten went to work to change the attitudes of white society.

Forten gained widespread recognition in 1813 when he published a booklet of five essays called *Series of Letters by a Man of Color,* in protest of a Pennsylvania bill banning African Americans from the state. The essays set forth Forten's radical view that the two races were equal in every respect and helped to defeat the bill.

Following a terrible "anti-Negro" riot in Cincinnati, Ohio, Forten and other African American leaders formed the American Society of Free Persons of Color and held the first annual Negro National Convention in 1830. These conventions called for the abolition of slavery, petitioning against unjust laws, and the creation of schools and employment opportunities for free African Americans.

By 1830, some white reformers had begun to accept the principles of true abolition: immediate (not gradual) emancipation and a commitment to helping the freed slaves take their place in society. When William Lloyd Garrison started his newspaper, *The Liberator,* in 1831, Forten was jubilant. "It has roused up a spirit in our young people that has been slumbering for years," he wrote Garrison. He solicited subscriptions from the African American community and sent money whenever the newspaper ran into financial difficulties.

Forten's adamant opposition to colonization and eloquent promotion of racial equality had a great influence on Garrison. The men corresponded frequently, and Garrison's inflammatory booklet *Thoughts on African Colonization,* published in 1832, included a large section written by free African Americans setting forth their objections to colonization.

In 1833, the country's leading abolitionists gathered in Philadelphia to found the American Anti-Slavery Society. Forten's home was open to all involved, both black and white. Garrison was a frequent visitor. Forten served for years on the society's Board of Managers and remained a loyal "Garrisonian" until his death in 1842.

Although he did not live to see the end of slavery, James Forten left five grown children to carry on his work. The torch was even passed on to his grandchildren, the best known of whom is Charlotte Forten. During the Civil War, she helped educate newly freed slaves in the Sea Islands of South Carolina.

Antislavery meetings began to be held in public commons in the North during the early 1830s. On January 1, 1831, William Lloyd Garrison published the first issue of *The Liberator,* calling for the immediate and unconditional liberation of slaves.

NATIVE AMERICANS AND SLAVERY

by Randy Krehbiel

No ethnic group viewed slavery from more different perspectives than the Native Americans. At various times, in various places, they were slaves, slave traders, slave owners, and antislavery crusaders.

Before the arrival of whites in America, some Native American tribes practiced a form of slavery using enemies captured in battle. Later, during the early days of colonization, Indians traded these captives to whites for weapons and manufactured goods. There is evidence that some colonists encouraged war between rival tribes not only to weaken them but also to increase the flow of cheap forced labor.

When southern colonists began to show a preference for black slaves imported from Africa and the West Indies, some Native Americans turned to tracking and trading black slaves who attempted to escape into the frontier wilderness of the western Carolinas, eastern Tennessee, and Kentucky. The more unscrupulous traders did not always wait for the slaves to escape on their own. A noted Chickamauga warrior named Chief Benge was tracked down and killed by the Virginia militia because he persisted in luring away and sometimes even kidnapping slaves in one area and selling them in another.

By the late 1700s, some of the Five Civilized Tribes of the Southeast were becoming slave owners. The Cherokees especially acquired large numbers of black slaves to work on the farms and plantations they were building in Tennessee and Georgia.

In 1817, when General Andrew Jackson declared war on the Florida Seminoles, who harbored escaped slaves from Georgia, he brought on war with Spain, which controlled Florida. On February 22, 1819, Spain ceded Florida to the United States. When Jackson became president in 1829, he wanted to move the Seminoles out of Florida, bringing about the Second Seminole War.

The Seminoles also had slaves, but their relationship with the slaves among them was different. Slaves were allowed to live wherever they pleased, on the condition that they pay their owners a yearly tribute. Free African Americans were relatively numerous, too. Most were runaways, but some were former Seminole slaves who had bought or been granted their freedom.

Many African Americans rose to positions of prominence as warriors and statesmen among the Seminoles. The Seminoles deeply distrusted whites, especially English-speaking ones, and avoided contact with them as much as possible. As a result, African Americans — who often spoke English, Spanish, and several Indian dialects — usually served as interpreters and negotiators with the U.S. government.

One of the most interesting of these men was known as Gopher John. He served the U.S. Army and the Seminoles as an interpreter in Florida in the 1830s. When he was rewarded with his freedom and sent west in 1842, he established a settlement of African Americans that became the present town of Wewoka, Oklahoma. In 1849, with the former Seminole chief Wildcat, he led a contingent of African Americans and Indians into Mexico to found a new settlement.

The Seminoles would hardly qualify as abolitionists, but they did come closer than any other group to treating African Americans as equals. Their refusal to return escaped slaves or conform to the rigid slave codes of the South led to three bloody wars with the United States and the Seminoles' partial removal to Indian Territory (now Oklahoma) beginning in 1832. The Seminoles were the last of the Five Civilized Tribes to be relocated to Indian Territory. The Cherokees, Choctaws, Chickasaws, and Creeks had already established thriving agrarian societies there similar to those of the southern states from which they had come.

In the years leading up to the Civil War, an antislavery movement began to grow among the Indians. Abolitionists were particularly active among the

Cherokees, who were also the largest slaveholders. Antislavery Cherokees tended to be the most conservative members of the tribe. They were encouraged by missionaries from the Northeast. In the late 1850s, these missionaries helped revive an ancient order known as the Keetowah Society. Its original purpose was to preserve the traditional ways of the Cherokees. Only full bloods could belong.

Members of the new Keetowah Society were called Pins because they identified themselves by wearing crossed pins on their shirts or jackets. The Pins believed that the Cherokees should follow the old ways, but they also were active abolitionists. During the Civil War, the Pins fought for the North.

In 1866, Albert Pike, who served both the U.S. and the Confederate governments as a representative to Indian Territory, reported that "the Pin organization...was established by Evan Jones, a missionary, and at the service of (chief) John Ross, for the purpose of abolitionizing other Cherokees and putting out of the way all who sympathized with the Southern State." Evan Jones and his son, John, were Baptist missionaries from Boston who were forced to leave Indian Territory in 1861 because of their antislavery statements. They returned after

The Second Seminole War lasted for seven years, ending without a victor. As shown here, the Seminoles were tracked down using bloodhounds.

the Civil War and became Cherokee citizens.

The Civil War split Indian Territory just as it did the United States. Each of the five nations had Union and Confederate fighting forces. In the most important battle in Indian Territory, a combined force of red, black, and white Federal troops defeated a larger Confederate army at Honey Springs in 1863.

Also in 1863, the council of the northern Cherokees issued its own Emancipation Proclamation. Unlike President Abraham Lincoln's version, which freed only the slaves in territory held by the Confederacy, the Cherokees' proclamation freed all slaves throughout the Cherokee Nation.

The Old Hill House in Andover, Massachusetts, was a stop on the Underground Railroad.

From Ellen Hansen, ed., *The Underground Railroad: Life on the Road to Freedom,* Perspectives on History Series, pp. 5–6. Copyright © 1993 Discovery Enterprises, Ltd., Lowell, Massachusetts.

THE UNDERGROUND RAILROAD

The Underground Railroad was neither "underground" nor a "railroad." It was a network of people and houses throughout sixteen northern U.S. states and Canada, organized to help escaped slaves reach safety.

At that time (about 1820–1860), such activities were against the law. Underground Railroad workers and fugitive slaves therefore had to carry on in secret — often in darkness or disguise. As many as 100,000 fugitive slaves traveled the Underground Railroad's "lines" (or routes) north to freedom.

Slaves, mainly people of African descent, had been seeking freedom from bondage since colonial times. Even as white colonists sought their own human rights and independence from Britain during the latter 1700's, blacks were forced to sue for their freedom in court or take great risks in running away from their masters. The invention of the cotton gin and the passage of the first national fugitive slave law (both in 1793) seemed to give new life to this "peculiar institution" of slavery, which was so tied into the economy of the South.

By the early 1800's, fugitive slaves had many sympathizers in the North, including free blacks, abolitionists, and church groups such as the Quakers, Congregationalists, and Methodists. These "agents" of the Underground Railroad ran "safe houses" to harbor the escaping slaves on their way north; served as "conductors" leading the fugitives to the next "station" or resting place; raised money, collected food and clothing for the cause; and worked politically (starting newspapers, giving speeches, working to get laws passed) to end slavery.

The courage and perseverance of the fugitive slaves, combined with these efforts by the "agents," formed the backbone of the Underground Railroad.

There are many names worthy of mention in any discussion of the Underground Railroad and the anti-slavery movement: Harriet Tubman, Frederick Douglass, Abraham Lincoln, William Lloyd Garrison, Levi Coffin, Robert Purvis, William Still, Lucretia Mott, Anthony Burns, Susan B. Anthony, Ellen and William Craft, David Walker, Elijah Lovejoy, Sarah and Angelina Grimké, Thomas Garrett, Harriet Beecher Stowe, James Brown, and Nat Turner, for example.

WILLIAM AND ELLEN CRAFT*

A quarter of a century ago, William and Ellen Craft were slaves in the State of Georgia. With them, as with thousands of others, the desire to be free was very strong. For this jewel they were willing to make any sacrifice, or to endure any amount of suffering. In this state of mind they commenced planning. After thinking of various ways that might be tried, it occurred to William and Ellen, that one might act the part of master and the other the part of servant.

Ellen being fair enough to pass for white, of necessity would have to be transformed into a young planter for the time being. All that was needed, however, to make this important change was that she should be dressed elegantly in a fashionable suit of male attire, and have her hair cut in the style usually worn by young planters. Her profusion of dark hair offered a fine opportunity for the change. So far this plan looked very tempting. But it occurred to them that Ellen was beardless. After some mature reflection, they came to the conclusion that this difficulty could be very readily obviated by having the face muffled up as though the young planter was suffering badly with the face or toothache; thus they got rid of this trouble. Straightway, upon further reflection, several other very serious difficulties stared them in the face. For instance, in traveling, they knew that they would be under the necessity of stopping repeatedly at hotels, and that the custom of registering would have to be conformed to, unless some very good excuse could be given for not doing so.

Here they again thought much over matters, and wisely concluded that the young man had better assume the attitude of a gentleman very much indisposed. He must have his right arm placed carefully in a sling; that would be a sufficient excuse for not registering, etc. Then he must be a little lame, with a nice cane in the left hand; he must have large green spectacles over his eyes, and withal he must be very hard of hearing and dependent on his faithful servant (as was no uncommon thing with slave-holders), to look after all his wants.

William was just the man to act this part. To begin with, he was very "likely-looking"; smart, active and exceedingly attentive to his young master — indeed he was almost eyes, ears, hands and feet for him. William knew that this would please the slave-holders. The young planter would have nothing to do but hold himself subject to his ailments and put on a bold air of superiority; he was not

Robert Purvis

....

Purvis's mother was a free African American and his father a wealthy English cotton broker who was sympathetic to the abolitionist cause. In 1831, Purvis helped organize the First Annual Convention of Free Colored People in Philadelphia and was one of five African Americans on the first Board of Managers of the American Anti-Slavery Society. (Also see the poster on page 208.)

From Ellen Hansen, ed., *The Underground Railroad: Life on the Road to Freedom,* Perspectives on History Series, pp. 7–10. Copyright © 1993 Discovery Enterprises, Ltd., Lowell, Massachusetts.

*As reported in William Still's book *The Underground Rail Road* (1871): 382–384.

William and Ellen Craft

to deign to notice anybody. If, while traveling, gentlemen, either politely or rudely, should venture to scrape acquaintance with the young planter, in his deafness he was to remain mute; the servant was to explain. In every instance when this occurred, as it actually did, the servant was fully equal to the emergency — none dreamed of the disguises in which the Underground Rail Road passengers were traveling.

They stopped at a first-class hotel in Charleston, where the young planter and his body servant were treated, as the house was wont to treat the chivalry. They stopped also at a similar hotel in Richmond, and with like results.

They knew that they must pass through Baltimore, but they did not know the obstacles that they would have to surmount in the Monumental City. They proceeded to the depot in the usual manner, and the servant asked for tickets for his master and self. Of course the master could have a ticket, but "bonds will have to be entered before you can get a ticket," said the ticket master. "It is the rule of this office to require bonds for all negroes applying for tickets to go North, and none but gentlemen of well-known responsibility will be taken," further explained the ticket master.

The servant replied, that he knew "nothing about that" — that he was "simply traveling with his young master to take care of him — he being in a very delicate state of health, so much so, that fears were entertained that he might not be able to hold out to reach Philadelphia, where he was hastening for medical treatment," and ended his reply by saying, "my master can't be detained." Without further parley, the ticket master very obligingly waived the old "rule," and furnished the requisite tickets. The mountain being thus removed, the young planter and his faithful servant were safely in the cars for the city of Brotherly Love.

Scarcely had they arrived on free soil when the rheumatism departed — the right arm was unslung — the toothache was gone — the beardless face was unmuffled — the deaf heard and spoke — the blind saw — and the lame leaped as an hart, and in the presence of a few astonished friends of the slave, the facts of this unparalleled Underground Rail Road feat were fully established by the most unquestionable evidence.

DAVID WALKER'S *APPEAL*

*N*ot all blacks during this time were slaves. Some, like David Walker, were born free blacks; others purchased their own freedom or had their freedom purchased for them by friends, family members, or religious groups.

David Walker believed that blacks should fight for their freedom by any means possible, including violent means. In this respect, he went further than most abolitionists at the time.

The following selection about David Walker is reprinted in its entirety from *The African Meeting House in Boston — A Sourcebook.* *

David Walker was a free black man, born in Wilmington, North Carolina on September 28, 1785. After travelling extensively in the South and observing first-hand the effects of slavery, he came to Boston in 1827. Here he opened a shop on Brattle Street where he sold both new and second-hand clothing. White clothing dealers tried to force him out of business, and Walker and two other black clothing dealers were subjected to police harassment. In 1828, they were indicted and tried for receiving stolen goods. Walker and one of the others were acquitted, and charges against the third were dropped.

Walker quickly became involved in the black community, working to improve education for black children, establish black churches, and increase employment opportunities for blacks. He became a leader in the Massachusetts General Colored Association, an organization founded in 1826 to abolish slavery and improve racial conditions for blacks. He was Boston's agent for and occasional contributor to *Freedom's Journal,* or *Rights of All,* as it was renamed by Samuel Cornish in 1829, after [John] Russwurm resigned and went to Liberia.

Walker is remembered, however, for a pamphlet that he published in 1829. Known as *Walker's Appeal,* the full title of the seventy-six page pamphlet was *Walker's Appeal, in Four Articles: Together with a Preamble, to the Coloured Citizens of the World, but in particular, and very expressly, to those in the United States of America, written in Boston, State of Massachusetts, September 28, 1829.* The four articles mentioned in the title address four separate issues: Article 1 deals with slavery and its evil consequences; Article 2, with the black's lack of education; Article 3 addresses the upholding of the slave system by the Christian ministry; and Article 4 is concerned with the colonization plan. Much of Walker's appeal is addressed particularly to slaves, urging them to rise up and take the freedom due them, by any means possible.

"Never make an attempt to gain our freedom or natural right, from under our cruel oppressors and murderers, until you see your way clear — when that hour arrives and you move, be not afraid or dismayed....

"...if you commence...kill or be killed. Now, I ask you, had you not rather be killed than to be a slave to a tyrant, who takes the life of your mother, wife and dear little children? ...believe this, that it is no more harm for you to kill a man, who is trying to kill you, than it is for you to take a drink of water when thirsty....

Walker also addressed part of his message to white Americans:

"If any are anxious to ascertain who I am, know the world, that I am one of the oppressed, degraded and wretched sons of Africa, rendered

From Ellen Hansen, ed., *The Underground Railroad: Life on the Road to Freedom,* Perspectives on History Series, pp. 11–15. Copyright © 1993 Discovery Enterprises, Ltd., Lowell, Massachusetts.

*Reprinted courtesy of the Museum of Afro American History from "The Appeal" by David Walker from *The African Meeting House in Boston — A Sourcebook.*

so by the avaricious and unmerciful, among the whites. If any wish to plunge me into the wretched incapacity of a slave, or murder me for the truth, know ye, that I am in the hand of God, and at your disposal. I count my life not dear unto me, but I am ready to be offered at any moment. For what is the use of living, when in fact I am dead. But remember, Americans, that as miserable, wretched, degraded and abject as you have made us in preceding, and in this generation, to support you and your families, that some of you (whites) on the continent of America, will yet curse the day that you ever were born. You want slaves, and want us for your slaves!!! My colour will yet, root some of you out of the very face of the earth!!!!!!"

The Appeal was the most militant and inflammatory anti-slavery document that had ever been published, and response to it was immediate and intense. The South was enraged; a reward was offered for Walker — $1,000 dead or $10,000 alive. Georgia and South Carolina passed laws against incendiary publications — Georgia made the circulation of such documents a capital offense. The governor of Georgia and the mayor of Savannah sent letters to Boston's mayor urging him to suppress the publication. The mayor replied that he didn't like the pamphlet either, but that no law had been broken and there was nothing he could do.

Four blacks were arrested in New Orleans for distributing the "diabolical Boston pamphlet." The vigilance committee of South Carolina offered a $1500 reward for the arrest of anyone distributing *The Appeal*. The document came under attack even among northerners and abolitionists; Benjamin Lundy claimed it would injure the cause, Samuel May attributed to it a rise in southern fury against the Abolitionists; Garrison, however, referred to it as "one of the most remarkable productions of the age" and the "forerunner of the Abolition struggle."

Reaction against Walker was so strong that he was urged to go to Canada, but he insisted on remaining in Boston, in spite of, or perhaps because of, the furor aroused by *The Appeal*. It was in its third printing in 1830, when Walker's body, possibly dead of poisoning, was found outside his shop. Although he had been in Boston only three years, Walker left his mark on the city and on the anti-slavery movement. He also left a son, Edward Garrison Walker, who became a lawyer prior to the Civil War, and in 1866 was elected to the Massachusetts House of Representatives, representing Charlestown. He and Charles L. Mitchell, elected at the same time, were the first blacks to sit on any state legislature.

From Ellen Hansen, ed., *The Underground Railroad: Life on the Road to Freedom,* Perspectives on History Series, pp. 20–24. Copyright © 1993 Discovery Enterprises, Ltd., Lowell, Massachusetts.

HOPPING 'ON BOARD' THE UNDERGROUND RAILROAD

One of the more memorable escapes from slavery was that of Henry "Box" Brown. He hit upon the idea of being crated up, and shipped direct to Philadelphia as freight. Brown stepped into the box a slave in Richmond, Virginia, and emerged twenty-six hours later in Philadelphia a free man.

The box measured three feet long, two feet wide, and two feet eight inches deep, and was lined with baize. Brown's only supplies were one small container of water, a few biscuits, and a handtool to bore holes for air. A friend nailed the box up and strapped the outside with five hickory hoops, marking the box "This side up with care" near the address.

Nonetheless, Brown spent a good deal of time on his head during the journey, as the box was transferred from dray to train to ferry to wagon. When the box arrived at its destination, the Anti-Slavery Society offices in Philadelphia, one of those expecting him rapped quietly on the box, calling out "All right?" "All right, sir!" came the answer from within. When the hoops were cut and the lid lifted, Brown stood up in the box, reached out his hand and said, "How do you do, gentlemen?"

Such a spectacular escape, though, was the exception. Most runaway slaves did just that — *run away.* They relied on their own courage, instinct, and stamina to escape the inhumane life of a slave.

The news passed quickly from plantation to plantation among the slaves: "There's an Underground Railroad that leads north — to freedom." But how did they make the initial escape from their plantations? Where did the slaves learn the routes to follow? Once on their way, how did they evade the slave hunters and bloodhounds pursuing them, and where did their arduous journey end?

Few were as bold as Ellen and William Craft, traveling in disguise by day and on major routes. Most runaway slaves traveled at night using the North Star as their guide, and made their escape alone or in small groups. Usually, they left on Saturday night. This gave them a head start: their absence wouldn't be noticed until Monday when they were summoned back into the fields to work.

Before reaching the free states and the nearest "safe house" on the Underground Railroad, the fugitives hid by day in barns, in haystacks, in the woods. At night, they'd press on, avoiding the well-traveled routes and sticking to backroads, fields, forests, swamps, and waterways.

Some slaves had learned the song "Follow the Drinking Ground" (meaning the Big Dipper) and so knew how to locate the North Star using that constellation. Others had seen anti-slavery pictures on handkerchiefs smuggled in with goods arriving from the North, or seen the "scatter sheets" (anti-slavery pamphlets) left by Underground Railroad workers along roadsides and other places accessible to slaves.

Word about the "underground" spread. Slaves "hired out" by their masters to work temporarily at other plantations spread the word. Friends and relatives visiting on a Sunday from a nearby plantation spread the word. And Underground Railroad workers whose jobs involved travel through the South, such as handymen, mechanics, preachers and salesmen, spread the word. These northern workers occasionally provided slaves with money toward their escape as well.

Word-of-mouth communication about the Underground Railroad worked best for two reasons: most slaves couldn't read, and those who could were not allowed to read anti-slavery material. The information which passed from person to person gave details about how to "ride the rails."

Slaves learned how to recognize a safe house in the North: a quilt (with a house and smoking chimney as one of its designs) hanging on a clothesline; a lamp (of a certain brightness) in the window; a ring of white bricks around a house's chimney.

They also learned of possible water routes to freedom, for instance getting "hired out" aboard a steamboat on the Ohio River or stowing away on coastal

This picture of a poor fugitive also was used on handbills offering rewards for runaway slaves.

shipping vessels headed for seaports in the North. Anti-slavery crews in northern ports then helped fugitives make the escape at that end.

Reaching a safe house in the North meant food, clothing, and added protection against capture. But it did not yet mean freedom, especially in states bordering the South.

When the Fugitive Slave Act passed in 1850, runaway slaves weren't safe until they arrived in Canada, which was beyond the reach of the slave hunters. Therefore, "traveling the rails" meant staying hidden, even once they were "on board" the Underground Railroad.

The Magee House in Canisteo, New York, served as a station on the Underground Railroad.

Slaves were hidden in the attics, storerooms, and cellars of safe houses; in secret chambers and behind false walls; under mattresses of feather beds.

While in transit to the next stopping place, Underground Railroad "conductors" hid slaves under bales of goods in wagons, as stowaways aboard ships, and in the woods. They were all risking capture. Capture meant a return to slavery for the runaways, and a fine of $1,000 and six months in jail for underground agents.

The Fugitive Slave Act of 1850 prompted the more well-known escaped slaves such as Ellen and William Craft, Frederick Douglass, and William Wells Brown, to flee to Europe to avoid capture. That act also spelled danger for free blacks in the North: free blacks and escaped slaves alike were being captured by slave hunters and brought down South to be sold into slavery. Many free blacks fled to Canada to avoid that risk.

The issue of slavery was tearing the nation apart. Abraham Lincoln, while campaigning for a Senate seat in 1858, put it this way: "'A house divided against itself cannot stand.' I believe this government cannot endure, permanently half *slave* and half *free.*"

The Civil War (1861–1865) began three years later. On September 22, 1862, President Lincoln issued the Emancipation Proclamation, which declared that as of January 1, 1863, "all persons held as slaves within any state...in rebellion against the United States shall be then...and forever free."

The Civil War had been ennobled: it was now being fought to save the Union *and* to abolish slavery. In 1865, the Civil War ended and the Thirteenth Amendment to the U.S. Constitution was ratified, abolishing slavery permanently.

The Underground Railroad, which had grandly served its purpose, was no longer needed.

ALL ABOARD WITH THOMAS GARRETT

by Alice P. Miller

The elderly couple walked sedately down the stairs of the red brick house, every detail of their costumes proclaiming their respectability. The small lady was wearing an ankle-length gray gown, a snowy white lawn kerchief, and a pleated gray silk bonnet, draped with a veil. The tall, white-haired gentleman wore the wide-brimmed beaver hat and long black waistcoat that was customary among Quakers.

When they reached the sidewalk, he assisted her into the four-wheeled barouche (carriage) that stood at the curb. Then he climbed into the barouche himself. The driver drove the horses away at a leisurely pace. Not until they were beyond the city limits did he allow the horses to prance along at a brisk pace across the few miles that separated Wilmington, Delaware, from the free state of Pennsylvania.

The gentleman was Thomas Garrett, a white man who had for many years been breaking the law by sheltering runaway slaves. And the lady at his side was runaway slave Harriet Tubman, clad in clothes donated by his wife. The preceding night, Tubman had slept in a small room secreted behind one wall of Garrett's shoe store, a room that never remained unoccupied for very long. It was Tubman's first visit to Garrett, but she would return many times in the future.

Runaway slaves remained with Garrett for one, two, or three nights until Garrett considered it prudent to send them along to the next station on the Underground Railroad. He provided them with clothing and outfitted them with new shoes from his store. He fed them hearty meals and dressed their wounds. He also forged passes for them so that any slave stopped by a slave catcher would have evidence that he or she was on a legitimate errand.

Some of the money he needed to cover the costs of his hospitality came out of his own pocket, but he was not a rich man. He could not have taken care of so many fugitives had it not been for donations made by fellow abolitionists in the North as well as supporters in foreign countries. There was never quite enough money, but no fugitive was ever turned away from his door. He would have gone without food himself before he would have refused food to a hungry slave.

Garrett, who was born in Upper Darby, Pennsylvania, in 1789, had been helping runaway slaves ever since 1822, when he rescued a young African American woman who was trying to escape from her master. At that time, he vowed to devote the rest of his life to helping fugitives, and he remained faithful to that vow.

Thomas Garrett

Garrett (1789–1871), an abolitionist and a Quaker, used his home in Wilmington, Delaware, as an Underground Railroad station.

Of all the stations on the Underground Railroad, his was probably the most efficiently run and the most frequently used. The fact that Wilmington was so close to Pennsylvania made it the most hazardous stop on the route. Slave catchers prowled the streets of Wilmington, on the alert for any indication that an African American might be a runaway. They kept a sharp eye on all roads leading north from Wilmington.

For many years, Garrett managed to get away with his illegal activities because he was a clever man and knew how to avoid detection by slave catchers. Sometimes he disguised a slave, as he had done with Tubman. Sometimes he dressed a man in a woman's clothing or a woman in a man's clothing or showed a young person how to appear like one bent over with age. Another reason for his success was that he had many friends who admired what he was doing and could be trusted to help. They might, for example, conceal slaves under a wagonload of vegetables or in a secret compartment in a wagon.

Slave catchers were aware of what he was doing, but they had a hard time finding the kind of evidence that would stand up in court. At last, in 1848, he was sued by two Maryland slave owners who hoped to stop his activities by ruining him financially.

The suit was brought before the federal circuit court of New Castle under a 1793 federal law that allowed slave owners to recover penalties from any person who harbored a runaway slave. The case was heard by Willard Hall, a U.S. district judge, and by Roger B. Taney, chief justice of the U.S. Supreme Court. Bringing in a verdict in favor of the owners, the jurors decided that the owners were entitled to fifty-four hundred dollars in fines.

Garrett did not have anywhere near that much money, but he stood up and addressed the court and spectators in these words: "I have assisted fourteen hundred slaves in the past twenty-five years on their way to the North. I now consider this penalty imposed upon me as a license for the remainder of my life. I am now past sixty and have not a dollar to my name, but be that as it may, if anyone knows of a poor slave who needs shelter and a breakfast, send him to me, as I now publicly pledge myself to double my diligence and never neglect an opportunity to assist a slave to obtain freedom, so help me God!"

As he continued to speak for more than an hour, some of the spectators hissed while others cheered. When he finished, one juror leaped across the benches and pumped Garrett's hand. With tears in his eyes, he said, "I beg your forgiveness, Mr. Garrett."

After the trial, Garrett's furniture was auctioned off to help pay the heavy fine. But he managed to borrow money from friends and eventually repaid those

Harriet Tubman

One of the most widely known conductors on the Underground Railroad was Harriet Tubman, an escaped slave who helped more than three hundred slaves flee to freedom. During the Civil War, she was a nurse, laundress, and spy.

loans, rebuilt his business, and became prosperous. Meanwhile, he went on sheltering slaves for many more years. By the time President Abraham Lincoln's Emancipation Proclamation went into effect in 1863, Garrett's records showed that he had sheltered more than twenty-seven hundred runaways.

During those years, he had many encounters with Harriet Tubman, as she kept returning to the South and coming back north with bands of slaves. Much of what we know about Tubman today is based on letters that he sent to her or wrote about her. A portion of one of those letters reads thus: "I may begin by saying, living as I have in a slave State, and the laws being very severe where any proof could be made of any one aiding slaves on their way to freedom, I have not felt at liberty to keep any written word of Harriet's labors as I otherwise could, and now would be glad to do; for in truth I never met with any person, of any color, who had more confidence in the voice of God, as spoken direct to her soul.... She felt no fear of being arrested by her former master, or any other person, when in his immediate neighborhood, than she did in the State of New York or Canada, for she said she ventured only where God sent her, and her faith in the Supreme Power truly was great."

In April 1870, African Americans in Wilmington held a huge celebration upon the passage of the Fifteenth Amendment to the U.S. Constitution. That amendment provided that the right of citizens to vote should not be denied or abridged by the United States or by any state on account of race, color, or previous condition of servitude. Jubilant African Americans drew Garrett through the streets in an open carriage on one side of which were inscribed the words "Our Moses."

Garrett lived for only ten months after that celebration. His African American friends carried his coffin on their shoulders to the Quaker cemetery, which became his final resting place.

THIS TRAIN DISAPPEARS

by Marion Schultz

The African American slave Tice Edwards had just escaped from a plantation in the Deep South. All night he ran, swift as a deer, following signs left by other fleeing slaves. By day, he hid in places marked by special signals that told him they were safe for hunted people. Then, just as he was about to cross the Kentucky River, his angry owner caught up with him and shouted for Tice to stop.

Tice did not answer. He plunged into the cold, swift river and swam as fast as he ever had in his life. His breath came in great sobbing gasps when he waded ashore on the opposite bank. Looking back over his shoulder, he saw his master rowing toward him in a skiff. Tice ran into the trees edging the river and was never again seen in the South. His owner said later, "Tice Edwards just plain disappeared right under my very nose. It was as though he had boarded an underground railroad."

The year was 1830, and by all accounts that was the first time the words "underground railroad" were used to describe the way slaves escaped from their bondage in the South to freedom in the North. In reality, it was neither a railroad nor underground.

Slaves like this boy and his family who escaped bondage and went to Union lines before the Emancipation Proclamation was issued were commonly called contrabands.

Many people who hated slavery — both southerners and northerners — had worked out a system. Slaves who were willing to risk their lives and attempt an escape to the North might have begun by singing the forbidden song:

Go down, Moses, into Egyptland,
Tell old Pharaoh, let my people go.

Then someone might have whispered,

"Follow the bent twigs through the woods.
The first safe place will have a white bar painted on a tree."

Slave catchers made a career of capturing escaped slaves in the North and returning them to their masters in the South. Protests against this practice increased after the Compromise of 1850, which strengthened the fugitive slave law. Abolitionists also complained that slave catchers sometimes kidnapped free African Americans and sold them into slavery.

These "safe places" were also called "stations," just as though they were part of a real railroad line. They might have been a smokehouse on a farm, a corncrib, or a woodpile. Sometimes a safe place was an empty schoolhouse locked up for the summer. Sometimes runaways were hidden under the floorboards of sheds while horses were noisily threshing out wheat above them.

Everyone took a great chance, of course, by helping a runaway slave. One old peddler selling his wares in the hills of the South was in reality a "conductor" on the Underground Railroad. His wagon, piled high with pots and pans, bolts of cloth, and needles and pins, had a secret space beneath the floorboards. In this space, many a slave was carried to safety while a patrol rode by searching for him, just a few feet away. If caught, the old peddler could have been fined a thousand dollars and jailed for as long as six months.

If the slaves were caught, they were branded with an R for runaway, so they could be easily identified if they tried to escape again. And they nearly always tried, again and again, because freedom was more precious to them than anything else on earth.

Sometimes the conductors disguised the runaways in an amusing fashion. They plastered their black skin with a flour-and-water paste, put white gloves on their hands, and dressed them in a woman's long skirt with a heavy veil draped over the head and face. This was an accepted style in those days, and no one gave the disguise a second look. Many a slave was then placed on a real train and taken in comfort to a safe haven in the North.

Yankee captains of steamboats running between the North and South often took a hand in the escapes. It was done very cleverly. At night, while cargo was taken on board, it was difficult to tell one hurrying figure from another in the light of flickering pitch pine flares. A stream of African Americans carrying bales or boxes trotted up one gangway and down a second empty-handed. But not all of them came down. Huddled in the hold, five or six runaways would be on their way to freedom.

One of the most famous conductors on the Underground Railroad was a slave herself, named Harriet Tubman. She escaped to the North when she was a young woman, but she returned to the South many times, enduring great hardships and narrow escapes to help fugitives along the "Freedom Trail." Often dogs were sent to track them down, and the fugitives would have to rub wild onions on their feet to disguise their scent. Their terror of the vicious bloodhounds was so great that the runaways might have given up if it had not been for their courageous leader. A reward of forty thousand dollars was offered for Tubman's capture, dead or alive, but nobody ever turned her in.

Of course, there had to be secret stations on the Underground Railroad in the North as well, because slave catchers always followed, hot on the trail of fugitives, and received a good reward for returning slaves to their masters. Many of the conductors in Pennsylvania and New York were Quakers who felt strongly that slavery should be abolished. These people risked a good deal to help the runaways reach safety in Canada. The usual route for slaves to follow was called "The Grand Trunk Line" and reached from Kentucky and Virginia across the Ohio River. To the north, Canada thrust down into Lake Erie with a climate so mild that peaches, grapes, and tobacco could be grown there. No slave catcher had authority on Canadian soil, and the fugitives were warmly welcomed as they started a new, free life.

Slaves who had fled their masters were photographed at Follie's Farm, near Cumberland Landing, Virginia, in 1862.

The Underground Railroad was a remarkable institution and lasted until the Civil War broke out. It combined a people's love of excitement and adventure with a daring chance to help the underdog. The slaves themselves were remarkable because they possessed great courage and even showed high spirits as they set out to face an unknown future. Very often, they would sing in the woods as they tramped along the road to freedom:

Farewell, old Marster, don't think hard of me.
I'm going on to Canada where all de slaves are free.

SOJOURNER TRUTH SPEAKS OUT

by Phyllis Raybin Emert

I am pleading for my people,
A poor downtrodden race,
Who dwell in freedom's boasted land,
With no abiding place.

I am pleading that my people
May have their rights restored
For they have long been toiling,
And yet have no reward...

Whilst I bear upon my body
the scars of many a gash,
I am pleading for my people
Who groan beneath the lash.

Sojourner Truth (c. 1797–1883) was a freed slave who was inspired to preach about emancipation and women's rights throughout the North.

From Phyllis Raybin Emert, ed., *Women in the Civil War: Warriors, Patriots, Nurses, and Spies,* Perspectives on History Series, pp. 11–13. Copyright © 1995 Discovery Enterprises, Ltd., Lowell, Massachusetts.

She was a freed slave who once was called Isabella. After renaming herself Sojourner Truth she became an outspoken orator in her fight against slavery, as well as in support of women's rights. Although she never learned to read or write, her speeches throughout the country often moved her audiences to tears.

"Well, children," said the six-foot-tall black woman, "I was born a slave in Ulster County, New York. I don't know if it was summer or winter, fall or spring. I don't even know what day of the week it was. They don't care when a slave is born or when he dies...just how much work they can do."

When Truth addressed a women's rights convention in 1851, she was met at first with jeers and boos from the men in the crowd. "Where there is so much racket there must be something out of kilter," Sojourner began. "I think that 'twixt the niggers of the South and the women at the North all talking about rights, the white men will be in a fix pretty soon. But what's all this here talking about?

"That man over there says that women need to be helped into carriages, and lifted over ditches, and to have the best place everywhere. Nobody ever helps me into carriages, or over mud puddles, or gives me any best place, and aren't I a woman?...

"I have borne five children and seen them all sold off into slavery, and when I cried out with a mother's grief, none but Jesus heard — and aren't I a woman?"

Before her speeches, Sojourner often sang anti-slavery hymns which she made up herself (see left).

When the Civil War began in 1861, Sojourner was already in her sixties. She was an active supporter of President Abraham Lincoln and believed he was a good friend to blacks everywhere. After the Emancipation Proclamation freed all slaves in the Confederacy in 1863, Sojourner spoke to an all-white audience of young people:

"Children, who made your skin white? Was it not God? Who made mine black? Was it not the same God? Now, children, remember what Sojourner Truth has told you and thus get rid of your prejudice and learn to love colored children, that you may be all the children of your Father in heaven...."

In 1864, Sojourner traveled to Washington from her home in Battle Creek, Michigan, and met privately with Abraham Lincoln. "It was about 8 o'clock A.M., when I called on the president. Upon entering his reception room we found about a dozen persons in waiting, among them two colored women. I had quite a pleasant time waiting until he was disengaged, and enjoyed his conversation with others; he showed as much kindness and consideration to the colored persons as to the whites — if there was any difference, more.

"I said to him, Mr. President, when you first took your seat I feared you would be torn to pieces, for I likened you unto Daniel, who was thrown into the lion's den; and if the lions did not tear you into pieces, I knew that it would be God that had saved you; and I said if he spared me I would see you before the four years expired, and he has done so, and now I am here to see you for myself.

"I must say, and I am proud to say, that I never was treated by any one with more kindness and cordiality than were shown to me by that great and good man, Abraham Lincoln.... He took my little book, and with the same hand that signed the death-warrant of slavery, he wrote as follows: 'For Aunty Sojourner Truth, Oct. 29, 1864. A. Lincoln.'"

The President's House, shown here in 1861, eventually came to be called the White House.

SOJOURNER TRUTH

by Peter Roop

Sojourner Truth was truly a traveler on the road to freedom, walking and riding thousands of miles, spreading her message of liberty and equality. Born around 1797 in New York State as Isabella, a black slave, she gained her freedom in 1827. She then turned her tremendous energies toward winning emancipation for all African Americans. One of her monumental accomplishments was gaining freedom for her son, who had been illegally sold into slavery in the South. Her legal victory was a rare case of an African American's rights being upheld in a court against the claims of a white.

When she was close to forty years old, Isabella began a journey throughout the North, the South, and the expanding West. Early on this journey, she changed her name to Sojourner

Truth, meaning a traveler for truth. She traveled from town to town, speaking at antislavery meetings. She argued that no man, woman, or child should ever be enslaved. Her moving speeches captivated and inspired audiences. "I can't read a book, but I can read the people," she was fond of saying.

Just as she delighted some people, Sojourner Truth infuriated others. A man once told her that he did not care about her speeches any more than he cared about a flea bite. She replied, "Maybe not, but the Lord willing, I'll keep you scratchin'."

At the end of the Civil War, Sojourner Truth struggled to get the government to assist ex-slaves who were rebuilding their lives as free people. Then in her seventies, she was still, in the words of a friend, "teaching, preaching, nursing, watching, and praying" for her people.

Sojourner Truth died in 1883. She was active to the end of her days in the fight for equal rights for African Americans and women.

An illustration from the original edition of *Uncle Tom's Cabin*, published in 1852.

UNCLE TOM'S CABIN*
by Harriet Beecher Stowe

In 1852, a forty-one-year-old New England–born writer named Harriet Beecher Stowe published a novel about slave life in the South. A deeply religious woman whose father was a famous preacher, Stowe claimed that the entire story came to her in a vision from God. She called her book *Uncle Tom's Cabin, or Life Among the Lowly*. It became an instant sensation, sold tens of thousands of copies, and outraged many northerners who had no idea that slaves could be so cruelly treated by their masters and overseers. Abolitionists used the book to argue more strongly than ever that slavery should be ended. The book aroused so much controversy that when President Abraham Lincoln met Stowe for the first time, he exclaimed, "So this is the little lady who made this big war!"

The child, a boy of ten months, was uncommonly large and strong of his age, and very vigorous in his limbs. Never, for a moment, still, he kept his mother constantly busy in holding him, and guarding his springing activity.

"That's a fine chap!" said a man, suddenly stopping opposite to him, with his hands in his pockets. "How old is he?"

"Ten months and a half," said the mother.

The man whistled to the boy and offered him part of a stick of candy, which he eagerly grabbed at, and very soon had it in a baby's general depository, to wit, his mouth.

"Rum fellow!" said the man. "Knows what's what!" and he whistled, and walked on. When he had got to the other side of the boat, he came across Haley, who was smoking on top of a pile of boxes....

"Taking her down south?" said the man.

Haley nodded and smoked on....

"They won't want the young 'un on the plantation," said the man.

"I shall sell him, first chance I find," said Haley lighting another cigar....

"Well, stranger, what will you take?"

"Well now," said Haley, "I could raise that ar chap myself, or get him raised; he's uncommon likely and healthy, and he'd fetch a hundred dollars, six months hence; and, in a year or two, he'd bring two hundred, if I had him in the right

From Phyllis Raybin Emert, ed., *Women in the Civil War: Warriors, Patriots, Nurses, and Spies,* Perspectives on History Series, pp. 7–11. Copyright © 1995 Discovery Enterprises, Ltd., Lowell, Massachusetts. Introduction by Harold Holzer.

*Penguin Books edition, NY, 1981, pp. 205–212, originally published in 1852.

spot; — so I shan't take a cent less nor fifty for him now."

"O, stranger! that's rediculous!, altogether," said the man.

"Fact!" said Haley, with a decisive nod of his head.

"I'll give thirty for him," said the stranger, "but not a cent more."

"Now, I'll tell ye what I will do," said Haley, spitting again, with renewed decision. "I'll split the difference, and say forty-five, and that's the most I will do."

"Well, agreed!" said the man, after an interval.

"Done!" said Haley. "Where do you land?"

"At Louisville," said the man.

"Louisville," said Haley. "Very fair, we get there about dusk. Chap will be asleep, — all fair, — get him off quietly, and no screaming, — happens beautiful, — I like to do everything quietly, — I hates all kind of agitation and fluster." And so, after a transfer of certain bills had passed from the man's pocket-book to the trader's, he resumed his cigar.

It was a bright, tranquil evening when the boat stopped at the wharf at Louisville. The woman had been sitting with her baby in her arms, now wrapped in a heavy sleep. When she heard the name of the place called out, she hastily laid the child down in a little cradle formed by the hollow among the boxes, first carefully spreading under it her cloak; and then she sprung to the side of the boat, in hopes that, among the various hotel-waiters who thronged the wharf, she might see her husband. In this hope, she pressed forward to the front rails, and, stretching far over them, strained her eyes intently on the moving heads on the shore, and the crowd pressed in between her and the child.

"Now's your time," said Haley, taking the sleeping child up, and handing him to the stranger. "Don't wake him up, and set him to crying, now; it would make a devil of a fuss with the gal." The man took the bundle carefully, and was soon lost in the crowd that went up the wharf.

When the boat, creaking, and groaning, and puffing, had loosed from the wharf, and was beginning slowly to strain herself along, the woman returned to her old seat. The trader was sitting there, — the child was gone!

"Why, why, — where?" she began, in bewildered surprise.

"Lucy," said the trader, "Your child's gone; you may as well know it farst as last. You see, I know'd you couldn't take him down south; and I got a chance to sell him to a first-rate family, that'll raise him better than you can."

...The wild look of anguish and utter despair that the woman cast on him might have disturbed one less practiced; but he was used to it. He had seen that same look hundreds of times. You can get used to such things, too, my friend; and it is the great object of recent efforts to make our whole northern community used to them, for the glory of the Union. So, the trader only regarded the mortal anguish which he saw working in those dark features, those clenched hands, and suffocating breathings, as necessary incidents of the trade, and merely calculated whether she was going to scream, and get up a commotion on the boat; for, like other supporters of our peculiar institution, he decidedly disliked agitation.

But the woman did not scream. The shot had passed too straight and direct through the heart, for cry or tear.

Dizzily she sat down. Her slack hands fell lifeless by her side. Her eyes looked straight forward, but she saw nothing. All the noise and hum of the boat, the groaning of the machinery, mingled dreamily to her bewildered ear; and the poor, dumb-stricken heart had neither cry nor tear to show for its utter misery. She was quite calm....

Tom drew near, and tried to say something; but she only groaned. Honestly, and with tears running down his own cheeks, he spoke of a heart of love in the skies, of a pitying Jesus, and an eternal home; but the ear was deaf with anguish, and the palsied heart could not feel.

Night came on, — night calm, unmoved, and glorious, shining down with her innumerable and solemn angel eyes, twinkling, beautiful, but silent. There was no speech nor language, no pitying voice or helping hand, from that distant sky. One after another, the voice of business or pleasure died away; all on the boat were sleeping, and the ripples at the prow were plainly heard. Tom stretched himself out on a box, and there, as he lay, he heard, ever and anon, a smothered sob or cry from the prostrate creature, — "O! what shall I do? O Lord! O good Lord, do help me!" and so, ever and anon, until the murmur died away in silence.

At midnight, Tom waked, with a sudden start. Something black passed quickly by him to the side of the boat, and he heard a splash in the water. No one else saw or heard anything. He raised his head, — the woman's place was vacant! He got up, and sought about him in vain.

The poor bleeding heart was still, at last, and the river rippled and dimpled just as brightly as if it had not closed above it.

...The trader waked up bright and early, and came out to see to his live stock. It was now his turn to look about in perplexity.

"Where alive is that gal?" he said to Tom....

"Well, Mas'r," said Tom, "towards morning something brushed by me, and I kinder half woke; and then I hearn a great splash, and then I clare woke up, and the gal was gone. That's all I know on 't."

The trader was not shocked nor amazed; because, as we said before, he was used to a great many things that you are not used to. Even the awful presence of Death struck no solemn chill upon him. He had seen Death many times, — met him in the way of trade, and got acquainted with him, — and he only thought of him as a hard customer, that embarrassed his property operations very unfairly; and so he only swore that the gal was a baggage, and that he was devilish unlucky, and that, if things went on in this way, he should not make a cent on the trip. In short, he seemed to consider himself an ill-used man, decidedly; but there was no help for it, as the woman had escaped into a state which never will give up a fugitive, — not even at the demand of the whole glorious Union. The trader, therefore, sat discontentedly down, with his little account-book, and put down the missing body and soul under the head of losses!

OH, FREEDOM LAND!*

by Colleen Burns Sharp

Have you ever wondered what happened to the runaway slaves after they escaped from slavery? Many of them traveled on the Underground Railroad all the way to Ontario, Canada, especially after the Fugitive Slave Act of 1850 made it unsafe for them to stay in the northern states. What was life like for the fugitives when they finally managed to reach the long-dreamed-of Freedom Land?

Most fugitives were poor and usually uneducated. Winters in Canada were hard, especially for those who had lived their entire lives in the warm and sunny

*All quotes from *The Refugee: or the Narratives of Fugitive Slaves in Canada* by Benjamin Drew (Boston: John P. Jewett and Company, 1856. Facsimile edition published by Coles Publishing Company, Ontario, Canada, 1972.)

South. They came to cities already overcrowded with runaway slaves and where prejudice against them sometimes seemed as bad as it had been in the States.

But the prejudice was easier to deal with because of Canadian law. John D. Moore, an African American who had never been a slave but who had come to Canada to escape the poor treatment he received in New Jersey and Pennsylvania, explained, "There is prejudice here...but they have not the power to carry it out here that they have in the States. The law here is stronger than the mob — it is not so there. If a man insults me here, he is glad to get out of the way for fear of the law; it was not so in the States where I lived."

In some places, people like Reverend Hiram Wilson in St. Catharines formed societies to help. These societies provided fugitives with food and shelter until they could find good jobs. But in other places, the runaways were not as lucky. Harriet Tubman's parents had to live in a rickety old shack in Hamilton, and the ex-slaves there had to take whatever work they could find.

No matter where the fugitives went, the work they found was not easy. Never having had the privilege of learning to read and write, they had to do hard manual labor to earn a living. In 1852, when the Great Western Railway began construction, many runaways made their way to Chatham to work on the railroad there. In other cities, they worked as bootblacks, blacksmiths, waiters, house cleaners, coach drivers, and cooks. They hired out for fifty or seventy-five cents a day.

The fugitives who could not find work in the crowded cities made their way to farms. There were homesteading places like Queen's Bush, where someone could clear a piece of land out to the wilderness and have a reasonable chance of buying it in time. Sometimes the surveyors did not even get around to pricing the land for a couple of years, so the farmers could make some money before they had to pay any out. Of course, life in the wilderness was not a dream. John Little, a fugitive who was not happy in Windsor, Ontario, told of his move to Queen's Bush:

"My wife and I had not a second suit of clothes apiece; we had one bed quilt and one blanket, and eighteen dollars.... I bought two axes in Hamilton...half a dozen plates, knives and forks, an iron pot, and a Dutch oven.... I bought 50 weight of flour and 20 pounds of pork. Then we marched right into the wilderness.... At night we made a fire, and cut down a tree, and put up some slats like a wigwam. This was in February, when the snow was two feet deep.... We made our bed of cedar boughs from a swamp. Thus we traveled, three or four days, seeing plenty of deer; wolves, as plenty as sheep are now, were howling about us, and bears were numerous.

"Myself and wife built us here a little log hut amid the snow.... We went to chopping day and night...we logged the trunks with our own hands, without cattle or horses or help.... I raised that year 110 bushels of spring wheat, and 300 bushels of potatoes.... I got the seed on credit of some Dutchmen in the towns, by promising to work for them in harvest."

Henry Bibb (1815–1854) spent most of his life trying to escape slavery. He was successful but was forced to live in Canada to avoid being captured under the Fugitive Slave Act. This poster offers a fifty-dollar reward for his return to Kentucky.

Things were far from perfect in Canada, but at least there were laws to protect people from abuse, and blacks were considered people in Canada, not property. They had to work hard. Dan Josiah Lockhart, an ex-slave from Virginia who settled in St. Catharines, said, "My work is as hard here as it was in slavery." But he added quickly, "The hardest thing about slavery is not the work. It is the abuse of a man and, in my case, of a man's wife and children."

Most important, despite all the hardships, Canada held the promise of a future. Black children could go to school with white children. What little money the ex-slaves were able to earn they could use to buy whatever they wanted. As early as 1856, Benjamin Drew, an abolitionist writing a book on the lives of the fugitives in Canada, could report that they were shopkeepers, farmers, mechanics, and businessmen. They owned property and were even able to hire others to work for them. The blacks began to form their own societies, called True Bands, to care for the poor and sick among them and the fugitives newly arrived from slavery. The runaways who came to Canada after 1854, when the True Bands were becoming active, had an easier time of it.

So in spite of all the obstacles — the hard labor, the prejudice, the poverty — the ex-slaves survived and prospered, and they treasured their newfound freedom. They found Canada, on the whole, a good place to live. John Holmes, an ex-slave from Virginia, could say after living in London, Ontario, for twenty-four years, "It is the best poor man's country that I know."

On Sundays, when not at work, slaves took time out for singing, dancing, and playing music.

SONGS OF SLAVERY*

by Ruth M. Hamel

When slaves in the South sang, it was not because they were happy. They sang to make the time pass more quickly as they worked; to pass on information about escape routes, where to get help, and who was in trouble; to warn of impending danger; and to express their hopes and sorrows.

One of the best-known slave songs, filled with information about escape, was "Follow the Drinking Gourd." The "drinking gourd" was the Big Dipper, and by using the two stars at the end of the cup, runaways could locate the North Star and follow it to freedom.

The chorus of "Follow the Drinking Gourd" says, "For the old man say, 'Follow the drinking gourd.'" According to legend, the "old man" was a sailor known as Peg-Leg Joe, who traveled throughout Alabama around 1840 to 1860 helping slaves escape. He showed them the marks his feet made in the soil (a natural left

*The original words of the songs have been edited.

foot and the round hole made by his peg leg) and told them to follow those marks. The words to Peg-Leg's song gave escaping slaves a "map" to follow. They walked in the shallow water of the riverbank and followed the North Star to the Alabama River, then on to the Mobile River. When they got to the Ohio River, they followed it to Pennsylvania, New York, and on to Canada. The song gave this advice:

> *The river's bank is a very good road,*
> *The dead trees show the way:*
> *Left foot, peg foot going on,*
> *Follow the drinking gourd.*
>
> *The river ends between two hills,*
> *Follow the drinking gourd;*
> *Another river on the other side,*
> *Follow the drinking gourd.*

One complaint appearing repeatedly in slave literature is that white owners often broke their promises to slaves. Often a white mistress would tell a slave that when she died, the slave would be free. If the promise was written into a will, the owner's family often ignored it. In many cases, no one but the slave knew of the promise. One verse of the song "Run, Black Man, Run" tells of this betrayal:

> *My old miss, she promise me,*
> *That when she die, she set me free;*
> *But she done dead this many year ago,*
> *And here I'm hoeing the same old row!*

Probably the most famous song from the Civil War is "John Brown's Body," which was set to the tune of a southern camp song titled "Say, Brother, Will You Meet Us?" In 1859, abolitionist John Brown raided a federal arsenal at Harpers Ferry, Virginia. Federal troops retook the arsenal, and Brown was hanged. Northern soldiers during the Civil War, both black and white, kept his memory alive by singing these words to the old tune:

> *He captured Harpers Ferry with his nineteen men so true,*
> *He frightened Old Virginia till she trembled through and through,*
> *They hanged him for a traitor, they themselves the traitor crew,*
> *But his soul goes marching on.*

In 1861, author Julia Ward Howe visited some of the army camps outside Washington, D.C. She heard the soldiers singing "John Brown's Body" and was moved by the music. That night she wrote a poem called "Battle Hymn of the Republic." She put the words to the music of "John Brown's Body." We still sing her song today.

Julia Ward Howe

Howe (1819–1910) was coeditor of the abolitionist paper *Commonwealth*. She spoke out in support of emancipation, slavery, and women's rights and founded a world peace organization. A poet, she wrote her most famous work, "Battle Hymn of the Republic," as she listened to soldiers sing "John Brown's Body." The hymn was published in the *Atlantic Monthly* in 1862.

WORDS OF FIRE: BLACK ABOLITIONISTS

by Craig Gingold and Pam Deyell Gingold

On July 4, 1852, the citizens of Rochester, New York, were addressed by one of the city's most distinguished citizens. "This Fourth of July is *yours*, not *mine*," he told them. "Your sounds of rejoicing are empty and heartless, your shouts of liberty and equality, hollow mockery." The speaker was former slave Frederick Douglass, one of the country's foremost abolitionists.

Like Douglass, most African Americans did not celebrate the Fourth of July. Instead, they celebrated August First, the date in 1833 when slaves were emancipated in the British West Indies. In many northern communities, free African Americans marked the occasion with brass bands and parades, followed by speakers and picnics. Their banners proclaimed the sentiments of the day: "Liberty, the birthright of all" and "Let the oppressed go free."

Although black abolitionists were overshadowed by the white antislavery movement, they played an essential role in the ending of slavery. Oppressed by the same racist society that had enslaved their fellow African Americans, free African Americans created and directed their own organizations to liberate their people. They constantly tried to impress white society with the righteousness of their cause and energized white abolitionists with their urgency.

Even when working with well-meaning whites, African American activists felt it was necessary to maintain their independence, a feeling that was expressed in the *Colored American* newspaper in 1839: "As long as we let them think and act for us...they will outwardly treat us as men, while in their hearts they still hold us as slaves."

Publishers Samuel Cornish and John Russwurm gave the African American community a public voice when they launched *Freedom's Journal,* the nation's first African American newspaper, in 1827 (four years before William Lloyd Garrison's *The Liberator* began publication). In all, some two dozen African American newspapers, most of them short-lived, helped African Americans agitate for the abolition of slavery in the years before the Civil War. These included *Mirror of Liberty, Night Watchman,* and *Frederick Douglass' Paper.*

In 1829, David Walker, an agent for *Freedom's Journal,* published a stirring booklet called *Walker's Appeal,* which denounced slavery, ignorance, and colonization. He implored free African

Frederick Douglass (1818–1895) was the son of an African American slave, Harriet Bailey, and a white father. After he escaped slavery, he took the name Douglass from Sir Walter Scott's book *The Lady of the Lake.*

Americans and slaves to take action rather than accept their miserable situation. His provocative words were so upsetting to whites that the booklet was outlawed in five southern states. (See page 103.)

Rising anti–African American prejudice in the North led to stricter segregation and outbreaks of violence. In response, in 1830 African American leaders called the first Negro National Convention, which soon became a growing movement, strengthening and unifying northern African Americans. The main goals of these conventions were to abolish slavery and achieve equality for African Americans. Delegates spoke out against colonization, promoted boycotts of slave-made products, and pressed for petition campaigns against oppressive laws. They urged African American communities to start local antislavery and educational societies. And they stressed the need to demonstrate that free African Americans were every bit as intelligent and "respectable" as whites.

After 1830, many African Americans also joined the growing movement of white abolitionists. They wrote articles, lectured, and served on boards of directors of white societies. Some African Americans became paid, full-time agents and lecturers for white antislavery organizations. Among the best known were Charles and Sarah Remond, William Wells Brown, and Frederick Douglass.

Escaped slaves such as Henry Bibb and William and Ellen Craft were especially popular speakers. Their personal stories, recounting the cruelties of slave owners and the details of their escapes, drove home the horrors of slavery for white audiences. Some, including Brown and Douglass, crossed the Atlantic and spoke to enthusiastic crowds in Great Britain. Many former slaves wrote or dictated narratives telling of their experiences, which sympathetic whites eagerly read.

At an African American convention in 1843, Reverend Henry Highland Garnet delivered an explosive speech that echoed David Walker's *Appeal.* Garnet said, "Brethren, arise, arise! Strike for your lives and liberties.... Rather die freemen than live to be slaves!" During the 1840s, Garnet, along with editor Charles B. Ray and Reverend Samuel R. Ward, was a fervent supporter of the abolitionist Liberty party, which sought government action against slavery. After 1848, most African Americans who could vote gave their support to the Free-Soil party.

Following the passage of the Fugitive Slave Act in 1850, many free African Americans recalled Garnet's fiery words. Robert Purvis in Philadelphia and David Ruggles in New York took the lead in setting up "vigilance committees," which gathered at short notice to rescue fugitive slaves from federal marshals, sometimes by force of arms. Purvis and William Still had already pioneered the escape network known as the Underground Railroad. Helped by hundreds of courageous "conductors," most of them African American, thousands of slaves escaped to freedom before the Civil War.

When the war broke out in 1861, northern African Americans were eager to join the Union army, but the government refused to let them take up arms. After Abraham Lincoln's Emancipation Proclamation took effect on January 1, 1863, African American soldiers (including liberated slaves) gave a great boost to the Union and helped make the war a crusade for freedom.

Sarah Parker Remond

Remond and her brother, Charles Lenox Remond, were popular speakers in the antislavery movement.

FIGHTER FOR FREEDOM

Frederick Augustus Washington Bailey never knew his birth date or who his father was. He saw his mother only four or five times after he was separated from her as an infant. When he was seven, his mother became ill and died, but no one told Frederick. Such details were not supposed to matter to slaves.

As a young teenager, Frederick recognized the injustice of slavery and realized how much these details did matter to his humanity. He determined to escape, changing his last name to Douglass to avoid detection when he gained his freedom. Thereafter, he dedicated his life to achieving freedom for others as he had for himself.

In 1841, three years after his escape, Douglass was asked to speak about his experiences as a slave. Thus began his career as an abolitionist, lecturer, writer, and publisher of an antislavery newspaper. With the onset of the Civil War, Douglass saw that his dream of freedom for African Americans might come true, and he traveled the lecture circuit calling for President Abraham Lincoln to grant slaves their freedom. After Lincoln issued the Emancipation Proclamation freeing the slaves in Confederate states, Douglass worked even harder for African American enlistment in the Union army so that African Americans could fight to ensure their freedom.

In 1865, the Thirteenth Amendment officially abolished all slavery, and Douglass, then forty-seven, thought about buying a farm and settling down to a quiet life. It soon become clear, however, that his work was not done, as African Americans continued to suffer inequalities and injustices. For the rest of his seventy-seven years, Douglass wrote and lectured in support of African American suffrage and equal rights and worked as a political leader and government official, remaining the foremost spokesman for African Americans.

When Douglass died on February 20, 1895, crowds gathered to pay their respects at the Washington, D.C., church where he lay in state. African American schools closed for the day, and newspapers around the world praised his accomplishments and humanity. The London *Daily News* noted, "From first to last his was a noble life. His own people have lost a father and a friend, and all good men have lost a comrade in the fight for the legal emancipation of one race and the spiritual emancipation of all."

FREDERICK DOUGLASS: THE EARLY YEARS

by Sharman Russell

Frederick Bailey, later to be known as Frederick Douglass, was born a slave in 1818 on a wealthy Maryland plantation. As an infant, Fred was separated from his mother and sent to live with his grandmother, whose job was to care for slave children until they were old enough to work. Fred's memory of his mother included only a few visits, late at night, when the tall, dark field hand would walk twelve miles to see her son. Of his father, Fred

Douglass, probably in his late twenties, about six years after his successful second attempt to escape slavery.

knew only that the man was white — possibly the master himself.

As a small child, Fred was happy playing near his grandmother's cabin and fishing in the nearby pond. Then one day, when he was about six years old, his grandmother took him to the plantation manager's house and left him there to join his older brother and sisters. Fred wept bitterly. His childhood was officially over.

In the master's household, the young slaves were fed cornmeal mush in a trough. In winter, the children wore only a single linen shirt, and Fred's feet were often cracked with frostbite.

One night, Fred fell asleep on the dirt floor of the kitchen closet and awoke to horrible screams. Through the cracks of the closet door, he could see his master using a cowhide whip to beat a black woman. Blood streamed down the woman's back onto the floor. Fred was to see this scene repeated again and again with this victim and others.

The oyster fleet in Baltimore harbor. Douglass worked in Baltimore's shipyards as a caulker, someone who forces sealant into the hulls of ships.

During the day, Fred's job was to drive the cows, keep the front yard clean, and run errands. A bright and engaging child, he soon made friends with his master's married daughter, Mrs. Lucretia Auld. With her help, he was sent to Baltimore to live with her brother-in-law Hugh Auld. By now, Fred's mother was dead. Fred knew that leaving the plantation was his chance to escape the brutal life of a field hand.

At first, Fred was happy in his new home, where his work was to care for the Aulds' young son. Fred's new mistress even began teaching him to read. But when Hugh Auld found out about this, he was furious. "Learning will spoil...him to be a slave," he told his wife. Fred listened to Master Hugh's lecture with great interest. If reading would make him unfit to be a slave, then he most assuredly wanted to read.

In the next few years, Fred learned to read and write on his own. Sometimes he even exchanged bread for lessons from poor white boys on the street. At the age of eleven, he had a bad scare when Lucretia's father, still his owner, died and he was sent back to the plantation. Fortunately, Fred was assigned to Lucretia Auld, who returned him to her brother-in-law in Baltimore.

Because a slave was considered property that could be sold or given away, a slave's life was insecure. When Lucretia Auld died, her husband demanded Fred's return. Fred was now fifteen years old. His new master, Captain Thomas Auld, starved his slaves and quoted from the Bible as he beat them. The strong-willed and religious Fred openly disdained his master's hypocrisy. Finally, Captain Auld decided to find someone who could "break" the boy. Edward Covey, a poor farmer with a reputation for breaking difficult slaves, offered to lease Fred for a year of labor.

After a year with Covey, Fred was rented out to another farm, where he was treated more kindly. By now, however, kindness was not enough for Fred. With

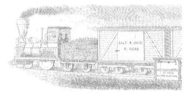

others, he plotted an escape, only to have one of his friends betray the plan. Again Fred was lucky. Instead of killing him or selling him to traders, Captain Auld returned the unruly boy to his brother in Baltimore.

For the next two years, Fred made a living as a caulker in the Baltimore shipyards. A caulker was a man who forced sealing matter into the hulls of ships. Although Fred was allowed to keep a little money, most of his earnings went to Hugh Auld. During this time, Fred began to meet and debate with a group of educated free African Americans. He also became engaged to a free African American servant named Anna Murray.

Although Fred was no longer starved or beaten, he was still a slave. He knew that to attempt a second escape was risky. If he was caught this time, he would be severely punished. Still, the idealistic twenty-year-old was determined to be free, and on September 3, 1838, he boarded a northbound train. For a disguise, he dressed as a sailor and carried a friend's "protection papers," which certified him as a seaman. Once in the North, he was reunited with Anna and changed his name from Bailey to Douglass. He would never call another man master again.

FIGHTING BACK

by Kenneth P. Czech

A life of misery faced sixteen-year-old Frederick Bailey. His owner had died, and his new master, Thomas Auld, was a cruel, insensitive man.

Young Fred had been living and working in Baltimore since age eight. He had learned to read and write there and was allowed to move freely about the city. Under his new master, however, Fred found himself transferred to the country, where hard labor as a plantation slave awaited him. He was angered by the poor food and refused to call Auld master. When he began teaching Sunday school to slave children against Auld's orders, the owner decided to teach him a lesson.

In January 1834, Auld hired Fred out to Edward Covey, a professional slave breaker. Covey heaped chore after chore on the youth, then beat him cruelly if the jobs were not done properly. The boy received less and less food, and his clothing became thin and ragged.

Fred became desperate. He had failed at begging Auld to take him away from Covey's farm, and hiding from Covey only brought more floggings. After a particularly savage beating, he decided he would not suffer such punishment and humiliation again. "I had been treated like a brute during the last six months and would stand it no longer," Frederick Douglass later wrote in his autobiography.

One morning, Covey ordered Fred to the hayloft of the barn.

As the youth began climbing the ladder, Covey attempted to slip a rope around his legs. Fred kicked free and tumbled off the ladder. When Covey grabbed him, Fred seized the slave breaker by the throat.

Covey struggled to break loose, then began screaming for help. His cousin, Bill Hughes, tried to rope the slave, but a kick sent him "staggering away in pain." As Covey stretched to reach a thick wooden club, Fred threw him into the "not overclean ground of the cow yard."

Fred hauled the slave breaker from the muck just as Covey's hired man returned to the farm. Covey begged for help, but the man did not want to get involved in the fight, especially when Fred warned him to stay away.

Then Caroline, Covey's powerful slave woman, entered the yard to begin the milking. He ordered her to strike Fred, but she pretended not to see the battle and continued on to the barn. After two hours of struggling, Covey realized he could not beat Fred. Panting from exertion, the slave breaker ordered the youth back to work but did not try to force him.

Fred believed that fighting was undignified, but he refused to be bullied again. He knew that Covey would not report him to the authorities because it would ruin his reputation as a slave breaker. Fred's service with Covey ended peacefully in December 1834, but he later wrote, "This battle with Mr. Covey was the turning point in my life as a slave. I was a changed being after that fight. I was nothing before; I was a man now. It inspired me with a renewed determination to be a free man."

★ ★ ★ ★ ★ ★ ★ ★ ★ ★

THE ABC'S

by Frederick Douglass

Frederick Douglass told this story of how he learned to read and write in his autobiography *Narrative of the Life of Frederick Douglass, An American Slave,* which he wrote in 1845. He twice revised and updated his life story, publishing it as *My Bondage and My Freedom* in 1855 and *The Life and Times of Frederick Douglass* in 1881.

Very soon after I went to live with Mr. and Mrs. Auld, she very kindly commenced to teach me the A, B, C. After I had learned this, she assisted me in learning to spell words of three or four letters. Just at this point of my progress, Mr. Auld found out what was going on, and at once forbade Mrs. Auld to instruct me further, telling her, among other things, that it was unlawful, as well as unsafe, to teach a slave to read.

To use his own words, further, he said, "If you give a nigger an inch, he will take an ell. A nigger should know nothing but to obey his master — to do as he is told to do. Learning would spoil the best nigger in the world. Now," said he, "if you teach that nigger how to read, there would be no keeping him. It would forever unfit him to be a slave. He would at once become unmanageable, and of no value to his master. As to himself, it could do him no good, but a great deal of harm. It would make him discontented and unhappy."

These words sank deep into my heart, stirred up

sentiments within that lay slumbering, and called into existence an entirely new train of thought. It was a new and special revelation, explaining dark and mysterious things, with which my youthful understanding had struggled, but struggled in vain. I now understood what had been to me a most perplexing difficulty — to wit, the white man's power to enslave the black man. It was a grand achievement, and I prized it highly.

Though conscious of the difficulty of learning without a teacher, I set out with high hope, and a fixed purpose, at whatever cost of trouble, to learn how to read. The very decided manner with which he spoke, and strove to impress his wife with the evil consequences of giving me instruction, served to convince me that he was deeply sensible of the truths he was uttering. It gave me the best assurance that I might rely with the utmost confidence on the results which, he said, would flow from teaching me to read.

What he most dreaded, that I most desired. What he most loved, that I most hated. That which to him was a great evil, to be carefully shunned, was to me a great good, to be diligently sought; and the argument which he so warmly urged, against my learning to read, only served to inspire me with a desire and determination to learn.

In learning to read, I owe almost as much to the bitter opposition of my master, as to the kindly aid of my mistress. I acknowledge the benefit of both....

My mistress was, as I have said, a kind and tender-hearted woman; and in the simplicity of her soul she commenced, when I first went to live with her, to treat me as she supposed one human being ought to treat another.... Slavery proved as injurious to her as it did to me.... Under its influence, the tender heart became stone, and the lamblike disposition gave way to one of tigerlike fierceness.

The first step in her downward course was in her ceasing to instruct me. She now commenced to practice her husband's precepts. She finally became even more violent in her opposition than her husband himself. She was not satisfied with simply doing as well as he had commanded; she seemed anxious to do better. Nothing seemed to make her more angry than to see me with a newspaper. She seemed to think that here lay the danger. I have had her rush at me with a face made all up of fury, and snatch from me a newspaper, in a manner that fully revealed her apprehension. She was an apt woman; and a little experience soon demonstrated, to her satisfaction, that education and slavery were incompatible with each other.

From this time I was most narrowly watched. If I was in a separate room any considerable length of time, I was sure to be suspected of having a book, and was at once called to give an account of myself. All this, however, was too late. The first step had been taken. Mistress, in teaching me the alphabet, had given me the inch, and no precaution could prevent me from taking the ell.

The plan which I adopted, and the one by which I was most successful, was that of making friends of all the little white boys whom I met in the street. As many of these as I could, I converted into teachers. With their kindly aid, obtained at different times in different places, I finally succeeded in learning to read. When I was sent on errands, I always took my book with me, and by doing one part of my errand quickly, I found time to get a lesson before my return. I used also to carry bread with me, enough of which was always in the house, and to which I was always welcome; for I was much better off in this regard than many of the poor white children in our neighborhood. This bread I used to bestow upon the hungry little urchins, who, in return, would give me that more valuable bread of knowledge....

I was now about twelve years old, and the thought of being a slave for life began to bear heavily upon my heart. Just about this time, I got hold of a book entitled *The Columbian Orator*. Every opportunity I got, I used to read this book. Among much of other interesting matter, I found in it a dialogue between a master and his slave. The slave was represented as having run away from his master three times. The dialogue represented the conversation which took place between them, when the slave was retaken the third time.

In this dialogue, the whole argument in behalf of slavery was brought forward by the master, all of which was disposed of by the slave. The slave was made to say some very smart as well as impressive things in reply to his master — things which had the desired though unexpected effect; for the conversation resulted in the voluntary emancipation of the slave on the part of the master....

The idea as to how I might learn to write was suggested to me by being in Durgin and Bailey's shipyard, and frequently seeing the ship carpenters, after hewing, and getting a piece of timber ready for use, write on the timber the name of that part of the ship for which it was intended.

When a piece of timber was intended for the larboard side, it would be marked thus — "L." When a piece was for the starboard side forward, it would be marked thus — "S.F." For larboard aft, it would be marked thus — "L.A." For starboard aft, it would be marked thus — "S.A." I soon learned the names of these letters, and for what they were intended when placed upon a piece of timber in the shipyard. I immediately commenced copying them, and in a short time was able to make the four letters named.

After that, when I met with any boy who I knew could write, I would tell him I could write as well as he. The next word would be, "I don't believe you. Let me see you try it." I would then make the letters which I had been so fortunate as to learn, and ask him to beat that. In this way I got a good many lessons in writing, which it is quite possible I should never have gotten in any other way.

During this time, my copy-book was the board fence, brick wall, and pavement; my pen and ink was a lump of chalk. With these, I learned mainly how to write. I then commenced and continued copying the Italics on *Webster's Spelling Book,* until I could make them all without looking on the book. By this time, my little Master Thomas had gone to school, and learned how to write, and had written over a number of copy-books. These had been brought home, and shown to some of our near neighbors, and then laid aside. My mistress used to go to class meeting at the Wilk Street meeting-house every Monday afternoon, and leave me to take care of the house. When left thus, I used to spend the time in writing in the spaces left in Master Thomas's copy-book, copying what he had written. I continued to do this until I could write a hand very similar to that of Master Thomas.

Thus, after a long, tedious effort for years, I finally succeeded in learning how to write.

THE BEGINNING OF DOUGLASS'S JOURNEY

by Lisa Belcher-Hamilton

Frederick Bailey felt his shoulders relax, but only a little. The twenty-year-old escaped slave had just bought a train ticket, although he did not have documents saying he was free. The train conductor was in a hurry, so the papers "proving" Fred was a sailor satisfied him. Only white and free African American men were allowed to be sailors. Actually, Fred had borrowed the papers from an African American friend who really was a sailor.

Fred stopped at many stations as he rode the train to Wilmington, Delaware, took a steamboat to Philadelphia, and rode a second train from there to New York City. Each time the train's noisy wheels started up again, Fred told himself, "I'm closer than ever to being a free man." After one stop, though, his heart began to pound. A new passenger had just boarded the train — a German American blacksmith who knew Fred well. The look in his eyes told Fred he was not fooled by the sailor's uniform. After a few moments of staring, the man looked away and ignored him for the rest of the trip. He had decided to help Fred with silence.

The nerve-racking journey finally ended in New York as dawn broke on the morning of September 4, 1838. Later Fred wrote, "If life is more than one breath, I lived more in one day than in a year of my slave life."

Fred was indeed a free man, but he had no place to go in this city, new to him and full of slave hunters anxious to collect large fees for finding escaped slaves. Fortunately, there were other people on the lookout for escaped slaves, people who worked for the Underground Railroad. The Underground Railroad was not made of railroad tracks but of a network of people who helped slaves find freedom in many ways. One of these people found Fred, and he asked in a kind voice, "Where are you headed?" Fred answered, "I always aim for the North Star," which was a code meaning he was looking for help through the Underground Railroad.

Anna Murray Douglass

Anna Murray Douglass, a free African American housekeeper from Maryland's Eastern Shore, was Frederick Douglass's first wife.

Fred's request for help was answered. First, the man and his friends sent for Fred's fiancée, Anna Murray, a free woman from Baltimore. The two were married a few days after Anna arrived. In the meantime, these friends found Fred a job in New Bedford, Massachusetts. They suggested that he change his last name to make it harder for slave catchers to find him, and so Frederick Bailey became Frederick Douglass.

Soon after the newlyweds arrived in New Bedford, they became active in the Underground Railroad. When they moved to Rochester, New York, Douglass became a stationmaster, someone who hid runaway slaves in his or her home until they could continue their journey. The Douglass's home had a secret passage between the eaves of the roof, and many escaped slaves stayed in the cramped space until they could get to Toronto, Canada, and freedom.

An even more dangerous job was that of conductor. Conductors escorted slaves from the South to the North, and if they were caught, the punishment was death by hanging. Conductors had to be creative and daring to avoid arrest. Once a white conductor named James Fairfield staged a mock funeral to help slaves escape. Fairfield pretended to be a minister, and the African American men acted as pallbearers, but the coffin they carried through town was empty. When they reached the cemetery, they threw the coffin aside and began their journey north.

Another famous conductor was Harriet Tubman, a former slave herself. One time she disguised herself as a man and drove a wagon full of slaves who were hidden under a load of manure. The slaves had to breathe through straws sticking up out of the manure.

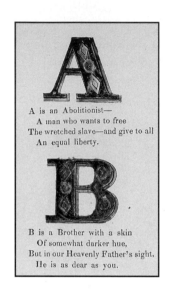

A is an Abolitionist—
A man who wants to free
The wretched slave—and give to all
An equal liberty.

B is a Brother with a skin
Of somewhat darker hue,
But in our Heavenly Father's sight,
He is as dear as you.

Two pages from the *Anti-Slavery Alphabet*, a children's book published in 1847.

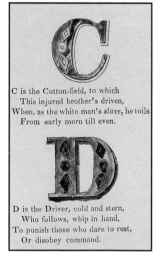

C is the Cotton-field, to which
This injured brother's driven,
When, as the white man's *slave*, he toils
From early morn till even.

D is the Driver, cold and stern,
Who follows, whip in hand,
To punish those who dare to rest,
Or disobey command.

Although no one is sure when the Underground Railroad began, it existed in George Washington's time. Washington had a slave who used it to escape from Mount Vernon to New Hampshire. Washington did not look for the slave because he was afraid capture would cause a riot. At that time, tradition dictated that an escaped slave was still considered the property of his or her owner. In 1850, that tradition became law. Because of this rule, some slaves chose to take the Underground Railroad all the way to Canada, where their freedom could not be challenged. Many born in slavery learned this song as children and sang it all their lives:

Oh righteous Father
Wilt thou not pity me
And aid me to Canada
Where all the slaves are free.

Frederick Douglass himself relied on the Underground Railroad to help him escape to England. When Douglass published his autobiography in 1845, he identified the family who had once (and by law still) owned him. Douglass's ship left only a few hours before slave hunters came to capture him. Once the ship landed, Douglass lectured about slavery in England, Scotland, and Ireland. While he spoke out for abolition and other social reforms, British admirers raised money to help him buy his freedom and his ticket home.

When Douglass returned to the United States, he was even more widely known than before he left. Susan B. Anthony was honored to have Douglass support her cause of women's rights, and she supported his work as well. As a Quaker, she considered slavery immoral. In fact, her father's house, where she lived, was a stop on the Underground Railroad. The two became close friends, fighting with many others for the rights of all women and men. They never forgot the importance of freedom and the vital role of the Underground Railroad.

ABOLITIONIST WRITER

by Karen H. Dusek

When Frederick Douglass was a boy, he wanted more than anything else to be free. Believing that he would never be truly free without an education, he learned to read and write.

Douglass's dream of personal freedom was realized in 1838, when he escaped to the North, but he would not be content until the dream came true for all Americans. His ability to read and write soon proved to be his most powerful weapon in his lifelong fight against slavery and prejudice.

Douglass became involved in the abolitionist movement a few months after settling in New Bedford, Massachusetts, with his new wife. Inspired by the writings of William Lloyd Garrison, publisher of the abolitionist newspaper *The Liberator,* Douglass began attending local antislavery meetings, where he was sometimes asked to speak.

Then, in August 1841, Douglass was invited to address a mostly white crowd during a major antislavery convention in Nantucket (an island off Massachusetts). No one seemed to notice his voice tremble as he described his life as a slave. In fact, Garrison himself was so moved by the power and richness of Douglass's words that he built his own speech around them.

Afterward, an agent for the Massachusetts Anti-Slavery Society urged Douglass to work for the society as a lecturer. Douglass hesitantly consented to try it for three months, wondering of what use he could possibly be.

As Douglass repeated his story before audiences across the country, his self-confidence grew along with his determination to end slavery. At first, he simply told about his experiences as a slave, but the more he read and heard about slavery issues, the more he wanted to discuss the way he felt about those issues in his speeches. Because many people believed that slaves could not think intelligently, Douglass's friends worried that his intellectual arguments against slavery would raise doubts that he had ever been a slave. They were right.

To prove that his stories were true, Douglass published his first autobiography, *Narrative of the Life of Frederick Douglass, An American Slave,* in May 1845. (Longer versions were published in 1855 and 1881.) In it he revealed the names of his former master and mistress, the Aulds.

People were curious about life as a slave, and the book was widely read. French and German editions were printed, as were nine editions in England,

William Lloyd Garrison

Massachusetts-born William Lloyd Garrison started his abolitionist career in Baltimore in 1829, working with Benjamin Lundy on the *Genius of Universal Emancipation.*

THE TRIP TO IRELAND

by Mary Dowling Daley

In August 1845, Frederick Douglass, twenty-seven years old, leaned over the railing of the *Cambria* en route to the British Isles. Douglass was escaping possible capture and return to the slaveholder who still owned him several years after his escape. As the ship made its way through the fog, Douglass's head was full of thoughts of Ireland and the one friend waiting for him.

Douglass knew that Daniel O'Connell had heard much about him from Douglass's friend abolitionist William Lloyd Garrison. The Garrisonians maintained an antislavery society in Dublin, and Douglass's speech three years earlier at Boston's Faneuil Hall had followed a message from O'Connell and sixty thousand other Irish supporters. The message urged the Irish of America to take up the antislavery cause.

O'Connell was known as the emancipator of millions of demoralized Irish Catholics. The Irish had been ruled by England for seven hundred years, and after 1691 the English imposed a series of cruel laws on Irish Catholics.

Some of these laws had been relaxed by the end of the eighteenth century, but Catholics could not sit in Parliament until 1829, when O'Connell finally won emancipation for his followers. O'Connell spoke about slavery in the United States. In 1836, he publicly accused the U.S. ambassador to Great Britain of being a slaveholder.

Douglass was not disappointed when he finally met the seventy-year-old O'Connell at Dublin's Conciliation Hall. When the "Great Dan" addressed the crowd of three thousand, Douglass later wrote, "his eloquence came down on the vast assembly like a summer thundershower on a dusty road." Arna Bontemps, one of Douglass's biographers, tells us that the Irish "fell head-over-heels in love with Douglass. They loved his wit, the sharpness of his argument, his manly beauty." The press of every Irish city praised Douglass. Historians agree that Douglass's nearly two years of brilliant speeches in Ireland, England, and Scotland greatly increased British hostility toward slavery.

which was strongly abolitionist.

The book ended the rumors about Douglass's past, but it also put his life in danger by identifying him to the Aulds, who still legally owned him. On the advice of friends, he left for England, where he would be safe, on August 16, 1845. The British welcomed him warmly. During his twenty-month stay in England, Ireland, and Scotland, he lectured and asked for support for the American abolitionist cause. His new friends responded by buying his freedom from the Aulds in December 1846 and offering to give him money to publish an antislavery newspaper.

Upon his return to the United States in April 1847, Douglass's friends, including Garrison, discouraged him from publishing a newspaper. Too many other African American men had tried and failed, they argued, and it would interfere with his lecturing. Douglass put off his plans, but he was growing frustrated. He wanted a means of expressing his ideas to thousands of people at one time, and he wanted to prove that African Americans were intellectually equal to whites.

On December 3, 1847, with money his British friends sent, Douglass began publishing the *North Star* in Rochester, New York, far from the competing abolitionist papers in New England. The decision cost him his friendship with Garrison and Garrison's followers, but Douglass did not regret it. For the first time in his life, he was on his own, free to make his own decisions and to voice his opinions, not only about slavery, but also about women's rights, temperance, and other social and political issues.

"I have come to think that it was the best school possible for me," he later wrote. "It obliged me to think and read, it taught me to express my thoughts clearly, and was perhaps better than any other course I could have adopted."

From the beginning, Douglass found himself in financial trouble. The two-dollar annual subscription rate did not cover expenses. He spent many hours lecturing to raise money and had to mortgage his house. Nevertheless, he was proud of the fact that his paper appeared every week on time.

Help came in the form of Julia Griffiths, a British woman who had helped raise funds for Douglass's press. Hearing of his difficulties, she traveled to Rochester with her sister and immediately set to work as Douglass's business manager. Within a year, she had raised the circulation from two thousand to four thousand and had paid off all the newspaper's debts. Douglass also was able to pay off his mortgage, and by May 1851 the paper had begun to show a profit.

To strengthen the paper further, Douglass merged it with John Thomas's *Liberty Party Paper* in the summer of 1851. Renamed *Frederick Douglass' Paper,* its masthead proclaimed its mission: "All Rights for All."

Despite financial support from abolitionist Gerrit Smith, the paper again began to founder in 1853. Douglass printed desperate pleas for unpaid subscription fees, and Julia Griffiths published a "gift book" of "essays, letters and speeches" by famous abolitionists to sell at "abolitionist fairs and bazaars." It was not enough, and in 1857 Griffiths returned to England to raise funds and sell subscriptions.

Profits from the new subscriptions were eaten up by the high cost of mailing overseas. Douglass solved that problem by publishing a special monthly edition called *Douglass' Monthly* for British subscribers. By leaving out local news and

....

Douglass's office in Rochester, New York, where the *North Star* was published.

ads, he reduced the size of the paper enough to lower shipping costs.

Still, his papers continued to lose money. In 1859, he was forced to reduce the size of his weekly, but he did not give up. He sensed that with the growing unrest, freedom for all Americans was at hand.

Finally, in July 1860, Douglass printed the last edition of his weekly. He continued to publish *Douglass' Monthly* until August 1863, seven months after President Lincoln's Emancipation Proclamation went into effect. The fight for freedom had been won, but Douglass did not rest. He continued to write and speak out against racial prejudice until his death in 1895.

*For the first time in his life,
he was on his own, free to make his own decisions
and to voice his opinions, not only about slavery,
but also about women's rights, temperance, and
other social and political issues.*

THE DOUGLASS 'STATION' OF THE UNDERGROUND RAILROAD
by Glennette Tilley Turner

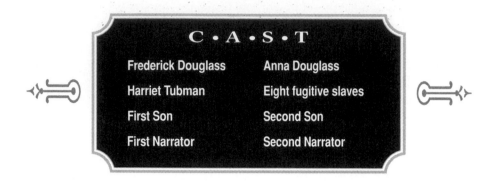

C · A · S · T

Frederick Douglass	Anna Douglass
Harriet Tubman	Eight fugitive slaves
First Son	Second Son
First Narrator	Second Narrator

First Narrator: It is late one night in early November, sometime after the 1850 Fugitive Slave Act has become law. Harriet Tubman and a party of eight fugitive slaves have just arrived outside the Douglass home in Rochester, New York.

Second Narrator: Harriet Tubman goes from a wooded area to the back door, trying to stay in the shadows of the house. Her knock is so quiet it can hardly be heard.

Harriet Tubman: *[Knock, knock. Pause. Knock, knock.]*

First Narrator: One of Douglass' sons looks out the window and whispers:

First Son: It's Moses.

Second Narrator: Frederick Douglass turns the lamplight off and goes to the door — just barely opening it.

Frederick Douglass: Come in, Moses.

First Narrator: Harriet Tubman steps inside, and whispers...

Harriet Tubman: I have eight. I had them wait in the woods 'til I knew it was safe to come in.

Frederick Douglass: One of my sons is the lookout. He let us know you were nearby and that the coast is clear.

Anna Douglass: Welcome, Harriet. Have them come in.

Second Narrator: Harriet Tubman signals to her company of slaves. One at a time they approach the house just as she had done.

First Narrator: Douglass barely opens the door and admits the slaves. Once they are inside, they gather near the fireplace to warm themselves after their long journey. Some are barefooted; others are wearing summer-weight clothes.

Second Narrator: Douglass silently shakes hands with the fugitives, then in a low voice says,

Frederick Douglass: Congratulations. Moses has brought you to the doorstep of freedom. The land of Canada is just across the lake. You'll be there by this time tomorrow night.

Anna Douglass: Meanwhile, here's food and some blankets so you can eat and then rest.

First Narrator: She gestures to an iron pot in the fireplace and blankets in the corner.

Frederick Douglass: I know from experience what it's like to escape. You really can't relax until you get to the Promised Land.

Second Narrator: The Douglass' second son appears at the door with a huge ladle and dishes up stew for everyone. In the meantime the first son has gone to take his turn as the lookout.

Anna Douglass to Harriet Tubman: How was your trip?

Harriet Tubman: *(eating like she's really hungry, but in a hurry to get through — talks between mouthfuls)* We had lots of close calls, but made it safely this far. Main thing was trying to race the snow. Didn't want that to catch us. Can't take the chance of leaving tracks.

Frederick Douglass to Harriet Tubman: Which route did you take this time?

Harriet Tubman: *(obviously worried about something as she talks)* Eastern Shore to Wilmington in Delaware. Some of the young ones got scared when they heard the slave catchers' dogs. We had to wade in water so the dogs would lose our scent.

Frederick Douglass: It must have been a relief to reach Thomas Garrett's house in Wilmington, wasn't it?

Harriet Tubman: *(trying to answer Douglass' question, although it is more and more obvious she has something else on her mind)* Yes, he gave us dry clothes and we slept a while. He had a Friend take us to Philadelphia in a wagon with a false bottom.

Frederick Douglass: Where William Still met you — right?

Harriet Tubman: Yes. *(then, putting her dish down abruptly)* Excuse me, Frederick, but what's the plan for us going from here to Canada?

Frederick Douglass: I've arranged for a friend to get you and your party on the morning train. You'll have to board before daylight, so you won't be seen. Hope you don't mind having to travel in the baggage car. It's getting harder and harder to cross the border.

Harriet Tubman: Let me stop you, Frederick. I thank you for what you're planning, but I won't feel safe 'til we get on the Canadian side. Can you possibly get somebody to take us across the lake tonight? All of a sudden I had this strange feeling the slave catchers are on our trail.

Anna Douglass: Can't you wait until morning? As tired as you all are, a good night's sleep would do you some good.

Harriet Tubman: Thank you, Anna. I am bone tired and the others are too, but I can't chance waiting. Morning may be too late.

Frederick Douglass: What makes you so sure slave catchers are trailing you?

Harriet Tubman: There's a $40,000 reward on my head and lots of people want to cash in. I don't know what gave me this feeling, but my hunches have been right too many times before to ignore them.

First Narrator: Douglass' second son has made an inconspicuous exit while his parents talked with Harriet Tubman. That son now reappears and announces,

Second Son: Excuse me for interrupting, but my brother and I have arranged to take you across the lake.

Harriet Tubman: Oh, thank you. *(turning to Frederick and Anna)* You certainly raised your sons well. Thank you all!

Second Narrator: Harriet gathers her things and wakens the fugitives in her group.

Harriet Tubman: Hurry now. It's time to go.

Frederick Douglass: *(shaking Harriet's hand)* Have a safe journey, Moses.

Anna Douglass: *(giving Harriet a hug)* God be with you.

First Son: *(in an urgent whisper)* The coast is clear. Let's go.

First Narrator: Harriet and the fugitives walk in the shadows as the Douglass' first son leads the way to the shores of Lake Ontario.

Second Narrator: There the second son is waiting to help them into a boat and they all set out for the Canadian shore.

THE AMERICAN MIND: EDUCATION, RELIGION, AND PHILOSOPHY

As the United States grew, so did Americans' hopes and dreams for the improvement of the **mind, spirit, and soul.**

Americans were determined that their children be better educated than those in any other country. But as usual, Americans never quite agreed on how best to achieve that goal. Some, for example, demanded that education and religion go hand in hand. Others insisted that religion be kept out of the schools altogether. It is a debate that continues to this day.

Meanwhile, Americans with new ideas about what we should know — and what we should forget — created both excitement and controversy as the eighteenth century ended and the nineteenth century began. Sadly, African Americans were forbidden to learn at all. But white Americans encouraged learning for themselves.

Not for many years would the gift of learning be granted to everyone, regardless of race, color, or gender.

THE STORY OF AMERICA'S SCHOOLS

by Henry Dubroff

Did you ever wonder what the first schools were like in your community? The first schools in most cities, towns, and frontier settlements all across America were one-room schoolhouses. Many were built more than one hundred fifty years ago, between 1820 and 1840. At that time, a new generation of Americans was growing up. Many people were concerned about who would be responsible for taking care of these large numbers of children. The simple question "How should children spend their time?" started a great debate. The question was answered in three different ways.

One group of people said that young people should spend their time at home. Children should help their families, they said, pointing out that most Americans

The teacher at this sod schoolhouse in Logan County, Nebraska, shown here with three pupils, kept a bed and cooking utensils in the school.

lived on farms where there was plenty of work to be done.

A second group, mostly businessmen and merchants, believed that children should work in mills and factories. America's Industrial Revolution had begun, and this group knew that there would be many jobs in manufacturing in the coming years. Some young people were already working in mills and factories. They were anywhere from seven to sixteen years old, and they worked up to thirteen hours each day.

A third group of people presented still another idea. They said that if young people were going to grow up to be voters, they needed to be able to read about current events and candidates running for office. The group argued that if people were going to manage stores or farms or work in factories, they needed to know arithmetic so that they could handle their money. To help create a better society, young people should know how to write and express their ideas. This group argued that each state should develop a system of public schools. The schools, called free schools or common schools, would be open to all, free of charge, and would be supported by taxes.

The free school movement had powerful voices on its side. "If a nation expects to be ignorant and free...it expects what never was and never will be," said our third president, Thomas Jefferson. About twenty years later, on the Illinois frontier, a young man named Abraham Lincoln was running for state office. He supported the free schools, saying that education was "the most important subject which we as a people can be engaged in."

One very important leader of the free school movement was Horace Mann, a Massachusetts-born educator who grew up in poverty but graduated from college in 1819 and became a lawyer. Mann was elected president of the Massachusetts Senate, but he gave up his post in 1837 to take a new job. He became head of the new Massachusetts Board of Education. In 1839, Mann opened the first common school in the United States at Lexington, Massachusetts. He continued to open common schools throughout the state. His example attracted national attention. Supporters of the free school movement liked his efforts to raise teachers' salaries, improve school buildings, and lengthen the school year. Before long, many states were attempting to do what Massachusetts had done. The free school supporters had won the debate.

Of course, the free schools were not the first schools in America. In New England, the Puritans wanted each person to know the Bible so that their clergy would be educated. In the 1600s, they established schools to teach religion and basic subjects. If communities could not afford to pay teachers' salaries, many women volunteered to teach children in their homes. These became known as dame schools. Other New England students were prepared for college at Latin grammar schools that were sponsored by churches. Still others attended private academies.

In the southern colonies, farms and plantations were very far apart, and very few schools were built. Wealthy families hired private tutors for their children. Poorer families taught their children at home or not at all. Plantation owners had differing views on the education of slaves. Some owners provided an education for them, but others feared that educated slaves would rebel. They passed laws that denied slaves an education.

Another very important part of education in the United States takes place completely outside school. It is called apprenticeship. Many young people sign up to work with a craftsperson for several years to learn a trade. Blacksmiths, silversmiths, carpenters, masons, and many other craftspeople learn their trades through apprenticeship. Apprenticeship has been practiced for centuries, and it is still an important part of craft training. A century ago, young people could become apprenticed at age eight or nine, but now they must be able to read and write before they will be accepted by craftspeople.

By the middle of the nineteenth century, however, the free school movement had taken hold. What was it like to go to a free school one hundred fifty years ago? Since most towns and villages had small populations, most schools were built of wood. But in Kansas, Nebraska, and other plains states, wood was scarce. Here the schools were built of sod. More than once, students arrived at school only to find that part of it had been eaten by grazing cattle! As Americans moved west, the idea of the free school moved, too.

Early one-room schools had dirt floors, no electricity, and no plumbing. There were few windows because glass was expensive, so the interior lighting was poor. Heat came only from a fireplace or wood stove, and in wooden schools a fire could spread with deadly speed. The furniture was rough and uncomfort-

KNOTT'S LITTLE RED SCHOOLHOUSE

Knott's Berry Farm's Little Red Schoolhouse was built in the 1870s in Beloit, Kansas. Standing at the door is Alda Reed, one of the sixteen women in the Old West Ghost Town who rotate school duty to answer questions and provide information about the building. The schoolhouse looks as it did one hundred years ago. Its interior features a pot-belly stove, handmade wooden desks and benches, and a hickory switch.

AN INDIAN SCHOOL IN KANSAS

by Darren Sextro

In 1830, one of the earliest Indian schools was erected in preterritorial Kansas by Reverend Thomas Johnson. He established the Shawnee Methodist Mission and Manual Labor School as a trade school because the Shawnee chiefs wanted their youngsters to learn how to farm and do carpentry work. The new mission was located near the heavily traveled Santa Fe and Oregon trails and was open to many tribes.

Students attended school six days a week. On Saturdays, there were only three hours of classes. Pupils rose at 4 A.M. and were in bed by 8 P.M. Many lived on the mission grounds, while others lived with their families nearby.

On September 30, 1862, the school was suspended when the U.S. government bought the land from the Indians. The students were forced to leave. During the Civil War, the school buildings were used as barracks for the Kansas Volunteer Cavalry. Afterward, the mission passed into private ownership, and in 1927 it was bought by the Kansas State Historical Society.

Indian school teachers met for their first conference at Pine Ridge Agency, South Dakota, in 1890.

able. Supplies were often limited, especially pens, pencils, and writing paper. Older students would often help younger ones learn their lessons. A single teacher frequently taught all the grades from one to eight.

Most teachers earned very little. In 1835, a teacher in Massachusetts earned $185 per year; in Colorado in the early 1900s, a teacher earned about the same. Sometimes teachers were paid in tobacco, peas, corn, or wheat. Many free school teachers were men. Horace Mann believed that both men and women should be teachers. He opened the first teacher training college, called a normal school, in Lexington, Massachusetts, in 1839.

At the close of the Civil War in 1865, the free school system existed everywhere except the South, where the idea of free schools caught on slowly and was introduced by Reconstruction governments. Not many people wanted to attend schools where African Americans and whites were forced to learn together. In the early 1900s, many southern communities established separate school systems for African Americans and whites in an attempt to solve this problem. (In 1954, the U.S. Supreme Court ruled that these systems treated African Americans unfairly and ordered them dismantled "with all deliberate speed.")

By the end of the 1800s, one-room schools were not big enough for many growing communities. In large cities, schools were expanded to enroll a flood of immigrants and teach them the English language, helping them to adjust to life in America. As industries grew, employers demanded that schools teach skilled trades or manual arts, as well as other necessary subjects such as book-keeping, shorthand, and typing. Gradually, one-room schoolhouses gave way to larger elementary schools — buildings with high ceilings and tall windows, central heat, large school yards, and separate classrooms for each grade of study. In the early 1900s, many communities started free junior high schools, high schools, and vocational schools. The school year was lengthened, and education was required until age sixteen in most states.

There are still one-room schoolhouses in some rural communities, but by the end of World War II in 1945, they were pretty much a thing of the past.

PRUDENCE CRANDALL'S SCHOOL

by Diane Norman

Education for African Americans began with religious instruction. The Puritans in the northern colonies felt that it was important for everyone, including African Americans, to read the Bible. Early efforts to teach English to African Americans in the South were restricted, and very few African Americans had a chance to learn to read and write. Local laws with stern penalties for teaching reading and writing to African Americans existed throughout the Colonies, but some African Americans received secret instruction in spite of these laws.

In the 1700s, several schools for African Americans were established. Cotton Mather opened a school for African Americans and Indians in Boston in 1717. In Pennsylvania, William Penn taught free African Americans and slaves. By 1788, New Jersey had passed a law requiring that slaves be taught to read. Throughout the Colonial period, there was an increase in the number of educated African Americans. Still, education in those days was a luxury — even for many whites — and the great majority of African Americans did not attend school.

At the same time that some people were allowing African Americans to obtain an education, others were denying such action. After the invention of the cotton gin in 1793, when slave importation increased dramatically, more people spoke out against educating slaves. One group that proposed sending African Americans back to Africa in an effort to curb slavery openly opposed education for African Americans on the grounds that it would interfere with the plan. The slave rebellion led by Nat Turner in 1831 (see page 93) made many people fearful that if African Americans became educated, they would be even more likely to rebel. Laws denying African Americans access to education were enacted in several states, in both the North and South.

In New Haven, Connecticut, a college for African Americans was proposed in 1831. The proposal failed because public sentiment against it was too strong, but a few African Americans were permitted to attend other colleges in New England.

It was at this point that Prudence Crandall came into the picture. Being a Quaker, she believed in equality, and this belief led to her struggle.

Crandall, a teacher of many years, ran a boarding school in Canterbury, Connecticut, for the daughters of wealthy local residents. Canterbury was a peaceful, prosperous, rural village where mills were beginning to play an important role. Crandall's school opened in November 1831.

Prudence Crandall

This illustration of Crandall appears in *Connecticut's Canterbury Tale*. It is based on an early-nineteenth-century oil painting that hangs in the library at Cornell University, in Ithaca, New York.

It had been open more than a year when Crandall did something considered unthinkable. She admitted a local African American girl to attend classes during the day.

Cotton Mather

William Penn

In 1788, New Jersey passed a law requiring that slaves be taught to read. The number of educated African Americans increased during this time. Earlier in the century, Cotton Mather (1663–1728), a clergyman and writer, ran a school for African Americans and Indians. William Penn (1644–1718) taught free African Americans and slaves.

Upon discovering this, white parents were furious. They called for the girl's removal. Crandall, shocked by their request, abruptly dismissed all twenty-five white pupils.

Crandall reopened her school several weeks later with twelve African American girls as her students. Her decision to do this was not impulsive. She had recently read *The Liberator,* an abolitionist newspaper, and it had changed her thinking forever. *The Liberator* condemned slavery and prejudice against African Americans, and it led Crandall to decide that she would educate African American children.

The townspeople were enraged and called for a town meeting. They hoped they could force the girls to leave by calling upon an old vagrancy law. A vagrant is defined as someone who wanders about without a settled home or regular income. Under the law, anyone warned by a town official to leave town had to prove that he or she had enough money to meet his or her expenses by posting a bond, or the person had to pay a fine of $1.67 each week. If the "vagrant" did neither, he or she would receive ten lashes of the whip.

Eliza Hammond from Providence, Rhode Island, was the first student warned. She refused to cooperate with town officials. She was spared the whipping, however, when Samuel May, a preacher from Brooklyn, Connecticut, came forward to post the required bond.

When the townspeople did not succeed in closing the school, they tried another approach. A bill was passed in the Connecticut state legislature requiring any school accepting African American pupils from out of state to get permission from local officials first. When Crandall still refused to close her school, she was told that she would be sent to jail unless she posted a bond. Crandall refused to do this and did not allow her supporters to do it for her, maintaining that the law was unjust. On June 27, 1833, she was jailed in Brooklyn. Although she remained in jail only one night, her strong stand drew much attention to both herself and her cause.

Following her release, she returned to the school to find local tensions reaching a new height. Rotten eggs and stones were thrown at the school, and the girls were constantly taunted and heckled. The school's well water was contaminated with manure, and no grocer would sell food to the school.

In late August, Crandall was put on trial for breaking the new law concerning out-of-state students. Lawyers for the state argued that African Americans could not be considered legal citizens and therefore had no right to an education. Lawyers defending Crandall argued that African Americans were, indeed, citizens and had the same rights as whites. After hearing the arguments, the jury could not reach a decision, and the judge ordered a new trial later in the year.

At the second trial, held in October, Crandall was found guilty. Her lawyers refused to give up, however, and they arranged for the case to be taken before the Supreme Court of Errors in Connecticut. In the meantime, the school would remain open.

The judges of the Supreme Court heard Crandall's case in July 1834. The conflict between the forces for and against educating African Americans had become so great that the judges were afraid to rule one way or the other. Instead they ruled that an error had been committed in the school trial held in August of the previous year and that the case would have to be thrown out of court.

Meanwhile, Crandall's school flourished. There were thirty-two girls and two new teachers. Crandall married a minister named Calvin Philleo. There was harmony within, but outside ill feelings toward the school remained.

On September 9, 1834, as the church bell tolled midnight, a group of men from the town crept out of the shadows, smashed the school's windows and sashes, and tore at the clapboards. There was little choice now but to close the school. But Crandall's pioneering spirit was not defeated. She later went to Rhode Island, New York, Illinois, and Kansas, where she continued teaching both African American and white pupils. After the Civil War, the Connecticut General Assembly voted an annual $440 pension to Crandall. The law that had been used against her was removed from the books.

THE LYCEUM MOVEMENT IN AMERICA

by Ellen Hardsog

Before Josiah Holbrook started the first American lyceum in Millbury, Massachusetts, in 1826, there was very little interest in educating people beyond the elementary grades. Many children learned the three Rs — reading, 'riting, and 'rithmetic — but only the wealthy could afford higher education. The average worker practiced his or her trade with more common sense and on-the-job training than book learning.

Holbrook's lyceum, named for the grove in Athens, Greece, where Aristotle had lectured his pupils, was an offshoot of the mechanics institutes, which were successful in England during the first quarter of the nineteenth century. The institutes offered science lectures for young tradesmen who wanted to improve themselves. Holbrook, a scientist and founder of two vocational schools, pictured his lyceum as the start of widespread public education and cultural enlightenment.

From the first lyceum in Massachusetts, the movement quickly spread throughout the country, until there were three thousand county and town lyceums. At first, local scholars gave free lectures, but it became more practical to hire traveling speakers. Some of the more famous lyceum lecturers were writers Nathaniel Hawthorne and Charles Dickens, statesman Daniel Webster, and philosopher Ralph Waldo Emerson, whose fee was five dollars and oats for his horse. They were certain to attract large audiences. The lecturers spoke about

A poster from the Worcester Lyceum announces the course of lectures for the winter of 1854–55. Notice that William Lloyd Garrison was speaking on January 18.

geology, travel, history, philosophy, education, and literature. Some gave scientific demonstrations. Music and art were seldom lyceum subjects, and politics was avoided until later years, when the lecturers used the lyceum platform to crusade for or against slavery.

Audiences enjoyed the lyceum lectures so much that they began to appreciate the importance of education for everyone. Holbrook also campaigned for better public schools, more museums, and more public libraries so that all people would have access to books. At Holbrook's suggestion, some towns published local histories and maps for the first time. The lyceum movement also encouraged the establishment of normal schools, which were specifically set up to train teachers.

When the Civil War broke out in 1861, Americans turned their attention to the problem of national survival, and the lyceum movement died. After the war, lectures became popular again, but they were handled by lecture bureaus instead of lyceums and were more entertaining than educational. Only a handful of lyceums remain today. The lyceum as Josiah Holbrook saw it was never revived, but its golden days left a permanent mark on American public education.

THE SHAKERS

The word "Shakers" probably means little, if anything, to most of us today. Those who know the word most likely associate it with simple, well-built furniture and craft items sometimes found in antique shops — furniture built by Shakers. A few of us may live near former Shaker villages and may have seen the plain, sturdy buildings Shakers once lived and worked in.

But if we want truly to understand who the Shakers were and what they accomplished, we need to look beyond the obvious handmade reminders — beyond the artifacts — of Shaker history. We also need to consider Shaker attitudes and beliefs.

The Shakers were a religious sect started in the mid-1700s in the midst of a religious revival. The group, whose actual name was The United Society of Believers in Christ's Second Appearing, believed that Christ's second coming would occur at some time during a thousand-year period starting in the mid-1700s. The group received the name "Shaking Quakers" and later "Shakers" because of the actions and movements of members during some of the group's early worship services.

The Shakers believed in pacifism and perfection, the ideals of Christ. They believed in leading simple lives and in remaining separate from "the world" —

The Shakers believed in pacifism and perfection, the ideals of Christ. They believed in leading simple lives and in remaining separate from "the world."

The village of the United Society of Shakers in Canterbury, New Hampshire.

that is, any people who were not Shakers and any land not owned by Shakers. After their arrival in America, the Shakers lived in small communities or villages that they built themselves, and all community members were considered part of one "family," sharing work and goods.

Shaker men and women shared leadership equally. Following another ideal of Christ, Shakers did not marry and have children; therefore, it was necessary for Shaker communities to gain new members through other means. Between the mid-1700s and mid-1800s, many adults converted to the Shaker religion and joined Shaker communities. These adults gave their possessions to be shared by the entire community, and husbands and wives agreed to live separately, in the Shaker manner.

Shaker children in New Hampshire take part in gymnastic exercises about 1870.

In addition, the Shakers often adopted and raised orphans. These children lived according to Shaker rules and received their education and training in various crafts from the Shakers. At the age of twenty-one, a person had to decide whether to join the Shakers officially or return to "the world." Some chose to remain, others to leave. Still others left the Shakers later in life.

The Shakers were an industrious and inventive people who met with much success as farmers and sellers of their superb goods. Their furniture and crafts were of the highest quality, and for this reason many reminders of their way of life can still be found today. It was the Shaker belief in perfection that determined the quality of their goods. Whatever task a Shaker set out to perform, however big or small, he or she tried to do the best possible job. Whether building a desk, raising livestock, or mending a shirt, a Shaker strove for perfection. When we realize this, it is easy to see the need to consider attitudes, as well as artifacts, when studying history.

The Shaker society began to decline after the mid-1800s, although the exact reasons for this are somewhat difficult to define. The Civil War proved quite costly to the western Shakers, even though Shaker men were not forced to fight. The Shakers' simple way of life was inconsistent with that of American society at the time, which was becoming more industrial and complex.

Today one active Shaker community remains (the Sabbathday Lake Shakers in New Gloucester, Maine), and several former Shaker villages are open to visitors. But if you visit one of these historic places, remember to look beyond the rocking chairs and farm buildings to the attitudes and beliefs that led to their creation. Then you will begin to appreciate the complete story of the Shakers in America.

Booker T. Washington delivered his most famous speech at the Cotton States Exposition in Atlanta, Georgia, in 1895. Washington stated his belief that African Americans should earn the trust and support of whites through hard work and education rather than by fighting for acceptance and civil rights.

STRUGGLE FOR AN EDUCATION: BOOKER TALIAFERRO WASHINGTON

by Lori Henshey

It was an exciting day in nine-year-old Booker Taliaferro's life. He and the other plantation slaves gathered close to the master's house in Franklin County, Virginia, to listen as a uniformed man read from a piece of paper. The rumors were true! The long and bloody Civil War was over, and the slaves were finally free. Shouts of joy came from the ex-slaves. Many danced and sang; others, heads bowed, whispered prayers of thanks. And amidst it all, young Booker's thoughts may have been simple: no more carrying water, cleaning yards, or taking corn to the mill under the hot Virginia sun.

Scenes similar to this occurred throughout the South in the early spring of 1865. But when the singing and dancing stopped, many ex-slaves wondered what freedom meant for them. Suddenly, they were responsible for taking care of themselves and their families, something they had never done before. They had no homes, jobs, or property. Most could not read or write, since southern laws strictly forbade the education of slaves. And few had money, clothes, or personal belongings.

After the Civil War, during Reconstruction, Congress created the Freedmen's Bureau. The bureau helped freedmen find jobs; supervised their work contracts; furnished them with clothing, food, and other supplies; and provided funding for hospitals. It also established and supervised schools throughout the South.

Ex-slaves made new lives as freedmen. With government aid, some were able to acquire small farms. Many flocked to northern cities. Some, especially the older ones, worked for their former masters as hired hands. Others attended the newly created schools. And some left their plantations to find faraway friends and relatives.

Booker's mother left Virginia with her children to join her husband, a former runaway slave, in West Virginia. They loaded their few belongings in a cart and began the three-hundred-mile walk to Malden, West Virginia, located in the Kanawha Valley near the present-day capital of Charleston. It was a long journey over densely forested mountains. They lived like mountaineers, sleeping in the open woods and cooking over a log fire.

Salt was plentiful in the Kanawha Valley, and it had first been mined there in the early 1800s. By the Civil War, the industry was at its peak. Great salt furnaces were operated to boil the brine, or salt water, and coal was mined to provide the necessary fuel. The town of Malden was home to many workers, and it was here that Booker's stepfather waited, having already obtained jobs for his stepsons, Booker and James, in the salt furnaces.

Booker soon became unhappy with his life, not because work in the furnaces was hard — he was used to hard work — but because he could not read or write. For most of his young life, Booker had had a strong desire to learn. Once, in Virginia, he had glimpsed the inside of a schoolhouse. And while Booker knew that, as a slave, he could never enter a classroom, he could not forget that vision. Now that he was free, nothing could stop him from learning. When an African American school opened in Malden, he was determined to attend.

Because Booker's family needed the money he brought home from the salt furnace, finding time for school was not easy. But Booker was not discouraged. Sometimes he worked all day and went to school at night, and sometimes he worked mornings and evenings and went to school during the day. But he always found time for school.

It was at this time that Booker gave himself a last name. He had been called Booker Taliaferro since birth, and he now added Washington as a third name, perhaps after our first president, George Washington. Booker Taliaferro Washington was a name that would become famous in our country's history.

Booker learned quickly, and soon he knew more than his teachers. When he heard about a school for African Americans in Hampton, Virginia, he promised himself that he would earn the money to go. He went to work as a house servant for General Lewis Ruffner, owner of both the salt furnace and the coal mine. While Booker worked for Ruffner, he gave much of his pay to his family and saved the rest. Mrs. Ruffner was a strict employer, but she taught Booker lessons in housekeeping that he would later find useful.

In 1872, Booker said good-bye to his family and left for Hampton with a small satchel of clothing and a little money. The five-hundred-mile trip was long and lonely. At that time, a railroad did not stretch the entire distance from Malden to Hampton, so he traveled part of the way by train and the rest by bumpy stagecoach. When the stagecoach stopped at an inn, Booker hoped to use some of his money to rent a bed for the night. When he asked the innkeeper for a room, however, he was told that the inn was not for African Americans. The boy, cold and weary, kept warm by walking around all night.

When Booker reached Richmond, Virginia, he was penniless and hungry. Up and down the city streets, vendors sold fried chicken and apple pie, which looked delicious to the hungry boy. Booker walked the streets until he was very tired. When he spotted a board sidewalk raised above street level, he crawled into the space and slept, using his satchel as a pillow.

The next day, Booker was hungrier than he had been the night before, and he knew that he had to find work. He saw a large ship docked in the James River and scurried out to speak with the captain. The captain gave Booker breakfast and hired him to help unload cargo. Booker worked on the ship until he had saved enough money to reach Hampton.

Booker arrived in Hampton in dirty, ragged clothes, and the head teacher at the

In 1881, Washington founded Tuskegee Normal and Industrial Institute in Tuskegee, Alabama. This vocational school taught African Americans trades such as farming and carpentry. The institute also helped educate farmers both at the school and on location. A nurse, home educator, and county agent joined this demonstration wagon on location.

school eyed him suspiciously when he asked to be admitted. Then she pointed to a nearby room and asked him to sweep it. Here Booker's experience as a house servant came in handy. He did not just sweep; he dusted and polished every crack and corner until the room shone. When the teacher saw his work and his enthusiasm, she let him enter the school and gave him a position as janitor.

Booker attended Hampton Institute from 1872 to 1875 and became a teacher there in 1879. In 1881, he founded Tuskegee Normal and Industrial Institute, later called Tuskegee Institute, in Tuskegee, Alabama. This vocational school taught African Americans useful trades such as carpentry and farming.

Booker Taliaferro Washington, already a great educator, became a respected political leader and the greatest spokesman for African American rights of his time. Until his death in 1915, he worked for the advancement of his race and sought a way for African Americans and whites to live together in harmony. For Washington and many African American men and women of his time, the struggle for an education paid off.

THE PREACHER AND THE BUSINESSMAN: FOUNDERS OF CHAUTAUQUA

by Laurel Sherman

John Heyl Vincent and Lewis Miller were born within a few years of each other, but they were so different that you might say they had only one thing in common — an interest in improving Sunday schools. That interest drew them together in the founding of Chautauqua.

John Heyl Vincent

Lewis Miller

In the early part of the nineteenth century, the Sunday school was a fairly new idea. It began as a place where children who worked in factories or in the fields six days a week went to learn reading, writing, and arithmetic. The Sunday school was the center of activity on a Sunday afternoon, and the children stayed four or five hours. Their teachers were frequently public school teachers who were paid extra to teach on this day.

John Heyl Vincent was born in 1832. His mother used to say that he was a born preacher. She remembered that when he was only four, she saw him with a Bible in his hands, urging anyone within hearing to take up Christianity. Like many children in the mid-nineteenth century, he attended school for only a few years and then went directly into teaching himself.

By 1850, he had decided to become a preacher and was given a license to "exhort." As a circuit preacher for the Methodist Church, he traveled on horseback from parish to parish, visiting communities too small to have a minister of their own. He held services and performed baptisms and weddings in each village. At the end of four weeks, he would find himself back in the first community, ready to start the circuit again. Eventually, he was appointed to a church in Newark, New Jersey, and later to churches in Illinois. In each of these places, his dream that ministers and church school teachers should have a better education continued to grow.

By 1864, Vincent was the editor of the newly formed *Northwestern Sunday School Teacher's Quarterly.* He next became a Sunday school agent (1866) and secretary of the Sunday School Union for the Methodist Church. In 1868, he became editor of the Methodist publication *The Sunday School Journal.*

Lewis Miller was born in 1829 in the new Ohio Territory. His father was among the pioneers who cleared the land acre by acre, planting crops between the tree stumps until the land was worn-out and they had to move on to a new field. Lewis loved this land. As a grown man, he could still remember "the glorious wave of bird songs that arose from those thickets...and...the myriad-tinted coloring which the autumn frosts painted upon this well-remembered spot."

He loved the outdoors and was determined to make the farmer's life easier. Like Vincent, he had only a few years of formal education, and by the time he was sixteen, he was teaching in a small school. It was as an inventor, however, that Miller became famous.

Improving standard harvesting machines, he eventually devised the Buckeye Mower and Reaper. Henry Ford, the inventor of the first mass-produced cars, said of one of Miller's machines, "There was never a better machine made." Farmers must have agreed with Ford. By 1863, the companies that produced the Buckeye moved their offices to Akron and Canton, Ohio, and within a year they were producing eight thousand reapers a year.

Miller was a rich man, and he had more time to devote to other interests, one of which was the quality of the Sunday school in his Methodist church. Even there, his inventive mind could not rest. One of his first contributions to the

The traveling chautauquas of the early twentieth century grew out of James Redpath's Lyceum Bureau. Although they should not be confused with the Chautauqua Institution in New York, they adopted the same format and name. The traveling chautauquas brought culture and entertainment to many American towns.

THE CHAUTAUQUA STORY

The Chautauqua Sunday School Assembly, which opened in 1874, later became more than a summer school for Sunday school teachers. It evolved into an educational and cultural retreat for all types of people. The rural location and lake also provided numerous recreational activities. Religion, which was the foundation of Chautauqua, remained important, and people of all denominations came to the New York institution.

Lewis Miller and John Vincent were strongly influenced by the climate of their day. During the late nineteenth century, America was experiencing substantial industrial growth. This growth created sharp class distinctions and also provided the emergence of a new class of people — the middle class. During this age, people had more leisure time, and educational and recreational activities became important. Most likely affected by the lyceum movement, which emphasized the notion of education for all, Miller and Vincent founded Chautauqua on this same principle.

It is in education that Chautauqua has made its greatest mark on American history. Chautauqua is more than a summer camp. It is an institution whose educational programs are strongly influential. Over the years, dozens of other chautauquas were formed, patterned after the New York institution. These were called "daughter" chautauquas. Besides the daughter chautauquas, traveling, circuit, or tent chautauquas traveled from town to town in the early twentieth century. These traveling chautauquas died out in the 1930s.

Today the Chautauqua Institution in New York carries on the traditions started by Miller and Vincent and emphasizes the importance of education for all. Chautauqua stresses that education is not only found in a classroom but also can be pursued in a relaxed atmosphere. For more than one hundred years, Chautauqua and her daughters have influenced Americans in religion, education, recreation, and the arts.

Akron Methodist Church was a design for a new Sunday school. The plan included a large central hall, where the children could gather before and after their lessons, with many smaller rooms off the hall for classes.

It was at this point that Vincent, the preacher, and Miller, the businessman, met. As a Sunday school agent, Vincent was used to holding winter conventions for Sunday school teachers and superintendents. When a national meeting was suggested, Vincent wanted to display the fine new building that Miller had designed. At about that time, Miller was thinking about a summer camp for Sunday school leaders. He felt strongly that an outdoor setting would be an inspiration to the teachers. When Vincent approached Miller with his winter convention idea, Miller responded that a summer assembly would be better.

Eventually, Vincent gave in and agreed to try the summer assembly, although he warned that the open-air setting would probably be too distracting for a religious gathering. Each took on a different responsibility: Vincent would be the head of the department of instruction, while Miller was to be president of the assembly.

The first Sunday School Assembly opened on August 4, 1874, on land leased from a camp meeting association on Lake Chautauqua in New York State. Although Miller and Vincent were different types of men — Vincent was a wonderful speaker and religious leader, and Miller was good at organizing and practical matters — they managed to create a successful first assembly.

At the end of this first assembly, the different natures of both men were quite apparent. As Vincent was delivering the final lecture, Miller was nowhere to be found. Only later did the people learn that the camp water pump had broken and only the ingenious Miller could get it working again. As always, the talents of these two men complemented each other perfectly, which was one secret of Chautauqua's success.

OLD-TIME TEXTBOOKS

by Elizabeth West

Imagine memorizing an entire book, then reciting it aloud from memory. If you were a student in 1800, you were expected to memorize your schoolbook. Of course, you probably had only one — if you had any at all. It might have been a good book, or it might have been awful, since schoolbooks were not carefully reviewed in those days.

The person sitting next to you in school would probably have used a different book. Schools did not supply books; pupils brought their own. If they did not have any books to bring, they might have used the Bible or shared with a classmate. A classroom of thirty pupils may have read from twenty different books.

The reading books usually dealt with religious subjects. Some began with a few pages of instruction, then quickly launched into biblical and moral selections. If you finished your book and did not have another, you reread the book you had. You did not necessarily read one easy book at age six and then another, harder book at age eight.

Today schoolbooks are checked carefully for factual accuracy, but in 1800 they were not. One author emphatically named the wrong mountain as the highest in the Andes; another stated that Asia was the country where Adam and Eve had lived; a third seriously reported on a talking dog who knew more than thirty words, including "coffee," "tea," and "assembly."

Since schoolbooks were not standardized, some books for beginners were very easy and others difficult. One well-known book, *The Tales of Peter Parley*, was in some ways like modern books for beginning readers. It used short words and sentences and had many illustrations. Most books, though, like Pierpont's *Introduction to the National Reader*, had small type and difficult words. There were no pictures, and sentences were long.

To a modern reader, the subjects covered in the early texts might seem curious. In addition to the usual biblical selections, Pierpont's book included "Avalanche of the White Mountains," a story about an entire family buried alive. This was followed by "The Village Funeral," "The Execution of Captain Nathan Hale," "Murderer's Creek," and "The Dangers of Robbing Birds' Nests."

By 1850, pupils studied more subjects and had a few more books. Besides a reader, they probably had an arithmetic book, a geography book, and perhaps a speller. Some of these were "progressive"; in other words, they progressed from easy to more difficult. A progressive speller began with simple words such as "cab," "tab," and "nab." It ended with more difficult ones such as "disquisition," "execration," and "malediction." Progressive arithmetic books started with simple addition and subtraction and went on to fractions, percentages, extraction of square and cube roots, and complicated geometric measurements. A favorite question found in many arithmetic books was to figure out the weight of Noah's ark. The answer differed from book to book.

The Chautauqua Kindergarten was established by 1876. It used the most progressive methods of teaching young children, including an annual hayride to watch "how doth the little busy bee improve each shining hour."

Reading books also were more complicated. Selections were still recited aloud, but recitation had become a separate subject. Chapters, and occasionally whole books, were devoted to pronunciation, rhythm, emphasis, and gestures. Sentences did not always run straight across the page but wandered up and down to show whether the voice should rise or fall. Pupils practiced tongue twisters, including "Peter Prickle Prangle picked three pecks of prickly pears from three prickly, prangly, pear trees." They also learned orthoepy, phonology, and vocal gymnastics. Orthoepy and phonology taught students how to pronounce words and sounds. Vocal gymnastics combined physical education and vocal exercises.

Special emphasis on recitation may seem overdone to us today, but it served a purpose back then. Paper was scarce, so most work was performed orally. Reciting a book proved that you knew it. Also, many people in rural communities could not read. It was assumed that people who could would recite aloud to others.

Standardized spelling books became popular around mid-century. Until Noah Webster published his spelling books early in the century, spelling was a haphazard affair. Webster standardized American spelling. Once spelling became standardized, spelling bees quickly became social fads as well as school activities. They were a form of entertainment.

Reading and education were actively promoted. Compulsory education laws that required regular school attendance were enacted. Textbooks became a valuable tool in this effort to promote schools.

Toward the end of the 1800s, textbooks began to look a lot like those we use today. Instead of one ungraded reader, pupils used a series of books. Illustrations were inserted routinely. Schools tried to lure pupils with interesting books. One author promised to leave out "insignificant details and repulsive statistics." Instead, he tried to include details he thought would interest his readers.

Textbooks are no longer the product of one person, but are usually produced by teams of writers, editors, and art directors. They are designed to be acceptable to large numbers of people, and their high standards for accuracy and attractiveness make them much more enjoyable to read.

Instead of memorizing one book by reading it over and over again, students today read many books, learning parts from each. Compared with the students of the 1800s, they have an incredible amount of information available to them. Textbooks are part of the reason.

TRANSCENDENTALISM: A NEW VIEW
by D.H. Deford and H.S. Stout

When you look at a tree, what do you see? A great chance to climb? A possible tree fort? Shade for a picnic lunch?

Imagine a group of people standing around the tree. One man is a carpenter. He looks at the tree and thinks of the lum-

Transcendentalist leader A. Bronson Alcott on the steps of the chapel at the Concord Summer School of Philosophy and Literature, founded in 1879 in Concord, Massachusetts. Alcott was the school's founder and dean.

ber it could provide to build a house. The woman standing next to him works in a paper factory. She sees the tree as raw material for paper pulp. Another person imagines a home for birds, squirrels, and insects, and someone else thinks of a beautiful piece of furniture.

Of course, any of these people also might think of your tree fort, and you might think of furniture, paper, or building a house. But different people often see things differently. What they see and how they understand it depends on their point of view.

In the early 1800s, most teachers at Harvard College in New England taught that the only way to know anything was through the physical senses — sight, hearing, touch, taste, and smell. They also said that to understand the "facts" gained through the senses, a person must think logically about those facts. This was their point of view. The Unitarian Church adopted this view.

A few people disagreed. These people, who became known as the transcendentalists, believed that people are born knowing what is good, even before they know the words to describe that goodness. (The term "transcendental" refers to knowledge transcending the five senses.)

They believed that the closer to nature people stayed, the better they would be.

They also thought that people have a sense, which some called intuition, that is not physical. Through this sense, people can know what is "true and right and beautiful" without logical thinking. According to transcendentalism, people could lose this sense when they spent all their time thinking the way the Harvard teachers thought.

Most of the first transcendentalists were Unitarian ministers who separated themselves from the Harvard teachers and the Unitarian Church because of their different views. But why did it matter so much to them?

Let's go back to the tree we considered earlier. The group of people around it might say, "Our town is growing and changing. That tree should be cut down and used to make a house." That point of view would make sense of chopping down the tree. But maybe you believe the tree needs to stand as a home for animals and a fun place for you. In that case, you might feel that the town is changing and growing in the wrong way.

The transcendentalists had this sort of problem. They saw the United States growing and changing quickly. Although many people thought the growth and changes were good, the transcendentalists did not. They saw slavery advancing, Native Americans being massacred, forests being cut down, and the United States at war with Mexico. And they felt that these changes grew out of a wrong point of view — the point of view taught at Harvard College.

The transcendentalists believed that the country would change for the better only when individuals improved. For that to happen, they thought, people needed to get away from Harvard's point of view. Only then would they return to the nat-

Nathaniel Hawthorne

....

After Hawthorne married Sophia Peabody, a friend and follower of Emerson, Thoreau, and Margaret Fuller and sister of Elizabeth Palmer Peabody (see page 159), in 1842, they moved to Concord, Massachusetts.

ural intuition with which they were born and which would show them what was true, right, and beautiful.

To encourage their point of view, transcendentalist leaders such as Reverend George Ripley, A. Bronson Alcott (Louisa May's father), and Orestes A. Brownson met as a group, first known as the Hedge Club (named for Frederic Henry Hedge, who was one of their number). They met to talk about new ways to see and understand the world and themselves. They considered philosophers from ancient Greece, the Orient, and Germany, and they reconsidered the religion of the Puritans. But they did much more than talk.

One of the more famous club members was the Unitarian minister Ralph Waldo Emerson. As a writer, minister, and lecturer, he became an important spokesman for the transcendentalists. He also led the way for a group of American writers that included Henry David Thoreau, Walt Whitman, Nathaniel Hawthorne, and Emily Dickinson.

Most transcendentalists took part in social reform movements, including those supporting equal rights for women and temperance (abstinence from alcohol) and those opposing war and slavery. Starting with *The Dial,* a magazine originally edited by Margaret Fuller and Ralph Waldo Emerson, transcendentalism fostered a series of journals meant to examine the movement's ideas.

A number of transcendentalists started experimental communities, such as Brook Farm and Fruitlands. These communities were intended to be utopias, or perfect societies. For instance, you might start a utopian community if you were as concerned about all trees as you were about the one we looked at earlier. In your utopia, trees would be saved for wildlife and fun. In the same way, the transcendentalists hoped to correct what they thought were wrong choices in the changing United States, at least in their own small communities. None of these lasted long, however.

In fact, by the Civil War, the transcendental movement had died out with the passing of its foremost leaders. But the point of view they held has not died. It lives on in the continuing American dream of a perfect society. It lives on, too, in some Americans' interest in Oriental philosophy and religion and in the conservation of nature. And it lives on in the literature of Ralph Waldo Emerson and the writers he inspired. Their work grew directly out of the transcendental movement, and it continues to be read and loved today.

RALPH WALDO EMERSON

by Julia F. Lieser

The United States of America was a raw young nation when Ralph Waldo Emerson was born in 1803. But Emerson grew with the country, becoming an innovative writer and thinker. His essays, lectures, and sermons, along with his books and poetry, earned him the title "The Wisest American." No longer need the new nation look to Europe for profound thinking and writing. Emerson spoke a new philosophy for the young country of his birth.

As a child, Emerson showed little promise of the greatness he was to achieve. A frail, solemn boy, he rarely joined in boisterous games with other children

Opposite: Ralph Waldo Emerson lived in Concord, Massachusetts, the home of his ancestors, and mingled regularly with other Concord residents such as Thoreau, Hawthorne, and A. Bronson Alcott. Shown here in the 1870s when he was in his sixties, Emerson was widely known as a writer and lecturer.

and developed a lifelong tendency not to indulge in unrestrained merriment. He was an average student, and although he entered Harvard at the age of fourteen, doing so was not unusual at the time.

Perhaps the restrictions placed on the children of clergy contributed to Emerson's restrained childhood. His father, descended from a long line of New England clergymen, was a Unitarian minister in Boston, where Emerson was born and grew up. Poverty was another factor that shaped his attitudes. Reverend William Emerson died when Ralph was only eight years old, leaving his widow with six children to raise, the youngest only a few months old.

After Emerson graduated from Harvard, finishing in the middle of his class, he was undecided about his future. Teaching in a school for girls operated by his brother occupied his time for a few years until he decided to follow in the family tradition and enter Harvard Divinity School.

After his ordination, he accepted a call to Boston's Second Church (Unitarian) and married Ellen Tucker. Neither of the Emersons' health was robust, and Ellen died of tuberculosis seventeen months after they were married. At this time, Emerson became aware of his growing disagreement with some of the doctrines of the Unitarian Church. When he stated his convictions publicly in a sermon, the congregation of Second Church had no choice but to accept his resignation. He had served only three years.

Sick, discouraged, and full of doubt, Emerson set sail for Europe. On this nine-month sojourn, he regained both his physical and mental health. While abroad, he met the English poets Samuel Taylor Coleridge and William Wordsworth, along with the Scottish essayist Thomas Carlyle, who became a lifelong friend.

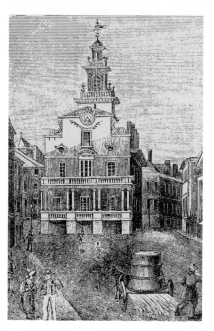

Boston's Old State House, built in 1748 on State Street, is shown here around 1848.

Back in Massachusetts, Emerson moved from the bustling city of Boston to the rural village of Concord, the home of his ancestors. He married Lydia Jackson, a marriage that produced four children, and became friends with his Concord neighbors Henry David Thoreau, Nathaniel Hawthorne, and Amos Bronson Alcott, all destined for fame. In the peaceful countryside, Emerson settled down to a life of writing and lecturing.

Emerson was a popular lecturer. Although not a forceful orator, he was an effective speaker who used few gestures, relying instead on timing, or pauses, for emphasis. A tall, spare figure with a pleasing baritone voice, he charmed audiences with his presence even when they did not understand the deeper meaning of his words.

Emerson published numerous books, ranging from discussions of his travels and his views on nature to poetry and collections of essays adapted from his lectures. He inspired and encouraged young writers, among them Thoreau, Walt Whitman, and the American philosopher William James.

During this period of his life, he and a group of friends who enjoyed philosophical discussions started meeting regularly, calling themselves the Hedge Club, after one of the members. Later known as the transcendentalists, this group also published *The Dial*, a magazine Emerson edited for a time.

Emerson traveled widely in the northern and midwestern United States on lecture tours and again visited Europe, where he lectured. He often accepted invitations to deliver sermons at church services and became a popular speaker at college functions, although his remarks to the senior class of Harvard Divinity School in 1838 stirred up such a violent controversy that he was not invited back for thirty years. He advised the future ministers to think for themselves and follow their own consciences.

Emerson was continually in the public eye until his health began to fail as he neared his seventieth birthday. He spent his last years quietly at home, where he died in 1882. He is buried in Concord's Sleepy Hollow Cemetery.

Although Emerson always felt himself to be lacking in warmth in his personal relationships, he nevertheless held the respect and admiration of people everywhere, even when they did not agree with his views. Convers Francis, a Harvard theologian and fellow transcendentalist, said of him, "[He is] such a calm, steady, simple soul, always looking for truth and living in wisdom, and in love for man."

Emerson's legacy to his readers, and the core of the philosophy by which he lived, was that each person must think for himself or herself and act on his or her own best instincts.

HENRY DAVID THOREAU: FOLLOWING A DIFFERENT DRUMMER

by Craig E. Blohm

To his neighbors, the spare, rustic man was a curious individual. He seemed always to march to a "different drummer," a phrase he himself had penned. But despite his critics, Henry David Thoreau would become one of the more influential transcendentalists.

Thoreau was born on July 12, 1817, in Concord, Massachusetts. We know few details of his youth, but one event does stand out. When he was five years old, his family took him on a picnic at the edge of a small, clear pond about a mile from Concord. This was Thoreau's first encounter with Walden Pond, but he would return there many times throughout his life.

Thoreau was a quiet, thoughtful boy. His older brother, John, was more outgoing and popular. Despite the difference in their personalities, the two became close friends. Some people thought that John was a more promising scholar, but it was Henry who went to college, entering Harvard at age sixteen.

During his college years, Thoreau began to realize that his talents leaned toward writing. Harvard's library was like heaven to a young man with literary interests, and Thoreau spent hours copying from library volumes. Sometime during this period, he met Ralph Waldo Emerson, the leading transcendentalist. Through his friendship with Emerson, Thoreau became acquainted with Ellery Channing, Bronson Alcott, and many other transcendentalists.

In 1837, the year Thoreau graduated from Harvard, he began keeping a diary, or journal. In it he recorded his innermost thoughts and observations of life,

Few portraits of Thoreau were made during his lifetime. The last, shown here, was taken in 1861 at the urging of his friend Daniel Ricketson. Thoreau died the next year.

nature, and humankind. It was a creative outlet the young writer would depend on throughout his life.

After college, Thoreau held a variety of jobs, but he worked only when absolutely necessary. He believed that work kept people from really living. "The mass of men lead lives of quiet desperation," he wrote, working for things that did not really satisfy them. "I am convinced...that to maintain one's self on this earth is not a hardship but a pastime, if we will live simply and wisely." Thoreau went to live at Emerson's home in 1841, earning his keep as a handyman. Finding kindred spirits in Emerson and the other transcendentalists, he continued writing, contributing many poems and essays to *The Dial*.

A reconstructed version of the cabin Thoreau built at Walden Pond is located at the Concord Museum in Concord, Massachusetts.

In 1842, a tragedy shattered Thoreau's life. John Thoreau died of lockjaw after cutting his finger in an accident. Henry was so stricken with grief at his brother's death that he actually acquired symptoms of lockjaw himself, a phenomenon known as a psychosomatic illness.

As Thoreau gradually regained his health, the idea of living a simple life close to nature continued to obsess him. He also wanted some time to write a book about a boat trip he had taken with John in 1839. Thoreau planned an experiment: He would live alone in a cabin at the edge of Walden Pond.

On July 4, 1845, Thoreau moved into the one-room cabin he had built with his own hands (the materials cost him only about twenty-eight dollars). During the two years he lived at Walden Pond, he spent his days writing and observing nature. In the winter, he watched fish swimming under the ice on the pond. He spent summers exploring the woods, observing the animals, and once witnessing a fierce battle between armies of red and black ants. The record of his observations would become his most famous book, *Walden*.

Not only was Thoreau sensitive to nature; he also had a keen social conscience. Being opposed to slavery, he protested by refusing to pay his poll tax for six years. He was arrested in 1846 and spent one night in jail. Released the next day when someone anonymously paid the tax for him, Thoreau was angry. As he would later write in his famous essay "Civil Disobedience," he felt that "under a government which imprisons any unjustly, the true place for a just man is also a prison."

Thoreau had only two books published during his lifetime: the account of his boat trip with John, called *A Week on the Concord and Merrimack Rivers,* and *Walden.** But since his death in 1862, his writing has been recognized worldwide. His views on peaceful resistance have inspired modern leaders such as Mohandas Gandhi and Martin Luther King, Jr. And even today, *Walden* gives new generations insight into the man who very deliberately followed a different drummer.

*After Thoreau's death, his friends edited his unpublished *Journals,* which have become almost as famous as his two books.

THE DIAL

by Ann M.B. Lake

The *Philadelphia Gazette* called the editors of *The Dial* "zanies" and "bedlamites." Why did the newspaper use such harsh words? Perhaps it was because this new magazine did not imitate European ideas and methods. Instead, it was filled with a freedom of expression not seen before in American publishing.

In 1840, transcendentalists Ralph Waldo Emerson, Margaret Fuller, and George Ripley felt that their group needed an outlet for their thoughts and feelings. They hoped that their new magazine, *The Dial* (from sundial), would occupy "a station on which the sight may fall; which is open to the rising sun; and from which it may correctly report the progress of the hour and the day." Its banner read, "The Dial: A Magazine for Literature, Philosophy, and Religion." Its purpose, stated in the first issue of July 1840, was "to furnish a medium for the freest expression of thought on the questions which interest earnest minds in every community."

It was decided that the magazine would be published quarterly with 136 octavo pages (meaning that the printer's sheets were folded into eight six- by nine-inch leaves). It would cost three dollars per year and would be published by Weeks, Jordan, and Company.*

It also was decided that Ripley would be the business manager, while Emerson and Fuller would be coeditors. In practice, however, Fuller did all the work for the first two years. She had been promised a salary of two hundred dollars a year for her efforts, but the magazine never made enough money to pay her. The contributors also were not paid for their articles, so *The Dial* often received low-quality work. With 136 pages to fill, Fuller often had to write additional articles herself. One of her fillers was a poem called "The Morning Breeze."

In spite of the lack of funds, Fuller persuaded some of the best New England writers to contribute. Emerson wrote both prose and poems; William Henry Channing, William Ellery Channing, and Bronson Alcott contributed essays; Henry David Thoreau donated his nature studies; and James Russell Lowell contributed poetry. Articles on religious reform came from Theodore Parker, and Fuller herself wrote poems and critical essays. The magazine also gave young writers a place to have their ideas printed. Over the life of *The Dial*, forty persons contributed articles.

Fuller differed from Emerson in that she felt the magazine should not reflect only what she agreed with or liked. Emerson, however, "would have everything in it good according to his own taste," which in Fuller's opinion was far too narrow an approach. Despite this difference, when Emerson took over as editor, very little changed.

The Morning Breeze

Ocean that lay
Like a sick child, spiritless, well nigh death
Now curls and ripples in eternal play
Beneath thy breath.

Margaret Fuller edited *The Dial* for two years, leaving that post to pursue a life of letters. In 1843, she traveled west, touring the Great Lakes and keeping a journal that became her first book, *Summer on the Lakes.* Her second book, *Woman in the Nineteenth Century*, deals with the topics of education and career.

*The Dial was first published by Weeks, Jordan, and Company and later by Elizabeth Peabody.

157

In 1842, burdened by the heavy responsibilities of *The Dial* and in poor health, Fuller asked Emerson to assume the editorship, promising to help as much as she could. Emerson's first issue was published in July 1842. At this point, *The Dial* had lost many subscribers, and the magazine was in financial trouble. Emerson asked his friends to recruit more subscribers, and he even used one hundred twenty dollars of his own money to get one issue printed. He changed publishers, hoping the new firm could cut costs, but nothing worked. By 1844, Emerson saw that the magazine would never have the public support it needed. The April 1844 issue was its last.

The Dial failed for a variety of reasons. Its strength, but also one of its weaknesses, was its originality. All the poetry, essays, private diaries, and spontaneous criticism had never been published before. Although this was a plus, it also meant that some of the articles were not as good as they might have been. In addition, although some of the contributors were widely known, none was so popular that the general public would buy the magazine just to read his or her views.

Other reasons for *The Dial*'s failure were the small number of transcendentalists and their diverse interests. Because they ranged from extreme idealists to conservatives, the magazine could not please all segments of the movement. For instance, although the magazine generally was criticized by its American readers as being too abstract, it was highly respected in England and Scotland.

The Dial survived only four years, but by the time the last issue was printed, there were four volumes of 544 pages each, and it had served a noble purpose. It had enabled the transcendentalists to speak to each other, brought their ideas more clearly into the open, and helped them realize what their own philosophy meant, to both themselves and others. The magazine also inspired a number of writers to express their thoughts in such a way that would influence succeeding generations.

The Dial was the first literary magazine in the United States, printing advanced works that commercial magazines would not even consider. Although it survived for only a short time, it inspired three other literary magazines with the same name over the years. More than a century later, scholars are once again examining this almost-unknown magazine, and a collection of its contents has been printed.

TRANSCENDENTAL COMMUNITIES: BROOK FARM AND FRUITLANDS

by Jill H. Lawler

During the period when transcendentalism flourished, several reform groups in the United States were inspired to establish utopian communities. Many of them were influenced by a Scotsman named Robert Owen, who in 1824 purchased more than thirty thousand acres in Indiana and Illinois and named his experimental community New Harmony.

The transcendentalists became caught up in the fervor for social experimentation. Their two communities, Brook Farm and Fruitlands, stand as examples of efforts to apply the philosophy of transcendentalism to everyday life.

The April 1842 edition of *The Dial* was Fuller's last as editor. Ralph Waldo Emerson became editor with the July 1842 issue.

Brook Farm

From the spring of 1841 until the fall of 1847, the Brook Farm Institute of Agriculture and Education existed in West Roxbury, Massachusetts. Its objective was to be a model community of teachers, students, and workers where "thought would preside over the operations of labor, and labor contribute to the expansion of thought." Elizabeth Palmer Peabody, a frequent visitor to Brook Farm, said that it provided the "leisure to live in all the faculties of the soul."

The leading forces behind this experiment were George and Sophia Ripley. Their enthusiasm attracted widely known thinkers and artists of the time, including Charles Anderson Dana, John Sullivan Dwight, George William Curtis, and Margaret Fuller's fourteen-year-old brother Lloyd (at the preparatory school).

Novelist Nathaniel Hawthorne invested his savings (one thousand dollars) in two shares of joint stock in the farm and became one of its earliest residents. At first enthusiastic about performing manual labor, Hawthorne became disillusioned with how little time was left to pursue his writing. He left the community in the autumn of 1841 and a decade later wrote the novel *The Blithedale Romance*, which might have been based on his Brook Farm experiences. Despite any ill feelings he might have had when he left, in the preface to this book he states, "The author has ventured to make free with his old and affectionately remembered home at BROOK FARM as being certainly the most romantic episode of his own life."

Many of the leading transcendental thinkers who did not become active participants in the community were frequent visitors. The stirring Unitarian minister Theodore Parker was at the farm two or three times a week, and on Sunday many of the "farmers" attended his church in Boston. Other notable visitors included Margaret Fuller, Ralph Waldo Emerson, Orestes Brownson, Bronson Alcott, and Christopher Cranch. Many people who were not so well-known also visited the farm out of curiosity. A visitors book kept in The Hive (the name given to the main farmhouse because everyone there was busy as a bee) was said to contain the names of four thousand visitors for a single year.

In the early years, life at Brook Farm combined hard physical labor with intellectual enlightenment and amusement. During the evenings, residents often would participate in entertainment such as charades and musical and dramatic performances. Some evenings were devoted to scholarship, with George Ripley lecturing on various philosophers or Sophia Ripley reading aloud from literary classics. A favorite pastime was dancing.

Residents were paid on the basis of time spent working rather than on the tasks performed, and they were allowed to choose their own tasks and their working hours. Emerson, who had disappointed Ripley by not becoming a member, pointed out one of the weaknesses of the community: "One man plowed all day, and one looked out the window all day, and perhaps drew his own picture; and both received the same wages."

Elizabeth Palmer Peabody

Peabody, publisher of *The Dial*, is shown here in her seventies. She also published the early works of Nathaniel Hawthorne and pamphlets of the Anti-Slavery Society, and she ran a bookshop in Boston that was a gathering place for literary figures. Somehow she found time to start one of the first kindergartens in the United States and the first kindergarten training school.

After six years, Brook Farm had attracted more than one hundred forty associates, but the community also was encountering many difficulties. During the latter half of its existence, it had been reorganized as a "phalanstery," which promoted the beliefs of the French socialist philosopher François Fourier. In 1847, the property was sold to the town of West Roxbury, which used it as a poor farm. During the Civil War, the site was used as a training encampment, parade ground, and munitions storage area. Later it was purchased and presented to the Lutheran Organization, which for many years ran a children's home on the site.

None of the original buildings from Brook Farm is still standing. A suspicious fire destroyed the Margaret Fuller cottage in 1985. This 175-acre tract is one of the largest pieces of undeveloped land left in the greater Boston area.

Fruitlands

Bronson Alcott, who was present when George Ripley first explained the idea for Brook Farm to Emerson and Margaret Fuller, did not think the community was "austere enough." In June 1843, he and an Englishman named Charles Lane led a

Philosopher A. Bronson Alcott, disillusioned with "modern" life, brought his family to this rural setting in 1843 for a short experiment in utopian community living. Ten-year-old Louisa May Alcott's journal of this experience is part of the Fruitlands collection. Today junior volunteers interpret life at the Fruitlands Farmhouse.

group of people they called the Consociate Family to Harvard, Massachusetts (about thirty miles west of Boston), where they had "made arrangements with the proprietor...of about a hundred acres which liberates this tract from human ownership." They named this community Fruitlands because a grove of ten apple trees was located on the property.

Among the members of this family were Alcott; his wife, Abigail "Abba" May, and four daughters; Charles Lane; William Lane; Abram Wood (who asserted his individuality by reversing the order of his names and became known as Wood Abram); Samuel Bower; Anna Page; and Joseph Palmer.

Life in this "New Eden," which Alcott called it, was certainly austere. The members were not allowed to eat meat or to use any product that had "caused wrong or death to man or beast." (Anna Page left after being scolded for eating fish at a neighbor's table.) They had intended to use only spades to till their fields, but the rocky New England soil proved too much for them, and they eventually allowed Palmer to use his oxen. Because he plowed the fields, they looked the other way when one of the oxen turned out to be a cow and Palmer sneaked forbidden drinks of milk. Because Alcott and Lane were busy traveling

about spreading the word of their experiment, most of the hard work was done by the Alcott women and the practical Palmer.

Alcott's daughter Louisa May, who later became famous as the author of *Little Women,* kept a diary of life at Fruitlands, which gives us a picture of how they spent their days: "I rose at five and had my bath. I love cold water! Then we had our singing lesson.... After breakfast I washed dishes, and ran on the hill till nine and I had some thoughts — it was so beautiful up there. Did my lessons — wrote and spelt and did sums.... We had bread and fruit for dinner. I read and walked and played till supper-time. We sung in the evening."

By December 1843, less than six months after Fruitlands' beginning, many of the original members of the community were gone, Lane and Alcott were in disagreement, and Mrs. Alcott had moved with her four daughters to a more comfortable home nearby. After the property was abandoned, Joseph Palmer bought the farm, renamed it Freelands, and for many years ran a hostel for the homeless on the site.

Although both Brook Farm and Fruitlands proved to be unsuccessful on both practical and financial grounds, many people believe they were successful as spiritual experiments. At the end of Hawthorne's *The Blithedale Romance,* the character Miles Coverdale states what is probably true of both these communities: "More and more I feel that we had struck upon what OUGHT to be a truth. Posterity may dig it up, and profit by it."

Fruitlands (top) and the Shaker Museum (above). The Shaker Museum was originally an office building at Harvard Shaker Village in Massachusetts and was moved to Fruitlands in 1920. The museum is set up to give visitors a sense of the Shaker philosophy and many Shaker activities, including weaving, basket making, and seed journeys (extended trips to collect seeds).

5

AMERICA TRANSFORMED: SCIENCE, EXPLORATION, AND TRANSPORTATION

Long before people began referring to that special talent called

"American know-how,"

nineteenth-century Americans showed that they knew exactly how.

They knew how to explore, invent, and devise the most extraordinary things. In so doing, they transformed their country and eventually changed the entire world.

No obstacle, whether formed by man or God, seemed too large to be overcome by American know-how. The United States boasted mighty rivers, so Robert Fulton invented the perfect vehicle to ride them: the steamboat. America's western territories seemed too vast to reach, so Americans blazed new trails, introduced the stagecoach, and finally built a thick web of railroads. And when this coast-to-coast nation seemed to be too big to permit its people to keep in touch, the Pony Express appeared to deliver its mail, followed by the telegraph, carrying coded messages so quickly that some people believed that mail would no longer be necessary.

American ingenuity should have brought the country closer together. But other forces were driving Americans farther apart. That was the great tragedy of American know-how in the Civil War era.

STEAMBOATING IN AMERICA

by Brenda Pollock

The golden age of steamboating came during the 1840s, when Mark Twain was a boy. In "Old Times on the Mississippi," Twain wrote about the fascination he and his friends had with this new form of travel: "When I was a boy there was

163

STEAMBOAT "CLERMONT" — 1861

The *Clermont*, the "first practical steamboat," was introduced in 1807 and used until the 1860s. Steamboats declined in use with the start of the Civil War and the coming of the railroad.

but one permanent ambition among my comrades in our village on the west bank of the Mississippi River. That was to be a steamboat man."

When Twain was born, hundreds of steamboats traveled the rivers, but only a generation before, people had scoffed at Robert Fulton when he launched the first successful steamboat. Inventors had tried for years to find a workable and safe way to harness steam power. Fulton, with help from Robert Livingston and a steam engine made by Englishman James Watt, became the first man to create a practical steamboat.

The people who laughed at Fulton's boat called it "Fulton's Folly," but its real name was the *Clermont*. On August 17, 1807, the *Clermont* went from New York City up the Hudson River to Albany. It made the 150-mile trip in a remarkable 33 hours. Fulton's boat had cabins for passengers and space for cargo, while two side paddle wheels drove it upriver.

A few years later, Nicholas Roosevelt, great-great-uncle of President Theodore Roosevelt, steamed all the way from Pittsburgh, Pennsylvania, to New Orleans, Louisiana. He was an inventor and engineer who wanted to prove that steam power was safe for travel. Roosevelt demonstrated his confidence in his steamboat, the *New Orleans*, by having his wife, who was expecting a child, accompany him on the trip. They stopped in Louisville, Kentucky, where their child was born, and then continued down the Mississippi. After three months on the water, they arrived safely in New Orleans.

After the success of the *Clermont* and the *New Orleans*, Robert Fulton continued to improve his boats, and other inventors added new concepts. Henry Shreve designed a boat with a broad, flat bottom, which made it possible for it to float in shallow water. He gave steamboats their "wedding cake" appearance

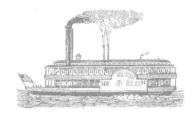

by putting the engines on the first deck, then adding another deck for the boilers. On top of that, he put the hurricane deck, the officers quarters, and the pilothouse. Because his boats were steadier than other steamboats, other designers copied his ideas.

Improvements continued. Soon steamboats could carry tons of freight, and passenger areas became more luxurious. Steamboat companies made their boats as grand as possible. The paddle wheel boxes sported brightly colored paintings, and the fancy woodwork made the boats look like gingerbread houses. Bells and three-toned whistles announced the arrival of a riverboat, and people ran down to the levees just to watch it pass.

Often the inside of the boat was as ornate as the outside. The large dining rooms had parquet floors and mirrors lining the walls. For the convenience of the passengers, the boats had a laundry, nursery, barbershop, bridal suite, and saloon.

Steamboats were extravagant, but they were workers, too. Farms located in the rich Ohio and Mississippi River valleys produced cotton, tobacco, hemp, and livestock. Steamboats became useful as a means of transporting these products to markets along the rivers. They also traveled up the Missouri River to facilitate the fur trade. They even carried soldiers and U.S. Army supplies as far north as Montana via the Yellowstone River.

In spite of their usefulness and elegance, however, there was great concern about their safety. Between 1810 and 1850, an estimated four thousand people were killed in riverboat accidents, which were caused by boiler explosions, low water, wind, storms, fires, and poor maintenance. (Mark Twain's younger brother, Henry, was killed in a steamboat explosion.)

There were no government regulations requiring owners to take safety measures. In addition, until 1850 there were no water pressure gauges, so engine crews had to rely on guesswork to run the boilers. Speed was emphasized more

Paddle-wheel steamboats still travel the Mississippi River today.

than good sense. Crews often raced with other boats or ran at high speeds just for the fun of it.

By 1860, there were about a thousand steamboats in use. But when the Civil War began in 1861, steamboat travel gradually declined. The Civil War encouraged development of steam power to drive locomotives, ushering in the railroad age. Trains could carry people and supplies faster than boats, and the routes did not have to follow waterways. The war also changed the plantation economy of the South, as America moved into an industrial boom. Soon railroads served every major city, and the steamboat was no longer needed.

Mark Twain eventually fulfilled his boyhood dream and became a licensed riverboat pilot. His career was cut short when Louisiana seceded from the Union in 1861. Traffic was uncertain and disrupted at that time, and passenger lines were finally shut down in 1862.

Mark Twain never forgot his days as a pilot. The Mississippi River, with its steamboats, was a powerful influence in his life.

THE GREAT RIVER

by Craig E. Blohm

When you think of the Mississippi River, what comes to mind? Perhaps you imagine steamboats with great churning paddle wheels, or barefoot boys poling rafts down the muddy river. These images come from the romantic era that Mark Twain so vividly brought to life in some of his writings. The Mississippi deeply affected Twain, as it did all those who lived on its banks.

The Mississippi River spans the width of the United States, its waters traveling 2,340 miles from Minnesota to the Gulf of Mexico.

Hernando de Soto came to America seeking gold. De Soto established a settlement at Tampa Bay in 1539, then traveled through the present-day states of Florida, Georgia, Tennessee, Alabama, and Mississippi. His party crossed the Mississippi River (shown here "discovering" it) and continued on through what are now Arkansas and Louisiana. De Soto died of fever in 1542 without finding the treasure he sought.

Even before recorded history, Indians in dugout canoes traveled the river, fishing and trading with neighboring tribes. They called it Mecha Sebe — "great river."

The first white man to see the Mississippi was a Spanish explorer, Hernando de Soto. In 1541, de Soto and his army crossed the river in their search for gold. Although de Soto never found his treasure, malaria-carrying mosquitoes found him. He died the next year and was

buried in the river.

Others followed. In 1673, Jacques Marquette and Louis Joliet paddled down the Mississippi, searching the region for converts to Christianity. Nine years later, French explorer René Robert Cavelier, sieur de la Salle, took possession of the region, naming it Louisiana after the French king, Louis XIV. It remained under French or Spanish rule until 1803, when President Thomas Jefferson purchased Louisiana Territory.

Life in the wilderness of the 1800s was never easy, but for the hardy pioneers who settled in the Mississippi Valley, the river had some special surprises in store. The Mississippi was a restless giant, often changing course or widening its channel as it flowed toward the gulf. When the Mississippi changed its course, many a prosperous town found itself without a livelihood, far from the river's banks. Some settlements were completely destroyed by the river. Kaskaskia, once an Indian village and later the capital of Illinois, now lies buried beneath the Mississippi's mud.

Floods, too, made living along the Mississippi uncertain. Melting snow or heavy rains caused the river to rise, sometimes more than fifty feet. Fields, farms, and towns for miles around were washed out. As early as 1727, man-made walls of earth, called levees, were built to hold back the river. These early dikes were too small to contain the rushing waters of the great river, and destructive flooding continued throughout the 1800s. Finally, in 1879, the Mississippi River Commission was established to coordinate flood prevention efforts.

On June 16, 1858, water from the Mississippi broke over the levee in St. Louis, Missouri, flooding everything in sight. Though not the highest flood to date — that had occurred in 1844 — it was the first flood captured by a photographer.

Commerce on the Mississippi flourished in the 1800s. In a land with few roads, the river was the only practical way to transport goods to market. Flatboats and keelboats carried produce, livestock, and passengers south to Natchez, Mississippi, and New Orleans, Louisiana. Beef, butter, hides, hay, cheese, and chickens were just a few of the goods that traveled down the Mississippi from as far away as New York.

When the first steamboat, the *New Orleans,* landed at its namesake city on January 12, 1812, a new age of trade began. By 1833, about a thousand steamboats traveled up and down the river. New towns sprang up along the muddy banks, and factories were built.

The steamboat years were the most colorful in the river's history. Well-dressed riverboat gamblers, rich plantation owners, and muscular roustabouts could be seen at nearly every large river port. It must have seemed as though the Mississippi Valley's prosperity would last forever. But war and a new invention brought an end to the boom years.

When the Civil War divided the country, the Union army sought to split the Confederacy by taking control of the Mississippi River. In 1862, Union admiral David Farragut captured the port city of New Orleans. By June 1863, the Mississippi, from the Gulf of Mexico to Vicksburg, Mississippi, belonged to the North. Union supply ships and gunboats replaced commercial traffic on the river. When the Confederacy fell, so did many of the large southern plantations that had made the Mississippi a great trading river.

The invention of the railroad was the final blow to the Mississippi's reign as queen of American commerce. Trains had begun to move west as early as 1840. In 1854, the first locomotive crossed the great river by ferry. Before long, bridges spanned the river, and trains began carrying goods more economically than steamboats. By 1877, only one steamboat line was left to serve the dwindling Mississippi River trade.

Although the steamboat is gone, the Mississippi River remains an active and mighty waterway. Today barges carrying cargo move up and down the river. People also visit the river to see an important part of America's natural heritage.

TAMING THE MIGHTY WATERS
by Karen H. Dusek

Trappers, explorers, and settlers of the American frontier quickly recognized the importance of the Mississippi River to trade and transportation and also as the source of the fertile soil that spread for miles from its shores. They soon learned that the mighty river could not be easily tamed, however. Strong currents, sandbars, fog, ice floes, snags, sawyers, planters, and rafts* were routine navigating hazards, while destructive floods regularly threatened the homes and families of those who settled near its shores.

Early settlers plowed up sandbars in the hope that the loosened sand would be washed away and built homemade levees in an effort to keep back floodwaters. It

The steam snagboat *A.H. Sevier* from *Taylor and Crooks Sketchbook of St. Louis,* 1858.

*Snags are logs in the river. Planters are snags held firmly in the river bottom by silt. Sawyers are snags that bob up and down with the motion of the river. Rafts are groups of logs floating together in a large mass.

soon became obvious, however, that more sophisticated techniques were needed to make the river safe for navigation and its shores safe for development.

The federal government stepped in in 1824 with the passage of the first River and Harbor Act. It made the Army Corps of Engineers responsible for "the improvement of seaports and internal waterways" and provided twenty-five thousand dollars for navigation improvement projects, mainly snag removal, on the Mississippi and Ohio rivers.

Before the 1830s, snags caused more than two-fifths of all the steamboat accidents on rivers in the West. Concerned about this problem in the 1820s, Secretary of War John C. Calhoun wrote steamboat captains asking for ideas about snag removal. Captain Henry Shreve replied that he had invented a boat that would pull snags from the water. His letter was never answered, but after two other men tried and failed, he was named superintendent of western waters and later allowed to try his snagboat, the *Heliopolis*.

The *Heliopolis* was an odd-looking two-hulled contraption. Known as "Uncle Sam's Tooth Pullers," snagboats could wrench loose logs anchored beneath ten to twenty feet of sand and weighing as much as seventy-five tons. They became the heroes of the Mississippi, saving steamboat owners thousands of dollars. In 1828, losses from snags on the Mississippi totaled more than one hundred thousand dollars. Just two years later, snags claimed only one small boat.

Despite Shreve's success, snags continued to take their toll. A steady supply was provided by the loose, unstable soil along the riverbanks, which gave way easily, especially on curves, where the water ran head-on into land. In some areas, as much as four hundred feet of soil eroded into the river each year. This not only added snags to the river, but it also caused other problems. Farmers lost valuable land. Harbors could not be built on river bends, where the water was deepest and therefore best suited for boat docks. Channels filled with silt, causing the river to change course. And huge sandbars formed, obstructing boat traffic.

Such a sandbar began to build near St. Louis during the 1820s when the river changed course, threatening to landlock the harbor. Plowing the bar proved useless, so the city asked the federal government for help. The Corps of Engineers sent two officers, Lieutenant Robert E. Lee and Second Lieutenant Montgomery C. Meigs, in response.

Dikes were built on opposite ends of a second sandbar, known as Bloody Island, to direct the current across the new bar (Duncan's Island) and, with luck, wash it away. The strategy seemed to be working when federal funds were

The Mississippi River Commission was created in 1879 to oversee navigation improvements. The waterfront at St. Louis is shown during an inspection trip by the Mississippi River Commission on October 25, 1909.

MIKE FINK: KEELBOAT KING
by Vivian Hartig

"Back out! Mannee! Throw your pole wide — and brace off — or you'll run against a snag!"

That's Mike Fink, king of the keelboatmen. See him standing tall at the front of the running board — hair bleached and skin darkened by the sun. They say he does the work of six men; they say he's half horse, half alligator.

Hear him sing as he and his men work their boat up the river:

> Hard upon the beech oar!
> She moves too slow!
> All the way to Shawneetown,
> Long while ago.

Mike is a legend around these parts. He can outshoot any man on the Mississippi. Why, he once beat ol' Davy Crockett in a shooting match. And his famous "shooting the cup" trick is the talk of the river. He can shoot a whiskey cup atop a man's head from one hundred paces.

Mike was a crack shot even when he was a boy. He won every contest he entered. He was so good that folks would offer him part of the prize beef not to compete!

Mike became an Indian scout when he was seventeen. It was the natural thing for him to do, growing up outside Fort Pitt in Pennsylvania and being so handy with a rifle. He roamed the woods west of the fort looking for Indians. They were a big problem in those days, but after "Mad Anthony" Wayne defeated them in 1794, the Indians left Fort Pitt in peace. So Mike was out of a job.

He joined a keelboat crew. Keelboating gave him the freedom and adventure he had had as a scout. The pay was good, too — about a dollar a day. Mike was on his way.

> As we go — as we go
> Down the O-hi-o,
> There's a tight place at Louisville
> You know, boys, know.

Mike soon became captain of his own boat, and what a beauty she was! Seventy-five feet from pointed bow to pointed stern, she rode high on the water, ready to take on the challenges of the Mississippi River.

Now, anything that floats can carry iron and glass bottles downriver, but nothing is faster than a keelboat. Even in low

Mike Fink, a keelboatman, was known for his rowdy ways and the fact that he could outshoot any man on the Mississippi.

water, Mike can make the run from Pittsburgh, Pennsylvania, to New Orleans, Louisiana, in less than three weeks. Of course, a keelboat is the only craft to make it back upriver. After loading up with cotton, tobacco, and sugar, Mike and his crew begin the backbreaking task of moving against the mighty Mississippi current.

If the wind's just right, they can set sail. But more likely, you'll see the crew running back and forth along the sides of the keelboat, pushing it forward with long poles. In some places, the river bottom is too muddy or deep for poling. Then Mike and his men tie long ropes, or cordelles, to the mast and pull the boat upstream. The banks of the Mississippi are uneven, muddy, and covered with rocks and trees. Cordelling thirty tons of cargo is a hard way to earn a living! Even with twenty men working, keelboats average only fifteen miles a day. That's more than four months from New Orleans back to Pittsburgh.

Time hangs heavy when you work hard every day, and Mike

cut off, bringing the project to a halt. Floods in 1844 and 1851 seriously damaged the work that had been done, but the project was finally completed in 1856. Duncan's Island eventually disappeared, as hoped, and Bloody Island became part of East St. Louis.

The river was not always that easy to control, however. In the 1830s, a sandbar near Memphis, Tennessee, grew to a length of one thousand feet in just two years. Shrubs and willows grew up so quickly that it looked as though the bar was there to stay. A navy yard was built on the convenient new island. Thirty years later, the island washed away, taking the navy yard with it.

Sandbars also caused problems for boat captains. In dry seasons, boats often ran aground. Cargo had to be transferred from oceangoing vessels to flat-bottomed riverboats before proceeding upriver. River interest groups begged the federal government to maintain a channel deep enough to allow safe year-round passage. Using a combination of dredging, canals, levees, jetties, and revetments ("mattresses" placed on riverbanks to help prevent erosion), the river was made navigable under most conditions.

The Mississippi River Commission was created in 1879 to oversee navigation improvements, but it was not until the devastating back-to-back floods of 1912 and 1913 that the federal government finally understood the connection between navigation and flood control. Flood control remained the responsibility of state and local governments until the Flood Control Act of 1917, which transferred responsibility to the federal government.

The flood of 1927, which killed about 300 people and 165,000 head of livestock and forced 700,000 people to evacuate, changed the way the Corps of Engineers looked at flood control. Since 1861, the Corps had considered levees the only reliable means of control, but this flood was so destructive that they began to experiment with other methods. Cutoffs, which shortened the river at

---

likes to add excitement to his trips. One day he passed a field full of sheep and thought fresh mutton would taste good. He rubbed some tobacco in the faces of several sheep, then called the farmer and pointed out how strangely the sheep were acting. He said they had the black murrain (plague) and should be shot to prevent infecting the entire flock. The farmer, knowing Mike's reputation with a rifle, begged Mike to shoot them. He did so, and threw the dead sheep into an eddy, where they were retrieved after dark. The next night, Mike and his crew enjoyed fresh mutton for dinner.

That Mike Fink — he's something else!

In 1811, the first steamboat appeared on the Mississippi. The ease with which it was able to move upriver made it popular with everyone but the keelboatmen.

In 1822, Mike Fink, disgusted with how civilized the river was becoming, joined a trapping expedition with two friends, Carpenter and Talbott. They left from St. Louis in the early spring and traveled into the Rocky Mountains, where they wintered at Fort Henry on the Yellowstone River.

It was there that Fink met his end. He was performing his famous cup-shooting trick when he aimed too low and shot Carpenter in the forehead. Talbott, in a rage, shot Fink.

Mike Fink may have died in the Rockies, but his legend will live forever on the Mississippi River:

> I can out-run, out-hop, out-jump, throw down, drag
> out, and lick any man in the country.
> I'm a Salt-River roarer; I love the wimming an' I'm
> chock full of fight.

curves, made it run faster and scour a deeper channel. Reservoirs held excess water, and man-made outlets let overflow water escape.

Despite the new emphasis on flood control, the damage caused by floods increased as time went on simply because the population was increasing at a steady pace. Record-setting floods in 1973 and 1993 forced the evacuation of thousands of people and caused millions of dollars' worth of damage, although the results would have been much worse if there had been no protection.

During the past two centuries, much of the Mississippi's wildness has been tamed with canals and locks, dams and jetties, levees and revetments. People who appreciated the river's wild qualities watched the effects these changes were having on the surrounding environment with increasing concern. In the 1960s, those concerns were addressed in a number of congressional acts, and the desire to control the great river gradually gave way to a desire to protect it.

The Falls of St. Anthony, Minnesota, shown here around 1884, was a busy trading post.

HOW MIGHTY IS THE MISSISSIPPI?

by Maurine V. Eleder

Flowing down through the center of the United States, the Mississippi River seems to cut the country in two. But throughout our history, it has actually helped to tie the nation together. Ten states border the Mississippi. Streams and rivers flow into it from more states in the Northwest (Montana), Southwest (Texas), Northeast (Pennsylvania), and Southeast (North Carolina). A lake surrounded by spruce bogs and pine forests in Minnesota's north woods marks its beginning, and the Louisiana bayou at the Gulf of Mexico marks its end.

As American settlers moved westward — first across the Appalachian Mountains and then across the Mississippi — it was difficult and expensive to transport supplies from the East Coast. The Mississippi and its more than two hundred fifty tributaries became river highways, providing a convenient and swift way to transport goods.

Fur traders using canoes were the first Europeans to use the river highway. As early as 1705, French fur traders floated fifteen thousand bear and deer hides from the Wabash River down the Mississippi to trading posts in Louisiana. Trading posts might be built where two rivers met or at portages, areas where the men had to carry the canoes over land.

The portage at the Falls of St. Anthony in Minnesota was a busy trading post. Acres of forest surrounded the post. It did not take long for enterprising men to realize they could earn a living by cutting trees and floating them down the river to sell. They lashed the logs together to form rafts 700 feet long and 135 feet wide. Crews of ten to twenty men guided them. A bustling lumber industry developed as huge sawmills, operated by waterpower, were built to cut timber into usable sizes.

A levee can also be a landing place. The St. Louis levee for steamboats is shown here in 1853.

Families from East Coast states such as Virginia and North Carolina took advantage of low-priced land in the western territories along the central Mississippi River. They used rafts and flatboats to carry furniture, clothing, and tools brought by wagons from the East. The flatboats were log "boxes" twenty to sixty feet long with sides two to three feet high. Carried by the current and guided by long oars at both ends, they were often taken apart at the end of the voyage and used to build houses. Keelboats, narrow and thirty to seventy-five feet long, could carry fifteen to forty tons of cargo. Towns often developed at the settlers' landings.

Plantation owners in the warm southern states grew acres of cotton, tobacco, and sugar cane. Instead of transporting the goods overland to the port of New York, they found it easier and cheaper to haul it to the Mississippi River and float it downriver to New Orleans, Louisiana, where it could be loaded aboard oceangoing ships and sold in England.

Ships from Europe docking at New Orleans brought Irish and German immigrants. They traveled up the river and its tributaries to settle in towns such as St. Louis, Missouri, and Cincinnati, Ohio. The growing population along the river and its tributaries meant more business for traders and merchants.

In 1762, Spain gained control of the lower Mississippi River. The Spanish limited the number of ships and collected fees for using the port of New Orleans. Four decades later, in 1803, President Thomas Jefferson arranged the Louisiana Purchase, giving the United States control of the entire river, which was already dominated by American boatmen.

The river itself caused problems with its strong downstream currents, boul ders, floods, shallow areas, rapids, and falls. Steamboats provided a solution to these problems.

Shipbuilders in Pennsylvania experimented with steam power for use on the river. The steam-driven *New Orleans* was launched in Pittsburgh in 1811. Its engine was not very powerful, and it could chug downstream at only three miles per hour. But engine builders made rapid progress. By 1817, the double-decked *Washington* made the roundtrip from New Orleans to Louisville, Kentucky, in forty-one days.

Panoramic view of New Orleans, with Federal ships anchored in the Mississippi River on April 25, 1862.

During the golden age of the steamboat (1830–1860), New Orleans had fifty boats lined up at its docks to handle hourly arrivals and departures of passengers and cargo. About a thousand steamboats traveled the river. They carried supplies for settlers and cargo to be exported, including lead, indigo, corn, and wheat. They also carried products imported from other countries, such as coffee, soap, shoes, and textiles.

As railroads were built and began carrying passengers and cargo both along the river and across it, steamboats gradually disappeared. But World War I brought new life to river trade when railroads and trucks were not able to handle all the cargo that needed to be moved. By 1931, barges moved twice as much cargo along the river as had been transported in any one year during the steamboat era. Today's river barges can weigh more than three hundred tons. They are lashed together with steel cables to form huge tows of fifty to sixty barges.

The Mississippi River spurred the growth of many cities. The "Twin Cities" of Minneapolis and St. Paul, Minnesota, owe much of their development to the river's waterpower. After the success of the early fur-trading and lumber industries, families from New England, New York, and the Great Lakes states were attracted to the area. Many settled on the prairie and grew wheat. Aided by loans from the prospering lumber industry, businessmen built flour mills — operated by Mississippi River waterpower — to grind the wheat. Traders shipped the grain and flour to other towns along the Mississippi. St. Paul, named after the church built by Father Lucian Galtier in 1841, became the main trading center on the upper Mississippi. Minneapolis, led by businessmen such as Dorilus Morrison, the Washburn brothers, and John S. Pillsbury, became a major milling center.

The Mississippi also helped increase the population and industry of Pittsburgh, more than five hundred miles east of the river. Pittsburgh's factories manufactured products for settlers, and its link to the Mississippi via the Ohio River made them easy and inexpensive to ship. The need for factory workers and dockworkers drew men and their families to the city.

Farther down the Mississippi, Memphis, Tennessee, was a major center for selling cotton and a favorite stopping point for showboats. Blues musicians traveled up and down the river, spreading a new type of music that changed America's popular music.

One of the largest oil refineries in the United States was built in Baton Rouge, Louisiana. Raw oil from fields in Texas, Louisiana, and Mississippi is brought down the river to be refined into gasoline, jet fuel, grease, and wax and is then shipped in barges or tankers all over the world.

The Mississippi River ends at New Orleans, a city rich in history. You can still visit the Vieux Carré (Old Square), which dates back to its founding by the French in 1722. Spain controlled the city and the river between 1762 and 1800, but the city never lost its French language and culture. In 1805, New Orleans was incorporated as a U.S. city. It has expanded on either side of the river and upward with modern skyscrapers. Steamboats, now an important part of the tourist industry, still travel the Mississippi, as well as the Ohio, Cumberland, and Tennessee rivers.

For more than two hundred years, New Orleans has been an important seaport. Today it ranks with New York as a major port of commerce in the United States. Industrial growth along the river between New Orleans and Baton Rouge now includes oil refineries, grain elevators, and petrochemical and other factories. "The mighty Mississippi" — builder of cities and industry — is not about to give up its title.

BUNTING, BURDINE, AND THE STAGECOACH LINES

by Shari Lyn Zuber

Competition was fierce among stagecoach lines and drivers on the National Road* during the early 1800s. Stagecoach service began in the Colonies in the early 1700s. After the American Revolution, stage companies grew as they provided the main form of public transportation in the new states. People traveling on business, going to visit family, or taking any other trip depended on the stagecoach to get them where they wanted to go if they did not wish to travel on horseback or did not own a suitable traveling coach.

A Concord Coach travels in Nova Scotia, Canada, around 1900.

When the first section of the National Road was completed in 1818, stagecoaches were soon rolling down it. In 1785, Congress had approved mail delivery by stage, so as the high-riding coaches began to carry passengers down the road, they also brought mail, newspapers, and presidential messages that kept people informed.

Stagecoach traffic was heaviest between the 1820s and the 1840s. Stage companies competed for passengers and postal contracts (which provided an exemption from paying road tolls). Three major lines eventually emerged: James Reeside's

*The National Road was originally intended to extend from Cumberland, Maryland, to the Ohio River, but it was later extended to Vandalia, Illinois. Construction began in 1811 and ended in 1839.

The old stage coach in its golden day
Rolled proudly on with its cheerful load.
And claimed from all the full right of way,
A monarch then of the turnpike road.
But now the day of its pride is o'er;
It yields the palm to the railway train;

The dear old friend so loved of yore,
We ne'er shall look on its like again.
Then, ho! for the days of the turnpike road,
The prancing steeds and the brisk approach,
The mellow horn, and the merry load
That used to ride in the old stage coach.

Coaches being shipped by the Abbot, Downing & Company of Concord, New Hampshire, to the Wells Fargo & Co. Terminus on April 15, 1868.

Good Intent Lines; the National Road Stage Company, under the presidency of Lucius W. Stockton; and the lines of Neil, Moore, and Company.

Sometimes this rivalry led to risk taking and daredevil stunts. Neil, Moore, and Company advertised itself as the "Citizens' Line," reducing fares and pushing for increased speed to keep up with the other companies. Stockton provided coaches to locations off the main road, as well as daily service and "rides in elegance." Reeside promised fast, safe service, although drivers were told to "make the time, or we'll find somebody who will." When Conestoga wagoners taking freight west or drovers taking livestock to market heard the long blast of the coach driver's horn, they were expected to clear the road and make way for the stagecoach.

Taverns along the road provided rest for weary travelers and became the source of legends about the feats of stage drivers. Two of the most famous drivers were Peter Burdine of Reeside's Good Intent Lines and Redding Bunting of Stockton's National Road Stage Company.

Burdine and Bunting feuded for years, each trying to outdo the other with a faster time or a more daring adventure. Burdine thought that he had Bunting beat when he was scheduled to drive the first Troy coach on the National Road to transport president-elect Andrew Jackson from Cumberland, Maryland, to Washington, D.C. Unfortunately, Jackson took his own carriage to the White House, but Burdine's coach did become known as the *General Jackson.*

Bunting finally accomplished a feat that Burdine could never equal. In 1846, Bunting was chosen to drive from Cumberland to Wheeling, Virginia, carrying

President James Polk's message that war with Mexico had begun. Leaving Cumberland at 2 A.M., his horses flew through the night, miraculously avoiding hazards masked by the darkness. With one stop at 8 A.M. for a change of teams and a quick breakfast, Bunting resumed the breakneck pace and stormed into Wheeling at 2 P.M., having completed the nineteen- to twenty-four-hour trip in only twelve hours.

In the 1850s, stagecoach travel declined as the faster and more comfortable railroads moved in. After the Civil War, stagecoaches rarely traveled the National Road, moving west across the Mississippi River.

THE SANTA FE TRAIL

Great trails carried Americans westward in the 1800s. Across Kentucky to Missouri, then on to Utah, Oregon, California, and the Southwest, these paths took settlers and American goods and ideas into the wilderness. Most routes were carved out for settlers who were heading for new homes and farmland, bringing furniture, dishes, linens, tools, seeds for the first year's crops, and a few treasured personal belongings.

But the Santa Fe Trail was different. It was mainly a trade route and saw few settlers, especially in the beginning. The westbound mule trains and wagon caravans that traveled it carried goods for sale and trade: cloth and clothing, buttons, buckles, handkerchiefs, writing paper, and sewing notions. Alongside those

The title of this painting, *Path of Empire*, refers to the great trails that Americans followed west in the nineteenth century.

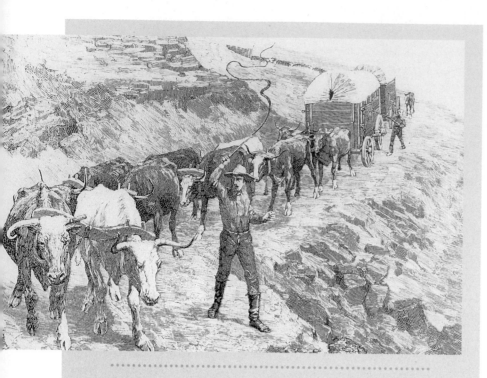

dry goods were pots and pans, soap, coffee, wine, scissors, shovels, axes, and hoes. After New Mexico became U.S. territory in 1848, freighters hauled tobacco, shoes, gunpowder, military supplies, and mining machinery.

All merchandise was welcome at the end of the trail — Santa Fe, New Mexico — which was cut off from civilization by desert on three sides and Spanish laws against foreign trade. Before American traders came to Santa Fe in the 1820s, the settlement received supplies only from Spain. Those goods traveled two thousand miles overland after being shipped to a Mexican port. So much handling made items expensive by the time they reached Santa Fe.

Once the route was open from the American frontier in Missouri, trade was less expensive and business boomed. By 1843, thirty travelers did $450,000 worth of business in Santa Fe. Santa Fe also was a stopping place for some traders who traveled on to Mexico. Many Mexican traders used the trail, too. By 1860, more than 9,000 men, 6,000 mules, nearly 28,000 oxen, and more than 3,000 wagons had made the forty- to sixty-day trek along the trail. Six years later, 5,000 to 6,000 wagons swept across the prairie. By this time, the trail had become a military route. U.S. Army forts were

PACK MULES AND MISSOURI OXEN

by Ellen Hardsog

The unsung heroes of the Santa Fe Trail were the mules and oxen that hauled tons of goods over the prairies and mountains. Pack mules were used by the first traders because they could work longer and harder than horses. Mules were strung together in trains of about twenty animals, each carrying up to three hundred pounds of goods. To handle bigger loads, traders used wagons pulled by four to eight spans of mules (two mules made a span).

Mules were suited for the trail. Their hides were tough, and they could live on buffalo grass and little water. A good mule could work for up to eighteen years. But mules were unpredictable and might run off when loose or stop dead with fright in the middle of a stream. When annoyed, they would kick viciously with their hind legs. Just as tough and ornery as the animals were their drivers. The muleskinners got their name because they boasted that their whips and language would take the skin off a mule's back.

In 1829, Major Bennett Riley introduced oxen to the trail. Traders discovered that oxen were better draft animals than mules. These steers from Missouri thrived on range grass and had large, sure hoofs. Indians would not steal them as they would horses and mules. If food ran out, the travelers could eat them. The men who drove the oxen were known as bullwhackers and were as colorful as the muleskinners. While oxen were easier to manage than mules, they suffered in hot weather and snow. Any unusual event could start a stampede.

built to protect traders from Indian attacks and provide a supply line for the Army. The trail also served as a mail and stagecoach route and a path for gold seekers, settlers, and other adventurers to follow.

But the dust and the glory of the Santa Fe Trail settled very quickly in the 1870s. Railroads had reached Kansas in 1867. Each year the tracks stretched closer to Santa Fe, and traders and travelers rode the train to the tracks' end. In February 1880, the first train steamed into Santa Fe, and the wagons no longer rolled across the prairie.

THE U.S. MAIL ON THE MOVE

by Jane Harrigan

Most of us today take daily mail delivery for granted. But between 1840 and 1880, U.S. mail service was very different from the way it is now. For the people who lived in the days of the Pony Express, receiving a letter was an important event.

First of all, people who mailed letters in 1840 did not use envelopes or stamps. They wrote their letters on one side of a thin piece of paper, often using a quill pen and ink they made themselves. When the letter was finished, the writer would fold the paper, seal it with wax, and address the outside. People tried to keep their letters short because postage rates were based on the number of pages and how far the letter was sent.

For example, mailing a one-page letter in 1840 could cost anywhere from six to twenty-five cents, depending on the distance the letter had to travel. Twenty-five cents may not sound very expensive, but in 1840 people could eat dinner in a restaurant for less money than it cost to mail some letters! Letters were a luxury that few people could afford.

Perhaps the biggest difference between today's postal system and the one in the 1840s was that postage was paid by the person who *received* the letter, not the person who sent it. When you went to the post office to pick up a letter, you had to pay the postmaster before he or she would give it to you. For this reason, many people did not use the U.S. mail to send letters even when they had important news to tell. They were afraid their relatives or friends could not afford to pay for the letter when it arrived. Instead, they would give letters to people who were traveling to the area where their family or friends lived. Many people also used "bootleg" mail services run by companies that carried letters for less money than the government.

RICHARD ERASTUS EGAN, UTAH PONY EXPRESS RIDER

As the postal system became more organized, rates were lowered and more people began using the mail. Stamps were introduced in 1847 so that the sender of a letter could pay the postage. But stamps were not required on letters until 1855, about the time envelopes became popular. At first, many people refused to use stamps. They believed that a letter might never reach its destination and the money for the stamp would be wasted.

Sometimes that fear was justified. The stagecoaches and horseback riders who carried mail faced the danger of attacks by Indians or outlaws. Because of mail theft, some postmasters advised people to cut their paper money in half and send only one half in a letter. When the person on the other end wrote back to say that he or she had received the first half of the money, the second half could be sent.

BILLY FISHER, JOHN FISHER, AND JOHNNY HANCOCK, UTAH PONY EXPRESS RIDERS

In the 1840s . . . postage was paid by the person who received the letter, not the person who sent it.

Sending money this way took a long time because letters moved much more slowly than they do today. In the 1850s, a letter sent by stagecoach in New York took twenty to twenty-five days to arrive in San Francisco. If the letter went by ship around the tip of South America, it could take as long as six months. And if it traveled by steamboat and train across the Isthmus of Panama, the letter would reach California in about thirty-five days. By the late 1860s, the transcontinental railroad had cut that time to about a week.

In both city and country, a trip to the post office was an adventure. Country post offices were often located in stores, and the family of the postmaster helped sort the mail and provide refreshments for the mail riders or stagecoach drivers. About once a week, on the day the mail was scheduled to arrive, farmers from miles around would come to town to shop, talk with neighbors, and see whether anyone had written them a letter.

Cities had big post offices, but city people got just as excited about mail as country people did. In San Francisco in the 1850s, people would start lining up at the post office the day before a steamship was scheduled to arrive with the mail. If a person went to the post office early and got a good place in line, other people might offer to buy his or her place for several dollars.

The reason for all this activity at post offices was that home delivery of mail did not start until 1863. Even then, home delivery was available only in big cities, and it was different from the way we receive mail today. When the mailman came to your house, you paid him a few pennies for each letter he gave you. That was the only way a mail carrier earned money. If no one was home, the mailman did not leave the mail.

Railroads helped people get mail faster and more often. Beginning in 1864, some postal clerks worked inside the trains as they chugged along. The clerks sorted the mail into separate bags for each town along the route. In small towns where the train did not stop, mail was put in a bag and hung from a big hook near the railroad tracks. As the train slowed down, the clerk would reach out the window, unhook the bag of mail the town was sending out, and replace it with a bag of mail addressed to the people in town. If the town had no hook near the tracks, a person would stand and hold out the bag of mail for the clerk to grab as the train went by.

As trains began carrying mail faster and post offices began opening in all the new towns springing up out west, people began relying on the mail more and more. Still, in 1880, twenty years after the Pony Express had come and gone, only about one-quarter of all Americans had mail delivered to their homes. And the average person spent only seventy-two cents a year to mail letters.

This 1830s guide helped drivers navigate the Overland Route, a stagecoach route that began at the Missouri River and ran to the Pacific coast (California).

THE PONY EXPRESS

In 1859, the established mail routes from the East to California were not very reliable. Most of the mail that was sent from coast to coast was loaded onto ships that carried it to the Isthmus of Panama (the narrow strip of land that connects North and South America). Today the Panama Canal has made it possible for ships to sail across the isthmus. But back in 1859, the mail had to be unloaded and carried through several miles of tropical jungle. It was then loaded onto other ships that completed the journey. This roundabout route took approximately twenty-two days.

Another route, called the Overland Route, began at the Missouri River and ran to the Pacific coast. A daily stagecoach service carried passengers, freight, and mail all the way to California. It usually took about twenty-five days to make the journey, but the service could not guarantee that the mail would get through. This fact was troublesome to many people.

The promise of both telegraph and railroad service across the continent made most people impatient for improvements in the way mail was delivered. In California, people were especially impatient because they knew that the northern and southern states were in strong disagreement over slavery and other issues. Should war break out between the two regions, the people of California worried that they might not receive any news for weeks. Telegraph service from the East went only as far as the Missouri River, and the mail routes would almost certainly be delayed.

That was one of the reasons an independent horse express across the Great Plains to California seemed like a good idea. William H. Russell, of the freighting firm Russell, Majors & Waddell, believed that the mail should have its own service that could guarantee delivery. He called it the Pony Express and boasted that it would get the mail from Missouri to California faster than any other company. He hoped that the Pony Express would solve the mail delivery problem until telegraph lines could be completed.

After a few months of preparation, Russell placed an advertisement in the *New York Herald* and the *Missouri Republican,* two prominent newspapers of the time. The ad explained how the Pony Express was supposed to work so that people would want to use it:

☞ PONY EXPRESS ☜

THE FIRST COURIER ON THE PONY EXPRESS WILL LEAVE THE MISSOURI RIVER ON TUESDAY, APRIL 3RD, AT 5 O'CLOCK P.M., AND WILL RUN REGULARLY WEEKLY THEREAFTER, CARRYING LETTER MAIL ONLY....

TELEGRAPHIC MESSAGES FROM ALL PARTS OF THE UNITED STATES AND CANADA, IN CONNECTION WITH THE POINT OF DEPARTURE WILL BE RECEIVED UP TO 5 O'CLOCK P.M. OF THE DAY OF LEAVING, AND TRANSMITTED...TO SAN FRANCISCO AND INTERMEDIATE POINTS BY THE CONNECTING EXPRESS IN EIGHT DAYS.

THE LETTER MAIL WILL BE DELIVERED IN SAN FRANCISCO IN TEN DAYS FROM THE DEPARTURE OF THE EXPRESS.

Today when we hear about express mail, we think of delivery by jets, not ponies, and certainly not by teenage boys sitting on top of a mail pouch, riding as fast as they can in a long-distance relay! But in 1860, the Pony Express did prove to be the fastest and surest way of getting mail to California.

The Pony Express has become one of the most famous organizations in American history. It is also probably one of the most misunderstood. The stories that have come down to us over the years are often more legendary than factual, partly because so many of the original records have been lost. It is important to remember that the Pony Express was organized at approximately the same time as the start of the Civil War. St. Joseph, Missouri, was often a place of disorder in 1860 and 1861. Newspapers and important documents were sometimes stolen or lost in fires. Without the information contained in these records, no one is certain about the exact mileage of the Pony Express route. We can only guess what trails the riders took from station to station. Also, we are reasonably cer-

tain that Johnny Fry made the first ride, but the precise account of what happened has been lost. Perhaps it is because the records are hard to find that the Pony Express has become even more intriguing.

Even though the Pony Express put William Russell and his partners out of business, Russell's two other ambitions came true. He did become famous, and he created, for a few short months, the fastest mail in the West.

THE FASTEST MAIL IN THE WEST

by Sue Macy

On January 27, 1860, John W. Russell received a telegram from his father. John worked for Russell, Majors & Waddell, a supply-hauling firm in Leavenworth, Kansas. His father, William H. Russell, was one of the company's founders.

William Russell's message, sent while he was traveling home from Washington, D.C., was brief. He wrote, "Have determined to establish a Pony Express to Sacramento, California, commencing 3rd of April. Time 10 days." Two days later, Russell arrived in Leavenworth to put his ideas into action.

What he really wanted, Russell admitted to one of his partners, was "to build

Johnny Fry

Top: The Pony Express Trail still runs through Wyoming, shown here approaching Rocky Ridge.
Above: Fry was the first Pony Express rider to head out of St. Joseph, Missouri, on April 3, 1860.

a worldwide reputation, even at considerable expense." He planned to do this by creating the fastest mail service the West had ever seen.

Russell, Majors & Waddell would buy 400 of the best horses on the frontier, hire 120 of the bravest young men available, and build station houses every 10 to 15 miles on a route approximately 2,000 miles long.

The men would carry the mail in a giant relay race across the West, changing horses at every station house and passing the letters to a new man every 75 miles.

Russell's scheme was the latest attempt to bring the West closer to the East. California had become the nation's thirty-first state in 1850, but communication between it and the rest of the United States was impossibly slow. In 1860, the nation's telegraph lines reached only as far west as the Missouri River. Messages to California could be tapped out on the telegraph from New York to Missouri in a matter of seconds. Then they had to be brought by stage or rider across 2,000 miles of mountains and deserts.

In the early 1850s, several small companies delivered mail to settlements in various parts of the West. This service was usually slow and unreliable. Then, in 1857, Congress hired a man named John Butterfield to transport letters and small packages west from St. Louis, Missouri. Butterfield's Overland Mail Company ran stagecoaches along a 2,800-mile route that cut across the southern part of the West. Mail was carried for ten cents for one-half ounce and reached San Francisco in twenty-five days. Passengers could ride, too, for a fee of one hundred dollars in gold.

Although Butterfield's service was a success, William Russell was sure he could do better. While in Washington in late 1859, Russell met with Senator William Gwin of California and got the push he needed. Gwin told Russell that his 380,000 fellow Californians needed quicker mail service than Butterfield's. He suggested that a route through the central United States might provide it. The central route was about 800 miles shorter than Butterfield's, although it was more mountainous and more likely to be blocked by snow in winter.

Gwin said that there was another need for a central mail route. At the time, the country was alive with talk of war. Some southern slave states were threatening to secede from the Union if Abraham Lincoln, the antislavery presidential candidate, was elected in November. If the South seceded, said Gwin, they would probably take over Butterfield's southern mail route. This might help them convince California to secede, too. A central mail route would keep communication open between California and the North, and it would probably help keep California in the Union.

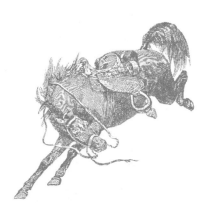

After hearing Gwin's arguments, Russell decided that a central mail route was a good gamble. On his way home from Washington, he got ready to sell his partners on the idea. William Russell, Alexander Majors, and William Waddell had been in business together for five years. In that time, they had become the best-known supply haulers in the West. In 1855, their first year together, the partners had sent out twenty wagon trains carrying 2.5 million pounds of supplies to U.S. Army forts and California settlements. In 1855 and 1856, the firm made $300,000 from Army deliveries alone.

Then the tide changed. In 1857, Russell, Majors & Waddell lost half a million dollars when one of its wagon trains was destroyed. Although the firm did well in other projects after that, it never made up for the loss. If the partners agreed to go ahead with the Pony Express, they would first have to raise the one hundred thousand dollars needed to get the mail service off the ground.

Majors and Waddell were not happy about Russell's scheme, but they gave in when Russell told them he had given his word to Senator Gwin. Russell quickly found an old friend, Ben Holladay, who was willing to put up the money for supplies and salaries. Then he divided the long route into five parts and chose a division leader for each.

It was up to these leaders to hire riders and station managers, buy horses, and see that station houses were built and stocked with food. They had a head start when it came to the station houses. About ninety were already standing, serving as stops for California-bound stagecoaches and supply wagons. The division leaders had to build only one hundred more in the sixty-five days before the Pony Express was scheduled to start running.

When it came to horses and men, the Pony Express took the best they could

1 · 2 · 3 · 4

Harry Roff (in the white pants), shown here with unidentified Pony Express officials, is credited by some as being the first rider out of California.

find. Division leaders paid as much as $200 each for Iowa thoroughbreds and California mustangs — horses known for their power and speed. The riders had to be light, strong, and fearless. Most were about twenty years old and weighed under 125 pounds. They were paid $50 a month, plus room and board. All of them had to sign a pledge written by Alexander Majors, in which they promised not to drink liquor, fight, or use bad language.

As April 3, 1860, approached, people on both ends of the Pony Express route started wondering whether the service would succeed. One California newspaper warned that the route was too dangerous, with unfriendly Indians and untraveled trails. Russell and his partners, the paper said, were "simply inviting slaughter upon all the foolhardy young men who have been engaged as riders."

At the same time, more optimistic people in California and the East prepared letters to be carried on the first run. Easterners put their mail on a special railroad train to St. Joseph, Missouri, the eastern starting point of the Pony Express. One of those who was not scared away by the high price of five dollars per half ounce was President James Buchanan. He sent a message to California's Governor John G. Downey congratulating him on the first successful run of the Pony Express.

On April 3, the first rider left St. Joseph at 7:15 P.M. — two hours late. It was not the speeches, the music, or the crowds of people gathered in the streets that delayed him. It was the messenger with the mail from the East. The man missed one of his train connections and had to be rushed in on a special express.

Despite the delay, the first westward Pony Express run brought the mail to Sacramento in nine days and twenty-three hours — one hour early. The eastbound run to St. Joseph took ten days to the minute. In the months to come, Pony Express riders would knock hours and even days off these times. Riders

WHO'S WHO OF THE PONY EXPRESS

by William Robertson

William Russell

☛ **William M. Gwin,** a senator from California, originated the idea of forming the Pony Express as a publicity stunt to attract attention to a central mail route from St. Joseph, Missouri, to Sacramento, California. He believed that such a route would be much faster than the southern one used by the Overland Mail Company. Gwin promised to obtain government money for anyone who would put his project into practice.

☛ **William Russell,** a financier and politician, was the brains behind the Russell, Majors & Waddell freight company, which dominated the overland transportation business in the West before the Civil War. Russell persuaded his business partners to invest five hundred thousand dollars in organizing the Pony Express in the hope that the government would award their company the contract held by the Overland Mail Company. When the Pony Express became a financial failure, Russell attempted to embezzle government bonds to pay off his debts. He was brought to trial but got off on a technicality.

☛ **Sam Hamilton** rode his horse out of Sacramento, California, at dusk on April 3, 1860, and headed east on the opening leg of the Pony Express's first run. At approximately the same time, another rider rode west from St. Joseph, Missouri, to initiate the ten-day mail service.

☛ **Boston Upson** carried the first mail over the summit of the Sierra Nevada. This feat required a great deal of courage. He had to fight his way through a blizzard, gale winds of sixty miles per hour, and snowdrifts fifteen to twenty feet deep. Despite the storm, he carried the mail fifty-five miles in eight hours, walking the last three miles into the summit relay station when his horse could not wade through the snow.

☛ **William F. Cody,** who joined the Pony Express at age fourteen, was credited with riding twenty hours nonstop and covering 322 miles from Red Buttes to Three Crossings, Wyoming. He later won fame as "Buffalo Bull," legendary hunter and scout.

☛ **Richard Erastus Egan** was another long-range Pony Express rider. To enable a friend to visit his sweetheart, Egan rode both his own and his friend's route more than 330 miles. Egan later became a Mormon bishop.

☛ **James Butler Hickok** worked as a station hand for the Pony Express at the age of twenty-three. He later gained notoriety as a scout and deputy U.S. marshal and earned the nickname "Wild Bill." Contrary to legend, Hickok was never a Pony Express rider because he weighed more than the limit of 125 pounds.

☛ **Pony Bob Haslam,** the most famous Pony Express rider, was chosen to carry news of President Abraham Lincoln's inaugural address of March 4, 1861, across western Nevada — a region inflamed by the Paiute Indian war. He delivered the message despite arrow wounds to the jaw and left arm. He was supposed to have traveled 120 miles in a little over eight hours. Haslam also was the record-holding distance rider, supposedly spending thirty-six hours straight in the saddle to cover 380 miles on another mail run.

☛ **Winnemucca,** chief of the Paiute Indians, raided isolated Pony Express stations, killing keepers, stealing horses, and destroying more than half the buildings between Carson City, Nevada, and Utah Lake. His raids slowed down the Pony Express considerably. Sometimes riders were wounded or could not get fresh horses.

San Francisco welcomes the Pony Express on the night of April 13–14, 1860.

would set amazing personal records when they rushed west with news of Lincoln's election, the secession of the southern states, and the outbreak of the Civil War. In March 1861, they would make their fastest trip ever, bringing copies of President Lincoln's inauguration speech from St. Joseph to Sacramento in seven days and seventeen hours.

During their eighteen months in the saddle, the Pony Express riders lived by the motto "The mail must go through." An Indian war in the spring of 1860 made this goal impossible for a few weeks, but in the end it was not the Indians or the weather that stopped the Pony Express. It was the telegraph.

On May 27, 1861, a construction crew put up the first telegraph pole in Omaha, Nebraska, connecting that city with the East. As they worked their way west, another crew started east from California. On October 24, 1861, the two crews met in Salt Lake City, Utah. They joined their wires and thus put the Pony Express out of business. Not even the fastest rider could outrace Samuel Morse's message machine.

When the Pony Express went out of business, Russell, Majors & Waddell did, too. Although the Pony Express had brought in about $500,000 in delivery charges, it had cost about $700,000 to operate. Ben Holladay, the man who had lent William Russell the money for the project, took over the company's property and paid its debts. He ran a stagecoach service on the central route for several years before finally selling out to another firm.

THEY RODE LIKE THE WIND

by Hazel Krantz

Leading his exhausted mustang pony and clutching the *mochila* (pouch) filled with mail, the sixteen-year-old boy staggered through the blizzard to an isolated cabin. After warming him with coffee and a good meal, the kindly settlers begged, "Stay the night. This is no weather in which to ride."

"No, thanks," the boy said, shaking his head. "This is the Pony Express. The mail has to go through."

For eighteen months, teenage boys galloped from St. Joseph, Missouri, to Sacramento, California, a distance of nearly two thousand miles, carrying important mail to settlers, gold prospectors, military forts, and businesses. They rode through blizzards and snowdrifts, over the glittering white salt desert of Utah and the badlands of Nevada, through cloudbursts and heat waves. They fought wolves and were on the lookout for terrifying buffalo stampedes. And for a long time, they kept their weapons ready for Indian ambushes.

When Russell, Majors & Waddell decided to offer the spectacular ten-day service from St. Joseph to Sacramento, they advertised as follows:
Eighty riders were employed at one time. Their boss was Major Howard Egan, an Irishman who had established the Egan Trail of three hundred miles across the desert of Utah and Nevada.

WANTED

YOUNG, SKINNY, WIRY FELLOWS

NOT OVER EIGHTEEN. MUST BE EXPERT RIDERS, WILLING TO RISK DEATH DAILY. ORPHANS PREFERRED.

The boys traveled light, frequently wearing buckskin shirts and pants, slouch hats, and moccasins. The leather mail pouch, called a *mochila* (Spanish for "knapsack"), rested on top of the lightweight saddle. The riders were paid fifty dollars a month.

Stations with fresh horses were spaced 10 to 15 miles apart. Sometimes the riders carried a horn, which they blew as they approached a station so that the keeper could prepare a fresh horse. The riders were supposed to ride a shift of about 75 miles, but sometimes there was no relief rider and they had to continue. One of the most famous riders, fifteen-year-old William Cody, later known as "Buffalo Bill," supposedly stayed in the saddle for 322 miles.

Each rider was supposed to take the following oath: "While I am an employee of Russell, Majors & Waddell, I will under no circumstances use profane language; I will drink no intoxicating liquors, I will not quarrel or fight with any other employee of the firm...so help me God." Then he was handed a leather-bound Bible. Experienced riders sometimes initiated newcomers with teasing and tricks, such as putting prickly pears in their bunks and salt in their coffee, stealing their pants, or jabbing their ponies to make them buck. After the oath was taken and the initiation was over, the riders got down to the business of delivering the mail.

The fastest ride on record was the one carrying President Abraham Lincoln's inaugural address of March 4, 1861, from St. Joseph, where it had been received by telegraph, to Sacramento. The trip took seven days and seventeen hours. Getting Lincoln's words to the people in California was of vital importance. The Civil

Samuel Finley Breese Morse

190

War was brewing, and people on both sides were trying to sway California to their beliefs. The heroes of this trip through March snows were William Campbell and "Pony Bob" Haslam. Haslam supposedly did the stretch of 120 miles from Smith's Creek to Fort Churchill in a little over eight hours, averaging close to fifteen miles per hour!

Most of the boys obeyed the rule about not drinking, although saloonkeepers sometimes tried to lure them with poisonous "mulekick" liquor. The riders did not fight each other, but one station hand got into a shootout with a gang at Rock Creek, Nebraska, which earned him the lifelong name "Wild Bill" Hickok.

Other than Indians, the biggest threat to the stations was horse stealing. One station worker, Jack Slade, knew how to deal with ranchers who stole his horses: He burned down their ranches. A quiet, gentlemanly man of good family, Slade sometimes had trouble controlling his temper, shooting out mirrors and lights, as well as some of the patrons, in saloons. It was said that he killed twenty-six men.

Not long after the Pony Express began operating, trouble broke out between the Nevada settlers and the Paiute Indians. Because many of the skirmishes took place along the Pony Express route, the mail service had to be stopped until the Paiutes were defeated. By the time the conflict was over, stations had been burned to the ground and many settlers and Indians killed.

Of the Pony Express riders, fourteen-year-old Billy Tate, an orphan rider, was killed in an ambush. Another rider, Elijah Nichols Wilson, was luckier. He got an arrow in the skull, just above the eye, but survived. He wore a hat thereafter to hide the scar.

Neither Indians, rough terrain, nor bad weather stopped the boys of the Pony Express. Only the expanding telegraph service, which made their wild rides unnecessary, was able to do that.

THE MAN WHO KILLED THE PONY EXPRESS

by Nancy Galloway

"What hath God wrought!" What strange words to change the course of history. Yet this was the message sent on May 24, 1844, by Samuel Finley Breese Morse. Morse sent the message from Washington, D.C., to his assistant more than forty miles away in Baltimore, Maryland.

A little more than seventeen years later, Morse's invention was to bring about the death of the Pony Express. In the fall of 1861, the first telegraph lines reached across the Great Plains, and before the new year had begun, a line had been opened through the Sierra Nevada. The telegraph was far less exciting than the Pony Express, but it could do in minutes what it took days for Pony Express riders to accomplish. At last, the dream of long-distance communication had been realized.

Morse did not start out to be an inventor. Born in Charlestown, Massachusetts, in 1791, he was the son of a Calvinist preacher and the oldest of three brothers. His first ambition was to be an artist. From the time he was very young, he found his greatest happiness in drawing and painting. In the summer of 1811, he made the first of several trips to Europe to study art. After returning

"What hath God wrought!" What strange words to change the course of history.

Opposite and above: Morse (1791–1872) was born in Charlestown, Massachusetts. He studied painting before he became interested in electricity and telegraphy. He also was Mathew Brady's first instructor in the daguerreotype process. Brady went on to become one of the Civil War's greatest photographers (see volume 2, page 147).

to the United States, Morse became an accomplished portrait painter. Among the people he painted were the Marquis de Lafayette, a Revolutionary War hero, and lexicographer Noah Webster. The portrait that Morse painted of Webster was later engraved and used as the frontispiece of the first Webster dictionary.

Morse had many interests and talents in addition to painting. His brothers, Richard and Sidney, started a family newspaper, the *Observer,* and Morse wrote many articles for the paper. Later, he helped establish another newspaper, the *Journal of Commerce.* When he later went to Europe, Morse was asked to be a special correspondent for the *Journal.*

Invention was an interest that occupied a lot of Morse's time. He was often compared with Leonardo da Vinci because his skills as an artist allowed him to sketch his ideas for inventions.

Morse's career as an artist led him to become one of the founders of the National Academy of Arts and Design, and in January 1826 he was elected president of the academy. He also was appointed professor of sculpture and painting at the City University of New York. This was the first professorship of fine arts at an American college.

But Morse's artistic ambitions also were the cause of bitter disappointments. He hoped to exhibit his paintings, charging a small fee for viewing them and thereby earning his living. His first attempt at such an exhibit was with his painting of Congress Hall. The painting had eighty-eight portraits of the members of Congress and also included spectators. Morse had spent more than a year completing the painting. He rented a hall in Boston for ten dollars a week and opened the exhibition, charging twenty-five cents admission. Later, he moved his exhibition to New York. Unfortunately, the exhibition was a financial failure. Morse lost money and was severely disappointed.

Morse finally was able to get enough commissions to finance another trip to Europe to study art. He sailed in November 1829 and spent three years traveling and painting in Europe. It was on his return voyage to the United States, in November 1832, that Morse became interested in the telegraph. A conversation aboard the ship centered on a new signaling device recently invented in Europe. Morse became intrigued with the idea of sending messages over long distances, and he began designing his own device using an electromagnet. During the long voyage home, Morse spent day after day sketching plans for his telegraph.

When he reached the United States, Morse enthusiastically began work on his telegraph at his brother's home. Over the next twelve years, with the financial backing of inventor Alfred Vail, Morse continued to work on the telegraph. Finally, in 1844, he achieved success. His invention made him world famous and financially secure. The telegraph paved the way for other electrical inventions, such as the telephone, television, and radio. In the name of progress, Samuel Morse had brought an end to the Pony Express.

Famous Civil War photographer Alexander Gardner (1821–1882) photographed this field telegraph battery wagon at Petersburg, Virginia, in September 1864. The field telegraph was vital to the success of the Army of the Potomac.

distinct advantage over the more agricultural South. On the other hand, the four-year war consumed manpower, financial resources, and the attention of the policymakers in Washington.

Still, those who favored building a railroad across the land were not content to stand quietly by. One of those was Theodore Judah, an easterner transplanted to California. Earlier proponents were dreamers and schemers without practical expertise or even interest in the awesome feat that building a railroad across empty plains and towering mountains would require. Judah, on the other hand, had railroad experience and the drive to finally get the project underway.

He needed, of course, financing. Eventually Judah formed a partnership with four Californians: dry goods merchant Charles Crocker, wholesale grocer Leland Stanford, and hardware store owners Collis P. Huntington and Mark Hopkins (The Big Four). It didn't hurt at all that Stanford became the Governor of California before the project was well underway. None of the men was wealthy (yet), so Judah went to Washington to seek funding.

Civil War era investors were making plenty of money peddling munitions and other military supplies. They were not especially interested in long-shot investments like a railroad. So Congressional generosity was necessary — and was given. The results were the Railway Acts of 1862 and 1864 that authorized government bonds and land grants for the companies building a transcontinental railroad. The Union Pacific, for example, was granted nearly 10% of the land area of Nebraska alone.

The big railroad backers (the Big Four of the Central Pacific and Thomas Durant of the Union Pacific) realized that there was a lot of money to be made in just building the railroads.

Charles Crocker

Collis Potter Huntington

Crocker and Huntington were two of the "Big Four" (Mark Hopkins and Leland Stanford were the other two) who organized the Central Pacific Railroad Company of California in 1861.

> *It didn't matter where the tracks were going or if they ever carried a single shipment of passengers and freight. Their fortunes were made.*

The Central Pacific was built without Theodore Judah. The engineer wanted to spend the time and money to build a proper railroad and do it right. His partners wanted to build it fast and cheap. When Judah was forced out, he headed back for Washington to seek different backers. On the trip across the Isthmus of Panama, he contracted a fatal illness and died shortly after reaching New York.

The Central Pacific owners stretched an investment of $150,000 into $200,000,000 in profits just in the building, not counting the seventeen and a half million acres of real estate that enriched them through their wheeling and dealing. Greed, cheating, and fraud were the games they played. The developers

WORKING ON THE RAILROAD
by Gloria A. Harris

The song "I've Been Working on the Railroad" is about African American railroad workers who laid ties, set rails, and did the jobs nobody else wanted. Even after the railroads were completed, many service positions were available to African Americans. The railroad industry was the biggest employer of African American men in the post–Civil War era. The jobs were usually difficult and often dangerous, and many railroad workers created inventions to improve their efficiency and safety.

Andrew Beard created the automatic coupler, called the Jenny Coupler, in the early 1890s. This invention allowed two railroad cars to be locked together just by being pushed against each other. A similar device is still used today.

In 1872, **Elijah McCoy** invented a self-lubricating cup that dripped oil continuously onto the engine's moving parts.

Granville T. Woods found a way to send a message to an engineer alerting him that a train was approaching. His telegraphony system combined the telegraph and telephone. In 1902, Woods obtained a patent for an improvement on George Westinghouse's automatic air brake. With this air brake, the cars and the locomotive stopped at the same time, preventing many accidents.

Landrow Bell received a patent for a better smokestack in 1871.

Humphrey H. Reynolds received a patent for a window ventilator in 1883.

William H. Jackson and **William Purvis** in 1897, **William F. Burr** in 1899, **Charles V. Richey** in 1897, and **Philip B. Williams** in 1900 all received patents for improvements on an electrically controlled and operated railway switch. Today trains switch from one track to another thanks in part to the work of these inventors.

Albert B. Blackburn received a patent for a railroad signal in 1888.

Richard A. Butler received a patent for a train alarm in 1897.

When the Central Pacific and Union Pacific met at Promontory Point, Utah, on May 10, 1869, Chinese workers were not included in the photographs of the event. Indeed, few of their coworkers had even bothered to learn their names, calling them all "John Chinaman." Although they are still anonymous today, the transcontinental railroad is said to have been "built on the backs of the Chinese."

of the Union Pacific were no better. Both railroad companies bribed federal, state and local officials, blackmailed towns along the proposed route, and lined their own pockets by forming separate companies to do the actual construction. The resulting scandals colored the country's history for decades.

The Central Pacific broke ground in Sacramento on January 8, 1863, to the amusement of bystanders. The Union Pacific broke ground on December 8, 1863, and never laid another foot of track for a full year. They started for real when Grenville Dodge came on board after the Civil War ended.

All the expected difficulties arose — and more. Indians attacked surveying crews, which often worked well ahead of the track builders; they also tore up survey stakes and caused accidents by blocking the tracks. The huge buffalo herds that thundered across the plains were another problem; they damaged track and knocked down telegraph poles, which they discovered made fine scratching posts during molting season.

Weather was another enemy of the railroad construction crews. Bitter snowy winters halted most construction in the Sierra Nevadas. Spring thaws in the mountains and on the plains turned streams and dry gulches into raging torrents that washed out track and trestles. Thunderstorms, wind, drought, avalanche, dust storms — all these tormented the railroads. And still they built.

The Central Pacific didn't have much trouble with the Native Americans; they allowed them to ride free whenever they wanted. By the spring of 1869, they had laid 690 miles of track over, around, and through the Sierra Nevadas into Utah. The Union Pacific, building over easier terrain, covered 1095 miles of plains, foothills, and Rocky Mountain passes into Utah.

The two lines met at Promontory Summit, Utah, on May 10, 1869. The continent was conquered.

The Union Pacific stops in Wyoming Territory to fill up its water tank. The windmill helped to regulate the water level of the territory's large water tank so that it could service incoming trains.

SETTING THE ROUTE: A POLITICAL VENTURE

Many obstacles stood in the way of building the railroad. First, there was all that emptiness in the middle of the continent. While visionaries could see benefits in opening the territory, many practical thinkers saw only a huge expense with little return. Among those who were convinced of the value of the railroad, many were interested mainly in their own profit. They wanted the road to start in their own backyard and travel to the west coast, and they were willing to vote against any proposal that took a different route. Politics, too, played an important role in the 1850s. Southern slave states didn't want the railroad to go north of them, cutting them out of the loop, and northerners didn't want to benefit the south by running the tracks west from their lands. It wasn't until 1862, when the southern states had seceded from the union, that the first Railway Act was finally passed. That legislation approved government grants for the building of the railroad, grants of both land and bonds to make the transcontinental a reality. Abraham Lincoln set the eastern terminus in Omaha, where he happened to own some land. The western end would be in Sacramento. Nobody thought to set the site at which the two, the Union Pacific building westward and the Central Pacific building eastward, would meet. That failing led to some of the most colorful exploits of the whole enterprise. Nor, despite surveys in the

1850s, was any exact route set. Parties of surveyors moved ahead of the track builders, finding the best way across the plains and through the mountains. The railroad builders threatened and blackmailed those few who were already on the plains or the mountains; if they didn't pay, the railroad bypassed them and the resulting economic boom went elsewhere.

"A railroad company approaches a small town as a highwayman approaches his victim. The threat, 'If you do not accede to our terms we will leave your town two or three miles to the side!' is as efficacious as the 'Stand and deliver,' when backed by a cocked pistol. For the threat of the railroad company is not merely to deprive the town of the benefits which the railroad might give; it is to put it in a far worse position than if no railroad had been built.... And just as robbers unite to plunder in concert and divide the spoil, so do the trunk lines of railroads unite to raise rates and pool their earnings, or the Pacific roads form a combination with the Pacific Mail Steamship Company by which toll gates are virtually established in land and ocean."*

From Jeanne Munn Bracken, ed., *Iron Horses Across America: The Transcontinental Railroad*, Perspectives on History Series, pp.16–17. Copyright © 1995 Discovery Enterprises, Ltd., Carlisle, Massachusetts.

*Henry George, "Progress and Poverty," 1879, pp. 192–193. Quoted in *The Robber Barons,* by Matthew Josephson, New York: Harcourt Brace and Co., 1934.

THE GATHERING STORM: AMERICA ON THE BRINK OF WAR

*"It is not alone a **fight** between the North and the South; it is a fight between freedom and slavery; between God and the devil; between heaven and hell." So wrote an Indiana congressman on October 21, 1856.*

That very same day, a Virginia man made clear why southern people believed just the opposite. "We have got to hating everything" that begins with the word "free," he revealed, "from free negroes up and down through the whole catalogue — *free farms, free labor, free society, free will, free thinking, free children, and free schools.*" All such things, he said, were "damnable."

Such quotes show how northern and southern anger intensified in the 1850s and threatened finally to boil over into secession and war. Well before blood was shed on the battlefield, it spilled over in places like Kansas and Virginia. To many worried Americans, the final split seemed unavoidable. It was just a matter of time.

Abraham Lincoln spoke for many Americans when he predicted in 1858 that "'a house divided against itself cannot stand.'"

What even Lincoln could not have known was that just two years later, the "house" would fall — and that he would be called upon to put it back together.

$100 REWARD

Ran away from the subscriber, living near the Anacostia Bridge, on or about the 17th November, negro girl ELIZA. She calls herself Eliza Coursy. She is of the ordinary size, from 18 to 20 years old, of a chestnut or copper color. Eliza has some scars about her face, has been hired in Washington, and has acquaintances in Georgetown.

I will give fifty dollars if taken in the District or Maryland, and one hundred dollars if taken in any free State; but in either case she must be secured in jail so that I get her again.

JOHN. P. WARING.

Nov. 28, 1857.

When California and New Mexico applied for admission to the Union, tensions between northern abolitionists and southern slaveholders increased. The Compromise of 1850, proposed by Henry Clay (center), was finally adopted after prolonged congressional debate.

THE FUGITIVE SLAVE LAW
by Harold Holzer

Congress passed the first American fugitive slave law in 1793. It was designed to protect slave "property" by punishing those who helped slaves escape to freedom.

As part of the Compromise of 1850, Congress created a new, tougher Fugitive Slave Act. Anyone who assisted a fugitive, or runaway, slave could now be fined one thousand dollars and imprisoned for six months. The law was designed to restore peace to the North and South. Instead, it outraged abolitionists, who openly disobeyed the law and continued aiding in such efforts as the Underground Railroad. Following are excerpts from that controversial law. Designed to keep the Union together, it served instead to drive the North and South farther apart.

Be it enacted by the Senate and House of Representatives of the United States of America in congress assembled,

...That when a person held to service or labor in any State or Territory of the United States, has heretofore or shall hereafter escape into another State or Territory of the United States, the person or persons to whom such service or labor may be due, or his, her, or their agent or attorney,...may pursue and reclaim such fugitive person, either by procuring a warrant...or by seizing and arresting such fugitive, where the same can be done without process, and by taking, or causing such person to be taken, forthwith before such court, judge, or commissioner, whose duty it shall be to hear and determine the case of such claimant in a summary manner; and upon satisfactory proof being made, by deposition or affidavit,...or by other satisfactory testimony, duly taken and certified...to make out and deliver to such claimant, his or her agent or attorney, a certificate setting forth the substantial facts as to the service or labor due from such fugitive to the claimant, and of his or

From Ellen Hansen, ed., *The Underground Railroad: Life on the Road to Freedom,* Perspectives on History Series, pp. 44–46. Copyright © 1993 Discovery Enterprises, Ltd., Lowell, Massachusetts.

her escape from the State or Territory in which such service or labor was due, to the State or Territory in which he or she was arrested, with authority to such claimant, or his or her agent or attorney, to use such reasonable force and restraint as may be necessary, under the circumstances of the case, to take and remove such fugitive person back to the State or Territory whence he or she may have escaped as aforesaid. *In no trial or hearing under this act shall the testimony of such alleged fugitive be admitted in evidence;* [emphasis added] and the certificates...shall be conclusive of the right of the person or persons in whose favor granted, to remove such fugitive to the State or Territory from which he escaped, and shall prevent all molestation of such person or persons by any process issued by any court, judge, magistrate, or other person whomsoever.

And be it further enacted, That any person who shall knowingly and willingly obstruct, hinder, or prevent such claimant, his agent or attorney, or any person or persons lawfully assisting him, her, or them, from arresting such a fugitive from service or labor, either with or without process as aforesaid, or shall rescue, or attempt to rescue, such fugitive from service or labor, from the custody of such claimant, his or her agent or attorney, or other person or persons lawfully assisting as aforesaid, when so arrested, pursuant to the authority herein given and declared; or shall aid, abet, or assist such person so owing service or labor as aforesaid, directly or indirectly, to escape from such claimant, his agent or attorney, or other person or persons legally authorized as aforesaid; or shall harbor or conceal such fugitive, so as to prevent the discovery and arrest of such person, after notice or knowledge of the fact that such person was a fugitive from service or labor as aforesaid, shall, for either of said offences, be subject to a fine not exceeding one thousand dollars, and imprisonment not exceeding six months, by indictment and conviction before the District Court of the United States for the district in which such offence may have been committed, or before the proper court of criminal jurisdiction, if committed within any one of the organized Territories of the United States; and shall moreover forfeit and pay, by way of civil damages to the party injured by such illegal conduct, the sum of one thousand dollars, for each fugitive so lost as aforesaid, to be recovered by action of debt, in any of the District or Territorial Courts aforesaid, within whose jurisdiction the said offense may have been committed....

APPROVED, September 18, 1850.

CAUTION!!
COLORED PEOPLE
OF BOSTON, ONE & ALL,
You are hereby respectfully CAUTIONED and advised, to avoid conversing with the
Watchmen and Police Officers of Boston,
For since the recent ORDER OF THE MAYOR & ALDERMEN, they are empowered to act as
KIDNAPPERS
AND
Slave Catchers,
And they have already been actually employed in KIDNAPPING, CATCHING, AND KEEPING SLAVES. Therefore, if you value your LIBERTY, and the *Welfare of the Fugitives* among you, *Shun* them in every possible manner, as so many *HOUNDS* on the track of the most unfortunate of your race.
Keep a Sharp Look Out for KIDNAPPERS, and have TOP EYE open.
APRIL 24, 1851.

THE CAPTURE OF THOMAS SIMS

Thomas Sims (above left) was a fugitive slave captured in Boston in April 1851. The Fugitive Slave Act passed in 1850 prohibited the testimony of runaway slaves and denied their right to a trial by jury. Thus, Sims was returned to his master. Abolitionist Thomas Wentworth Higginson argued against the law in court, while members of the Vigilance Committee tried to arrange Sims's rescue by less legitimate means. Their plan failed, and Sims was sent back to slavery.

Attempts to return slaves often provoked such organized resistance at a time when people in the North were becoming antagonistic toward the South. On April 24, 1851, African Americans were cautioned not to speak with watchmen and police officers for fear of kidnapping (above right). They were told to keep their "top eye" open.

Stephen A. Douglas

Douglas was the author of the controversial Kansas-Nebraska Act.

POPULAR SOVEREIGNTY

by Harold Holzer

Stephen A. Douglas never imagined that his support for a belief called "popular sovereignty" would divide the country and send it hurtling toward war. But that is just what it did.

Douglas was a Democratic senator from Illinois. He believed that voters in each new federal territory had the right to choose for themselves in free elections whether to accept slavery or not. Douglas did not invent the idea, which its supporters called popular sovereignty, but he became its strongest champion.

In the beginning, most Americans approved of the idea of popular sovereignty. For one thing, democratic elections were an important part of the national tradition. For another, many antislavery voters believed that northerners would vote overwhelmingly to reject slavery whenever it was proposed for a northern territory.

Some opponents, however, worried that whenever such elections were scheduled, slave owners would move into a territory just to make certain that slavery was approved there. They nicknamed Douglas's program "squatter sovereignty."

By 1858, Abraham Lincoln had become the most vocal foe of popular sovereignty. He declared that it was part of a conspiracy to make slavery legal everywhere in the country. Under no circumstances, he argued, could slavery be allowed to spread into the new federal territories.

Lincoln challenged Douglas in the 1858 Illinois Senate election, and the two rivals engaged in a series of seven political debates across the state. Both men discussed the notion of popular sovereignty in detail. Douglas won the election, but popular sovereignty was doomed.

After Lincoln defeated Douglas for the presidency in 1860, Douglas proved that he had never meant his policies to achieve anything but the preservation of the Union. In ill health, he undertook a national speaking tour to plead that the southern states give up secession and return to the Union.

Douglas died in early 1861, and by then the once-promising idea of popular sovereignty was dead, too. The philosophy designed to keep the Union together had, ironically, helped drive it apart.

BLEEDING KANSAS

by Harold Holzer

When Congress passed the Kansas-Nebraska Act in 1854, America's long-simmering anger over slavery boiled to the surface. The new law, sponsored by Senator Stephen A. Douglas of Illinois, gave to the citizens of each new territory the right to vote yes or no on slavery. Attention turned immediately to the western state of Kansas, which sought to become the nation's newest state.

For years, abolitionist groups had been urging their followers to migrate to Kansas, just in case such a vote on slavery was ever scheduled. As a result, Kansas boasted a sizable antislavery population. But a good many other Kansas residents were passionate supporters of the right to own slaves.

On May 21, 1856, violence erupted. A proslavery mob attacked antislavery men in the town of Lawrence. Then, just two days later, the antislavery zealot John Brown marched a band of six followers, including four of his sons, to Pottawatomie. There he ordered unarmed slave owners dragged from their homes and slaughtered with swords.

For the next several months, the bloodshed continued unchecked. Kansas threatened to explode into a small civil war all its own. Finally, President Franklin Pierce ordered federal troops sent to Kansas to quiet the disturbances.

By the time James Buchanan became president in 1857, Kansas appeared calm enough to begin creating a state constitution so that it could finally enter the Union. But appearances proved deceiving.

As reported in *Leslie's Illustrated Newspaper* on September 12, 1863, William C. Quantrill and his Confederate army attacked Lawrence, Kansas, on August 21, 1863. About 150 people were killed, and the town was nearly destroyed.

The territorial legislature was overwhelmingly proslavery, so the first constitution it drafted granted all Kansas citizens the right to own slaves. The next step in the statehood process called for a constitutional convention to produce a final document. But outraged antislavery voters refused to participate in the election for delegates to the constitutional convention. Only proslavery men were elected, and the result produced yet another uproar in Kansas.

Before the controversy died down, four different Kansas constitutions were written and submitted to the voters for their approval. All were rejected. In 1858, Kansas came very close to being admitted to the Union as a slave state. But this time, Congress voted no. The debate in the House of Representatives became so furious that at one point some fifty aging congressmen engaged in a fistfight that threatened to grow into a riot. Congressman Alexander H. Stephens of Georgia, destined to become vice president of the Confederacy three years later, observed that "if any weapon had been on hand," the harmless fight "would probably have been a bloody one." When the elderly gentlemen calmed down, the House voted to turn down Kansas's bid for statehood by a vote of 120 to 112.

Not until 1861 was Kansas finally admitted to the Union — as a free state. During the Civil War, much blood would be shed in the troubled western state. But the state had earned its sad nickname years before the war began: "Bleeding Kansas."

Charles Sumner

Sumner (1811–1874), U.S. senator from Massachusetts, was an abolitionist who approved of Lincoln's Emancipation Proclamation.

THE CANING OF CHARLES SUMNER
by Harold Holzer

Charles Sumner of Massachusetts was first elected to the U.S. Senate in 1851. A lawyer, Harvard professor, and long-time abolitionist, the brilliant Boston man was superbly qualified for his post. And no senator ever hated slavery more passionately.

To no one's surprise, Sumner bitterly opposed the 1854 Kansas-Nebraska Act. "My soul is wrung," he lamented. He decided that he must take to the Senate floor to voice his objections.

Sumner's speech, which he titled "The Crime Against Kansas," took two full days to deliver. The senator attacked the new law with anger and defiance and added severe, personal criticism of many southern senators who supported it. They were no better, he raged, than "murderous robbers...picked from the drunken spew and vomit" of a dying civilization.

Sumner reserved some of his harshest words for Andrew P. Butler of South Carolina. Some of Butler's friends urged him to challenge Sumner to a duel, but Butler refused, believing that Sumner would reject such a fight anyway. Southerners seethed in anger over Sumner's brutal charges.

Then a few days later, Butler's cousin, Congressman Preston Brooks, approached Sumner as he sat at his desk on the Senate floor. Few of Sumner's colleagues were in the chamber at the time. Brooks angrily told Sumner that his "Crime Against Kansas" speech had insulted Brooks's entire state.

Sumner began to rise in his chair to reply to Brooks, but the young congressman suddenly raised the heavy, gold-tipped wooden cane he had brought with him. He began striking Sumner violently in the head. Brooks struck his victim at least thirty times, leaving his head a bloody pulp. The attack was so vicious that at one point, trying desperately to get out of his chair to fight back, Sumner actually ripped his bolted-down desk from the floor. But he was defenseless against the blows of Brooks's cane. The attack left him unconscious and critically injured.

The North immediately expressed its outrage over the attack, but the South praised Brooks lavishly. The congressman reported happily that some southerners had even asked him for pieces of his cane, regarding such souvenirs as "sacred relics." Brooks was fined three hundred dollars for the attack but otherwise went unpunished.

Sumner barely recovered from the assault. He was taken home and remained ill for nearly four years. Proud Massachusetts voters reelected him to the Senate even though he could not serve. They wanted to send a message to the South that they would not back down from their antislavery beliefs.

Sumner eventually returned to the U.S. Senate in triumph. Throughout the Civil War, he remained a strong supporter of the Union. He prodded Lincoln to emancipate the slaves and urged him to deal harshly with the defeated South.

But Sumner never completely regained his health. In 1874, he suffered a heart attack at his desk on the Senate floor — not far from where he had been attacked by Brooks twenty years before. Sumner had been working tirelessly on a new civil rights bill. He died the next day at the age of sixty-three.

THE DECISION THAT LED TO CIVIL WAR

by Harold Holzer

Four years before the Civil War began, the first shots were fired — not on a battlefield, but in the Supreme Court. This occurred in 1857 when the Court considered a crucial question: Should a slave living in a free state be considered free?

The Court's answer to this question was no, and it sent shock waves through every state, slave and free alike. According to the ruling, which became known as the Dred Scott decision, a slave would always be regarded as property, no matter where he or she happened to be.

The Dred Scott decision set back the abolitionist cause and widened the gap between North and South concerning the explosive issue of slavery. The case aroused such passions that it helped bring on the Civil War, which ultimately signaled the end of slavery forever. Although the Dred Scott decision ruled against one slave's hope for freedom, it helped bring about freedom for all slaves in the United States.

When the case began, Virginia-born Dred Scott had spent all of his fifty-one years in slavery. He had been owned by a St. Louis family, which had sold him to a local Army surgeon. The doctor then took Scott from the slave state of Missouri to the free state of Illinois and later to the free territory of Wisconsin. Scott was then taken back to Missouri by his owner, who died there.

Automatically, the surgeon's widow inherited Scott. But when his former St. Louis owners learned what had happened, they launched a legal battle to have Scott and slaves like him declared free. They argued that he had spent so much time in free territory that he should now be free himself. Scott, who could neither read nor write, had to sign the legal papers with an X.

The case was heard first in 1846 by a state court in Missouri, which granted Scott his freedom. The victory was short-lived, however, as the ruling was soon overturned by a higher court.

Over the next ten years, the case dragged on from court to court. During all that time, Scott remained a virtual prisoner, at one point kept in custody by a local sheriff and even rented out to others to perform slave labor. Not until 1857 was the U.S. Supreme Court ready to rule on his case.

The chief justice at the time was Roger Brooke Taney, a Maryland native in his eighties whose parents had owned slaves of their own. A high-ranking public official since the days of Andrew Jackson, Taney had been chief justice for more than twenty years. Many critics thought him far too old and backward to continue serving.

Nonetheless, he still had great influence on his fellow justices. When Taney's court ruled on Dred Scott's case, its judgment was that he remain a slave. Taney went beyond Scott's case to rule that no African American descendant of any slave could ever be a U.S. citizen and declared that Congress had no

Scott was born into slavery in Southampton County, Virginia. His lawsuit to obtain freedom on the grounds that he had been moved from slave territory to territory that was considered free under the Missouri Compromise resulted in the famous Supreme Court case *Scott v. Sandford* (1857). In the Court's decision, Chief Justice Roger B. Taney held that Scott was not a citizen and could not sue in court and that the Missouri Compromise was unconstitutional.

Dred Scott

right to pass laws to curtail the spread of slavery in federal territories.

Public reaction was swift and strong. Southerners expressed delight with the decision, claiming that it affirmed once and for all their right to keep slaves. Northerners expressed outrage, charging that the ruling was unjust and inhumane. In Illinois, future president Abraham Lincoln worried aloud that slavery would be permitted outside the South.

Ironically, Scott was freed later in 1857 when the Army surgeon's widow married a congressman who opposed slavery. He died sixteen months after the Supreme Court's ruling, a free man.

Chief Justice Taney served another seven years. He lived to see his political enemy, Lincoln, become president, and in fact had to administer the oath of office to Lincoln at his inauguration. Lincoln proceeded to ignore Taney as he waged the war that destroyed the slavery system the chief justice had tried to protect.

It might be said that Dred Scott was used by those who opposed slavery to test how far the legal system would go to keep people in bondage. It is true that Scott probably understood little about the impact of his case, but thanks in part to his quiet patience, opposition to slavery grew.

Robert Purvis and Charles Remond (see pages 101 and 121) were the featured speakers at a public meeting to discuss the Dred Scott decision.

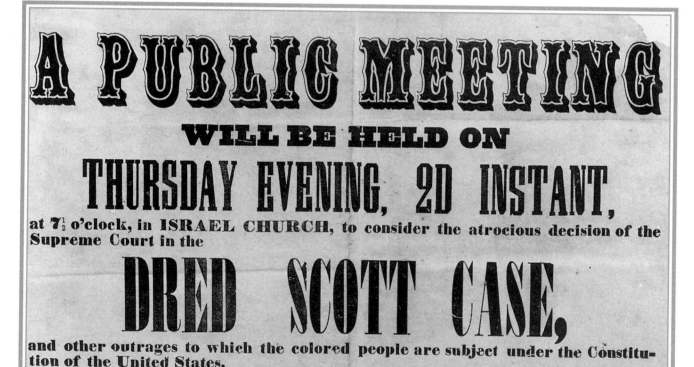

A PUBLIC MEETING

WILL BE HELD ON

THURSDAY EVENING, 2D INSTANT,

at 7½ o'clock, in ISRAEL CHURCH, to consider the atrocious decision of the Supreme Court in the

DRED SCOTT CASE,

and other outrages to which the colored people are subject under the Constitution of the United States.

C. L. REMOND,
ROBERT PURVIS,

and others will be speakers on the occasion. Mrs. MOTT, Mr. M'KIM and B. S. JONES of Ohio, have also accepted invitations to be present.

All persons are invited to attend.   Admittance free.

JOHN BROWN'S RAID AT HARPERS FERRY

by Kathleen Burke

"To arms, men." At this command, on the drizzly night of October 16, 1859, a band of eighteen men set out toward the small river town of Harpers Ferry in northern Virginia. Beneath their heavy gray cloaks they concealed spears and muskets. With these weapons, the men planned to seize the village arsenal where guns belonging to the U.S. Army were stored. They intended to use these rifles to help slaves from the surrounding countryside rise in rebellion and escape from bondage.

The leader of the determined group was a gaunt, bearded figure, fifty-nine-year-old John Brown. An impassioned opponent of slavery since boyhood, Brown had plotted this raid for months as he traveled as far north as Canada in search of volunteers and money. In Canada, he met with Harriet Tubman, heroine of the Underground Railroad, who described the mountainous Virginia terrain where Brown and his followers now gathered.

On this night, Brown and his men, including his sons, twenty-four-year-old Watson and twenty-year-old Oliver, were silent as they trudged down the muddy road. After more than three months spent hiding in a Maryland farmhouse, they were resolved to succeed in their desperate mission or die trying.

After two hours' march, Brown's raiders crossed the railroad bridge that spanned the Potomac River and led to the arsenal. They took as hostage the night watchman, who stared in disbelief as Brown announced, "This is a slave state; I want to free all the Negroes in this state; I have possession now of the United States Armory, and if the citizens interfere with me I must burn the town and have blood."

Soon the bloodshed began. As the night train headed for Baltimore approached the Potomac bridge, one of the town's few waking citizens flagged down the express and warned of the raid. The station's baggage master, an African American named Hayward Shepherd, ventured out on the tracks to investigate. When he disregarded orders to halt, one of Brown's raiders felled him with a single shot. He died the next morning.

By 7 A.M., the men had ranged throughout the town and taken more than fifty hostages. Word of the assault spread quickly. Church bells sounded the alarm, alerting militiamen from surrounding hamlets that they were called to march on Harpers Ferry.

Some of Brown's followers urged him to escape. The men could flee with their guns into the Blue Ridge Mountains and plan other attacks on slaveholding southerners. But Brown refused. Perhaps he thought, as he had avowed earlier, that slaves would "rise all over the southern states" to join his rebellion. In fact, slaves had no way of knowing of the events taking place at Harpers Ferry.

By midmorning, escape was impossible. The band of eighteen was outnumbered by two hundred rifle-toting militiamen.

John Brown

Brown (1800–1859) was an ardent abolitionist all his life. Before the raid on Harpers Ferry, he kept a station on the Underground Railroad in Richmond, Pennsylvania. In 1855, he and his sons moved to Kansas to help in the fight to have the territory admitted to the Union as a free state.

HARPERS FERRY — 1865

Brown tried to arrange a truce. He sent his son Watson and another of his men, A.D. Stevens, out to the street under a white flag. The militiamen opened fire. Stevens was taken prisoner and Watson crawled back to the arsenal, bleeding from a chest wound. Later that afternoon, Oliver Brown was shot. Oliver died that night; Watson would not live beyond the next day.

As night fell, more than five hundred townspeople, volunteers, and militiamen surrounded the arsenal. Later that evening, federal troops, ordered to Harpers Ferry by President James Buchanan, arrived from Washington. Their commander was Colonel Robert E. Lee, accompanied by Lieutenant J.E.B. Stuart. Both these southern-born Army officers were to become famous Confederate generals during the Civil War.

Lee and Stuart hoped that Brown and his companions would give up their hostages and surrender peacefully. But Brown steadfastly refused to give in unless his men were guaranteed safe conduct across the river. One of the hostages later recalled Brown in these final hours, calling him "the coolest and firmest man I ever saw in defying danger and death.... With one son dead by his side and another shot, he held his rifle...and commanded his men with utmost composure."

At daybreak, Lee's troops battered down the doors with sledgehammers and stormed the arsenal. "They came rushing in like tigers," recalled one witness. The assault lasted only three minutes. Two more of the raiders were killed, and

Opposite: *John Brown's Blessing* by Thomas Satterwhite Noble shows Brown blessing an African American child as he leaves the jail for his hanging.

"This is a slave state; I want to free all the Negroes in this state; I have possession now of the United States Armory, and if the citizens interfere with me I must burn the town and have blood."

Brown himself was wounded by a bayonet.

As their tragic venture ended, ten of Brown's men had lost their lives. Six of the surviving raiders were captured and executed for their part in the incident. Only five of his followers, those left as lookouts outside the town, escaped to the North. None of the hostages was injured.

Brown recovered and was tried for treason against the State of Virginia, for murder, and for inciting rebellion. His trial began on October 25, exactly one week after the raid. He was convicted and sentenced to hang. On December 2, 1859, at Charles Town, Virginia, he went to the gallows.

But even as he was led to his execution, Brown did not waver in his burning opposition to slavery. He handed a note to his guard that read, "I, John Brown, am quite certain the crimes of this guilty land will never be purged away but with Blood."

The crime he condemned was the enslavement of African Americans, and his prophecy came true. Less than two years later, on April 12, 1861, the first shots were fired as the nation, divided on the issue of slavery, entered the long and bloody Civil War. Many of the northern soldiers who marched in that war remembered Brown's strike against slavery. As they went into battle, they often joined in renditions of "John Brown's Body," a song based on his doomed exploits at Harpers Ferry.

JOHN BROWN: 'IN SYMPATHY A BLACK MAN'
by Nancy Norton Mattila

"Lean strong, and sinewy, of the best New England mold, built for times of trouble and fitted to grapple with the flintiest hardships. Clad in plain American woolen, shod in boots of cowhide leather, and wearing a cravat of the same substantial material, under six feet high, less than 150 pounds in weight, aged about fifty, he presented a figure straight and symmetrical as a mountain pine.... [His] eyes were bluish-gray, and in conversation they were full of light and fire."

This is the way Frederick Douglass described John Brown after their first meeting. Douglass had been intrigued by this mysterious white man, whose name people spoke in whispers. So when Brown invited Douglass to his home in Springfield, Massachusetts, in November 1848, Douglass accepted.

Brown was a militant abolitionist who proposed a radical plan to run slaves off their Virginia plantations. This could be done by using bands of armed men stationed at intervals in the Allegheny Mountains. Healthy slaves would be urged to join the slave army; the rest would be sent north by the Underground Railroad. Brown insisted that this "Subterranean Pass Way" would soon destroy the value of slavery by making owners' "property" insecure and easy to lose. Douglass was impressed with Brown's sincerity and found his plan generally constructive.

For the previous five years, Douglass had followed the moderate course of William Lloyd Garrison, speaking and writing against slavery. Although this "moral suasion" had convinced many northern reformers of the need for abolition, progress was slow. After his meeting with the militant Brown, however, Douglass's belief in the peaceful abolition of slavery was weakened.

After leaving Springfield, Douglass sent a letter to the abolitionist newspaper *North Star* telling of his interview with Brown. He wrote, "Though a white gentleman, [he] is in sympathy a black man, and as deeply interested in our cause, as though his own soul had been pierced with the iron of slavery." Douglass came to admire Brown's cheerfulness, courage, military skill, and lack of self-interest.

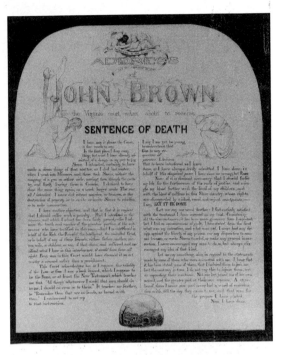

In 1855, Brown led the fight against proslavery Missourians and southerners fighting to bring Kansas into the Union as a slave state. A poor man himself, he traveled back and forth across the eastern half of the country soliciting money and weapons. Although Douglass gathered audiences to hear Brown's appeals for funds for Kansas, Douglass noted that Brown "never lost sight of what he called his greater work — the liberation of all the slaves in the United States."

Douglass welcomed Brown into his home in Rochester, New York, for three weeks in February 1858. Brown spent most of his visit writing letters soliciting funds. He also penned a plan proposing a new military state for the escaped slaves, with himself as commander in chief. In the preamble, Brown declared war on slavery. In addition, he suggested a reckless-sounding plan to which Douglass paid little attention: attacking the federal arsenal at Harpers Ferry, Virginia, to get guns.

In Brown's address to the Virginia court before he was sentenced to death, he did not plead for mercy but instead predicted years of bloodshed over the slavery issue.

About eighteen months later, Brown called on Douglass to bring money to him in Chambersburg, Pennsylvania. There he told Douglass his exact plans for the raid on Harpers Ferry. Douglass warned Brown that the scheme was bound to fail, but Brown refused to listen. "Come with me, Douglass. I will defend you with my life," Brown begged. "I want you for a special purpose. When I strike, the bees will begin to swarm, and I shall want you to help hive them."

Douglass's refusal to join Brown in his attempt to obtain U.S. government weapons probably saved his life. After the October 16 attack and Brown's arrest, Douglass's friends advised him to leave for Canada. After he was summoned to appear in court in Virginia, they agreed that his chances of not being hanged were slim because of his long-standing friendship with Brown. On November 12, 1859, Douglass sailed for England.

Even though some African Americans blamed the failure of Brown's raid on Douglass (insisting that Brown had relied on the men and weapons he never brought), Douglass said that he had never agreed to join the raid and had argued adamantly against it. Meanwhile, to save Brown's life, sympathizers tried in vain to plead insanity. Douglass considered this an insult to the man whose conviction in the fight against slavery had so impressed him. In an editorial in the November 1859 issue of *Douglass' Monthly,* he wrote, "It is an appalling fact in the history of the American people, that they have so far forgotten their own heroic age, as readily to accept the charge of insanity against a man who has imitated the heroes of Lexington, Concord, and Bunker Hill.... [T]he future will write his [Brown's] epitaph upon the hearts of a people freed from slavery, because he struck the first effectual blow."

LAST CHANCE FOR COMPROMISE

by Harold Holzer

Even before Abraham Lincoln could take the oath of office as the sixteenth president of the United States, seven southern states announced that they were seceding from the Union. America faced the greatest crisis of its young history. There appeared only one chance to head off rebellion and civil war. That chance rested with Congress.

In December 1860, Senator John J. Crittenden of Kentucky proposed a compromise that he thought might reverse secession and hold the country together. Crittenden suggested that six new amendments be added to the U.S. Constitution. They would have the effect of saving the Union by protecting the institution of slavery forever.

The first amendment proposed to outlaw slavery north of the old Missouri Compromise dividing line of 36°30´. South of that line, slavery would be officially protected by the U.S. government.

Another of Crittenden's proposed amendments called for the protection of the interstate slave trade. Yet another would have made it illegal for Congress to outlaw slavery in the city of Washington, D.C., until nearby Maryland and Virginia banned slavery first or until the city's voters approved of emancipation. Even then, slave owners would be paid for their freed slaves.

Still another amendment would have prevented Congress from officially prohibiting slavery in any new territories controlled by the federal government. To guarantee the force of these new amendments, Crittenden proposed a final amendment that would prevent any future amendment from overriding the earlier ones.

The compromise seemed tempting to moderate Republican and Democratic leaders alike, who wanted nothing more than to nip the rebellion in the bud and welcome back to the capital their southern colleagues from the seceded states. But Lincoln made it clear that he would not compromise on the issue about which he cared most deeply: the extension of slavery. Under no circumstances, he declared, would he support measures that made legal the introduction of slavery into the territories.

Besides, Lincoln was convinced that a showdown could no longer be avoided. As he put it, "Stand firm. The tug has to come, & better now than any time hereafter."

The "tug" came. The Crittenden Compromise, the last chance to save the Union with slavery and without war, went down to defeat.

John Jordan Crittenden

Crittenden (1787–1863), U.S. senator from Kentucky, proposed a compromise (which he is holding) to prevent civil war.

The First Guns:
Attack on Fort Sumter

by Harold Holzer

When Abraham Lincoln took the oath of office as president of the United States on March 4, 1861, he urged peace and calm. "There needs to be no bloodshed or violence," he insisted.

But Lincoln also pledged to maintain full control over federal forts in the South. This promise angered citizens in states that had already seceded from the Union. They vowed to seize the federal forts within their territories. A crisis seemed unavoidable, and it appeared likely that the crisis would come at Fort Sumter in Charleston, South Carolina.

Sumter was an old stone fort that sat on an island in Charleston harbor. When Lincoln became president, Sumter was manned by 127 Union soldiers led by Major Robert Anderson. But the fort began running out of supplies. None had been delivered for months.

The situation forced Lincoln to make the first crucial decision of his presidency: Should he order supplies sent to the fort, or should he allow his troops to leave peacefully once their food and water ran out? Lincoln pondered the difficult choice for days, knowing all too well that if he chose to resupply Sumter, it might trigger war. In the end, he decided that he must fulfill the promise of his inaugural address. Sumter would be resupplied.

The supply ships never arrived. Before dawn on April 12, 1861, South Carolina forces, under the command of Brigadier General P.G.T. Beauregard, began bombarding Fort Sumter from the surrounding shoreline and nearby forts. Major Anderson bravely refused

Robert Anderson

Pierre Gustave Toutant Beauregard

Above: Anderson (1805–1871) was the commander of Union forces in Charleston, South Carolina. Hailed as the defender of Fort Sumter, he later served as brigadier general in the regular army.

Left: Beauregard (1818–1893) was the Confederate general responsible for firing on Fort Sumter.

Fort Sumter as viewed from the sandbar in Charleston harbor.

FORT SUMTER — 1861

early demands that he surrender, even though he faced far more firepower than he could muster from inside Sumter's walls.

For thirty-four hours, Beauregard kept up the attack. Shells set fire to the fort's wooden barracks thirteen different times. Many of Anderson's men were overcome by smoke. Finally, shortly after noon on April 13, a shell tore away the flagpole inside the fort. When the flag fell out of sight, the southern forces ceased fire and sent a colonel out to the fort in a rowboat to ask for its surrender. This time, Anderson had no choice but to give up the fight. The major asked only that he be permitted to raise the American flag one more time before leaving.

On April 14, Anderson assembled his battered men, ordered the flag hoisted on a newly repaired pole, and began a one-hundred-gun salute. Midway through the ceremony, a gun exploded, killing a Union soldier standing nearby. He was the only casualty of the bombardment of Fort Sumter. Anderson and his men left the fort and rowed out to the supply ships that had been sitting outside the harbor.

News of the bombardment and surrender of Fort Sumter excited and inspired southerners and outraged northerners. In Charleston, citizens celebrated their vic-

tory in the streets, waving Confederate flags and cheering. But in New York City, angry residents purchased hundreds of thousands of American flags and waved them defiantly in Union Square Park to welcome Major Anderson home.

The day after Sumter fell, Lincoln called for seventy-five thousand troops to put down the rebellion. The Civil War had begun.

Until South Carolina opened fire on Fort Sumter, America's sectional conflict had been a war of words. Now Americans would fight Americans on battlefields north and south, and hundreds of thousands of lives would be lost. Fort Sumter itself would come under renewed attack — only then it would be northern troops shelling a fort held by southerners. By late 1863, Union forces had reduced Fort Sumter to little more than rubble.

In response to the attack on Fort Sumter, a Union rally took place in New York City's Union Square Park.

On April 14, 1865, exactly four years after its surrender, Robert Anderson, by then a general, returned to the fort where the Civil War had begun. The war had been over for nearly a week. As veteran soldiers cheered, the American flag was hoisted above the fort for the first time since Anderson had left in 1861.

The recapture of Fort Sumter might have inspired celebrations throughout the North, but only a few hours later, Lincoln was assassinated in Washington, D.C., and the recapture of the fort was all but forgotten.

7

BROTHER AGAINST BROTHER: THE GREAT BATTLES OF THE WAR

The first guns were fired by the South. On April 12, 1861, South Carolina opened fire on a U.S. fort in Charleston harbor.

No one died in the attack, but one of the shells that burst inside the fort shot away its flagpole. Down came the American flag and with it the Union as well.

No one in 1861 could have begun to imagine the kind of war to come. Over the next four years, cities would be destroyed, refugees would flee war zones and starve, and tens of thousands of lives would be sacrificed, as the largest battles ever fought on earth brought death and destruction sweeping across the country.

No two battles were the same. Each had its own heroes, its own strategies and terrain, its own special turning point. The only thing all had in common was death — death on a scale never before seen.

One of the fiercest warriors of the war was Union general William T. Sherman. He burned Atlanta, Georgia, and then led his troops on a devastating march through the state. Sherman brought the South to its knees and became a hero in the North, but he never gloated about his triumphs. "War," he explained, "is all hell." The following pages explain why.

HIGHLIGHTS OF THE CIVIL WAR

On March 4, 1861, Abraham Lincoln was worried as he prepared to take office as the sixteenth president of the United States. He had just completed a two-thousand-mile trip from his home in Illinois, visiting five northern states and making more than twenty speeches in an attempt to calm the people who had elected him.

At the time of Lincoln's inauguration, seven southern states had already seceded from the Union. They refused to accept Lincoln as their president. They elected their own Jefferson Davis as the first president of the newly formed Confederate States of America. And now, as Lincoln prepared to take office, four more slave-

Soldiers relax in front of their hut at winter quarters.

In 1991, at Boston Harbor, the Fifth Massachusetts Battery of Light Artillery encamped at Fort Warren. The fellow on the right, wearing a frock coat with many buttons and "bars" on his shoulders, is the commander. At the beginning of the war, everyone wore shell coats, which came to the waist and had many buttons and fancy piping (to the commander's right). By the end of the war, everyone was wearing the sack coat with four buttons (left). Soldiers were differentiated by their hats and piping — red for artillery, yellow for cavalry, and blue for infantry.

holding states were ready to join their seven southern neighbors.

Two presidents; two constitutions; two nations, each insisting on its own sovereignty. Was it lawful for states to withdraw from the Union and form their own confederation? Was the U.S. Constitution only a compact that states might or might not agree to uphold? Could certain states, through legal proceedings, bring their participation in the Union to an end?

For years, these questions had been debated without resolution. The North and South had grown apart, developing different ways of life with different kinds of problems. To the South, compromise no longer seemed possible. The southern states wanted to govern themselves as a separate nation. To the North, the formation of the Confederate States of America was widely thought to be treason. Confrontation between North and South seemed unavoidable. And on April 12, 1861, when the Confederates attacked Fort Sumter in Charleston, South Carolina, the war finally began.

The Confederates called the confrontation the War Between the States. The Federal War Department under President Lincoln called it the War of the Rebellion. Those who tried to understand the war from a constitutional point of view called it the War of Secession. But no matter what they called it, few people believed that it would last very long — maybe three months at the most. The North hoped that the South was not serious about its new confederacy, and the South hoped that the North would soon give in and let it go its separate way.

But each side underestimated the other. And it was not long before the whole country realized that there was nothing more brutal and tragic than the hand-to-hand combat of a civil war.

In 1861, when the war began, there were approximately eighteen million people living in the North, and the North controlled almost two-thirds of the nation's railroads. The North had nine-tenths of the nation's industry and most of the raw materials needed to keep its factories going.

The South had only half as many people as the North, and one-third of its population were slaves. With fewer troops, fewer guns and ammunition, and fewer supplies to keep the solders clothed and fed, the South appeared to be at a tremendous disadvantage.

However, the South had one important advantage over the North that probably kept the war going. The South fought almost the entire war, with the exception of two battles, on its own soil. The North was forced to invade the South, shipping supplies across enemy lines and camping in unfamiliar, unfriendly territory.

There are volumes that recount the terrible battles that took place between 1861 and 1865. One out of every five soldiers who took part was killed in battle or died in camp. Compare that number with one out of twelve who died in World War I or one out of eleven who died in World War II. It is easy to see how terribly violent and destructive a civil war can be.

When General Ulysses S. Grant took command of the Union army, he planned to keep attacking the South until the Confederates were worn down, no matter how many lives were lost. To trap the Confederate army, he turned his western army over to General William T. Sherman, with orders to move in behind Confederate general Robert E. Lee. Sherman began his march across Georgia, destroying Confederate supplies that lay in his path.

In the meantime, Grant's own army began a battle with Lee's that became one of the worst in American military history. Throughout the summer of 1864, Grant tried to get his army across the Rappahannock River in northern Virginia while Lee resisted his attempts. At Cold Harbor, just ten miles from Richmond, Virginia, Grant lost twelve thousand men in half an hour. In fact, Grant lost more men than Lee had in his entire army, but he was able to replace his losses with fresh troops. Lee also suffered heavy losses. His army was reduced to half its original size, and there were no replacements.

Early in April 1865, Lee abandoned Petersburg and Richmond to the Union

One out of every five soldiers who took part [in the war] was killed in battle or died in camp.

The Battle of Fredericksburg was reenacted in Massachusetts in 1994. Above: Members of the Fifth Massachusetts Battery stand ready at their gun. Top: This three-inch cannon is an example of the most common type of cannon used in the Civil War.

army. He tried to move his army west, but his movements were blocked. On April 9, surrounded by Union troops, Lee surrendered to Grant at Appomattox Court House, Virginia. Sherman forced the remaining Confederate resistance to surrender near Durham, North Carolina. The war was finally over.

Then began the work of rebuilding a tattered nation still divided by different ways of life and very different needs. This period is called Reconstruction. The question of whether it was lawful for a state to secede from the Union had been resolved by war. The practice of slavery in America had been abolished. During Reconstruction, new questions had to be answered. What role was the South going to play in our nation's future? How were the newly freed slaves going to be integrated into society? These were difficult questions that our nation's leaders would have to answer — questions made much more complicated when the most important leader, President Abraham Lincoln, was assassinated on April 14, just five days after Lee's surrender.

'YOUNG ELLSWORTH': THE FIRST UNION OFFICER TO DIE

by Harold Holzer

The first Union officer killed during the Civil War was a dashing young colonel named Ephraim Elmer Ellsworth. His death was mourned throughout the North, and he became an inspiration to the entire Union.

Ellsworth was famous even before the war began. As a very young man, he had formed a unit of Zouaves — fierce, old-fashioned-looking soldiers who wore colorful red pantaloons. Ellsworth's U.S. Zouave Cadets won the national drill team competition. The little colonel then took them on a national tour, accompanied by a brass band. He attracted much favorable attention.

Ellsworth also was a friend of the Lincoln family. He accompanied the Lincolns to Washington for the 1861 inauguration. He remained close to the family when they moved into the White House and was a particular favorite of the Lincolns' young sons Willie and Tad.

When the war broke out, Ellsworth formed a new unit made up of tough city firemen: the New York Fire Department Zouaves. They saw their first action on May 24, 1861. The regiment was ordered across the Potomac River from Washington and into Alexandria, Virginia, a hotbed of anti-Union feeling. "We have no means of knowing what reception we are to meet with," Ellsworth wrote to his mother the night before leading his men there.

As it happened, the Confederate troops who were guarding Alexandria left before Ellsworth's men arrived. He met no armed resistance, but he did encounter a symbolic act of rebellion that bothered him greatly.

Flying defiantly from a tall pole atop a hotel in the city was a large Confederate flag. Its sight offended Ellsworth greatly. Taking several men with him, he raced up the hotel's steps, ripped down the flag, and headed downstairs clutching the trophy to his chest. The infuriated innkeeper, James W. Jackson, took a shotgun and fired at Ellsworth as he headed back toward the lobby. The colonel was killed instantly.

One of the men who climbed the stairs with Ellsworth that day was a news-

Ephraim Elmer Ellsworth

Opposite: Alonzo Chappel's *Death of Ellsworth* shows innkeeper James Jackson (on right) shooting Ellsworth after he tore down the Confederate flag from atop a Virginia hotel. Almost immediately, Corporal Francis E. Brownell, who tried to stop Jackson, killed him.

paper reporter. He quickly spread the news of Ellsworth's heroic act. Before long, the North was flooded with tributes: poems, songs, photographs, engravings, and lithographs. "Remember Ellsworth!" and "Avenge Ellsworth!" became rallying cries for soldiers in the early battles of the war.

Ellsworth was given one final, and rare, honor. His funeral was held in the White House. Abraham Lincoln himself attended the service.

In a letter to Ellsworth's parents, Lincoln made clear how much he admired the young man. "So much of promised usefulness to one's country, and of bright hopes for one's self and friends," he wrote, "have rarely been so suddenly dashed, as in his fall."

Other commanders would fight more dangerous enemies, lead many more soldiers, and perform with equal bravery. But few Civil War heroes ever won as much affection or inspired as much mourning as Ephraim Elmer Ellsworth, the first Union officer killed during the long war.

This Confederate soldier and his wife were part of a centennial reenactment of the First Battle of Bull Run.

PICNIC WAR: THE BATTLE OF BULL RUN

by Harold Holzer

Three long, tense months passed after the surrender of Fort Sumter, and still Union and Confederate soldiers had not faced each other in battle. From both the North and the South came demands for a fight. Each side seemed eager to taste war. Each seemed sure of victory.

In midsummer, Confederate forces occupied a busy little railroad center in northern Virginia. The town of Manassas was less than thirty miles south of Washington, D.C. The Union decided to attack.

The plan was anything but secret. On the morning of the expected battle, hundreds of Washington's residents, including many public officials, packed picnic baskets and confidently set out in their carriages for Manassas to watch Union troops defeat the Confederates. Many expected to see a victory that would end the war. What they saw instead would surprise and sicken them.

The battle began early on the morning of July 21, 1861, when Union forces under General Irvin McDowell attacked the enemy near a little stream called Bull

Run. For hours, Union troops attacked relentlessly. Finally, around noon, Confederate resistance broke, and southern troops began fleeing in disarray. The Union seemed on the verge of a great victory that might indeed have ended the rebellion in a single day. But the Confederates sent reinforcements, and General Thomas Jonathan ("Stonewall") Jackson's heroic refusal to retreat further inspired the Confederate troops to fight back.

At 2 P.M., northern and southern forces began a long, bloody struggle along Henry Hill. The fighting proved intense and confusing. Because most of the soldiers on the field that day were outfitted in state uniforms, not the Union blue and Confederate gray that became common later in the war, it was difficult to know friend from foe. Northern troops fired mistakenly at fellow northerners, and southerners, too, occasionally directed their guns at their comrades. But amidst the heat, horror, dust, and roar, the southern lines refused to crack.

The ruins of Stone Bridge at Bull Run, March 1862.

Just before 4 P.M., a fresh group of Confederate reinforcements arrived and charged up the Union line. The Union troops began slowly retreating across Bull Run. Then a Confederate shell exploded on a Union carriage as it was crossing a bridge, blocking the line of retreat. Union troops suddenly panicked and began fleeing in all directions. Men and horses ran directly at the civilians who were parked at what they thought was a safe distance, eating their picnic lunches. Blankets and baskets were overturned, and the civilians ran for their lives. All through the night, they walked or rode slowly back to Washington, defeated and humiliated.

The Battle of Bull Run, as it became known in the North (where battles were named for the nearest waterway) ended General McDowell's brief career as commander of Union forces. The Battle of Manassas, as it was called in the South (where battles were generally named for the town where they occurred) made southern heroes of Confederate commanders P.G.T. Beauregard and Joseph E. Johnston and transformed "Stonewall" Jackson into a legend.

By losing, the Union came to grips with the fact that the war would not be over quickly; it would be a long and bloody struggle.

The final casualty count at Bull Run was surprisingly low: 460 Union and 387 Confederate troops killed. Losses would be far worse in battles to come. And neither side fought with great brilliance. Both northern and southern troops were untrained and disorganized. Nevertheless, Bull Run was not only the first but also one of the most important battles of the entire Civil War. By winning, the Confederates forced the world to take their new nation seriously and served notice on the North that they could fight successfully for their independence. By losing, the Union came to grips with the fact that the war would not be over quickly; it would be a long and bloody struggle.

THE BLOODIEST DAY IN HISTORY:
THE BATTLE OF ANTIETAM

by Harold Holzer

September 17, 1862, was the bloodiest day in our nation's history. More than twenty-six thousand soldiers were killed, wounded, or reported missing in one morning and afternoon of fierce combat at the Battle of Antietam.

Completed by September 1867, Antietam National Cemetery in Sharpsburg, Maryland, contains the remains of 4,776 Union soldiers and 1,836 unknown soldiers. Veterans from the Spanish-American War, World Wars I and II, and Korea also are buried here, but not Confederate soldiers of the Civil War. The Confederate remains are buried in Rose Hill Cemetery in Hagerstown, Maryland; Elmwood Cemetery in Shepherdstown, West Virginia; and Mt. Olivet Cemetery in Frederick, Maryland. If you visit the cemetery, be sure to see the monument known as "Old Simon," the iron guns, and the Irish Brigade Plaque.

No single day's casualties ever rose higher during the Civil War — or, for that matter, in any war Americans ever fought either before or after.

The Battle of Antietam also was historic for other reasons. For one thing, it marked the defeat of Robert E. Lee's Confederate army in its first invasion of the North. Even more important, Antietam gave President Abraham Lincoln the victory he needed to announce the most revolutionary act of the century: the Emancipation Proclamation.

Antietam was the name of a small creek that flowed from north to south in the village of Sharpsburg, Maryland. (Southerners thereafter referred to it as the Battle of Sharpsburg.)

On September 4, 1862, Lee's Army of Northern Virginia crossed the Potomac River from Virginia and invaded Union territory. It was a bold move, designed to alarm northerners. Some Confederate leaders believed that their army should devote itself only to defending southern territory. But Lee insisted that if he could win a victory in Maryland, he might be able to march all the way to Philadelphia and capture the city where American independence had been born. Then he would force the Lincoln administration to ask for peace and recognize the Confederacy as a legitimate, separate government.

Once he marched into Maryland, Lee divided his army and planned several battles at once. But when his troops suffered small defeats at different locations, Lee seemed ready to declare his invasion a failure and retreat back into the South as early as September 14. The following day, "Stonewall" Jackson captured the historic town of Harpers Ferry, Virginia (now West Virginia), only a few miles away. Lee changed his mind about abandoning his campaign. Instead, he massed his army around the town of Sharpsburg and prepared for a showdown with the Union's Army of the Potomac.

The northern forces were led by General George B. McClellan. "Little Mac," as his adoring soldiers called him, had fared poorly when he had tried attacking Lee's army in Virginia during the summer of 1862. Now his forces outnumbered Lee's overwhelmingly. He brought eighty thousand troops to Sharpsburg, while Lee could mass only forty thousand by the morning of September 17. McClellan decided to attack both outside flanks of the Confederate army, then follow with a massive assault on the Confederate center.

Joseph Hooker (1814–1879) held subordinate commands in the Union army until Antietam, when he became a brigadier general in the regular army.

The battle began around dawn, when General Joseph Hooker charged against Lee's left from the woods north of town. Hooker's men raced out of the woods, across a farm, and into a corn field filled with man-size cornstalks only days away from being harvested. "In a second the air was full of the hiss of bullets," remembered one New York private. Jackson defended the corn field until Hooker's men forced them out, but then a Confederate counterattack drove the Union soldiers back into the corn. Thousands of troops found themselves trapped in the mass of giant cornstalks, unable to tell friend from foe, shooting at whatever moved, and running in any direction they could to escape the whiz of bullets that tore at the leaves.

A Boston newspaperman recalled the horror of the scene, writing, "I counted fourteen bodies lying together, literally in a heap, amid the corn rows on the hillside. The broad, green leaves were sprinkled and stained with blood." At one point, twenty-two hundred Union soldiers fell in just twenty minutes.

George B. McClellan (1826–1885) served as general in chief of the Union army but was dismissed after Antietam. Lincoln could not get him to attack and concluded that he had "the slows."

Meanwhile, at the southern end of the battlefield, Confederate troops lay in a sunken farm road, defending it heroically for a time against attack by Union forces. Then a massive Union charge mowed down the Confederates, filling the road with blood. Dead and wounded soldiers lay on top of each other, some struggling to crawl away from the mass of human bodies. "Words are inadequate to describe the scene," wrote one northern journalist. "What a ghastly spectacle." The sunken road became known in history as Bloody Lane.

With Bloody Lane theirs, Union forces had a clear opportunity to attack the weakened center of Lee's lines. Had they done so, they would certainly have won the battle and perhaps even ended the war. But McClellan, timid as always, refused to attack the center. Instead, he ordered General Ambrose E. Burnside to cross a stone bridge across Antietam Creek and attack from the south. Burnside's men fought their way ahead toward Sharpsburg with little resistance and at 3 P.M. seemed on their way to victory. But then Confederates under General Ambrose P. Hill attacked Burnside unexpectedly, driving his men all the way back to the creek and into full retreat across the bridge.

Ambrose E. Burnside (1824–1881) served under McClellan at Antietam and succeeded him as general in command of the Army of the Potomac. After the Battle of Fredericksburg in December 1862, he was relieved of his command and replaced by Hooker. Burnside was known for his long side-whiskers, which came to be called sideburns.

At sunset, nearly five thousand soldiers lay dead, and nearly nineteen thousand more were wounded. The bloodiest single-day battle in American history had ended without a clear victor. That night, however, Lee moved his crippled army back across the Potomac River, ending his first invasion of the North in failure. McClellan boasted to his superiors, "I fought the battle splendidly...it was a masterpiece of art."

President Lincoln disagreed. He wanted McClellan to follow Lee into Virginia and destroy his exhausted troops before they could regain their strength. When McClellan hesitated, Lincoln left Washington to visit the general at his headquarters near the heights above Harpers Ferry, not far from the Antietam battlefield. The two men conferred on October 3, but Lincoln could not convince his cautious general to take action. That night, Lincoln watched thousands of Union campfires brightly burning and complained bitterly, "That is not the Army of the Potomac. It is McClellan's bodyguard!" Lincoln finally concluded of McClellan, "He has got the slows." A few weeks after the Battle of Antietam, Lincoln replaced him.

Even though the Battle of Antietam did not bring the Union the clear-cut triumph McClellan claimed, it proved enough of a victory to permit Lincoln to announce an action he had been planning for two months: a proclamation of emancipation of the slaves. When he had first told his cabinet of his intentions in July, his ministers had warned him that if he announced emancipation before winning a battle, northern citizens would regard it as "a last shriek on the retreat." Lincoln reluctantly postponed his announcement. Finally, five days after Antietam, he was able to issue his proclamation, changing forever the nature of the war and of all American history. The day that cost more American lives than any other also made possible the proclamation that saved millions of Americans from a life of slavery.

Thomas Nast's *The Emancipation of the Negroes* appeared in *Harper's Weekly* in January 1863. Nast (1840–1902) was famous for the Civil War drawings he produced for *Harper's*.

PLEASANT HILL AND THE BATTLE OF PERRYVILLE

by Thomas Pond

It has been said of Shaker communities that they were "without jail, without poor, without saloons, nor did they learn the art of war therein." The Shakers lived peacefully from the time of their arrival in this country. They refused to fight in the Revolutionary War, which made some of their neighbors angry. A few state legislatures — mostly around the time of the War of 1812 — had passed laws making Shakers exempt from service in the militia. Other states, however, punished Shakers for their refusal to do military service.

After the colony at Pleasant Hill, Kentucky, was founded in 1805, the Shakers made a good name for themselves in the community. Frequently, they gave generous gifts to public charities for the relief of suffering. They performed labor on the public roads and bridges used by the colony, keeping these byways in excellent condition. Because the roads and bridges were used by the whole community, everyone benefited from the Shakers' work.

sands of fighting men, and his troops had consumed many badly needed supplies. The South had lost its momentum and all hope of obtaining European support.

Two years later, General Robert E. Lee surrendered his army to General Ulysses S. Grant at Appomattox Court House, Virginia, but in many people's minds, the war had been lost at Gettysburg.

FROM FARMLAND TO BATTLEFIELD

by Caryl Simon-Katler

Throughout the month of June 1863, thousands of Civil War soldiers marched north from Virginia to Pennsylvania. Dressed in blue, gray, and even homespun brown uniforms, they trekked twenty to thirty miles a day through the scorching heat. Hiking for hours over dusty, unpaved roads, the soldiers stopped for infrequent meals of pork and dry biscuits.

Where were they heading at such speed? To the next battle in the Civil War. And where would it take place? No one knew.

Still they struggled on, many dying of sunstroke under the hot June sun. Although they did not know it, they were converging on Gettysburg, Pennsylvania, destined to become one of the bloodiest battlegrounds of the war. In its twenty-five-square-mile area, one hundred sixty thousand Americans would fight during the first three days of July 1863. Of those, fifty thousand would be wounded, captured, or killed.

What drew them to Gettysburg? This quiet Pennsylvania farm town lay seventy miles northwest of Washington, D.C., and was located at the intersection of nine major roads. Confederate general Robert E. Lee planned to invade the North; Union general George Meade intended to make his stand in Maryland. When Union and Confederate soldiers clashed near Gettysburg, coincidence, not strategy, brought them together.

What did Gettysburg look like in 1863? This was farm country, with rural roads, split-rail and stone fences, barns, and log, frame, stone, and brick houses. Bluebells and hollyhocks bloomed abundantly in the gardens, and the fertile land supported corn, wheat, and peach and apple orchards.

Artillery reserves are shown going into action at Gettysburg along Cemetery Ridge, with Culp's Hill in the background. This artillery helped stop George E. Pickett's charge on the third day of the battle and turned the tide for the Union.

Signal cannon

Founded in 1786, the town was named for James Gettys, who had laid out two hundred ten lots on his father's old farm. By the Civil War, Gettysburg was home to more than two thousand inhabitants. Located in a prosperous market region, it featured two colleges — the Lutheran Theological Seminary, high on Seminary Ridge, and Pennsylvania College.

Gettysburg was set amid rolling hills, ridges, and valleys. Seminary Ridge lay to the west and Culp's Hill to the southeast. Cemetery Hill and Little and Big Round Tops framed the shallow valley, which measured two miles from north to south and half a mile wide. It was an ideal spot for nineteenth-century warfare, which focused on strategic heights and maneuvers.

When the two armies met, they fought in a wheat field and a peach orchard, where the fruit was just beginning to ripen. They also fought in Devil's Den amid a jumble of rocks and trees. Bullets passed within inches of homes, and many civilians fled their burning farms. The remains of the thousands of soldiers who died littered the fields and yards, and the town's colleges, churches, and homes, as well as surrounding farmsteads, were converted into hospitals for the wounded.

THE BATTLE OF GETTYSBURG
GENERAL CRAWFORD'S CHARGE OF THE REBEL LINES

An illustration from *Harper's Weekly,* August 8, 1863.

Gettysburg's citizens suffered, too. Houses were occupied by Confederate troops, and one civilian, Jennie Wade, was killed while caring for her sister and her sister's newborn child near Cemetery Hill. A Confederate bullet pierced two doors of the house she was in and struck her while she was baking bread.

Schoolteacher J. Howard Wert was able to collect battle souvenirs — a fife, shaving mirror, drum ornament, and blanket insignia — within yards of his family home. Other families also retrieved battle relics, and many solid-shot cannonballs became doorstops and paperweights.

When the battle ended, artists and photographers descended on Gettysburg. Alexander Gardner rumbled into town with two horse-drawn darkrooms and began recording the scene. By the time Mathew Brady arrived, the dead had been buried, so he documented the landscape, taking panoramic shots of Little Round Top and Cemetery Hill. In 1866, after the Civil War had concluded, artist Peter Frederick Rothermel tramped the fields with former soldiers. He sketched faces and locations, then created a series of paintings immortalizing the battlefield.

The town of Gettysburg also had changed. Bullet holes scarred the trees, farm fields had been ruined, and lives had been torn apart, as the quiet village had been transformed into a battleground.

Today the 3,500-acre Gettysburg National Military Park surrounds the town itself. Seminary Ridge, Culp's Hill, Little and Big Round Tops, Devil's Den,

Cemetery Hill, Wheat Field, and Peach Orchard are all located within the park's borders. The seventeen-acre national cemetery contains more than thirty-five hundred graves of Union soldiers who died at Gettysburg. Thirty miles of roads wind through the park, battlefield guides lead informational tours, and a seventy-five-foot observation tower offers extraordinary views of the site. A visitors center features displays, while more than a thousand markers and monuments highlight significant battlefield locations. Gettysburg is every inch a Civil War site. It is hard to believe that the town was once just a peaceful farm community in the Pennsylvania countryside.

THE LEGENDS AND FOLKLORE OF GETTYSBURG

by Hilda Brucker

On many starry nights during the Civil War, northern and southern troops alike gathered around their campfires for an evening of storytelling. Sharing tales of bravery and heroic feats helped the soldiers keep up their morale, and talking openly about their fears and the horrors they had seen seemed to ease their burdens. Some of the tales they told began to circulate, passed among the troops by word of mouth, sent home in letters, or published in small-town newspapers. After the war was over, favorite stories continued to be retold at family gatherings and meetings of veterans' organizations. Although their historical accuracy is no longer known, many charming stories have been preserved as part of the legacy we call folk history.

Folk stories of the Civil War seem to share certain common characteristics. Ordinary people often became the heroes of these tales, and the good or bad qualities of public figures such as President Abraham Lincoln often were exaggerated until the people resembled the characters of ancient mythology. The following are three tales from Gettysburg that focus on General Robert E. Lee. They all show that he was respected by northerners and southerners alike.

The last Confederate gun at Gettysburg.

THE SALUTE

Under the scorching June sun, General Lee led his Confederate troops northward. As the tired soldiers marched across the fields of Pennsylvania, a young Pennsylvania Dutch girl came running out of a farmhouse, fiercely waving a Union flag. Calling his troops to a halt, Lee studied the face of the girl standing defiantly before him. Then he raised his arm and ceremoniously saluted her before resuming his march.

Later, as the troops were setting up camp for the night, the southern general overheard a conversation between two soldiers who were criticizing him for his salute of the enemy flag. Lee corrected them, saying, "I saluted not the enemy, but the bravery of a young patriot and the flag of a great nation that I once served."

THE WOUNDED UNION SOLDIER

It was clearly a victory for the Union forces, and General Lee had no choice but to call retreat. As he led his defeated Confederate soldiers from the Gettysburg battlefield on that fateful day in 1863, a wounded Union soldier taunted him with a cry of "Hurrah for the Union." To the astonishment of the young private, Lee swung his horse around and dismounted. Kneeling in the dirt beside the boy, the defeated general lightly touched his fingertips to the bloody wound that had caused the soldier to fall. "My son," he said gently, "I hope you will soon be well."

As Lee rode away, the wounded soldier burst into tears, both because of this unexpected act of kindness and because he feared he would die there. The soldier did not die, but recovered to tell his story.

A statue of Major General G.K. Warren stands watch over Little Round Top at Gettysburg National Military Park.

★ ★ ★ ★ ★ ★ ★ ★ ★

REPORT OF COLONEL JOSHUA L. CHAMBERLAIN
by Joshua L. Chamberlain

Joshua Chamberlain commanded the Twentieth Maine Union Infantry. Before he was a brave leader and good war reporter, Chamberlain had been a college professor. His regiment played a key role in the Battle of Gettysburg, and his account helps us to see how the men of both armies had to work together to be effective.

After an hour or two of sleep by the roadside just before daybreak, we reached the heights southeasterly of Gettysburg about 7 A.M., July 2. Massed at first with the rest of the division...we were moved several times farther toward the left..., expecting every moment to be put into action and held strictly in line of battle....

Somewhere near 4 P.M. a sharp cannonade, at some distance to our left and front, was the signal for a sudden and rapid movement of our whole division in the direction of this firing, which grew warmer as we approached. Passing an open field in the hollow ground in which some of our batteries were going into position, our brigade reached the skirt of a piece of woods, in the farther edge of which there was a heavy musketry fire, and when about to go forward into line we received...orders to move to the left at the double-quick, when we took a farm road crossing Plum Run in order to gain a rugged mountain spur called Granite Spur, or Little Round Top.

The enemy's artillery got range of our column as we were climbing the spur, and the crashing of the shells among the rocks and the tree tops made us move lively along the crest.... Passing to the southern slope of Little Round Top, Colonel Vincent indicated to me the ground my regiment was to occupy, informing me that this was the extreme left of our general line, and that a desperate attack was expected in order to turn that position, concluding by telling me I was to "hold that ground at all hazards." That was the last word I heard from him.

In order to commence by making my right firm, I formed my regiment on the right into line, giving such direction to the line as should best secure the advantage of the rough, rocky, and stragglingly wooded ground.

The line faced generally toward a more conspicuous eminence southwest of ours, which is known as Sugar Loaf, or Round Top. Between this and my position intervened a smooth and thinly wooded hollow. My line formed, I immediately detached Company B, Captain Morrill commanding, to extend from my left flank across this hollow as a line of skirmishers, with directions to act as occasion might dictate, to prevent a surprise on my exposed flank and rear.

The artillery fire on our position had meanwhile been constant and heavy, but my formation was scarcely complete when the artillery was replaced by a vigorous infantry assault upon the center of our brigade to my right, but it very soon involved the right of my regiment and gradually extended along my entire front. The action was quite sharp and at close quarters.

In the midst of this, an officer from my center informed me that some important movement of the enemy was going on in his front, beyond that of the line with which we were engaged. Mounting a large rock, I was able to see a considerable body of the enemy moving by the flank in rear of their line engaged, and passing from the direction of the foot of Great Round Top through the valley toward the front of my left. The close engagement not allowing any change of front, I immediately stretched my regiment to the left, by taking intervals by the left flank, and at the same time "refusing" my left wing, so that it was nearly at right angles with my right, thus occupying about twice the extent of our ordinary front, some of the companies being brought into single rank when the nature of the ground gave sufficient strength or shelter. My officers and men understood my wishes so well that this movement was executed under fire, the right wing keeping up fire, without giving the enemy any occasion to seize or even to suspect their advantage. But we were not a moment too soon; the enemy's flanking column having gained their desired direction, burst upon my left, where they evidently had expected an unguarded flank, with great demonstration.

We opened a brisk fire at close range, which was so sudden and effective that they soon fell back among the rocks and low trees in the valley, only to burst forth again with a shout, and rapidly advanced, firing as they came. They pushed up to within a dozen yards of us before the terrible effectiveness of our fire compelled them to break and take shelter.

They renewed the assault on our whole front, and for an hour the fighting was severe. Squads of the enemy broke through our line in several places, and the fight was literally hand to hand. The edge of the fight rolled backward and forward like a wave. The dead and wounded were now in our front and then in our rear. Forced from our position, we desperately recovered it, and pushed the enemy down to the foot of the slope. The intervals of the struggle were seized to remove the wounded (and those of the enemy also), to gather ammunition from the cartridge boxes of disabled friend or foe on the field, and even to secure better muskets than the Enfields, which we found did not stand service well. Rude shelters were thrown up of the loose rocks that covered the ground.

Captain Woodward, commanding the Eighty-third Pennsylvania Volunteers, on my right, gallantly maintaining his fight, judiciously and with hearty cooperation made his movements conform to my necessities, so that my right was at no time exposed to a flank attack.

The enemy seemed to have gathered all their energies for their final assault. We had gotten our thin line into as good a shape as possible, when a strong force emerged from the scrub wood in the valley [to the left], as well as I could judge, in two lines in *échelon* by the right, and opening a heavy fire, the first line came on us as [if] they meant to sweep everything before them. We opened on them as well as we could with our scanty ammunition snatched from the field.

It did not seem possible to withstand another shock like this now coming on. Our loss had been severe. One-half of my left wing had fallen, and a third of my regiment lay just behind us, dead or badly wounded. At this moment my anxiety was increased by a great roar of musketry in my rear, on the farther or northerly slope of Little Round Top, apparently on the flank of the regular brigade [Weed], which was in support of Hazlett's battery on the crest behind us. The bullets from this attack struck into my left rear, and I feared that the enemy might have nearly surrounded the Little Round Top, and only a desperate chance was left for us. My ammunition was soon exhausted. My men were firing their last shot and getting ready to "club" their muskets.

It was imperative to strike before we were struck by this overwhelming force in a hand-to-hand fight, which we could not probably have withstood or survived. At that crisis, I ordered the bayonet. The word was enough. It ran like fire along the line, from man to man, and rose into a shout, with which they sprang forward upon the enemy, now not 30 yards away. The effect was surprising; many of the enemy's first line threw down their arms and surrendered. An officer fired his pistol at my head

with one hand, while he handed me his sword with the other. Holding fast by our right, and swinging forward our left, we made an extended "right wheel," before which the enemy's second line broke and fell back, fighting from tree to tree, many being captured, until we had swept the valley and cleared the front of nearly our entire brigade.

Meantime Captain Morrill with his skirmishers (sent out from my left flank), with some dozen or fifteen of the U.S. Sharpshooters who had put themselves under his direction, fell upon the enemy as they were breaking, and by his demonstrations, as well as his well-directed fire, added much to the effect of the charge.

Having thus cleared the valley, and driven the enemy up the western slope of the Great Round Top, not wishing to press so far out as to hazard the ground I was to hold by leaving it exposed to a sudden rush of the enemy, I succeeded (although with some effort to stop my men, who declared they were "on the road to Richmond") in getting the regiment into good order and resuming our original position.

Four hundred prisoners, including two field and several line officers, were sent to the rear. These were mainly from the Fifteenth and Forty-seventh Alabama Regiments, with some of the Fourth and Fifth Texas. One hundred and fifty of the enemy were found killed and wounded.... We went into the fight with 386, all told — 358 guns. Every pioneer and musician who could carry a musket went into the ranks. Even the sick and foot-sore, who could not keep up in the march, came up as soon as they could find their regiments, and took their places in line of battle.... Some prisoners I had under guard, under sentence of court-martial, I was obliged to put into the fight, and they bore their part well, for which I shall recommend a commutation of their sentence.

The loss, so far as I can ascertain it, is 136–30 of whom were killed, and among the wounded are many mortally. [*Official Records of the Union and Confederate Armies in the War of Rebellion*, volume 27, part 1, pp. 622–626.]

PICKETT'S CHARGE

by Heather Mitchell

A solemn silence stretched uneasily between the Union and Confederate troops that morning of July 3, 1863, following the early-morning battle over Culp's Hill at the far right of the Union line. The stillness was broken by the cries of the wounded and the groans of dying horses, but the artillery was quiet — for the moment.

The bloody and bitter Battle of Gettysburg had been raging for two days, and this, the third and final day, would decide the outcome of the greatest battle of the Civil War and, ultimately, of the war itself.

The Union troops were worried. Confederate forces had attacked nearly every segment of their line, and victory seemed just out of the Confederates' reach. The Confederate army, properly known as the Army of Northern Virginia, had thrashed the North soundly many times, most recently at Chancellorsville, Virginia, only two months before. It seemed as though nothing could get in the Confederates' way.

General George Meade, who had assumed command of the North's Army of the Potomac just three days before Union and Confederate forces accidentally clashed at Gettysburg, had held a meeting with his generals the night before. They had voted to "stay and fight it out," defending Gettysburg as Union domain, but not to lead any attacks against the southern forces. They would let the Confederates take the offensive if they wanted, but the Federals would remain in their trenches and behind the stone walls of Cemetery Ridge.

General Robert E. Lee, waiting with his army across the fields, had two options: Either the Army of Northern Virginia could make a final, spectacular attack to try to break the Union line, or the Confederates could admit defeat and retreat back to their home territory. Lee and his troops were unwilling to give up so easily. They knew that if they won this battle, they could march farther into the North,

Top: Meade's headquarters during the Battle of Gettysburg.
Above: Photographer Timothy H. O'Sullivan (1840–1882), one of the greatest Civil War photographers, captured General George G. Meade (fifth from left) and other Union generals about 1865. O'Sullivan first worked with Mathew Brady and then with Alexander Gardner.

James Longstreet

J.E.B. Stuart

Above: Longstreet (1821–1904), promoted to lieutenant general in October 1862, commanded the right wing of the Confederate army at Gettysburg. It is generally thought that when he reluctantly gave the order to charge at three o'clock on the last day, it cost Lee the battle. Later in life, he was critical of Lee's performance at Gettysburg, making him unpopular in the South.

Right: Stuart (1833–1864) was known as the "eyes" of Lee's army, but he did not arrive at Gettysburg in time to give Lee the vital information he needed.

or perhaps capture Washington, D.C., more than seventy miles away. If they held Washington, they could very well win the war. It was a big gamble, and the stakes were high, but in the end Lee decided that taking the offensive was worth the risk.

The day before, the Confederates had made repeated attacks on the Union flanks (sides). Today, General Lee planned to make a full-scale assault on the center of the Union line, scattering and destroying the Army of the Potomac once and for all.

Of course, the disadvantages of the plan had to be weighed. Only one fresh division of southerners was available. Major General George Pickett's all-Virginia infantry, guarding supply wagons for the first two days of battle, had seen no action at Gettysburg. Despite the loss of thousands of men, Pickett's infantry was itching to fight. General Pickett, with his drooping mustache and long, curled hair, looked like a swashbuckling cavalier, and he, too, was eager to see battle and perhaps win everlasting glory at Gettysburg.

Another problem was that Lieutenant General James Longstreet, the corps commander, opposed the plan altogether and tried unsuccessfully to convince Lee to launch an attack on the Union's left flank instead. Finally, the attacking Confederates had to cross a nearly mile-long stretch of open ground before they could confront the enemy. The Federals had dug in infantry equipped with long-range rifles to defend their position on Cemetery Hill, and they were backed by cannon besides. The strategy of pitting massed troops against weapons designed to slaughter large numbers of soldiers could spell wholesale destruction for the South.

But General Lee's plan seemed solid enough. A fierce barrage of cannon fire would weaken the Union forces. This would be followed by General Pickett's three brigades spearheading the assault on the Union center. To tie up the loose ends, General Richard S. Ewell would go after the Federals' right flank, and Major General J.E.B. Stuart's famous cavalry would circle around to the rear, ready to surprise the enemy when they retreated.

Lee, it seemed, had thought of everything. But for all his wisdom, he had underestimated the enemy. The Federals, used to marching deep into enemy territory amid the resentment of the southern populace, had often been defeated by the heroic and often outnumbered Confederates. Now the tables were turned. The Federals in Pennsylvania found themselves local heroes and this time were defending their homeland against the southern invaders.

A little after one o'clock that afternoon, the blast and roar of cannon fire interrupted the hazy stillness. The thundering of nearly three hundred cannon could be heard far and wide.

Meanwhile, nearly twelve thousand Confederate soldiers had been forming their lines all along Seminary Ridge under the cover of ridges and woods. At three o'clock, General Longstreet reluctantly gave the order for the charge to advance. "I could see the desperate and hopeless nature of the charge and the hopeless slaughter it would cause," he wrote long after. "That day at Gettysburg was one of the saddest of my life."

With parade-ground precision, the Confederates marched valiantly forth — Pickett's men on the right, John Johnston Pettigrew's soldiers on the left — supported by even more troops in the rear. A mass of gray infantry flowed unfalteringly toward the Union line in a solid wave nearly a mile wide. The Federals had never seen such a sight. They waited silently, holding their fire until the Confederates were a little closer.

When the order to fire was given, it did not take the Federals long to act. They fired, and gray-clad soldiers fell in clumps. The survivors surged forward, faster now. The famous "rebel (Confederate) yell" rang out as the men in gray closed the gap between themselves and the Union line. At first it seemed as though the torrent of men could not be stopped, but as they continued to fall, a Union victory seemed closer at hand. The few Confederates who made it behind the Union lines had little chance of survival. Many surrendered, and those who did not fought valiantly to the end.

George E. Pickett

Meanwhile, J.E.B. Stuart's cavalry was repulsed at the rear of the battlefield by Union troops, including General George Custer's horsemen. When Stuart's men saw that the battle was lost, they turned back to Seminary Ridge.

General Lee rode into the field to praise and rally the survivors of Pickett's Charge. "It's all my fault," he told his men sadly. "It is I who have lost this fight, and you must help me out of it the best way you can." He believed that General Meade would order a counterattack to take advantage of the disorganized state of Lee's army and perhaps destroy the Army of Northern Virginia once and for all. But the expected counterattack never came. Meade neglected to follow through on his victory. Instead, he gave the enemy time to regroup and allowed them to withdraw to Virginia the following day under cover of a heavy rainstorm. Meade has been criticized for that error ever since.

Hell for Glory, a contemporary painting by Keith Rocco, depicts Pickett's Virginia Division at Gettysburg, with Brigadier General Richard Garnett's brigade on its left flank. Garnett is shown on his bay horse Red Eye.

Both the Union and the Confederate forces suffered enormous losses that day at Gettysburg. Of the nearly twelve thousand Confederate soldiers who took part in Pickett's Charge, perhaps only half returned to fight again.

Historians say that Pickett's Charge is representative of the entire Confederate war effort. Just as the men in Pickett's Charge carried a sense of unbeatability onto the fields around Gettysburg, the entire South believed it was indestructible. In both cases, a deep sense of matchless valor met with disaster

Union soldiers enjoyed reading news fresh from the front. Newspapers were delivered by newsmen on horseback, who unrolled the single sheets and distributed them.

NEWS FROM THE BATTLEFIELD

by Janine Richardson

C.C. Coffin and Samuel Wilkeson were among the more than three hundred reporters who followed the Union armies from battle to battle during the Civil War. They provided on-the-spot accounts of major battles, and their information was often the first report the War Department and President Abraham Lincoln had of how a battle was progressing.

C.C. Coffin was not just an ace reporter; he was a gifted musician as well. His knowledge of notes and tones helped him distinguish what ammunition was whizzing around his head. Known as being brave and steadfast under fire, this well-educated New Hampshire native was one of the few news correspondents to stay on the job throughout the war. His reports of the Battle of Gettysburg appeared in the *Boston Journal*.

Also reporting from Gettysburg was Samuel Wilkeson. Wilkeson had been involved in journalism since his grammar school days, when he had published a weekly newspaper. Later trained as a lawyer, Wilkeson had left his legal practice to pursue a newspaper career. At the beginning of the war, he was the *New York Tribune*'s Washington correspondent.

Aside from reporting the details of each battle, reporters like Coffin and Wilkeson compiled lists of the dead and wounded, interviewed prisoners of war, and sketched pictures of the people and events they saw. During the terror and confusion of battle, they took care of the wounded and offered whatever other assistance they could provide. Reporting was a hazardous job, for sickness and injury struck those observing the battle as well as those fighting it.

The Civil War had created a boom in news publishing and had changed the appearance and nature of newspapers. The pace of news reporting quickened as people demanded the latest accounts of fast-breaking events. Americans were emotionally, physically, and financially caught up in this great conflict, and they wanted to know the latest news from the front. After a great battle, a newspaper's circulation often increased to five times its normal level. The war inspired the creation of Sunday papers, and several daily editions were common. These afternoon and evening editions were called "extras" because initially they were extra editions put out after significant events.

The armies also provided a huge market for newspaper sales. Pickets (front-line sentinels) commonly swapped newspapers, along with tobacco and other prized items, with their enemy counterparts.

During the war, news publishing also became more profitable, and technical innovations came into widespread use. Expensive telegraphed reports mushroomed from two to three columns per paper to two to three pages. Improvements in typesetting and printing also were made, and headline sizes were increased greatly to produce a dramatic effect. As bylines became widely used, formerly anonymous reporters became celebrities.

The pace of news reporting quickened as people demanded the latest accounts of fast-breaking events.

With the papers rolled up on their horses, these newsmen from the *World* and the *Herald* pass the road guards in the hope of reaching the troops first.

Both Samuel Wilkeson and C.C. Coffin arrived at Gettysburg on July 3, 1863, the third day of the battle. They witnessed the Confederate bombardment and Pickett's Charge, which marked the climax of the Battle of Gettysburg.

On that day, the armies had gathered on two roughly parallel ridges — the Confederates on Seminary Ridge and the Federals on Cemetery Ridge. At about 1 P.M., Robert E. Lee's artillery on Seminary Ridge opened fire. "Every size and form of shell known to British and American gunnery shrieked, whirled, moaned, and whistled and wrathfully fluttered over our ground," Wilkeson wrote. "Not an orderly — not an ambulance — not a straggler was to be seen upon the plain swept by this tempest of orchestral death thirty minutes after it commenced."

The Federal guns returned the fire, but shortly after 2 P.M., either as a ruse or to preserve ammunition, they were slowly silenced. At the pause of gunfire, about twelve thousand Confederate soldiers moved across the mile-long valley separating the two ridges. They marched at a walk — one hundred yards a minute. Blasted by the Union artillery, they continued on.

Describing the horrendous hand to hand combat that ensued, C.C. Coffin

A *New York Herald Tribune* wagon (at left) and reporters in the field.

wrote, "Men fire into each other's faces, not five feet apart. There are bayonet thrusts, sabre-strokes, pistol shots; cool, deliberate movements on the part of some, — hot, passionate, desperate efforts with others.... There are ghastly heaps of dead men."

When the battle was over, victory belonged to the Federals, but both armies had suffered devastating losses. Wilkeson sat beside the body of his nineteen-year-old son while he wrote his account of Gettysburg. Lieutenant Bayard Wilkeson had been injured on the first day of the battle and had died from lack of medical attention to his wounds.

Coffin galloped away in search of telegraph wires to relay his story. Most had been cut, so he boarded a hospital train and made his way back to Boston. Once there, he locked himself in a room, wrote his copy, then threw himself down on a stack of newspapers and slept for twenty-four hours.

SHERIDAN'S RIDE

by Harold Holzer

No event of the Civil War thrilled the North more thoroughly than the inspiring gallop through the Shenandoah Valley of Virginia that became known as Sheridan's ride. The hero who rode his way to glory was Union general Philip Henry Sheridan. "Little Phil," as he was known to his adoring troops, made up for his small stature with a healthy dose of bravery and aggressiveness. Sheridan was also an able military strategist. His Shenandoah Campaign in the Virginia valley had been wildly successful. Union forces had triumphed at both Winchester and Fisher's Hill. The fighting appeared to be over.

But on October 19, 1864, the day of his famous ride, Sheridan was fast asleep in his headquarters at Winchester when Confederate forces launched a surprise attack against the Union at Cedar Creek, some twenty miles away. The booming artillery woke the general from his slumber.

Sometime after 8 A.M., Sheridan mounted his horse and rode into town to investigate. He soon grew worried. The "unceasing roar" of battle, as Sheridan later described it, not only continued but grew louder. This could only mean that Union troops were being forced into retreat and moving closer and closer back toward Winchester.

Now joined by three hundred cavalrymen, Sheridan rode quickly up to a hill outside Winchester and was shocked by what he saw. Slowly coming toward him was what Sheridan described as "a panic-stricken army — hundreds of slightly wounded men, throngs of others unhurt but demoralized...all pressing to the rear in hopeless confusion." For a moment, Sheridan thought he should try to stop the retreat and order the men to take a stand and fight back from here in Winchester.

But quickly Sheridan decided instead "that I ought to try now to restore their broken ranks, or, failing that, to share their fate."

Sheridan ordered twenty of his cavalry to follow him, and astride his horse, Rienzi, he began galloping rapidly toward Cedar Creek. Waving his hat in the air as he sped by the exhausted troops, he inspired them first to wave back, then to turn around and head with him back toward the front. "Every mounted officer who saw me," Sheridan proudly remembered, "galloped out...to tell the men at a distance that I had come back."

When he finally arrived at the scene of the fighting, Sheridan found his exhausted troops clinging to a line of rail fences on a hillside. The general daringly galloped Rienzi toward the line, then leaped across the fence and up the hill, again waving his hat to his soldiers. The troops responded by leaping up from their positions, waving back, and planting themselves more confidently in their dangerous positions.

Sheridan's ride electrified his army as it was on the verge of collapse. Sheridan took advantage of the emotion of the moment by ordering a counterattack. At 4 P.M., Union troops burst through enemy lines and sent the Confederates into a full retreat. Somehow, Sheridan had turned a certain defeat into a ringing victory. Casualties were high — more than eighty-five hundred men on both sides — but the triumph earned Sheridan a commendation from Congress and the praise of President Abraham Lincoln himself.

Several weeks after the Battle of Cedar Creek, a poet-artist named Thomas Buchanan Read became so inspired by a newspaper sketch of Sheridan's ride that he locked himself in a room and within hours composed a long, dramatic poem about the incident. Just days later, his good friend actor James Murdoch appeared on-stage in Cincinnati, Ohio, to recite it before a wildly enthusiastic audience. Overnight, the poem became popular throughout the North. It was performed before

SHERIDAN'S RIDE

He dashed down the line 'mid a storm of huzzahs,
And the wave of retreat checked its course there, because
The sight of the master compelled it to pause,
With foam and with dust the black charger was gray;
By the flash of his eye, and the red nostril's play,
He seemed to the whole great army to say,
"I have brought you Sheridan all the way
    From Winchester down to save the day!"

Hurrah! Hurrah for Sheridan!
Hurrah! Hurrah for horse and man!
And when their statues are placed on high,
Under the dome of the Union sky...
Be it said in letters both bold and bright:
    "Here is the steed that saved the day,
By carrying Sheridan into the fight,
    From Winchester, twenty miles away!"

excited crowds and published in newspapers all over the Union. Although the verses might seem a bit overdone to modern readers, they were perfectly suited to their time and place. Civil War era readers adored them.

Read went on to paint a famous portrait of Sheridan and Rienzi, thus further ensuring Sheridan's reputation (see page 245). A copy of the canvas now hangs in the U.S. Military Academy at West Point, New York.

Sheridan surely deserved the adoration showered on him after his great ride. He not only exhibited extraordinary energy and courage, but the battle also proved decisive. The Confederates never tried to recapture the Shenandoah Valley again.

More important, Sheridan's triumph was a symbolic one. In an age in which machines were rapidly overshadowing human beings in waging war, he showed that one brave and daring individual could turn the tide of battle.

MODERN WAR AT HAMPTON ROADS: THE *MONITOR* VS. THE *MERRIMAC*

by Harold Holzer

The Civil War has long been called "the first modern war" — the first in which machines and weapons counted even more than individual courage and classic strategy. If this is so, then it might be said that the modern war began in earnest on March 9, 1862. On that day, two ugly, fearsome ironclad warships faced each other in a duel at sea off Hampton Roads, Virginia.

This 1863 engraving captures the famous naval battle between the *Monitor* and the *Merrimac* on March 9, 1862.

When it was over, neither vessel had damaged the other, but together the ships had changed naval warfare forever.

Ironclads had already been introduced in Europe, and both Union and Confederate leaders began planning to build ironclad warships as early as 1861. Late that year, the Confederacy commenced to build an armor-plated vessel on the hulk of the *Merrimac,* a wooden ship that the Union had abandoned in Norfolk, Virginia, and burned all the way down to the water line. Since the Confederate navy proposed that its first iron-plated warship be built low to the water, the burned-out but still-floating hulk of the *Merrimac* seemed the ideal foundation for its first experiment.

Southern engineers proceeded to build a ship entirely covered on its sides and deck by armor plates designed to resist the most powerful enemy shells. It would ride beneath the surface of the water, leaving fully exposed only a powerful ram at the bow and a heavily armored gun casemate that looked almost like a small, floating building. The vessel, completed in early 1862, was renamed the CSS *Virginia,* although most historians have always referred to it by its original name, the *Merrimac.*

Meanwhile, a persistent Swedish-born inventor named John Ericsson had convinced the Lincoln administration that the Union, too, needed to develop iron-plated ships to combat the *Merrimac.* The Union paid $275,000 to build its first ironclad based on Ericsson's design. It took the determined inventor only one hundred days to complete the vessel, which was launched from Brooklyn, New York, in January 1862.

The *Monitor* was much smaller than the *Merrimac,* but it was faster and easier to maneuver. It boasted only three guns, but they fired from a turret that revolved. No one knew which vessel would survive in a one-on-one fight, but doubters nicknamed Ericsson's marvel "the Yankee cheesebox on a raft" and predicted that it would neither float nor survive heavy shelling.

On March 8, 1862, without the benefit of either a trial run or a training mission, Confederate captain Franklin Buchanan steamed the slow-moving *Merrimac* into the deep waters off Hampton Roads and launched a fierce attack on the all-wooden ships of the old Union navy off the coast of Newport News, Virginia. At least two great warships proved defenseless against the surprise attack.

First, the *Merrimac* rammed the USS *Cumberland.* The Confederate ironclad struck the wooden ship so viciously that the point of its iron ram broke off and remained in the side of the *Cumberland.* The ramming left a huge hole in the wooden warship below the water line, and within moments the Union vessel sank.

Next the *Merrimac* aimed its deadly iron ram at another wooden ship, the USS *Congress.* But fearing the same fate as the *Cumberland,* the captain of the *Congress* sailed the ship into shallow water and ran it aground, where the heavy, low-lying enemy ironclad could not follow. But the *Congress* was hardly safe. Instead of ramming the ship, the *Merrimac* opened fire with a blistering attack that quickly set the wooden ship on fire and destroyed it.

Thus, in a matter of minutes, the U.S. Navy suffered the most devastating losses in its history. Not until the Japanese attack on the American fleet at Pearl Harbor in 1941 would a worse defeat occur. In Washington, Lincoln's cabinet worried that the *Merrimac* would destroy the entire Union navy the next day and then head for the Potomac River, sail into Washington, D.C., and shell the northern capital into submission. Nothing, they were convinced, could stop it from winning the war single-handedly. They were wrong.

The next morning, March 9, the *Merrimac* prepared to resume its attack, as the rest of the Union squadron anticipated destruction. Turning its attention first on yet another defenseless ship, the USS *Minnesota,* the *Merrimac* prepared to ram. At

A Federal recruiting poster issued at New Berne, North Carolina, in November 1863.

John Lorimer Worden

Top: The crew of the original USS *Monitor* relax on deck.
Above: Worden (1818–1897) commanded the *Monitor* during the battle with the *Merrimac*. He was wounded in the face and temporarily blinded.

first, the old Union ship seemed destined for the same fate as the *Congress*. But suddenly, just before 9 A.M., the long-awaited Union ironclad *Monitor* appeared over the horizon to save what was left of the Union fleet and challenge the *Merrimac*.

Like two dueling gladiators, the vessels circled each other and opened fire. For the next two hours, they kept up a relentless, brutal attack. Smoke spewed from both steam-powered vessels. Shells burst across the water line and exploded on both decks. Unhurt, the *Monitor* steamed off at 11 A.M. to take on more ammunition. One eyewitness described the shelling as "merciless" but "ineffective." The armor plates protected both ships, and the shelling did no noticeable damage to either vessel.

At noon, the *Monitor* reappeared, and the classic battle began anew. Once again, the two vessels shelled each other ferociously. At one point, a Confederate shell exploded just outside the narrow slit through which the *Monitor*'s captain, John Worden, watched the action. The explosion blinded Worden temporarily, and once again the *Monitor* steamed toward shore. It was midafternoon, and the tide was too low to allow the heavy Confederate ironclad to pursue its foe. The *Merrimac* steamed out to sea, ending the battle.

Neither ironclad could claim a clear victory, but both sides knew that naval warfare would never be the same again. For the next two months, the two ships followed each other. The *Merrimac* tried to force the *Monitor* into deep water for another fight. The *Monitor* hoped to steer the *Merrimac* into shallow water to run it aground and destroy it. Neither plan worked.

On May 9, 1862, Union forces captured Norfolk, Virginia. The *Merrimac* suddenly found that it had no home port to call its own and nowhere to turn for supplies or ammunition. Fearing that his helpless ship would be captured and taken over by the Union navy, the *Merrimac*'s captain steamed the ship toward shore and then burned it. The ironclad that the Union could not sink was thus sunk by its own crew.

The *Monitor* fought on for the Union, participating in several battles, and then headed for the Washington Navy Yard for repairs. It was relaunched that November and headed back to the scene of its great duel at Hampton Roads. But on the night of December 29, 1862, a huge storm struck the area, and the *Monitor* sank without a trace, going down with all sixteen crew members.

By the time the *Merrimac* and *Monitor* were destroyed, both sides in the war had launched new ironclads. The Union built at least sixty *Monitor*-type ships, and the Confederacy launched some twenty-two. At every naval battle to come, on the open seas or on mighty rivers, iron-plated ships fought alongside or against wooden ships. Union ironclads also began pounding away at southern harbors such as Charleston, South Carolina.

The great duel between the *Monitor* and the *Merrimac* changed the Civil War and naval warfare everywhere in the world. Their heroic duel launched the iron age at sea and made technology as important as heroism in all wars to come.

THE BATTLE OF THE SAILING SHIPS:
THE *KEARSARGE* VS. THE *ALABAMA*

by Harold Holzer

One of the most famous naval battles of the Civil War actually made very little difference in the outcome of the war. The battle involved two ships, both of them outdated wooden vessels with billowing sails, and did not even take place in the United States. It occurred off the coast of northern France. But Americans loved the romantic story of the one-on-one duel between the USS *Kearsarge* and the CSS *Alabama* in June 1864. The *Kearsarge* won the battle, and the victory so thrilled northerners that the news may have helped President Abraham Lincoln win reelection later that year.

The *Kearsarge* was launched in 1862. A wooden, seven-gun sailing ship also equipped with steam power, it was immediately ordered to Europe. There the ship stood guard near Gibraltar to prevent a Confederate vessel from sailing off to the American South. In 1863, under the command of Captain John A. Winslow, the *Kearsarge* began patrolling European waters.

Built in England and launched around the same time, the Confederate ship *Alabama* was nearly the same size as the *Kearsarge* and boasted eight guns. The *Alabama* was placed under the command of a dashing captain named Raphael Semmes, whose long, waxed mustache made him look like a hero of old.

For the next two years, Semmes sailed the *Alabama* all around the world — into the Atlantic Ocean, down the coast of Brazil, westward into the Indian Ocean, around the southern tip of Africa, and then back into the Atlantic again. The Confederate warship never once docked inside the Confederacy itself, instead taking on supplies in ports of call around the globe.

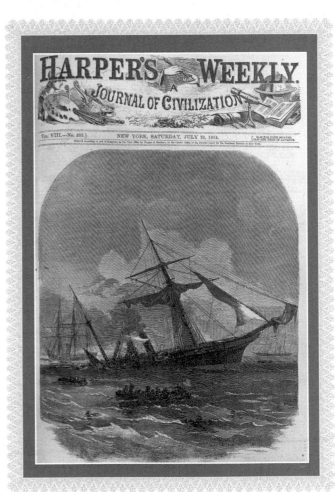

On July 23, 1864, the cover of *Harper's Weekly* featured the June 19 sinking of the Confederate raider *Alabama* off Cherbourg, France.

Under Captain Semmes, the *Alabama* operated as a so-called commerce raider. It attacked Union warships and merchant ships alike, stealing their cargo and sinking them. In its twenty-one months at sea, the *Alabama* captured or destroyed between fifty-five and sixty-nine "enemy" ships. Some were Union warships, but many were all-but-defenseless whalers and other nonmilitary vessels. Altogether, the *Alabama* looted cargo worth some $6.5 million, a huge sum in the 1860s. To angry northerners, the *Alabama* was no better than a pirate ship.

Union military leaders insisted that a way be found to destroy the dangerous *Alabama*. The North got its chance in June 1864, when the *Alabama*, too long at sea and badly in need of repair, limped into the harbor of Cherbourg, France, to

CHARLES FRANCIS ADAMS: A YANKEE DIPLOMAT

by Thomas R. Harris, Jr.

Charles Francis Adams, son of President John Quincy Adams, was elected to the House of Representatives in 1858. He served on the Committee of Thirty-three, created to solve the secession crisis. Adams tried to work out a compromise, but feelings on both sides were too strong.

Soon after Abraham Lincoln became president in 1861, he appointed Adams minister to Great Britain. Britain was the world's leading nation, and its textile mills made cloth from cotton imported from the American South. The South hoped — and the North feared — that Britain would give its support to the Confederacy.

In May 1861, when Secretary of State William Seward sent a dispatch to the British government making it sound as though the United States was "ready to declare war with all the powers of Europe," Adams delivered the message with such tact that relations between the two nations were not damaged. A short time later, a Union ship stopped a British steamer and arrested two Confederate agents who were on board. When the British public heard the news, they demanded war. Adams persuaded Seward to find a peaceful solution to the problem.

During the early years of the war, a Confederate agent named James Bullock arranged for several warships to be built in British shipyards. Adams collected enough evidence to convince the British government to stop one of those ships, "hull 290," from sailing. To the Union's dismay, the ship, renamed the *Alabama,* slipped out of Liverpool in 1862 and attacked Union merchant ships around the world for the following two years. But Adams was able to keep two other ironclads commissioned by the Confederacy from being delivered.

Following the war, Adams began gathering information on the damage done to Union vessels by Confederate ships built in England. These claims, known as the "*Alabama* claims," resulted in Britain's paying more than fifteen million dollars in damages to the United States.

The surrender of the *Alabama.*

be overhauled. News of its arrival reached the nearby *Kearsarge.* Within three days, Captain Winslow maneuvered the Yankee warship into international waters outside the French harbor, blocking the *Alabama*'s exit.

Captain Semmes might have chosen to remain in port, ignoring the enemy warship poised in the waters beyond. But instead he decided to try fighting his way out of the harbor. It was a poor decision. On Sunday, June 19, the *Alabama* sailed out of the harbor to meet the *Kearsarge* face to face. Hundreds of French citizens, sensing a great battle, gathered on the hills of Cherbourg to watch the action. Among them, it is believed, was the great French impressionist Edouard Manet, who would later paint a famous canvas of the battle.

When they were within sight, the two graceful wooden ships began circling each other in steadily narrowing arcs. They opened fire at 11 A.M., blasting away even before their shells could reach their target. They quickly closed in on one another, and by the eighth circle, they were close enough to do serious damage.

In a cascade of dark smoke, the *Kearsarge* struck the *Alabama* with a series of devastating shells below the water line. Casualties on board the *Alabama* mounted, and seawater poured into the decks below. By noon, the Confederate ship began tilting over on its side. After only one hour of furious fighting, the *Alabama* sank, "graceful," one Union sailor admitted, "even in death."

Captain Winslow and the *Kearsarge* captured sixty-three prisoners, but Captain Semmes and thirty-eight survivors escaped the Yankees. They were rescued by an English yacht that had been sailing nearby to observe the action.

When news of the destruction of the *Alabama* reached the American North a few weeks later, the Union erupted in celebration. Not only was the dreaded pirate ship finally on the bottom of the ocean, but the North had proved that in face-to-face, one-on-one battle, its men were as brave and heroic as the southerners. Captain Semmes tried to poison the good cheer by claiming that the *Kearsarge*'s crew had "cheated" by lowering heavy chains down the ship's sides before the battle. The chains acted like armor, Semmes charged, and gave the *Kearsarge* an unfair advantage. But Semmes seemed to believe that the rules of knighthood applied to modern warfare. Even in the Confederacy, one long-time admirer, diarist Mary Chesnut, labeled Semmes a "fool."

Before long, pictures of the sea battle began appearing in northern newspapers. Prints designed for display in northern homes rolled off the presses of the Union's picture publishers. Artists began producing painting after painting of the encounter.

Of all the sea battles of the Civil War, the only one to inspire as many artists was the much more crucial fight between the ironclads *Monitor* and *Merrimac*. The battle between the *Kearsarge* and the *Alabama* reminded Americans of the past, when beautiful sailing ships dominated the oceans. Such ships looked far more graceful than ugly ironclads, and their heroic sailors and officers fought on deck, visible to all, not inside armor-plated gun turrets. Americans seemed to prefer imagining that Civil War naval warfare looked more like the fight between the *Alabama* and the *Kearsarge* than the battle between the *Monitor* and the *Merrimac*.

Poet Thomas Buchanan Read was so inspired by the old-fashioned duel of wooden ships on the open sea that he wrote a patriotic verse he called "The Eagle and the Vulture." Read summed up the emotions of the entire North when he wrote:

Captain John A. Winslow and officers on board the USS *Kearsarge* after sinking the *Alabama*, 1864.

The Cherbourg Cliffs were all alive
With lookers-on, like a swarming hive;
While compelled to do what he dared not shirk,
The pirate went to his desperate work;
And Europe's tyrants looked on in glee,
As they thought of our Kearsarge sunk in the sea.
But our little bark smiled back at them
A smile of contempt, with that Union gem,
The American banner, far-floating and free,
Proclaiming her champions were out on the sea;
Were out on the sea, and abroad in the land,
Determined to win under God's command.

America's interest in the battle of the *Alabama* and the *Kearsarge* continued for years to come. After the war, the reunited country demanded that England pay the United States $19 million for the damage done to Union vessels and property by Confederate warships built by the British. For years, England refused to pay, but eventually it was forced to hand over $15.5 million in gold. To the surprise of no one who remembered the classic sea battle that sank the dreaded Confederate raider, Americans nicknamed the case the "*Alabama* claims."

THE SAVIOR OF THE UNION

During the Civil War,

his admirers called him "Uncle Abe," "Father Abraham," and the "Great Emancipator."

His enemies called him "tyrant," "baboon," and "imbecile." History has judged him the "Savior of the Union" — the man who led the fight to save American democracy and blessed the struggle with some of the most beautiful words ever written in the English language.

Politician, president, orator, poet — Abraham Lincoln was all these things. And he not only preserved the Union, he also became its greatest symbol. He rose from a log cabin to the White House and believed that every American had the right to do the same.

Lincoln's greatest contribution may well have been the example of his own life. "I am living witness," he told a regiment of Ohio soldiers visiting the White House in 1864, "that any one of your children may look to come here as my father's child has."

Opportunity, he declared, was a "jewel" worth fighting for, and American democracy alone offered it.

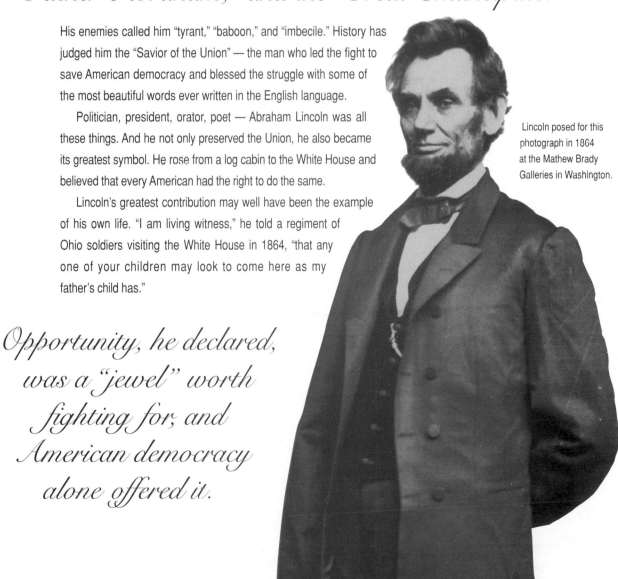

Lincoln posed for this photograph in 1864 at the Mathew Brady Galleries in Washington.

Lincoln Time Line

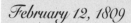

by Jane L. Symens

February 12, 1809

Abraham Lincoln is born near Hodgenville, Kentucky.

1816

Family moves to Indiana.

October 5, 1818

Lincoln's mother, Nancy Hanks Lincoln, dies.

December 2, 1819

Lincoln's father, Thomas Lincoln, marries Sarah Bush Johnston.

March 1, 1830

Family moves to Illinois.

July 1831

Lincoln moves to New Salem (near Springfield); becomes a surveyor, storekeeper, and postmaster.

April–July 1832

Serves in the Black Hawk War.

1834–1841

Serves in the Illinois legislature.

September 9, 1836

Gets law license while still in New Salem.

April 15, 1837

Moves to Springfield and becomes law partner with John Stuart.

Spring 1841

Becomes law partner with Stephen T. Logan.

November 4, 1842

Marries Mary Todd.

August 1, 1843

Son Robert Todd is born (dies 1926).

December 1844

Lincoln becomes law partner with William ("Billy") Herndon.

March 10, 1846

Son Edward ("Eddie") Baker is born (dies 1850).

March 4, 1847–March 3, 1849

Lincoln serves as U.S. representative.

December 21, 1850

Son William ("Willie") Wallace is born (dies 1862).

April 4, 1853

Son Thomas ("Tad") is born (dies 1871).

1856

Lincoln becomes involved in the new Republican party.

August 21–October 15, 1858

Participates in seven debates with Democrat Stephen A. Douglas, against whom he is running for the U.S. Senate.

November 2, 1858

Loses Senate election.

May 18, 1860

Is nominated for president by the Republican party.

November 6, 1860

Is elected president.

December 20, 1860

South Carolina secedes from the Union.

February 18, 1861

Jefferson Davis is inaugurated president of the Confederate States of America.

March 4, 1861

Lincoln is inaugurated U.S. president at age fifty-two.

April 12, 1861

Fort Sumter, in Charleston harbor, South Carolina, is fired upon; the Civil War begins.

January 1, 1863

Lincoln's Emancipation Proclamation goes into effect.

November 19, 1863

Lincoln delivers the Gettysburg Address.

November 8, 1864

Is elected to a second term as president.

March 4, 1865

Is inaugurated for second term as president.

April 9, 1865

Robert E. Lee surrenders, effectively ending the Civil War.

April 14, 1865

Actor John Wilkes Booth shoots the president at Ford's Theatre.

April 15, 1865

Lincoln dies at 7:22 a.m.

May 4, 1865

Is buried in Springfield, Illinois.

December 18, 1865

Thirteenth Amendment, abolishing slavery, is adopted.

FROM LOG HOUSE TO STATEHOUSE: YOUNG ABE LINCOLN

by Edison McIntyre

Abraham Lincoln's rise to the presidency did not come easily. In fact, young Abe lost his first election, finishing eighth among thirteen candidates. Lincoln had known setbacks before, and he would have others, but he possessed a determination to succeed that was born in the rugged country where he grew up.

In 1806, twenty-eight-year-old Thomas Lincoln married twenty-two-year-old Nancy Hanks. The couple settled near Elizabethtown, Kentucky, where their daughter, Sarah, was born in 1807.

The Lincolns owned a series of farms, but Thomas grew barely enough food to feed his family. He made most of his living as a skilled carpenter. He built the one-room log cabin near Hodgenville where his son Abraham was born in 1809.

In later years, Abe remembered little about Kentucky. He was just seven years old when his family decided to leave Kentucky and move farther west, across the Ohio River to Indiana. The Lincolns settled in what is now Spencer County, a few miles north of the river. Although Indiana became a state that year, 1816, the land along the Ohio was dense forest with few trails or settlements. Abe and his family spent their first winter there in a rough lean-to shelter while Thomas built a cabin.

Around the time of Abe's eighth birthday, the Lincolns moved into their new home. Abe was tall and strong for his age. He took up an ax to cut down the surrounding trees and hitched up a team to plow the fields he had cleared. He hauled water to the new house from the nearest spring, a mile away.

The farm began to yield good crops, and as more settlers came to the area, Thomas found more work as a carpenter. But 1818 was a cruel year. A disease called milk-sick struck the community. It killed Nancy, who was then just

Above: Lincoln worked at New Salem as a postmaster and a storekeeper until his shop, as he put it, "winked out."

Left: New Salem Village, outside Springfield, Illinois, re-creates life during Lincoln's time. Here a reenactor weaves a basket.

thirty-four years old.

Death at such an early age was common in the 1800s. Abe's younger brother, also named Thomas, died when only a baby; Sarah died at age twenty while bearing her first child. When Abe was ten, he nearly died after being kicked by a horse. He learned quickly the hard lessons of life.

Abe also learned to value knowledge. Thomas and Nancy had little formal education. In fact, Thomas could hardly sign his name, while Nancy signed with an X. Still, they had great respect for learning. Nancy loved to tell Bible stories to Sarah and Abe, and before the family left Kentucky, she sent Abe to a small school near their home.

About a year after Nancy died, Thomas went back to Elizabethtown. When he returned to Indiana, he brought with him his second wife. Sarah Bush Johnston Lincoln, a widow with three children, was warm and loving; she quickly adopted Abe and Sarah as her own.

Like his mother, Abe's stepmother encouraged him to learn all he could. Over the years, he received less than twelve months of schooling, but at age twelve he could read, write, and do a bit of arithmetic. An eager student, Abe often walked several miles to borrow books. He read the Bible, *Aesop's Fables, Robinson Crusoe, Pilgrim's Progress,* a biography of George Washington — anything he could find. He enjoyed listening to his father and other adults talk late into the night about farming, politics, and life.

Abraham and Mary Lincoln purchased their home in Springfield in 1844 from the minister who married them and expanded it several times over the years. It was the only home they ever owned.

By age fourteen, Abe was old enough to work away from the Lincoln farm when his father could spare him. Over the next few years, he had several jobs — clearing land, splitting logs for fence rails, helping to run a ferry — and he gave most of his earnings to his father. When he was nineteen, he helped guide a flatboat loaded with produce down the Mississippi River to New Orleans. It was his first trip to a big city.

In 1830, the Lincoln family moved west again, this time to Illinois. Soon afterward, Abe left home and began working in a general store in New Salem, a small settlement near Springfield. He enjoyed roughhousing with his new friends and loved to wrestle, but he also spent many hours reading. He joined a debating group and, in 1831, voted for the first time.

The following year, Lincoln decided to run for the Illinois legislature. His campaign was severely delayed when he volunteered to serve in the Black Hawk War. He returned to New Salem in late July and campaigned hard, but he lost the election. Still, Lincoln got 277 of the 300 votes in his hometown, and that encouraged him to run again. In 1834, with overwhelming support from New Salem, Lincoln won a seat in the legislature. It was just the beginning for the frontier boy who would eventually be one of our most famous presidents.

1854: YEAR OF DECISION

by George L. Painter

During the early 1850s, Abraham Lincoln devoted most of his attention to his law practice, which was growing into one of the largest in the state of Illinois. In 1854, he once again became active in the political arena. This occurred after congressional passage of the Kansas-Nebraska Act, which Senator Stephen A. Douglas of Illinois had spearheaded through Congress.

The act established the territories of Kansas and Nebraska, which had previously been referred to simply as Kansas. The organization of this vast region had been delayed by controversy between the North and the South over the question of whether slavery would be allowed to spread into territories where it was not already established.

In Congress, four previous attempts to organize a single territory had been unsuccessful, chiefly because of slaveholding states' opposition to the Missouri Compromise. Enacted by Congress more than thirty years earlier, the Missouri Compromise had become a time-honored barrier to the extension of slavery. Under its terms, Missouri had been allowed to enter the union as a slave state and territories from the Louisiana Purchase south of latitude 36°30´ were permitted to have slavery. The institution was prohibited north of that line, including the area known as Kansas.

Because the West was being settled rapidly, Senator Douglas regarded the territorial organization of Kansas as an urgent matter. In an attempt to win over slaveholding states, he introduced legislation that left the question of slavery up to the territorial settlers. Douglas called this the principle of popular sovereignty.

This feature of the Kansas-Nebraska Act contradicted the provisions of the Missouri Compromise. An amendment to the original version of the bill explicitly repealed the earlier legislation. The bill was signed into law on May 30, 1854.

Douglas saw the settlement of the West as essential and regarded slavery as a less important issue, although he expressed the hope that Kansas and Nebraska would remain free. Abraham Lincoln took a very different view of the Kansas-Nebraska Act. The legislation alarmed him because it allowed the introduction of slavery into territory where the Missouri Compromise had prohibited it for more than three decades.

Although Lincoln had taken stands opposing slavery in his earlier service in the Illinois House of Representatives and U.S. Congress, prior to 1854 he did not regard it as a momentous national issue. He later explained that he held this view because he believed that the institution would eventually disappear. The Kansas-Nebraska Act shattered Lincoln's hope. From 1854 on, slavery became a focus of his public statements on political issues.

After the act was passed and Congress went into recess, an outraged public made their feelings known. Senator Douglas noted that on a journey from Washington to Illinois, "all along the Western Reserve of Ohio I could find my effigy upon every tree we passed." Douglas then embarked on a speaking tour throughout Illinois to support Democratic candidates for Congress and the state legislature. In his speeches, he also defended the legislation with which he was now identified.

Stephen A. Douglas

He introduced legislation that left the question of slavery up to the territorial settlers.

This photograph of Douglas was taken around 1861, the year of his death. Three years later, his widow signed a copy and presented it to the Lincolns, who kept it in their photo album.

In September 1854, Lincoln again became a candidate for the Illinois House of Representatives. Although he was not running directly against Douglas, the Kansas-Nebraska Act was the major point of contention in the 1854 campaign. In a sense, all candidates opposed to that act were running against its sponsor.

In comparison with the Lincoln-Douglas debates that formed so prominent a feature of the Illinois senatorial campaign of 1858, the 1854 debates between the two men were played out on a smaller scale. These events received much less attention, both from the public and press at the time and subsequently from historians. They also were less significant in the development of Lincoln's political career. Nonetheless, these debates, along with other speeches he delivered that year, represented a milestone in the expression of Lincoln's position on slavery.

As part of the debates, Lincoln delivered a major three-hour speech at Peoria on the evening of October 16. Although a self-contained statement, it was intended to answer a speech given earlier in the day by Douglas. Some historians have called Lincoln's Peoria speech his first great address.

In Peoria, Lincoln attacked Douglas's Kansas-Nebraska Act. He said, "I think, and shall try to show, that it is wrong; wrong in its direct effect, letting slavery into Kansas and Nebraska — and wrong in its prospective principle, allowing it to spread to every other part of the wide world, where men can be found inclined to take it."

The Peoria speech was the most open and forceful statement of the immorality of slavery that Lincoln had made, and this stand would remain an important part of his future discussions of the issue. The speech included another theme that would continue to be a significant element of Lincoln's political statements: preservation of the Union. Lincoln called upon his fellow citizens to limit the spread of slavery by returning to the principles of the nation's founders: "If we do this, we shall not only have saved the Union; but we shall have so saved it, as to make, and to keep it, forever worthy of the saving."

After Peoria, Lincoln continued to campaign, delivering speeches in Chicago and other communities. On November 7, he was elected to the Illinois House of Representatives for the fifth time, but he decided to press on and try to win a seat in the U.S. Senate instead.

Unfortunately, his bid for the Senate was unsuccessful. Nonetheless, Lincoln continued to speak out against the expansion of slavery, and his speeches from 1854 on attracted more favorable attention.

Certainly, Lincoln's political activities in 1854 were the beginning of a chain of events that led to his election to the presidency in 1860. As passage of the Kansas-Nebraska Act had influenced Lincoln in 1854, so would Lincoln have a profound effect on the course of history through his actions as president.

"A house divided against itself cannot stand." I believe this government cannot endure, permanently half *slave* and half *free*. I do not expect the Union to be *dissolved* — I do not expect the house to *fall* — but I *do* expect it will cease to be divided. It will become *all* one thing, or *all* the other.

Speech in Springfield, Illinois, June 16, 1858

THE LINCOLN-DOUGLAS DEBATES

by Craig E. Blohm

In the mid-1800s, Ottawa, Illinois, was a small railroad town seventy miles southwest of Chicago. With a population of around six thousand, Ottawa led a rather quiet existence on the Illinois frontier. But at dawn on August 21, 1858, a great commotion stirred the sleepy town. From all directions, people converged on Ottawa. By train, by wagon, and on foot came such a multitude that soon a huge pall of dust rose over the town. From far and near, people had come to hear the first debate between Abraham Lincoln and Stephen Douglas.

The seven Lincoln-Douglas debates, held in various towns around the state, were arranged as part of the 1858 Illinois senatorial campaign. Stephen Douglas, the incumbent senator, was a powerful Democrat thought by many to be a good choice for the presidency in 1860. He was a stocky man, about five feet tall, with a barrel chest and a head that was rather large in proportion to his body. Nicknamed the "Little Giant," Douglas had been senator since 1847 and was chairman of the Senate Committee on Territories. In 1854, he authored the Kansas-Nebraska Act, a controversial bill that would help bring his long-time rival, Abraham Lincoln, back into the political arena.

Physically, Lincoln was about as different from Douglas as one could imagine. More than six feet tall, lean and rawboned, Lincoln was the favorite son of the newly formed Republican party. In contrast to Douglas, however, Lincoln's career as a lawyer and one-term member of the House of Representatives was singularly unremarkable. But the differences between the two men went deeper than appearance or career. On the ideological level, Lincoln and Douglas differed on the most important issue of the day: slavery.

In drafting his Kansas-Nebraska Act of 1854, Douglas made his opinion on slavery clear. According to the bill, slavery would be allowed in Kansas and Nebraska if the people of the territories wanted it. This was what Douglas called "popular sovereignty." To ensure passage of his bill, Douglas also included wording that repealed the Missouri Compromise of 1820 (an act that prohibited slavery above the southern border of Missouri, an area that included Kansas and Nebraska). It was obvious where Douglas stood on the issue of slavery: He did not feel it was wrong if the people wanted it.

Lincoln's reaction to the Kansas-Nebraska Act was immediate. He began speaking out against the act, publicly condemning slavery for the first time in a speech in Peoria, Illinois. But although he felt slavery was wrong, he was not an abolitionist (one who wanted slavery outlawed totally). He did, however, oppose the spread of slavery. The young Republican party, itself against slavery, was looking for someone to oppose Douglas in the senatorial race. By a unanimous vote, the Republicans nominated Lincoln as their candidate. The stage was now set for the debates between the "Little Giant" and the "Rail-splitter."

By noon, the sun shone brightly in the dusty sky over Ottawa. Brass bands played, cannon boomed, and flags flapped on the rooftops of stores and houses. About twelve thousand people jammed the town square, anxious to see and hear the two opponents. Reporters stood by to record every word with a new

As I would not be a *slave*, so I would not be a *master*. This expresses my idea of democracy.

Fragment written around August 1858

method of note taking called shorthand. For the first time, a political debate would be available to a mass audience through the newspapers. At 2:30 P.M., everything was ready; the debate began.

Douglas, who spoke first, was an experienced orator. He accused Lincoln of being an abolitionist and of favoring a civil war. He explained his doctrine of popular sovereignty as the answer to the question of slavery in the United States.

After an hour, it was Lincoln's turn. His sometimes shrill voice and informal manner were in distinct contrast to Douglas. Lincoln avoided specific replies to Douglas's accusations, preferring to think out his answers and respond at the next debate. He did, however, accuse Douglas of being part of a conspiracy to extend slavery in the territories, a charge that never was proved. Lincoln spoke for an hour and a half, then Douglas replied for thirty minutes more.

After three hours of oratory, the debate ended, and each speaker's followers crowded around, cheering and applauding their candidate. This first debate had done little more than clarify the candidates' differing positions on slavery. Now it was on to Freeport and a debate that would spell trouble for Senator Douglas.

> He who would *be* no slave, must consent to *have* no slave.
>
> Those who would deny freedom to others, deserve it not for themselves,
>
> and, under a just God, can not long retain it.
>
> Letter to Boston supporters, April 6, 1859

August 27 dawned chilly and damp in Freeport, but the weather could not dampen the enthusiasm of the almost fifteen thousand people who crowded into Goddard's Grove, the site of the second debate. This time Lincoln spoke first, responding to the accusations Douglas had made at Ottawa. Then Lincoln posed four questions to the Little Giant, one of which set a trap for Douglas.

Lincoln asked Douglas to restate his endorsement of the Dred Scott decision, a Supreme Court ruling that made the outlawing of slavery in any territory unconstitutional (see page 207). This seemed to conflict with the doctrine of popular sovereignty and put Douglas in a bind. Lincoln already knew how Douglas would answer; the point was to get him to say it for the reporters, and thus the entire nation, to hear.

The trap worked. It was true, Douglas said, that the Dred Scott decision made the spread of slavery legal. But, he added, the people of a territory could render this decision meaningless by not passing laws to protect slavery. Douglas's answer angered many southern Democrats, splitting the party and ultimately costing him the presidency in 1860.

Other debates took the candidates across the Illinois plains: Jonesboro, Charleston, Galesburg, Quincy, and finally Alton. By the end of the campaign, Lincoln and Douglas each had made approximately sixty speeches and had traveled thousands of miles by train, by wagon, and on foot. Now the only thing that remained was November 2, Election Day.

When the votes were finally counted, Lincoln had 125,430 popular votes to Douglas's 121,609. But because the state legislature actually decided who would

Opposite: Artist John D. Whiting captures "Long Abe" and the "Little Giant" as they might have looked debating in one of the town squares where they met face to face in 1858.

be senator and the legislative districts favored the Democrats, Douglas retained his Senate seat by a legislative vote of 54 to 46.

Disappointed that he had not become the U.S. senator from Illinois, Lincoln returned to his law practice in Springfield. Because of the national prominence he had gained through the debates, however, Lincoln soon would go to Washington in a much greater capacity: as the sixteenth president of the United States.

'THE ANIMAL HIMSELF': HOW ARTISTS SAW LINCOLN

by Harold Holzer

When Abraham Lincoln first ran for president, few people outside his hometown of Springfield, Illinois, knew what he looked like. But there was great curiosity about his appearance. Many people wondered whether Lincoln could really be as ugly as some newspaper stories hinted.

Were Lincoln a candidate today, he would travel around the country to speak and be seen. But in Lincoln's day, candidates for president did no campaigning of their own. They remained at home. Afraid that he would lose the election, Lincoln's friends decided that they must show the country good-looking pictures of their man, whether he deserved them or not.

Photography was still quite new. Action photos and color photos had not yet been invented. In any case, most photographs only made Lincoln look grimmer. Fortunately, people still relied on paintings, prints, and statues to show them the heroes of the day. Many of these were made of Lincoln.

Just before he was nominated for president, a sculptor named Leonard Wells Volk made a life mask of the candidate by applying wet plaster to Lincoln's face while the subject breathed through straws. Volk used the life mask as a model to sculpt a bust of Lincoln that became a bestseller.

Above: Leonard Wells Volk cast this life mask of Lincoln in 1860. It was widely reproduced after Lincoln's death five years later.

Right: Thomas Hicks painted this portrait of Lincoln in June 1860 in Springfield. It was the first painting for which Lincoln ever sat.

The first artist to paint his portrait was Thomas Hicks of New York. Hicks traveled all the way to Springfield, where Lincoln posed for him while opening his daily mail. Lincoln liked the finished painting. He thought it showed a nicer expression than he wore in life, but added jokingly, "That, perhaps, is not an objection."

Not all artists tried to make Lincoln look better. Adalbert Volck of Boston (no relation to the sculptor who had made the Lincoln life mask) hated Lincoln. During the Civil War, he produced many etchings that attacked the president and the Union cause. One showed Lincoln as he looked when he passed through Volck's hometown on his way to his inauguration in Washington. It exaggerated Lincoln's secret passage and made him look like a coward.

Lincoln posed for many artists and sculptors. They helped create his image as "Savior of the Union" and "Great Emancipator." But Lincoln pretended not to take all their attention too seriously — although he always made himself available to pose. He would joke that some portraits looked "just like the critter" or like "the animal himself."

Deep down, however, Lincoln knew that good pictures could help him win both popularity and votes. Many artists made "attempts upon my life," Lincoln later jested. But few captured the real Lincoln. Most made him look either too handsome or too homely.

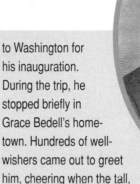

When Lincoln grew his new whiskers, artists quickly added beards to their old, clean-shaven Lincoln portraits.

WHY LINCOLN GREW A BEARD
by Harold Holzer

Little Grace Bedell did not change the face of history, but she certainly changed the face of someone who did. It was Grace, an eleven-year-old from the village of Westfield, New York, who inspired our sixteenth president, Abraham Lincoln, to grow his famous beard.

The year was 1860, and a clean-shaven Lincoln was running for president. Grace admired him, but when she first saw his picture on a campaign poster, she was horrified. The portrait made him look grotesque, with a lined face, crooked jaw line, and sour expression. Worried that he was too homely to win the election, Grace wrote Lincoln a delightful personal letter with a delightful suggestion.

"I hope you wont think me bold to write to such a great man as you are," she began, "but want you should be President of the United States very much." Grace went on to explain: "I have got 4 brother's and part of them will vote for you any way, and if you will let your whiskers grow I will try to get the rest of them to vote for you. You would look a great deal better for your face is so thin. All the ladies like whiskers and they would tease their husbands to vote for you and then you would be President."

Grace was thrilled to receive an immediate, hand-written reply. Lincoln asked, "As to the whiskers, having never worn any, do you not think people would call it a silly piece of affec[ta]tion if I were to begin It now?" Nevertheless, only a few weeks after he won the election, Lincoln began to grow a beard.

The next February, he began a long train journey from Illinois to Washington for his inauguration. During the trip, he stopped briefly in Grace Bedell's hometown. Hundreds of well-wishers came out to greet him, cheering when the tall, bearded man stepped out onto the platform of his railroad car. "I am glad to see you," he announced. "I suppose you are (glad) to see me, but I certainly think I have the best of the bargain!" The crowd laughed, and then Lincoln astonished everyone by remembering that a little girl from this town had once sent him "a very pretty letter."

"She asked me to let my whiskers grow, as it would improve my personal appearance," Lincoln said. "Acting upon her suggestion, I have done so. And now, if she is here, I would like to see her." A little boy pointed toward the back of the crowd and cried out excitedly, "There she is, Mr. Lincoln!" All eyes turned to the beautiful black-eyed girl, now "blushing all over her face."

With that, Lincoln stepped down from the train. The crowd parted respectfully as he made his way back to where Grace waited. Then, as the audience erupted into "yells of delight," the future president bent over and gave her "several hearty kisses."

In the bloody Civil War soon to come, Americans would regard their leader not as the beardless, rough frontiersman of 1860, but as the bewhiskered statesman they called "Father Abraham." It was a new image for Lincoln, and Grace Bedell had helped inspire it.

TRYING TIMES: THE CIVIL WAR PRESIDENT

by Harold Holzer

Lincoln faces General George B. McClellan during their famous meeting at Antietam on October 3, 1862. The president was a foot taller than his general.

Lincoln in McClellan's tent at Antietam

When Abraham Lincoln left his home in Illinois to begin the long journey to his inauguration as president, he told his neighbors he faced a task "greater than that which rested upon Washington." It was one of the most accurate predictions he ever made. No U.S. president before or after faced a graver crisis or emerged with a greater reputation.

Lincoln took his oath of office on March 4, 1861, assuring southerners that they had "no quarrel" with him. But quarrel they did. Southern states had already seceded and formed the Confederate States of America, presenting the most severe challenge to national authority in the country's brief history. Then, in April, when Confederate forces opened fire on Fort Sumter, South Carolina, Lincoln promptly called for volunteers to defend the Union. The Civil War had begun.

In a special Independence Day message to Congress that year, Lincoln called the struggle ahead "a people's contest." He was determined to preserve majority rule, warning that if democracy was defeated in America, it would surely never rise again anywhere in the world.

Words alone did not win victories. Just weeks later, Union forces were crushed at the Battle of Bull Run. A despairing Lincoln realized that the struggle would be long, costly, and bloody, but he steadfastly rejected suggestions that he abandon the war and allow the South to leave the Union in peace.

Union impatience was understandable. The North boasted more men and better technology. The South claimed a brilliant corps of generals, including Robert E. Lee, whom Lincoln had tried to recruit to head the Union army. The Union lost again at the Second Battle of Bull Run (August 1862) and the Battle of Fredericksburg (December 1862), and Union forces failed to capture the Confederate capital of Richmond after a long campaign in Virginia.

In September 1862, General Lee, fearing that southern supplies would eventually run out, invaded Maryland. There, Union forces finally triumphed at the Battle of Antietam, the bloodiest single day in the history of American warfare. Lincoln seized on the victory to issue the Emancipation Proclamation. He clearly hoped it would change the course of the war by threatening southern productivity at home — where slaves still worked on farms and plantations while white men fought in the Confederate army.

Lincoln defended his momentous decision by declaring, "We cannot escape history." Although emancipation certainly did change history, it did not immediately change the course of the war. In May 1863, Lee handed the Union one of its worst defeats at the Battle of Chancellorsville.

Meanwhile, many antiwar northerners were demanding peace and openly urging disloyalty to the Union. Lincoln created more controversy by allowing military arrests of civilians and prolonged confinement of suspects awaiting trial. The government defended both as attempts to crack down on treason.

Lincoln also ordered America's first military draft — a highly unpopular, badly conceived system in which wealthy men could buy their way out of service. In July 1863, New York City erupted in riots triggered by the draft. Mobs lynched innocent African Americans and even burned an orphanage for African American children.

Earlier in July, the North won a major victory at the Battle of Gettysburg and captured Vicksburg, Mississippi, the same week. But as 1863 drew to a close, Lincoln probably ranked as the most unpopular president in history.

That November, Lincoln did with words what he had been unable to do with bullets. In a two-minute speech at Gettysburg, he rallied the North to what he called a "new birth of freedom" for America, vowing that "government of the people, by the people, for the people" would not "perish from the earth." It remains the greatest presidential speech ever given.

Lincoln also assumed an increasingly active role as commander in chief. It took him years to find the right generals — he hired and fired them with shocking swiftness in 1861 and 1862 — but he eventually found reliable leaders such as Ulysses S. Grant and William T Sherman.

Bottom: If you were rich enough, you could avoid the draft by paying a fee or finding a substitute. Poorer men were forced to enlist. To encourage men to volunteer, cash bonuses were offered. This Chicago poster from December 1863 offers cash to veterans and volunteers.

Below: Lincoln's draft was not popular. In New York in July 1863, riots broke out because of it.

In 1864, Lincoln made two major decisions. First, he allowed the presidential election to proceed as scheduled — something unheard-of in countries torn by rebellion. In addition, Lincoln decided to run again for the presidency. No president since Andrew Jackson had been reelected to a second term.

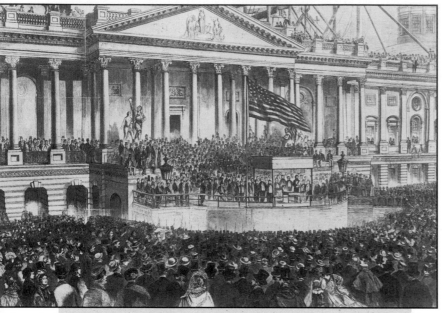

In *your* hands, my dissatisfied fellow countrymen, and not in *mine,* is the momentous issue of civil war.... We are not enemies, but friends. We must not be enemies.

First Inaugural Address, March 4, 1861

The inauguration of the sixteenth president of the United States at the U.S. Capitol in Washington, D.C., March 4, 1861. Lincoln reads his inaugural address prior to taking the oath of office with Chief Justice Roger B. Taney.

The 1864 campaign was one of the ugliest in U.S. history. Lincoln was challenged by one of his former generals, George B. McClellan. McClellan's backers accused Lincoln of supporting intermarriage between African Americans and whites, a ploy designed to panic voters.

Until the last few weeks of the campaign, Lincoln believed that he would lose the election. He even asked his own cabinet to sign, sight unseen, a pledge to cooperate with the next president. And he secretly plotted with African American leader Frederick Douglass to spread news of emancipation in the South to encourage slaves to flee their masters before the next president could overturn the order.

Two months before Election Day, Union forces captured Atlanta, Georgia, turning the tide of the war. Lincoln went on to defeat McClellan, winning fifty-five percent of the popular vote and 212 of 233 electoral votes.

Lincoln's finest moment may have come at his second inaugural on March 4, 1865. He defended the sacrifice of lives that had been necessary to rid America of the evil of slavery and called for an era of "malice toward none" and "charity for all" to "bind up the nation's wounds" and create "a lasting peace, among ourselves."

The war ended a month later, and Lincoln began working on plans to reconstruct the devastated Union. He even hinted publicly that he would extend the right to vote to those African Americans who had fought to preserve the Union.

One of those who heard Lincoln offer that hope was an actor named John Wilkes Booth. An embittered Confederate sympathizer, Booth and several other conspirators fatally shot Lincoln at Ford's Theatre on Good Friday, April 14, 1865. Nine hours later, Lincoln died in a boarding house across the street.

A man may have died, but a legend was quickly born. Hated by many while he lived, Lincoln was now universally celebrated as a latter-day Moses who had led African Americans to freedom and a beloved martyr who had died at the moment of his greatest triumph. More than ever, he seemed to symbolize American opportunity, for as Lincoln had put it, if he could rise from log cabin to White House, "any man's son" could hope to do the same.

LINCOLN'S OTHER WARTIME TRIUMPHS
by Harold Holzer

Abraham Lincoln won his greatest fame for saving the Union during the Civil War and issuing the Emancipation Proclamation. But in four years in the White House, Lincoln dealt with many other issues, and his handling of them still benefits Americans today.

During Lincoln's administration, for example, the nation began the program that led to today's state college system. The Morrill Act of 1862 required that money raised by the sale of public lands granted to each state be used for agricultural education. These land-grant schools later formed the basis for many state university systems still in operation.

Also in 1862, Congress passed, and Lincoln signed into law, the Homestead Act, which offered Americans up to one hundred sixty acres of free land. This law did much to encourage the settlement of the West.

Before Lincoln became president, the United States had only primitive communication and transportation systems. But during his term in office, the country introduced its first free mail delivery service and its first coast-to-coast telegraph operation. Meanwhile, enormous progress was made in linking the nation together by rail.

The fact that the United States could make such progress during a rebellion shows the strength not only of its president but also of the country itself.

'I LAUGH, BECAUSE I MUST NOT CRY'
by Carolyn Liberator Lavine

Abraham Lincoln often had a look of sadness on his face, but he enjoyed few things more than a good joke. It was an ironic side to the stoic leader. A childhood friend once said that even as a young boy, Lincoln was "so funny he could make a cat laugh." Years later, a newspaper called President Lincoln "Chief Joker of the Land." Humor was his way of coping with the stress of a nation at war with itself.

Because he was skinny and not very handsome, Lincoln liked to tell jokes about himself. One favorite was his reply to Stephen Douglas during a debate, after Douglas called him a two-faced liar. "If I had another face," Lincoln said to the audience, "I ask you would I be wearing this one?"

A humorous story Lincoln told was about his first meeting with Mary Todd at a grand ball. Bowing to her, he nervously said that he would like to dance with her "in the worst way." A footsore Mary Lincoln later told a friend, "He certainly did."

As president, Lincoln often used wit with people who annoyed him. When General George B. McClellan kept refusing to engage the enemy in battle, Lincoln sent him a letter saying, "If you don't intend to use the army, won't you lend it to me?" McClellan, upset by Lincoln's barbs and constant requests for reports from the front, turned the tables and sent the president a dispatch asking what to do with "six captured cows." His commander in chief was quick to reply, "Milk them."

Lincoln certainly did not take the war lightly. In fact, the president, who suffered through spells of depression, felt a keen sense of responsibility for the bloodshed. To remain an effective president, he used his humor. "I laugh, because I must not cry," he once said.

Today, more than one hundred years later, humorous Lincoln stories are still being told. Some really happened. Others are made up. But that would not have bothered Lincoln. When told that his favorite book, *Aesop's Fables,* was "all lies," he replied, "Mighty darn good lies," and continued reading.

Common looking people are the best in the world: that is the reason the Lord makes so many of them.

Reply to a critic of his appearance — in a dream! — December 23, 1863

LINCOLN'S CONFEDERATE COUNTERPART: JEFFERSON DAVIS

by Harold Holzer

Two American presidents served during the Civil War. One led the Union from Washington; the other led the Confederacy from Richmond.

Jefferson Davis was Lincoln's Confederate counterpart. Like Lincoln, he was tall, bearded, and Kentucky born. But there the similarities ended. Ironically, while Lincoln's grandfather had been born in Virginia, part of the Confederacy, Davis's grandfather had come from Pennsylvania, part of the Union.

Jefferson Finis Davis was born on June 3, 1808. He studied first at schools in Kentucky and then at the U.S. Military Academy at West Point, New York. Davis graduated in 1828, ranked ninth from the bottom in his thirty-two-man graduating class. The young cadet spent the next seven years in the military, finally leaving the U.S. Army in 1835 to become a planter in Mississippi. He married Sarah Knox Taylor, whose father was the great general and future president Zachary Taylor. Tragically, Sarah died only a few months after their marriage.

Ten years later, Davis married Varina Howell of Natchez, Mississippi. That same year, Davis began his political career as a Democrat. In his first try for public office, he was elected to Congress. Soon thereafter, he left the House of Representatives to fight in the Mexican War as a colonel. He served with particular bravery at the Battle of Buena Vista, defeating an enemy cavalry charge and suffering a wound in his foot.

Jefferson Davis and his wife, Varina. When Varina met her husband-to-be, she wrote her mother, "Would you believe it, he is refined and cultivated and yet...a Democrat."

Davis later said that his Mexican War service was one of the most satisfying experiences of his life.

When he returned to civilian life, Mississippi sent its war hero to the U.S. Senate. The state's voters rejected his 1851 bid to become governor. Two years later, Franklin Pierce became president, appointing Davis secretary of war. Davis was an enormously effective member of the Pierce cabinet. He helped modernize the U.S. Army and began exploring new routes for the proposed transcontinental railroad. He kept his hand in national politics, supporting the controversial Kansas-Nebraska Act of 1854.

In 1857, Davis returned to the Senate, where he became a strong advocate of southern rights. When his home state seceded from the Union in January 1861, Davis made one final speech in the Senate and then returned home. He probably hoped that he would be asked to lead the troops in the new Confederate army. To his surprise, the Confederate States of America instead named him its provisional president. Other, more ardent supporters of secession and rebellion had been considered likely to get the post.

Davis and his family moved to the temporary Confederate capital at Montgomery, Alabama, for his inauguration on February 18, 1861. On February 22, 1862,

THE CAPTURE OF AN UNPROTECTED FEMALE, OR THE CLOSE OF THE REBELLION.

When Davis was captured by Union troops in Georgia, he was wearing his wife's raincoat as a disguise. Cartoonists quickly made him the butt of their jokes, suggesting he had worn a hoop skirt and bonnet to avoid capture. This is an 1865 Currier & Ives print.

he took office as permanent president in the new Confederate capital of Richmond, Virginia. Davis was the first, last, and only president of the Confederate States of America.

There is no question that the task he faced was nearly impossible. He was expected to organize a new national government alongside southern leaders who hated national government as a matter of principle. He was expected to select generals who could win on the battlefield despite the overwhelming might of the North. He was expected to win diplomatic recognition for his country from the reluctant nations of Europe. And he was expected to inspire his people to keep fighting even when their supplies of arms, clothing, and food began to dwindle.

Unfortunately, Davis was not the perfect man for the job. Unlike Lincoln, he was stubborn and defiant. He was unable to compromise or change with the times. He was not a great writer or a particularly inspiring public speaker, even though he gave more speeches during his presidency than Lincoln, who was far better known as an orator. Even his wife admitted that he was not a good politician.

What was worse, Davis fancied himself a great military leader, based solely on his limited experience in the Mexican War. When the First Battle of Bull Run broke out in northern Virginia, he raced by train to the scene and made an appearance on the field so soon after the shooting had ended that some southerners believed he had led the army himself. Over the next four years, he argued endlessly with most of his generals about how best to fight the Yankees, and he hired and fired no fewer than six secretaries of war in only four years. The only

Jefferson Davis

A lithograph showing Davis (center) and some of his generals around 1861. Davis liked to think of himself as a military leader as well as president.

general with whom he maintained a good relationship was Robert E. Lee.

Davis also worried far too much about defending the Confederate capital of Richmond, and he did too little, too late to stop the Union advances in the West. He could do little to help the Confederacy break the Union naval blockade that choked the South and caused food shortages. But in one of his finest hours, he took to the streets personally to plead for an end to the Richmond bread riots of April 1863. His bold threat to shoot the rioters unless they dispersed ended the worst civil disturbance in Confederate history. It should be noted that when Lincoln faced draft riots in New York City, he never placed himself in personal danger to plead for calm.

The proud Davis and his government were, nevertheless, doomed to failure. The president began to lose popularity as the war news grew worse, but he refused to admit that he had made any errors. With no organized political parties in the Confederacy and no new elections scheduled, Davis absorbed all the unhappiness of a population sick and tired of war, hunger, and death.

In April 1865, Lee sent word to Davis that his army could no longer prevent the Union from capturing Richmond. Davis received the news in church and immediately hurried out and left the capital. Some criticized him for fleeing, but Davis truly believed that he could continue to lead a Confederate government-in-exile from whatever city he occupied.

Lincoln hoped that Davis would escape out of the country, but Union troops captured him in Georgia on May 10, 1865. Just before he was discovered, his frantic wife, Varina, threw a raincoat over his shoulders to disguise him. Union troops recognized him anyway. When northern newspapers heard about the deception, they gleefully reported that Davis had been captured wearing women's clothes. Artists then exaggerated the story further by creating cruel cartoons showing Davis wearing a hoop skirt and a bonnet. Davis's humiliation in defeat was complete.

Davis might then and there have lost the loyalty of the southern people. But a few days later, when Union guards tried to place him in chains in Fortress Monroe, Virginia, Davis put up a brave fight. Overnight, he once again became a southern hero. In addition to winning the respect of the southern people, he had earned their affection as well.

Davis was never placed on trial for treason, as his captors first intended. Instead, he was released from prison in 1867 and for years thereafter traveled the country insisting passionately that the rebellion had been justified. In 1881, he wrote a long book called *The Rise and Fall of the Confederate Government,* which critics charged showed Davis at his worst, refusing to accept any responsibility for what had gone wrong with the Confederate war effort.

A few years before he died, Davis made a final tour of the old Confederacy. Soon the whole South was "aflame," in the words of one admiring eyewitness. Dedicating a monument to the Confederate dead, Davis undoubtedly spoke for many unreconstructed southern whites when he declared of their struggle and defeat, "Is it a lost cause now? Never!" Davis died in 1889 at the age of eighty-one.

Davis never won the love of his people to the degree that Lincoln did. He lacked humor, compassion, and keen political sense. But when the South looked for a first president who would launch the new country with dignity and strength, he seemed the best available choice. The Confederacy needed a George Washington, but it got Jefferson Davis.

AMERICA'S TWO CIVIL WAR VICE PRESIDENTS

	ANDREW JOHNSON, UNITED STATES	ALEXANDER H. STEPHENS, CONFEDERACY
Born	December 29, 1808	February 11, 1812
Birthplace	North Carolina	Georgia
Raised	Tennessee	Georgia
Education	None; self-taught	University of Georgia; graduated first in class
Married	Eliza McCardle, 1827	Bachelor
Early occupation	Tailor	Teacher, lawyer
Prewar government service	Mayor, state legislator, congressman, governor of Tennessee, U.S. senator, war governor of Tennessee	State legislator, congressman 1843–1861
Nickname	"The Tennessee Tailor"	"Little Aleck"
Notable acts as vice president	Served only six weeks; drunk at inauguration, which he did not wish to attend	Split with President Jefferson Davis, returned home to Georgia, worked for war wounded, attended peace conference with Lincoln in 1865
After Civil War	U.S. president 1865–1869; argued with Congress over Reconstruction; impeached in 1868 but acquitted by one vote; returned to U.S. Senate in 1874	Imprisoned in 1865; elected to U.S. Senate in 1866 but denied seat because of war record; returned to House of Representatives in 1873; wrote book; elected governor of Georgia in 1882
Died	July 31, 1875	March 4, 1883

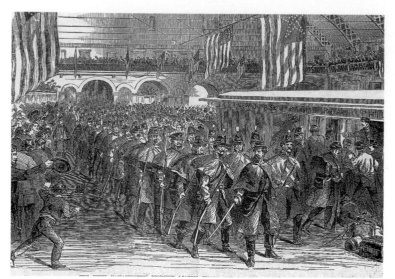

The Sixth Massachusetts Regiment leaves Jersey City for Washington on April 18, 1861.

A CRUCIAL DECISION

by Ellen Hardsog

During the early months of the Civil War, Abraham Lincoln attempted to keep from offending the Confederacy in regard to slavery, hoping that the country could be reunited and a long, bloody war avoided. When Union army leaders attempted to free slaves in conquered areas, Lincoln would not allow it, fearing that such action would convince the Confederacy not to rejoin the Union. Northern politicians sharply criticized him for such actions.

Things changed in 1862. The Union army was losing more battles than it was winning. Fewer volunteers were answering the president's call to sign up. Many northern whites did not wish to risk their lives for the cause of freeing the slaves. "Enlist the Negroes!" cried the abolitionists, but most whites did not agree that African Americans should be armed and allowed to fight.

Lincoln's generals complicated matters by welcoming runaway slaves into the army camps to dig trenches, build forts, and cook. The runaways were able, willing workers, but no one knew how to regard them — as free men or property. It was time for the president to make a decision.

Through the summer of 1862, Lincoln labored over this decision. When he presented a paper outlining his plan to his cabinet, they approved it but cautioned him to wait for a northern victory before announcing it. On September 22, Lincoln delivered the now-famous Emancipation Proclamation. The proclamation stated that unless the Confederacy surrendered by January 1, 1863, "all slaves in states or districts in rebellion against the United States on January 1, 1863, will be thenceforth and forever free." If the Confederacy surrendered, slavery would not be abolished.

But the Confederacy did not surrender, and on January 1, 1863, abolitionists and freed slaves celebrated the historic change in American history. When the celebration was over, however, they realized that the proclamation had not ended all slavery. Slaves in states that had not seceded from the Union were not free, nor were slaves in Confederate areas already occupied by the Union army. Not until 1865, when the Thirteenth Amendment to the U.S. Constitution was passed, was slavery abolished throughout the United States.

Following the Emancipation Proclamation, thousands of free African Americans rushed to join Union troops. The renewed strength of the Union army and the loss of plantation workers crippled the South, although the war dragged on for another two years. Lincoln's Emancipation Proclamation helped end slavery in America, but African Americans' struggle for equal rights continues today.

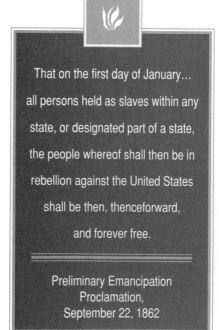

That on the first day of January... all persons held as slaves within any state, or designated part of a state, the people whereof shall then be in rebellion against the United States shall be then, thenceforward, and forever free.

Preliminary Emancipation Proclamation, September 22, 1862

THE 'GREAT EMANCIPATOR'

by Harold Holzer

Nothing Abraham Lincoln ever did as president aroused so much celebration — and so much anger — as the Emancipation Proclamation. When it was issued in 1863, many white Americans were outraged, complaining bitterly that it changed the goal of the Civil War from saving the Union to freeing the slaves — a mission many people could not accept. Ironically, most complaints about the proclamation today come from African Americans, who contend that it accomplished nothing. They argue that the slaves freed themselves by fleeing from plantations on their own.

Lincoln's proclamation was a moral landmark. It also was a stroke of political genius that began the long-overdue process of crushing slavery.

To some, it may seem to have offered too little, too late, as it was not issued until the war was nearly two years old and at first it freed slaves only in states over which Lincoln had no control. But Lincoln knew that he could not issue his revolutionary document until a majority of white northerners were prepared to accept it and until he was sure it would not drive still-loyal slave states like Maryland into the Confederacy. As for limiting its reach, Lincoln had no legal authority to free slaves in Union states. Instead, the order was based on the commander in chief's power to seize the property of those in rebellion. Unquestionably, the slaves themselves had to accomplish with their feet what Lincoln had begun with his pen.

Many times in the months to come, advisors urged Lincoln to cancel his proclamation, but he steadfastly refused. Lincoln knew that his order had only begun the work of ending slavery. "The harpoon is in the monster," he said. Now the monster had to be destroyed. To do this, Lincoln encouraged passage of the Thirteenth Amendment to the U.S. Constitution, outlawing slavery everywhere. Despite its passage, if Lincoln were alive today, he would likely be the first to admit that the work of ending slavery still remains unfinished.

Unfortunately, Lincoln's commitment to the destruction of slavery has come into question. In reality, Lincoln truly deserved the title that a grateful America bestowed on him in 1863: "Great Emancipator."

Although the words themselves were not inspirational, the text of Lincoln's Emancipation Proclamation inspired many artists. This lithograph shows the "Great Emancipator" posing before his historic document.

ollowing are the actual texts of the two Emancipation Proclamations. They are not as eloquent as some of Lincoln's other writings, but he wanted them to be able to pass legal tests if challenged in the courts. First is the so-called Preliminary Emancipation Proclamation of 1862. It gave the South one hundred days' notice to return to the Union or lose its slaves forever. Next is the final proclamation, issued on January 1, 1863, just as the first document promised. African Americans celebrated it as their "Day of Jubilee." Some called the proclamation America's "second Declaration of Independence."

★ ★ ★ ★ ★ ★ ★ ★ ★

PRELIMINARY EMANCIPATION PROCLAMATION, SEPTEMBER 22, 1862

I, Abraham Lincoln, President of the United States of America, and Commander-in-chief of the Army and Navy thereof, do hereby proclaim and declare that hereafter, as heretofore, the war will be prossecuted [sic] for the object of practically restoring the constitutional relation between the United States, and each of the states, and the people thereof, in which states that relation is, or may be suspended, or disturbed.

That it is my purpose, upon the next meeting of Congress to again recommend the adoption of a practical measure tendering pecuniary aid to the free acceptance or rejection of all slave-states, so called, the people whereof may not then be in rebellion against the United States, and which states, may then have voluntarily adopted, or thereafter may voluntarily adopt, immediate, or gradual abolishment of slavery within their respective limits; and that the effort to colonize persons of African descent, with their consent, upon this continent, or elsewhere, with the previously obtained consent of the Governments existing there, will be continued.

That on the first day of January in the year of our Lord, one thousand eight hundred and sixty-three, all persons held as slaves within any state, or designated part of a state, the people whereof shall then be in rebellion against the United States shall be then, thenceforward, and forever free; and the executive government of the United States, including the military and naval authority thereof, will recognize and maintain the freedom of such persons, and will do no act or acts to repress such persons, or any of them, in any efforts they may make for their actual freedom.

That the executive will, on the first day of January aforesaid, by proclamation, designate the States, and parts of states, if any, in which the people thereof respectively, shall then be in rebellion against the United States; and the fact that any state, or the people thereof shall, on that day be, in good faith represented in the Congress of the United States, by members chosen thereto, at elections wherein a majority of the qualified voters of such state shall have participated, shall, in the absence of strong countervailing testimony, be deemed conclusive evidence that such state and the people thereof, are not then in rebellion against the United States.

That attention is hereby called to an act of Congress entitled "An act to make an additional Article of War" approved March 13, 1862, and which act is in the words and figure following:

Be it enacted by the Senate and House of Representatives of the United States of America in Congress assembled, That hereafter the following shall be promulgated as an additional article of war for the government of the army and the United States, and shall be obeyed and observed as such:

Article —. All officers or persons in the military or naval service of the United States are prohibited from employing any of the forces under their respective commands for the purpose of returning fugitives from service or labor, who may have escaped from any persons to whom such service or labor is claimed to be due, and any officer who shall be found guilty by a court-martial of violating this article shall be dismissed from the service.

SEC. 2. *And be it further enacted,* That this act shall take effect from and after its passage.

Also to the ninth and tenth sections of an act entitled "An Act to suppress Insurrection, to punish Treason and Rebellion, to seize and confiscate property of rebels, and for other purposes," approved July 17, 1862, and which sections are in the words and figures following:

SEC. 9. *And be it further enacted,* That all slaves of persons who shall hereafter be engaged in rebellion against the government of the United States, or who shall in any way give aid or comfort thereto, escaping from such persons and taking refuge within the lines of the army; and all slaves captured from such persons or deserted by them and coming under the control of the government of the United States; and all slaves of such persons found *on* (or) being within any place occupied by rebel forces and afterwards occupied by the forces of the United States, shall be deemed captives of war, and shall be forever free of their servitude and not again held as slaves.

SEC. 10. *And be it further enacted,* That no slave escaping into any State, Territory, or the District of Columbia, from any other State, shall be delivered up, or in any way impeded or hindered of his liberty, except for crime, or some offence [sic] against the laws, unless the person claiming said fugitive shall first make oath that the person to whom the labor or service of such fugitive is alleged to be due is his lawful owner, and has not borne arms against the United States in the present rebellion, nor in any way given aid and comfort thereto; and no person engaged in the military or naval service of the United States shall, under any pretence [sic] whatever, assume to decide on the validity of the claim of any person to the service or labor of any other person, or surrender up any such person to the claimant, on pain of being dismissed from the service.

And I do hereby enjoin upon an order all persons engaged in the military and naval service of the United States to observe, obey, and enforce, within their respective spheres of service, the act, and sections above recited.

And the executive will in due time recommend that all citizens of the United States who shall have remained loyal thereto throughout the rebellion, shall (upon restoration of the constitutional relation between the United States, and their respective states, and people, if that relation shall have been suspended or disturbed) be compensated for all losses by acts of the United States, including the loss of slaves.

In witness whereof, I have hereunto set my hand, and caused the seal of the United States to be affixed.

Done at the City of Washington, this twenty second day of September, in the year of our Lord, one thousand eight hundred and sixty two, and of the Independence of the United States, the eighty seventh.

By the President: ABRAHAM LINCOLN

WILLIAM H. SEWARD, Secretary of State.

FINAL EMANCIPATION PROCLAMATION, JANUARY 1, 1863

Whereas, on the twentysecond [sic] day of September, in the year of our Lord one thousand eight hundred and sixty two, a proclamation was issued by the President of the United States, containing, among other things, the following, towit [sic]:

"That on the first day of January, in the year of our Lord one thousand eight hundred and sixty-three, all persons held as slaves within any State or designated part of a State, the people whereof shall then be in rebellion against the United States, shall be then, thenceforward, and forever free; and the Executive Government of the United States, including the military and naval authority thereof, will recognize and maintain the freedom of such persons, and will do no act or acts to repress such persons, or any of them, in any efforts they may make for their actual freedom.

"That the Executive will, on the first day of January aforesaid, by proclamation, designate the States and parts of States, if any, in which the people thereof, respectively, shall then be in rebellion against the United States; and the fact that any State, or the people thereof, shall on that day be, in good faith, represented in the Con-

gress of the United States by members chosen thereto at elections wherein a majority of the qualified voters of such State shall have participated, shall, in the absence of strong countervailing testimony, be deemed conclusive evidence that such State, and the people thereof, are not then in rebellion against the United States."

Now, therefore I, Abraham Lincoln, President of the United States, by virtue of the power in me vested as Commander-in-Chief, of the Army and Navy of the United States in time of actual armed rebellion against authority and government of the United States, and as a fit and necessary war measure for suppressing said rebellion, do, on this first day of January, in the year of our Lord one thousand eight hundred and sixty three, and in accordance with my purpose so to do publicly proclaimed for the full period of one hundred days, from the day first above mentioned, order and designate as the States and parts of States wherein the people thereof respectively, are this day in rebellion against the United States, the following, towit:

Arkansas, Texas, Louisiana, (except the Parishes of St.

Bernard, Plaquemines, Jefferson, St. Johns, St. Charles, St. James[,] Ascension, Assumption, Terrebonne, Lafourche, St. Mary, St. Martin, and Orleans, including the City of New-Orleans) Mississippi, Alabama, Florida, Georgia, South-Carolina, North-Carolina, and Virginia, (except the fortyeight [sic] counties designated as West Virginia, and also the counties of Berkley, Accomac, Northampton, Elizabeth-City, York, Princess Ann, and Norfolk, including the cities of Norfolk & Portsmouth[)]; and which excepted parts are, for the present, left precisely as if this proclamation were not issued.

And by virtue of the power, and for the purpose aforesaid, I do order and declare that all persons held as slaves within said designated States, and parts of States, are, and henceforward shall be free; and that the Executive government of the United States, including the military and naval authorities thereof, will recognize and maintain the freedom of said persons.

And I hereby enjoin upon the people so declared to be free to abstain from all violence, unless in necessary self-defence [sic];

and I recommend to them that, in all cases when allowed, they labor faithfully for reasonable wages.

And I further declare and make known, that such persons of suitable condition, will be received into the armed service of the United States to garrison forts, positions, stations, and other places, and to man vessels of all sorts in said service.

And upon this act, sincerely believed to be an act of justice, warranted by the Constitution, upon military necessity, I invoke the considerate judgment of mankind, and the gracious favor of Almighty God.

In witness whereof, I have hereunto set my hand and caused the seal of the United States to be affixed.

Done at the City of Washington, this first day of January, in the year of our Lord one thousand eight hundred and sixty three, and of the Independence of the United States of America the eighty-seventh.

By the President: ABRAHAM LINCOLN

WILLIAM H. SEWARD, Secretary of State.

'A FEW APPROPRIATE REMARKS'

by Harold Holzer

The entrance to Gettysburg's National Cemetery.

As Union and Confederate forces battled ferociously at Gettysburg in July 1863, the Union's commander in chief, Abraham Lincoln, waited in Washington for news from the front.

Hour after hour during those anxious days and nights, an eyewitness remembered, Lincoln's tall form could be found at the War Department, bent over stacks of telegrams from the battle. On the third day, his burden grew even heavier. His fragile wife, Mary, was thrown from her carriage in a freak accident and suffered a head injury. Finally, after seventy-two hours of unrelieved tension, Lincoln learned that the North had prevailed at Gettysburg. Privately, he was disappointed that his generals did not follow up their victory by pursuing the Confederates as they fled south. Publicly, he sent the army the "highest honors" for their "great success." He seemed to sense that, flawed or not, the Battle of Gettysburg would be a turning point in the Civil War.

The citizens of Pennsylvania, also aware of their new place in history, moved quickly to create a national cemetery for the thousands of casualties at Gettysburg. A dedication ceremony was planned, and Lincoln received an invitation to attend. He was not, however, asked to deliver the major speech of the day. That honor was given to a New England statesman and professional orator named Edward Everett. Lincoln, one organizer worried, was incapable of speaking "upon such a great and solemn occasion." The president was asked merely to give "a few appropriate remarks." Aware that the event was momentous, Lincoln accepted the halfhearted invitation.

As the day grew near, Lincoln's wife urged him to reconsider. Their young son Tad had fallen ill, and Mrs. Lincoln was near hysteria. (Only a year earlier, their middle child, Willie, had died.) On the morning of his father's departure, Tad was so sick that he could not eat breakfast. Lincoln himself felt unwell, but he decided to go anyway. With little fanfare, he boarded a train for the slow journey to Gettysburg.

The legend that the president waited until he was on the train to prepare his speech and then scribbled it on the back of an envelope is untrue. Lincoln carefully wrote at least one version of his speech on White House stationery before he left and probably rewrote it in his bedroom in Gettysburg the night before delivering it.

On Thursday, November 19, 1863, a balmy Indian summer day, the six-foot-four Lincoln mounted an undersize horse and joined a mournful procession through the town and toward the new cemetery near the battlefield. An immense throng had

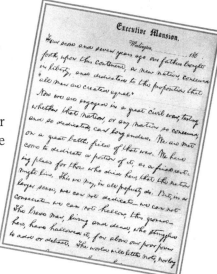

This version of the Gettysburg Address in Lincoln's hand was given to his private secretary, John G. Nicolay, and is called the Nicolay draft.

THE GETTYSBURG ADDRESS

Four score and seven years ago, our fathers brought forth on this continent, a new nation, conceived in Liberty, and dedicated to the proposition that all men are created equal.

Now we are engaged in a great civil war, testing whether that nation, or any nation so conceived and so dedicated, can long endure. We are met on a great battlefield of that war. We have come to dedicate a portion of that field, as a final resting place for those who here gave their lives that that nation might live. It is altogether fitting and proper that we should do this.

But, in a larger sense, we can not dedicate — we can not consecrate — we cannot hallow — this ground. The brave men, living and dead, who struggled here, have consecrated it, far above our poor power to add or detract. The world will little note, nor long remember what we say here, but it can never forget what they did here. It is for us the living, rather, to be dedicated here to the unfinished work which they who fought here have thus far so nobly advanced. It is rather for us to be here dedicated to the great task remaining before us — that from these honored dead we take increased devotion to that cause for which they gave the last full measure of devotion — that we here highly resolve that these dead shall not have died in vain — that this nation, under God, shall have a new birth of freedom — and that government of the people, by the people, for the people, shall not perish from the earth.

Lincoln spoke for only two minutes at Gettysburg — so briefly that a photographer there to take his picture did not have time to focus his camera. Artists have been trying to re-create the event ever since.

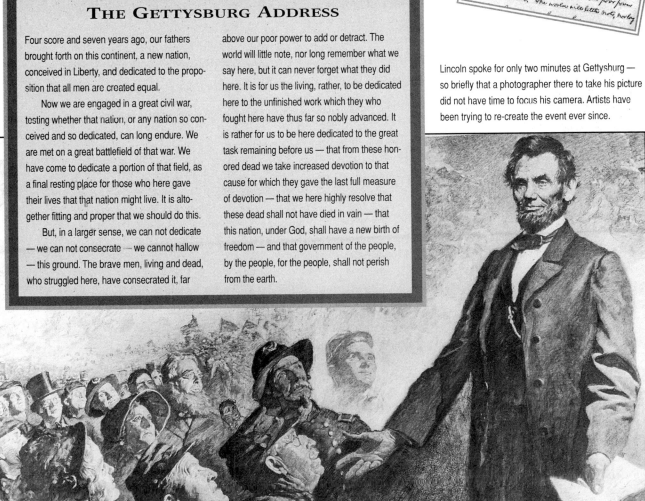

gathered there, and as Lincoln arrived on the speakers' platform, every man in the crowd respectfully removed his hat. The president was greeted with "a perfect silence."

For two hours, Edward Everett held the spectators spellbound with his rich voice and soaring words. A hymn followed, then Lincoln rose to speak. "Four score and seven years ago," Lincoln began in a high-pitched voice. He spoke for about two minutes, ending with the words "government of the people, by the people, for the people, shall not perish from the earth."

Almost as soon as he had begun, he sat down. Some eyewitnesses recalled a smattering of applause, but others heard "not a word, not a cheer, not a shout." A stenographer leaned over to Lincoln and asked, "Is that all?" Embarrassed, Lincoln replied, "Yes — for the present." A photographer in the crowd, fussing with his camera, had not even had time to take a picture.

Lincoln thought his speech was a failure. "People are disappointed," he grimly told the man who had introduced him. To add to his misery, he came down with a mild case of smallpox on the trip back to Washington.

Many who listened to the speech felt differently, however. While some newspapers dismissed the speech as "silly," "dull," and "commonplace," one correctly predicted that the Gettysburg Address would "live among the annals of man." Perhaps the best compliment of all came from Edward Everett. A few days after they both had spoken at Gettysburg, he wrote to Lincoln saying that he wished he had come "as close to the central idea of the occasion, in two hours, as you did in two minutes." Lincoln replied, telling Everett how pleased he was that "the little I did say was not entirely a failure."

Lincoln was asked to write out his speech several times once he returned to Washington. Admirers wanted copies to keep or to sell for charity. The last of those copies appears on page 277. It is the final text of Lincoln's greatest speech, exactly as he wanted the words to be remembered. Today Lincoln's Gettysburg Address is considered one of the great speeches of all time.

Thomas "Tad" Lincoln (1853–1871) with his father (top) and in uniform (above).

AN UNLIKELY PAIR: MR. AND MRS. LINCOLN

by Linda Norbut Suits

On the evening of November 4, 1842, in the parlor of her sister's home, Mary Todd married Abraham Lincoln. Although her family objected to this match with the rugged and penniless lawyer born on the frontier, Mary said, "I would rather marry a good man — a man of mind — with a hope and bright prospects ahead for position — fame & power than to marry all the houses — gold...in the world."

From their first meeting in 1839, at a ball in Springfield, Illinois, the differences between Mary Todd and Abraham Lincoln would be glaring. He was tall and lean and had been born in a log cabin. She was short and plump, with a more refined upbringing. But their relationship was one of genuine love.

History has not always been kind to Mary Todd Lincoln. She was a complicated and often misunderstood woman, and she remains so today. Too often she is remembered for her fights, wild spending, and later insanity. What is not mentioned is her intelligence, kindness, and immense love for her husband and family.

Mary Ann Todd was born on December 13, 1818, to wealthy parents in Lexington, Kentucky. She was the fourth of seven children. Her mother died when she was six, and less than eighteen months later, her father married Elizabeth Humphreys. Mary did not get along with her stepmother, who had nine more children. She became lost in the crowd and later described her childhood as "desolate."

Mary was a good student, and her escape from her situation was boarding school. Because she did not get along with her stepmother, she soon considered Madame Mentelle's school her home. In all, Mary attended school for ten years, much longer than most girls at the time, who usually received only enough education to make them good wives and mothers.

In 1837, Mary spent three months in Springfield, Illinois, visiting her older sister Elizabeth Todd Edwards. Elizabeth and her husband were prominent in Springfield society, and Mary enjoyed her visit. She returned to Springfield to stay in 1839, and it was then that she met and married Abraham Lincoln.

The Todd family opposed the match because Abraham did not fit their idea of a suitable husband. He was not wealthy and did not travel in the same social circles as the Todds. Mary's sister also felt that they were incompatible in "natures, mind — education — raising &c."

But Mary believed that she and Abraham had much in common. Both had lost their mother at an early age. Both were intelligent and loved to read. And most important, both liked to discuss politics.

Mary was known to have a sharp tongue, and the Lincolns, like many couples, argued. The cause of many of their disagreements was Abraham's long absences, sometimes up to six months, while he was a lawyer on the Eighth Circuit. They also quarreled about his lack of refined manners. Yet their marriage was strong and built on mutual affection. While a congressman in Washington, D.C., Abraham wrote, "When you were here, I thought you hindered me some in attending to business; but now, having nothing but business — no variety — it has grown exceedingly tasteless to me.... I hate to stay in this old room by myself."

Mary's greatest difficulties began after the Lincoln family moved into the White House. Many northerners saw her as a traitor because she was from the South. Conversely, many of her siblings sided with the Confederates, who saw her as a traitor because she was married to the despised president of the Union.

Mary Lincoln ran up such huge bills for gowns like these that she worried that her husband would be financially ruined unless he was reelected president.

Mary Lincoln

Opposite bottom: Abraham and Mary Lincoln were never photographed together. Mary was nearly a foot shorter than Abraham and self-conscious about the difference in height. Many of their admirers took separate photographs of the president and first lady and framed them side by side.

LINCOLN'S SONS

by Edison McIntyre and Ann Woodbury Moore

Although the Lincolns had four sons, only their oldest child, Robert, lived to adulthood. Eddie, the Lincolns' second son, did not live past the age of four. He died in February 1850 of consumption, or pulmonary tuberculosis. Their third son, Willie, was eleven when he died in 1862 after a long illness. Willie and his younger brother, Tad, enjoyed the distinction of being the first presidential children to live in the White House.

Tad (few people called him by his given name, Thomas) was the youngest Lincoln son, born on April 4, 1853. He was a month shy of his eighth birthday when his father was inaugurated. When he and ten-year-old Willie were shown around their new home, their mother wrote that they eagerly "interviewed" all the servants, sizing up the possibilities for the fun they could have in the mansion.

Though a trial for the staff, the young boys' presence in the White House was a delight for their father. The boys loved playing jokes on others. Once, while experimenting with the White House bells, they made all the bells ring, summoning all of Lincoln's secretaries. Willie's death in the winter of 1862 was a severe blow to the family. Tad's prankish nature, however, continued to amuse his father, and with Robert at college, Tad became the immediate focus of all his parents' love. Consequently, he ran wild and studied little. After his father's assassination, Tad lived with his mother in Chicago and later in Europe before he died after a long illness in 1871, at the age of eighteen.

Lincoln's sole surviving son, Robert Lincoln, was born on August 1, 1843, and lived to be eighty-three years old. He graduated from Harvard in 1864 and enlisted in the Union army in February 1865, joining General Ulysses S. Grant's staff as a captain. After his father's death, he moved to Chicago, where he became a prominent lawyer and businessman.

Robert served as secretary of war from 1881 to 1885 and as minister (ambassador) to Great Britain from 1889 to 1893, but he repeatedly refused to enter politics, saying, "I have seen enough of the inside of Washington official life to have lost all interest in it." Oddly, he was nearby at the assassinations of three U.S. presidents — his father, James A. Garfield, and William McKinley. Once, when asked if he would attend an official function, Robert reportedly replied, "No, I'm not going and they'd better not invite me, because there is a certain fatality about (them) when I am present."

Although critics accused him of being pompous and aloof, Robert's friends found him loyal, kind, generous, and — like his father — an excellent storyteller.

Robert Lincoln

Abraham Lincoln studied law on his own, but he sent his son Robert to Harvard Law School. When this photo was taken, the younger Lincoln was a successful attorney and businessman.

Despite her education and grace, easterners saw her as an uncouth westerner. The newspapers usually wrote only about her fine clothes and extravagant spending and not about her visits to hospitals and other charitable activities.

Because of the war and his other presidential duties, Abraham spent little time with Mary. She wrote, "I consider myself fortunate, if at eleven o'clock, I once more find myself, in my pleasant room and very especially, if my tired and weary Husband is *there.*"

Mary also had much tragedy in her life. While still in Springfield in 1850, the Lincolns' second son, Eddie, died shortly before his fourth birthday. Twelve years later, in the White House, their third son, Willie, died when he was eleven. Willie's death affected Mary deeply. She even tried to contact his spirit and said that he came to the foot of her bed at night. The final blow was her husband's assassination while he was sitting next to her at Ford's Theatre.

After Abraham's death in 1865, Mary traveled all over the United States and Europe with her youngest son, Tad, trying to find peace. Sadly, Tad died in 1871 after a long illness, and Mary's mental state continued to deteriorate. Eventually, her lone remaining son, Robert, began court proceedings to judge her sanity. She was found insane and spent nearly four months in a mental hospital.

After her release and more travel, she returned to Springfield in 1880 and spent her remaining days with her sister Elizabeth. Ironically, she lived in the very house where Abraham had given her the wedding ring engraved "Love Is Eternal." She died on July 16, 1882.

THE LINCOLN ASSASSINATION

by Christina Mierau

For several months, actor John Wilkes Booth's band of conspirators had plotted to capture Abraham Lincoln and hold him hostage in exchange for Confederate prisoners held by the North. Several early attempts had failed, and with General Robert E. Lee's surrender on April 9, 1865, Booth became desperate. "Our cause being almost lost," he wrote in his diary, "something decisive and great must be done."

His opportunity to act came on Friday, April 14. Booth, an acclaimed actor, was at Ford's Theatre when word arrived from the White House: President and Mrs. Lincoln would attend that night's performance of *Our American Cousin*. The president was fatalistic about security, saying that no security system could stop an assassin, and he traveled with little protection.

Calling together his coconspirators, Booth mapped out a plan. As Lincoln was assassinated at Ford's Theatre, Secretary of State William Seward and Vice President Andrew Johnson would be killed as well. With one bold stroke, they surmised, the North would collapse in chaos.

That night, Booth strolled into Ford's Theatre just after ten o'clock. Tipping his hat to the doorman, he crossed the lobby and climbed the stairs to the mezzanine. Finding the area unattended (the guard had taken a seat in the audience), Booth approached the door that led to the private boxes. Slipping into the dimly lit corridor, he shut the door and barred it from the inside.

Booth saw Lincoln seated in a rocker, silhouetted against the glowing stage lights beyond. The actor's hand closed around the handle of his revolver as he boldly stepped into the box. Leveling the pistol behind the president's left ear, the assassin fired.

Confronted by Major Henry Rathbone, a guest in the presidential box, Booth dropped his gun, drew his dagger, and slashed the officer's arm to the bone. Booth quickly vaulted the railing, landing on the stage twelve feet below. As he jumped, his heel caught on a flag, and he landed awkwardly, breaking his left leg. Despite his pain, the actor got to his feet, held his dagger aloft, and cried, *"Sic semper tyrannis!"* (Thus always to tyrants!) before fleeing to the rear of the theater.

Someone shouted, "Stop that man!" but pursuit was futile. Despite his injury, Booth had already mounted his waiting horse and escaped into the night.

Top: Sergeant Boston Corbett shot John Wilkes Booth to death and instantly became famous. He later went mad.
Above: Ford's Theatre in Washington, D.C.

With malice toward none; with charity for all; with firmness in the right, as God gives us to see the right, let us strive on to finish the work we are in; to bind up the nation's wounds; to care for him who shall have borne the battle, and for his widow, and his orphan — to do all which may achieve and cherish a just, and a lasting peace, among ourselves, and with all nations.

Second Inaugural Address, March 4, 1865

THE LINCOLN MEMORIAL

by Beth Haverkamp

More than half a century after Lincoln's assassination, a monument honoring him was built. Construction of the monument, designed by architect Henry Bacon, began in 1914. Shown here in 1920, it was dedicated on Memorial Day, 1922. The architectural style of the Lincoln Memorial is similar to that of the Parthenon, a temple to the goddess Athena in Athens, Greece. The design attempts to evoke the timelessness of Lincoln's ideas. Surrounding the outer walls are thirty-six Doric columns representing the states in the Union at the time of Lincoln's death. The columns symbolize the unity Lincoln fought so hard to preserve throughout the Civil War. Inside the memorial chamber are a colossal statue of Lincoln, designed by sculptor Daniel Chester French; chiseled inscriptions of the Gettysburg Address and Lincoln's Second Inaugural Address; and two murals depicting his life, words, and principles.

*"Payne" or "Paine" was an alias. The man's real name was Lewis Thornton Powell.

The following morning, at 7:22 A.M., Lincoln died in a boarding house located across the street from the theater. A massive hunt for the assassin and his accomplices was launched. Lewis Payne,* one of Booth's coconspirators who had gone to Seward's house and brutally wounded the secretary of state, was arrested. George Atzerodt, who was sent to kill Johnson, also was caught, although he had lost his nerve and never attacked the vice president. Dozens more were taken into custody as Secretary of War Edwin Stanton vowed swift retribution for Lincoln's murderers.

Booth and David Herold, another conspirator, eluded capture. But when Booth's broken bone began "tearing the flesh at every jump," the two sought help at the Maryland home of Dr. Samuel Mudd. The doctor, who later denied any knowledge of the assassination, set Booth's leg and offered the travelers food and rest.

In the early hours of April 26, federal troops cornered Booth and Herold inside a tobacco shed in Bowling Green, Virginia. Herold was captured without a fight, but Booth refused to surrender and was shot. Just before he died, he whispered, "Tell Mother I died for my country."

Booth's coconspirators were tried by a military court without benefit of a jury. Payne, Atzerodt, and Herold were sentenced to "hang by the neck until dead." Another alleged conspirator, Mary Surratt, also was hanged. The assassination plot had been hatched in her boarding house, although many still doubt her involvement.

Samuel Arnold and Michael O'Laughlin, who had deserted Booth long before the assassination, were sentenced to life in prison, as was Dr. Mudd. Edward Spangler, a stagehand at Ford's Theatre, was accused of helping Booth to escape. He was sent to prison for six years.

GIVING THANKS:
THE STORY OF THE FIRST *REAL* THANKSGIVING
by Harold Holzer

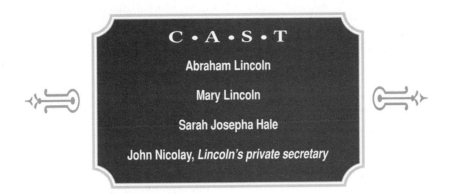

C • A • S • T

Abraham Lincoln

Mary Lincoln

Sarah Josepha Hale

John Nicolay, *Lincoln's private secretary*

Introduction

Almost everyone knows the story of the "first Thanksgiving" — the feast shared by the Pilgrims and Native Americans more than three hundred fifty years ago. But few people know that this was also nearly the last Thanksgiving. In the years to come, the feast was seldom repeated or even remembered.

Over the years, several U.S. presidents issued orders calling for occasional Thanksgiving holidays. But there would be no official annual Thanksgiving Day until Abraham Lincoln declared one in the midst of the Civil War in 1863. Not all the credit belongs to Lincoln, however. The very next year, he nearly forgot to declare another holiday. He had to be reminded to issue a new proclamation by the woman who had suggested it the year before: Sarah Josepha Hale, editor of the magazine *The Lady's Book.* No one deserves more credit than Hale for creating the Thanksgiving holiday as we know it today. Ever since Lincoln's time, presidents have declared a new Thanksgiving Day with a special proclamation each and every November. They no longer have to be reminded to do so.

Act I

Late summer, 1863. The scene is the president's office in the White House. President Lincoln is holding his regular afternoon "open house," during which visitors are allowed to come in to see him. As the scene opens, Lincoln is just finishing a talk with one of these visitors.

Abraham Lincoln: Madam, I am deeply impressed with your story. If your son ran away from the army just to help you harvest your crops, I do not want him punished any more than you do. Give me your letter, and I will write a note on it: *(writes)* "Pardon young Jack Michaels. Send him back into the army. The harvest is done, but there is a war still to be fought. Signed, A. Lincoln." Take this to your boy's captain, and all will be well. *(in a louder voice)* Now, who is next?

Sarah Josepha Hale: I believe I am, Mr. President.

Lincoln: Ah, yes, Madam. I saw you waiting. And what can I do for you? Has your son been sentenced to be punished for deserting the army?

Hale: No, Mr. President.

Lincoln: A husband, then?

Hale: No, sir.

Lincoln: You want a pass through army lines to visit the South?

Hale: Not at all, Mr. President.

Lincoln: Surely you do not come here to ask for a job in my government?

Hale: Hardly! I already have a job.

Lincoln: You do? How unusual for a woman! But wait, I am being rude. You must forgive me. You see, everyone who comes here to see me either wants me to pardon a relative, give them a pass, or give them a job.

Hale: Not me, Mr. Lincoln.

Lincoln: Indeed! You say you are a working woman, Mrs. —

Hale: Hale. Mrs. Sarah Hale.

Lincoln: I know that name.

Hale: I am editor of *The Lady's Book,* a magazine for women.

Lincoln: Of course! Mrs. Lincoln reads that magazine all the time. I must tell her you are here. *(shouts)* Nicolay!

John Nicolay: *(coming into the room)* Yes, sir?

Lincoln: Nicolay, call the lady. There is someone here I want her to meet. *(Nicolay leaves.)* Now, Mrs. Hale, what can I do for you?

Hale: I am afraid that I, too, have come to ask you a favor.

Lincoln: How may I serve you? Wait, I do believe I hear Mrs. Lincoln.

Mary Lincoln: *(entering)* I was in my parlor, entertaining the Union Ladies' Guild, when I got your message. I rushed here the minute —

Lincoln: Mother, this is Mrs. Hale. Mrs. Hale of —

Mary: Mrs. Sarah Hale?

Hale: Yes.

Mary: Why, Mrs. Hale, I do declare! You are a favorite of mine. Has my husband told you? I just adore your magazine. I rely upon it for so many recipes and dress patterns. Why, I simply would not know how to spend my money if I did not have *The Lady's Book* to inform me of the latest fashions.

Lincoln: Mrs. Hale, it seems that it is *you* who owes *me* a favor!

Hale: Whatever do you mean, Mr. President?

Lincoln: If it were not for your magazine, I would be a great deal wealthier today — and Mrs. Lincoln would be getting a lot more wear out of her clothes!

Mary: *(to Mrs. Hale)* Pay no attention, my dear Mrs. Hale. Men are all alike, even presidents. They simply have no idea about the pressures upon women to look their best at all times. But I *do* go on. You are here to ask for our help. Tell us what we can do.

Hale: Thank you, Mrs. Lincoln. I come here today not for myself, but on behalf of others. On behalf of all my readers. Indeed, on behalf of all the people in our great country. I am here to ask you to proclaim a day of Thanksgiving so that all in our country may give thanks for our blessings.

Lincoln: Mrs. Hale, you must know that I have already proclaimed a day of Thanksgiving *seven* different times since I have been president. Why, only five months after I came to this White House, I asked for a "national day of humiliation, prayer, and fasting." Then, in November 1861, I closed all the offices of the government for yet another Thanksgiving day. And the very next year, I asked for a special day of thanks for our great victories on the battlefield against the Confederates.

Hale: Yes, Mr. President, but —

Lincoln: And this very year, Mrs. Hale, we have already had *three* Thanksgiving days. One in March, one in April, and the third right after we won the Battle of Gettysburg and captured Vicksburg. It was, as I remember, a day of "national thanksgiving, praise, and prayer" for those great victories. Don't you remember?

Hale: Of course, Mr. Lincoln. But I fear I am not making myself understood. Much as I rejoiced with you and the rest of the country each time we won a great victory on the battlefield, I think that Thanksgiving should be different.

Mary: How so?

Hale: I believe we should celebrate Thanksgiving on the same day each and every year. I believe we should give thanks not only when we win battles but also for all the great bounties we enjoy in our land. For the rich harvest, the great cities, the lovely countryside, and the chance every American has to rise as high as his talent and hard work allows.

Lincoln: Now I begin to see your point.

Federal soldiers in the South celebrate Thanksgiving at Fort Pulaski, Georgia.

Hale: Mr. President, our families need a day when they can all sit down together — a day to pause and express our gratitude. Can we not have such a day?

Lincoln: Mrs. Hale, I am glad that you have come. I shall tell you something today — something quite exciting and wonderful. But I must ask you to promise not to repeat it.

Hale: I promise.

Lincoln: This very morning, our soldiers have scored yet another great victory. And so today I will not only issue another order asking for a special day of Thanksgiving, but I also will send a letter to Congress asking it to begin work on a law to free all the slaves in our land.

Hale: But, Mr. President, I thought your Emancipation Proclamation did exactly that.

Lincoln: No, Mrs. Hale, the proclamation freed only the slaves in the South. And since the South is still at war with us, the emancipation had the effect of freeing only some of the slaves. I hope the new law I propose will free the rest.

Hale: How wonderful!

Lincoln: And I believe you have another good idea, Mrs. Hale. I shall order a Thanksgiving celebration for later this year. Here, let me write the order now: *(writing)* "The year that is drawing towards its close has been filled with the blessings of fruitful fields and healthful skies. In the midst of a civil war of unequalled severity, peace has been preserved with other nations, order has been maintained, the laws have been respected and obeyed. These are great gifts for which we are thankful to the Most High God, who has remembered mercy. Therefore I invite my fellow citizens in every part of the United States to set apart and observe the last Thursday of November as a day of Thanksgiving. I pray we may heal the wounds of the nation and restore it as soon as possible. Signed, Abraham Lincoln."

Mary: Truly wonderful, Father!

Hale: Oh, yes, Mr. President. It is exactly what we hoped for!

Lincoln: As soon as it is issued, I shall send you a copy of the proclamation — the copy I wrote with my own hand. Keep it as my gift to you.

Hale: If you would permit, I will take it and sell it to raise money to care for our wounded soldiers.

Lincoln: Do so, good lady. You know, I have many things to be thankful for this very day, including the fact that you have come to see me without any hope of personal gain.

Hale: Thank you, Mr. Lincoln. Good-bye!

Mary and Lincoln: Good-bye!

Act II

October 1864. The scene is the Lincolns' dining room. The president is eating lunch with Mary. Lincoln is about to be reelected, the war is nearly over, and generally he is much happier than he has been in years.

Lincoln: Mary, we are very lucky.

Mary: Yes, Father. Why, no president since Andrew Jackson has been elected to a second term. And now my husband!

Lincoln: You speak too soon. The election will not take place for another two weeks.

Mary: Twiddle-twaddle! You know as well as I do that you will be reelected. The early state votes are in, and your party has won them all. Do not be coy with me.

Lincoln: I *am* very hopeful. But it would not do for me to celebrate my victory before the election.

Nicolay: *(entering)* Excuse me, Mr. President.

Mary: Honestly, Mr. Nicolay, can we never have a single meal in peace?

Lincoln: There, there, Mary. We better get used to these interruptions if we are to be here another four years. Yes, Nicolay, what is it?

Nicolay: Your afternoon appointments are ready in your office. One of them is Mrs. Sarah Hale.

Mary: *Our* Sarah Hale?

Nicolay: Yes, Madam. From *The Lady's Book.*

Lincoln: Well, John, do not make her wait with the others. Bring her in here. After all, Mary has not bought a new fashion for at least a day, and Mrs. Hale may have such good ideas that the first lady can act upon them before dinner.

Nicolay leaves, then reappears with Mrs. Hale.

Nicolay: Mrs. Hale!

Mary: My dear, please come in and join us.

Lincoln: By all means, Mrs. Hale, come sit with us. Now tell us, what can we do for you? Why, we have not seen you since that day more than a year ago when we made a Thanksgiving Day together.

Hale: *(sits at the table)* Yes, sir, it has been more than a year. And that is exactly why I am here.

Lincoln: Indeed? Have I forgotten something?

Mary: I think I know, Father. Don't you recall? Mrs. Hale

did not want just *one* Thanksgiving Day. She wanted one *every* year. And it is that time of year again.

Hale: Yes, Mr. President, exactly. And this year, I have done something to save you time. I have dared to write down the proclamation myself so that you will not have to.

Lincoln: Well, Mrs. Hale, you have done everything but cook the meal!

Hale: Mr. President, it is so important. If you sign it now, your proclamation will have time to reach people in Europe and Asia, as well as the people throughout our wide land. You could order all Americans in foreign countries to observe the holiday — and all Americans on ships at sea. Just think of it — Americans on land and sea, wherever our flag flies, uniting in a national Thanksgiving Day. Won't it be a glorious festival?

Lincoln: I suppose so, but —

Mary: How can there be any but's?

Lincoln: Well, Mother, I am a little worried about this once-a-year-holiday idea.

Hale: Why, sir?

Lincoln: Well, Mrs. Hale, last time you asked me to make Thanksgiving a regular November holiday, many newspapers criticized me. They said that a president who makes war should not ask God for his blessings on a day of Thanksgiving. In fact, one person drew a cartoon of me dressed as a wild Indian. And the caption said, "It may be Thanksgiving, Abe, but don't you think you should wash off your war paint before going to church?"

Hale: I remember that cartoon. It was unfair.

Lincoln: Unfair it may be, but it was printed in the newspaper anyway. Oh, I do not mind criticism. Or even being poked fun at. What worries me is the thought that perhaps they are right. Perhaps I have no right to ask God to bless us — no right even to give thanks to him — while so many of our young men are fighting a bloody war and dying for their country.

Mary: Or perhaps it is *just* the right time to do so, Father. What better reminder that *our* side is the *right* side — the side of freedom, not slavery?

Hale: Yes, Mr. President.

Lincoln: But we have had two more Thanksgiving days this year, ladies. A day of "common thanksgiving and prayer" in March and another in August. Do we really need yet another in November?

Hale: We do, sir. We have promised our readers in the November issue of *The Lady's Book* that our *annual* Thanksgiving, begun last year, will continue this year. Can you disappoint them, sir?

Mary: How can you even consider it, Father?

Lincoln: I suppose you are right. Give me your proclamation, Mrs. Hale.

Hale: *[hands it to him]* Oh, thank you, sir.

Lincoln: It is good, but I would change a few lines. Let it read this way: *[writes]* "It has pleased God to continue our country's life for another year, defending us against unfriendly enemies and giving us many victories over the enemy who is of our own household. Our soldiers in their camps and our citizens in their homes have been blessed with unusual health. New citizens have come to settle in our country from across the oceans. He has inspired us with courage during the civil war — into which we have been thrown because we believe so deeply in freedom and humanity. And now He has given us hope of a final victory and an end to our dangers and afflictions. Now, therefore, I, Abraham Lincoln, President of the United States, do set apart the last Thursday of November as a day which I desire to be observed by all my fellow-citizens, wherever they are, as a day of Thanksgiving and Praise to the Almighty. Signed, Abraham Lincoln."

Hale: Oh, thank you, sir.

Lincoln: And once again, you shall have the proclamation as your own.

Hale: Sir, I shall again sell it for charity. The last proclamation you gave me brought many thousands of dollars for our soldiers' hospitals.

Lincoln: I am glad to hear it, Mrs. Hale.

Mary: Father, isn't it fine that Thanksgiving will now occur each and every year?

Lincoln: Yes, Mary, I never doubted it. I only worried that we had no right to say God was on our side and against the people of the South. After all, *they* worship God, too. And they believe He watches over *them,* not us.

Hale: Mr. Lincoln, shall we again fast and eat no food on this Thanksgiving Day?

Lincoln: Perhaps we should celebrate instead. Celebrate the end of the war with a great feast. Perhaps even the war will be at an end by Thanksgiving Day, and we can sit down and break bread with our enemies — the way the Pilgrims and Indians did more than two hundred years ago.

Hale: A feast — how marvelous!

Mary: I shall consult Mrs. Hale's *Lady's Book* this instant to choose the best new recipes for meats and cakes.

Lincoln: And corn. Do not forget corn, our national vegetable.

Hale: Oh, Mr. Lincoln, I do hope we can have such a Thanksgiving every year.

Lincoln: Mrs. Hale, I promise you will not have trouble with me again. You shall have your holiday *every* November, do not fear. I shall ask Congress to set it aside as a holiday by law. And even if I do not live to see another Thanksgiving —

Mary: Do not talk so, Father.

Lincoln: — I feel sure there will always be a Thanksgiving. Long after I am forgotten, this day will live on as our country's moment of prayer and thanks to our God.

Hale: I believe that Americans will always remember you as the father of the Thanksgiving holiday — the president who made it a day for all Americans, every year, to celebrate together.

Lincoln: I doubt it. They will remember the holiday, I hope. They may even remember the Pilgrims, who feasted long before we did. But I doubt whether anyone will remember that "Old Abe" Lincoln made Thanksgiving a holiday.

Hale: I pray you are wrong.

Lincoln: It is *you* they should remember, Mrs. Hale. *You* are the one who has made Thanksgiving the holiday I know it will become.

Hale: I suspect that I, certainly, will be forgotten. But if the holiday lives on, I will be happy enough.

Lincoln: Well said, Mrs. Hale.

RESOURCES

These resources are geared to the eight- to fourteen-year-old unless otherwise indicated.

BOOKS

General

Archer, Jules. *A House Divided: The Lives of Ulysses S. Grant and Robert E. Lee.* Scholastic, 1995. This book documents the lives of the two Civil War generals who led opposing armies but showed respect and admiration for each other.

Batty, Peter, and Peter Parish. *The Divided Union: The Story of the Great American War, 1861–1865.* Salem House, 1987. The companion book to the Arts and Entertainment television series on the Civil War. Illustrated with more than two hundred color and black-and-white photographs. For older readers.

Bolotin, Norman, and Angela Herb. *For Home and Country: A Civil War Scrapbook.* Lodestar, 1995. An overview of the war.

Climo, Shirley. *A Month of Seven Days.* HarperCollins, 1987. A southern girl tries to save her family from a Yankee captain who uses their home for his headquarters.

Donahue, John. *An Island Far From Home.* Carolrhoda, 1994. The twelve-year-old son of a Union army doctor corresponds with a fourteen-year-old Confederate soldier imprisoned at George's Island, Massachusetts, and learns about the tragedies of war.

Donald, David Herbert. *Lincoln.* Simon & Schuster, 1995. This book traces Abraham Lincoln's career as a lawyer, politician, statesman, husband, father, and commander. For older readers.

Dorf, Philip. *Highlights and Sidelights of the Civil War.* Southfarm, 1994. A collection of stories, anecdotes, and incidents of the war.

Harwell, Richard B., ed. *The Confederate Reader: How the South Saw the War.* Dover, 1989. This anthology of documents offers a glimpse of life in the South from newspaper accounts of the initial attack on Fort Sumter to an address by Jefferson Davis in 1864. For older readers.

Hastings, William H., ed. *Letters From a Sharpshooter.* Historic Publications, 1993. A collection of letters written to and by seventeen-year-old private "Willie" Greene as he tries to get out of "the biggest mistake of his life" but ends up between the lines, in the very center of the Civil War.

Hunt, Irene. *Across Five Aprils.* Silver Burdett, 1984. The war tears a family and a community apart.

Kassem, Lou. *Listen for Rachel.* Avon, 1986. A young girl from Tennessee finds her life changed during the Civil War.

Kent, Zachary. *The Civil War: "A House Divided."* Enslow, 1994. This book discusses the war and Reconstruction.

Lyman, Darryl. *Civil War Quotations: Including Slogans, Battle Cries, and Speeches.* Combined Books, 1995. The Civil War's most memorable sayings are collected in this book.

Lyon, George Ella. *Cecil's Story.* Orchard, 1991. The story of a young boy left behind while his father serves as a soldier in the Civil War.

Marrin, Albert. *Unconditional Surrender: U.S. Grant and the Civil War.* Atheneum/Simon & Schuster, 1994. A portrait of the Union general who went on to become president.

Marrin, Albert. *Virginia's General: Robert E. Lee and the Civil War.* Atheneum/Simon & Schuster, 1994. A biography that presents the personal and wartime view of one of the important generals.

Meltzer, Milton. *Voices From the Civil War: A Documentary History of the Great American Conflict.* HarperCollins, 1989. Materials from primary and secondary sources are linked by the author's commentary.

Murphy, Jim. *The Boys' War: Confederate and Union Soldiers Talk About the Civil War.* Clarion, 1990. Using diaries, letters, journals, and photographs, this book explores the role of underage boys who fought in the war.

Nixon, Joan Lowery. *A Dangerous Promise.* Delacorte, 1994. Two orphans run away to become Union army drummer boys.

Nixon, Joan Lowery. *Keeping Secrets.* Delacorte, 1995. This book is part of the "Orphan Train Adventures" series about the Kelly family in the 1800s.

O'Dell, Scott. *The Two Hundred Ninety.* Houghton Mifflin, 1976. A young boy becomes a crewman aboard the Confederate ship *Alabama.*

Poe, Clarence, ed. *True Tales of the South at War: How Soldiers Fought and Families Lived, 1861–1865.* Dover, 1995. This anthology re-creates life in the South during the war with primary documents, including letters, diary entries, and commentaries by children. For older readers.

Ray, Delia. *Behind the Blue and Gray: The Soldier's Life in the Civil War.* Lodestar, 1991. This book portrays the everyday life of the common soldier with more than fifty early photographs of soldiers at work and play.

Ray, Delia. *A Nation Torn: The Story of How the Civil War Began.* Lodestar, 1990. Vintage photographs and prints enhance this account of the issues and events that led to the war.

Robertson, James I., Jr. *Civil War! America Becomes One Nation.* Knopf, 1992. An overview that explores the major battles, military leaders, and effects of the war on the country.

Sandler, Martin W. *Civil War.* HarperCollins, 1995. More than one hundred photographs and prints from the Library of Congress bring the Civil War to life.

Smith, Carter. *Prelude to War.* Millbrook, 1993. The events leading up to the Civil War are documented with reproductions of photographs and prints.

Wisler, G. Clifton. *Mr. Lincoln's Drummer.* Lodestar, 1994. The story of eleven-year-old Willie Johnston, who became a drummer boy and was the youngest person to receive the Medal of Honor.

Young, Robert. *The Emancipation Proclamation: Why Lincoln Really Freed the Slaves.* Dillon, 1995. This book suggests military, political, and moral reasons for Lincoln's Emancipation Proclamation.

Battles

Beatty, Patricia. *Charley Skedaddle.* Morrow, 1987. A Union drummer boy rethinks his ideas about the glory of war.

Beller, Susan Provost. *To Hold This Ground: A Desperate Battle at Gettysburg.* McElderry, 1995. The many smaller battles within the larger Battle of Gettysburg are explored.

Fleischman, Paul. *Bull Run.* HarperCollins, 1993. This historical novel consists of vignettes focusing on the lives and thoughts of sixteen people who participated in the Civil War.

Fleming, Thomas. *Band of Brothers: West Point in the Civil War.* Walker, 1988. A fictionalized portrait of several West Point graduates and their roles in the war.

Fritz, Jean. *Just a Few Words, Mr. Lincoln: The Story of the Gettysburg Address.* Putnam, 1993. A close-up study of Abraham Lincoln's Gettysburg Address and his family life. For younger readers.

Fritz, Jean. *Stonewall.* Putnam, 1979. This biography documents Thomas "Stonewall" Jackson's military career.

Gauch, Patricia Lee. *Thunder at Gettysburg.* Putnam, 1990. A fictionalized account of the battle through the eyes of a young girl who is inadvertently drawn into the war.

Haskins, Jim. *The Day Fort Sumter Was Fired On: A Photo History of the Civil War.* Scholastic, 1995. This book traces the course of the war from Bull Run to Robert E. Lee's eventual surrender at Appomattox Court House, Virginia.

Johnson, Neil. *The Battle of Gettysburg.* Four Winds, 1989. An account of the reenactment of the Battle of Gettysburg that brought together fourteen thousand people in 1988.

Keith, Harold. *Rifles for Watie.* HarperCollins, 1957. This Newbery Medal book tells the story of a young boy's wartime experiences.

Lincoln, Abraham. *The Gettysburg Address.* Houghton Mifflin, 1995. Lincoln's famous words are illustrated in black-and-white drawings by Michael McCurdy.

Murphy, Jim. *The Long Road to Gettysburg.* Clarion, 1992. The Battle of Gettysburg from the points of view of two young soldiers.

Perez, N.A. *The Slopes of War.* Houghton Mifflin, 1984. A young soldier from West Virginia fights against his relatives in the Battle of Gettysburg.

Tracey, Patrick Austin. *Military Leaders of the Civil War.* Facts On File, 1993. This collection recounts the lives and achievements of eight commanders from the Union and the Confederacy.

Reconstruction

Beatty, Patricia. *Be Ever Hopeful, Hannalee.* Morrow, 1988. A southern working-class family begins to rebuild after the war.

Calvert, Patricia. *Bigger.* Scribner, 1994. The story of a young boy's search for his father at the end of the war.

Cox, Clinton. *The Forgotten Heroes: The Story of the Buffalo Soldiers.* Scholastic, 1993. How these African Americans helped open the West.

Hakim, Joy. *A History of Us: Reconstruction and Reform.* Oxford University, 1994. One volume in a series that explores the history of America.

Lyons, Mary E. *Stitching Stars: The Story Quilts of Harriet Powers.* Scribner, 1993. A story quilt serves as a diary of the spiritual life of a former slave in 1886.

Mettger, Zak. *Reconstruction: America After the Civil War.* Lodestar, 1994. A chronicle of how the country began to rebuild.

Reeder, Carolyn. *Shades of Gray.* Macmillan, 1989. A young boy comes to term with his uncle's choice to be a conscientious objector.

Stalcup, Brenda, ed. *Reconstruction.* Greenhaven, 1995. This volume in the "Opposing Viewpoints" series details Reconstruction and the growing power of African Americans.

Civil War Sites

Davis, William C. *Civil War Parks: The Story Behind the Scenery.* KC Publications, 1995. This book covers twenty-six Civil War–related sites of the National Park Service.

Davis, William. *Gettysburg: The Story Behind the Scenery.* KC Publications, 1995. Learn how Gettysburg National Military Park developed and the history behind the bloody battle there.

Waldron, Larry. *Lincoln Parks: The Story Behind the Scenery.* KC Publications, 1995. This book explores the seven National Park Service sites honoring Abraham Lincoln.

African Americans

Armstrong, Jennifer. *Steal Away.* Orchard, 1992. A novel about the friendship between a Vermont child and her slave.

Banim, Lisa. *A Thief on Morgan's Plantation.* Silver Moon, 1995. As the Civil War begins, young Constance Morgan is sent south from Philadelphia to live with relatives she has never met. Soon after she arrives, she finds herself embroiled in a conflict in which a young slave is accused of stealing a family heirloom.

Beatty, Patricia. *Who Comes With Cannons?* Morrow, 1992. Truth is orphaned and sent to live with her uncle's family, who are part of the Underground Railroad.

Berry, James. *Ajeemah and His Sons.* HarperCollins, 1992. A novel that portrays the early slave trade in Jamaica.

Bial, Raymond. *The Underground Railroad.* Houghton Mifflin, 1995. A historic look at the Underground Railroad and some of the stories of slaves who escaped to the North. A map of the railroad and an antislavery chronology are included.

Blos, Joan. *A Gathering of Days: A New England Girl's Journal, 1830–1832*. Scribner, 1979. The diary of a young girl who befriends a runaway slave and struggles with her conscience.

Chu, Daniel, and Bill Shaw. *Going Home to Nicodemus: The Story of an African American Frontier Town and the Pioneers Who Settled It*. Julian Messner, 1994. The story of the first all–African American town on the Great Plains.

Collier, James Lincoln, and Christopher Collier. *With Every Drop of Blood*. Delacorte, 1994. An adventure story of an unlikely friendship that develops when a white Confederate soldier is captured by a band of African American Union soldiers.

Cooper, Michael L. *From Slave to Civil War Hero: The Life and Times of Robert Smalls*. Lodestar, 1994. Smalls fought for the Union, campaigned for equal rights, and was elected to the U.S. Congress.

Cox, Clinton. *Undying Glory*. Scholastic, 1993. The history of the Fifty-fourth Massachusetts Colored Infantry.

Everett, Gwen. *John Brown: One Man Against Slavery*. Rizzoli, 1993. This story is told from the point of view of Brown's daughter Annie.

Forrester, Sandra. *Sound the Jubilee*. Lodestar, 1995. The story of three hundred freed slaves who lived on Roanoke Island, North Carolina, during the Civil War.

Fox, Paula. *The Slave Dancer*. Macmillan, 1973. A white cabin boy recounts the horrifying details of life aboard a slave ship.

Fritz, Jean. *Brady*. Peter Smith, 1960. A novel about the Underground Railroad told by a young white boy who helps African American slaves move from one station to the next.

Fritz, Jean. *Harriet Beecher Stowe and the Beecher Preachers*. Putnam, 1994. A biography of the famous author of *Uncle Tom's Cabin*.

Goldman, Martin. *Nat Turner and the Southampton Revolt of 1831*. Watts, 1992. Explores Turner's early years as a slave and the bloody events of his 1831 revolt.

Hamilton, Virginia. *Anthony Burns: The Defeat and Triumph of a Fugitive Slave*. Knopf, 1988. An account of a runaway slave in 1854 Boston.

Hamilton, Virginia. *Many Thousand Gone: African Americans From Slavery to Freedom*. Knopf, 1993. A collection of original slave narratives that recount a courageous struggle for freedom.

Hansen, Joyce. *The Captive*. Scholastic, 1994. This story follows young Kofi from his years as a slave in Massachusetts to his later life of freedom.

Hansen, Joyce. *Which Way Freedom?* Walker, 1986. This novel describes the contributions of African American soldiers to the Union cause.

Haskins, Jim. *Get on Board: The Story of the Underground Railroad*. Scholastic, 1993. A comprehensive look at the Underground Railroad and the stories behind many journeys.

Hurmence, Belinda. *A Girl Called Boy*. Houghton Mifflin, 1982. A young African American girl is mysteriously transported to the mid-1800s and finds out firsthand the tragedies of slavery.

Katz, William Loren. *Breaking the Chains: Afro-American Slave Resistance*. Atheneum, 1990. This book documents the heroism of slaves before and during the Civil War.

King, Wilma. *Toward the Promised Land: From Uncle Tom's Cabin to the Onset of the Civil War*. Chelsea House, 1995. This book is part of the "Milestones in Black American History" series.

Lester, Julius. *Long Journey Home: Stories From Black History*. Dial, 1993. A collection of stories about African American slaves.

Lyons, Mary E. *Letters From a Slave Girl: The Story of Harriet Jacobs*. Scribner, 1992. This novel is told through Jacobs's letters describing her life in slavery and her dreams of freedom.

McFeely, William S. *Sapelo's People: A Long Walk Into Freedom*. Norton, 1995. A sensitive portrait of the journey from slavery to freedom of the people of this island. For older readers.

Meltzer, Milton. *All Times, All Peoples: A World History of Slavery*. HarperCollins, 1980. A history of slavery and attempts to explain its cause.

Meltzer, Milton. *The Black Americans: A History in Their Own Words*. HarperCollins, 1984. This collection of primary source documents gives an overview of the African American struggle before and after the Civil War.

Meltzer, Milton, ed. *Frederick Douglass: In His Own Words*. Harcourt Brace & Co., 1995. The Civil War as seen in Douglass's writings and speeches. For older readers.

Mettger, Zak. *Till Victory Is Won: Black Soldiers in the Civil War*. Lodestar, 1994. The story of the Fifty-fourth Massachusetts Colored Infantry and other brave African American regiments and individuals.

Petry, Ann. *Harriet Tubman: Conductor on the Underground Railroad*. HarperCollins, 1996. A portrait of one of the pioneers of the Underground Railroad.

Piggins, Carol Ann. *A Multicultural Portrait of the Civil War*. Marshall Cavendish, 1993. African Americans, immigrants, and Native Americans discuss the causes of the war and their lives.

Polacco, Patricia. *Pink and Say*. Philomel, 1994. A heart-wrenching picture book for older readers about an African American Union soldier's rescue of a white comrade who was left for dead.

Robinet, Harriette Gillem. *If You Please, President Lincoln*. Atheneum, 1995. This historical novel documents a fourteen-year-old slave's journey to a small island off Haiti, where, instead of freedom, he finds he is part of a colonization project.

Rogers, James. *The Antislavery Movement*. Facts On File, 1994. A chronicle of the activism behind the antislavery and civil rights movements.

Schlissel, Lillian. *Black Frontiers: A History of African-American Heroes in the Old West*. Simon & Schuster, 1995. The story of African Americans who settled the West from 1865 to the early 1900s.

Washington, Booker T. *Up From Slavery: An Autobiography*. Airmont, 1965. The famous story of an eloquent former slave.

Yates, Elizabeth. *Amos Fortune, Free Man.* Dutton, 1967. A Newbery Medal book about a slave who was able to purchase his freedom and buy a small farm.

Native Americans

Cottrell, Steve. *Civil War in the Indian Territory.* Pelican, 1995. This book outlines the events that led to the involvement of Native Americans in the war and the effects of their participation.

Hauptman, Laurence M. *The Iroquois and the Civil War: From Battlefield to Reservation.* Syracuse University, 1992.

Women

Burchard, Peter. *Charlotte Forten: A Black Teacher in the Civil War.* Crown, 1995. This biography is based on the letters and diaries of Charlotte Forten, the daughter of prominent abolitionists.

Chang, Ina. *A Separate Battle: Women and the Civil War.* Lodestar, 1991. Brief biographies of Angelina Grimké, Sojourner Truth, Harriet Tubman, Louisa May Alcott, and Mary Chesnut, with a discussion of women's roles in the war.

Collins, David R. *Shattered Dreams: The Story of Mary Todd Lincoln.* Morgan Reynolds, 1994. The tragedies of Mary Lincoln's life unfold in this biography.

Colman, Penny. *Spies! Women in the Civil War.* Shoe Tree, 1992. A collection of brief sketches of Belle Boyd, Rose O'Neal Greenhow, and other women spies.

Hamilton, Leni. *Clara Barton.* Chelsea House, 1988. This biography documents Barton's early days setting up supply camps during the Civil War and her involvement in the American Red Cross.

Houston, Gloria. *Mountain Valor.* Philomel, 1994. This story is based on the life of Matilda Houston, one of the author's ancestors, who masqueraded as a boy to protect her family's farm in Appalachia.

Lyon, George Ella. *Here and Then.* Orchard/Jackson, 1994. A realistic novel about a girl who takes part in a Civil War reenactment and discovers the plight of Eliza Hoskins, a nurse during the war.

Ray, Delia. *A Separate Battle: Women in the Civil War.* Lodestar, 1991. Details women's experiences during the war as slaves, abolitionists, women's rights leaders, teachers, and refugees.

Reilly, Wayne E., ed. *Sarah Jane Foster: Teacher of the Freedmen. A Diary and Letters.* University Press of Virginia, 1990.

Reit, Seymour. *Behind Rebel Lines: The Incredible Story of Emma Edmonds, Civil War Spy.* Harcourt Brace & Co., 1988. The fictionalized biography of a feminist patriot who posed as a Confederate soldier to spy on the Union army.

Rutberg, Becky. *Mary Lincoln's Dressmaker.* Walker, 1995. This biography weaves together the life stories of Mary Todd Lincoln and Elizabeth Hobbs Keckley and their remarkable friendship. For older readers.

Shura, Mary Francis. *Gentle Annie: The True Story of a Civil War Nurse.* Scholastic, 1991. The fictionalized biography of a nurse on the front lines.

Zeinert, Karen. *Elizabeth Van Lew: Southern Belle, Union Spy.* Dillon, 1995. This biography is part of the "People in Focus" series.

The Arts

Alcott, Louisa May. *Little Women.* Little, Brown, 1968. This novel was originally published in 1868 and portrays the sacrifices a family made during the war.

Currie, Stephen. *Music in the Civil War.* Shoe Tree, 1992. A collection of sheet music, etchings, and historical references to composers, musicians, and drummers of the Civil War.

Reef, Catherine. *Walt Whitman.* Clarion, 1995. A biography of one of America's great poets. Whitman was an activist and nurse in the Civil War and wrote about the enormous suffering the war caused.

Stowe, Harriet Beecher. *Uncle Tom's Cabin.* Penguin Classics, 1981.

Photography

Barnard, George. *Photographic Views of Sherman's Campaign.* Dover, 1977.

Freedman, Russell. *Lincoln: A Photobiography.* Clarion, 1987. This photo history covers Abraham Lincoln from boyhood through the presidential years.

Gardner, Alexander. *Gardner's Photographic Sketch Book of the Civil War.* Dover, 1959.

Hamilton, Charles, and Lloyd Ostendorf. *Lincoln in Photographs: An Album of Every Known Pose.* Rev. ed. Morningside, 1996. The most complete collection of Abraham Lincoln's photos.

Russell, Andrew. *Russell's Civil War Photographs.* Dover, 1982.

Sullivan, George. *Matthew Brady, His Life and Photographs.* Cobblehill/Dutton, 1994. This biography of Civil War photographer Mathew Brady documents his technical skill alongside reproductions of his famous portraits of the war's leaders.

DISCOVERY ENTERPRISES

Discovery Enterprises, Ltd., publishes educational materials for students and teachers in grades 3 to 12. The "Perspectives on History Series" focuses on specific periods in American history and includes concise anthologies of primary source documents on each subject, with an overview of the period by the editor. Civil War era titles include *Women in the Civil War: Warriors, Patriots, Nurses, and Spies; Westward Expansion: Exploration and Settlement; The Underground Railroad: Life on the Road to Freedom; Forward Into Light: The Struggle for Woman's Suffrage; Iron Horses Across America: The Transcontinental Railroad; Reconstruction: Binding the Wounds.* These books, available singly or in sets, link American history with classic literature on the subject. Also popular from Discovery Enterprises are original plays for upper-elementary and middle school students, biographies, and curriculum materials for educators. For information or a catalog, contact Discovery Enterprises, Ltd., 31 Laurelwood Drive, Carlisle, MA 01741 (1-800-729-1720).

JOURNALS

The American History Herald. Steck-Vaughn Co., 8701 North MoPac, Austin, TX 78759.

America's Civil War. Cowles History Group, Inc., 741 Miller Drive SE, Suite D-2, Leesburg, VA 22075.

The Children's Chronicle. P.O. Box 1601, Plainville, MA 02762. A newsletter designed to help children understand American history during the 1860s.

The Civil War News. Route 1 Box 36, Tunbridge, VT 05077.

Civil War Times. P.O. Box 8200, Harrisburg, PA 17105-8200.

Prologue: Quarterly of the National Archives. National Archives, Washington, DC 20408. This magazine brings attention to the resources and programs of the National Archives, the regional archives, and the presidential libraries.

TEACHER RESOURCES

The Battle of First Manassas. Teaching With Historic Places. The Preservation Press, National Trust for Historic Preservation, 1785 Massachusetts Avenue NW, Washington, DC 20036. Study personal accounts of soldiers who fought in the first battle of the Civil War and discover how the day set the tone for the many bloody battles to come.

Civil War Cards. Atlas Editions, 33 Houston Drive, Durham, CT 06422. This collection of color-coded index cards documents the war from the beginning of the antislavery movement through Reconstruction.

The Civil War (Jackdaw No. 106) compiled by David Johnson. Jackdaw Publications/Golden Owl Publishing, P.O. Box A03, Amawalk, NY 10501. Replicas of primary source documents, including letters, recruiting notices, and newspaper articles, for classroom use.

The Civil War: Literature Units, Projects, and Activities by Janey Cassidy. Scholastic Professional Books, Scholastic Inc., 555 Broadway, New York, NY 10012-3999.

Civil War Teaching Resource Kit. Museum of American Financial History, 26 Broadway, New York, NY 10004. This multimedia kit focuses on the financial roots of the Civil War. It includes a syllabus of financial events following the conflict and twenty color slides featuring rare items from the original exhibit at the Museum of American Financial History.

Lincoln Life Lincoln-Douglas Debates. National Forensic League, P.O. Box 38, Ripon, WI 54971. High school students debate significant moral and value issues facing society.

Teaching Guide to TAD, Life in the White House During the Civil War. The Family Channel, CIC Dept., P.O. Box 2050, Virginia Beach, VA 23450-2050.

Woman Suffrage Illustrated Timeline. National Women's History Project, 7738 Bell Road, Windsor, CA 95492. The history of the woman suffrage movement is depicted in a dramatic and informative eight-panel display set.

CD-ROMs

The African American Experience CD-ROM. Primary Source Media, Woodbridge, CT 06525. Provides students with insight into the culture and history of African Americans from the beginning of the American slave trade to the Anita Hill hearings.

The Civil War. Primary Source Media, Woodbridge, CT 06525. Offers primary documents and images from 1820 to 1877, with a full examination of the war itself, its causes and repercussions, and Reconstruction.

Civil War: A Nation Divided. Softkey International, 1 Athenaeum Street, Cambridge, MA 02142. A reference tool with a multimedia time line from 1861 to 1866 that puts the war in perspective.

The Civil War: A Newspaper Perspective CD-ROM. Accessible Archives, Inc., 697 Sugartown Road, Malvern, PA 19355. This database contains the full text of major articles from more than twenty-five hundred issues of the *New York Herald, Charleston Mercury,* and *Richmond Enquirer* published between November 1, 1860, and April 30, 1865.

The Civil War CD-ROM. Empire Interactive, United CD-ROM, P.O. Box 159, Savoy, IL 61874. This CD-ROM allows you to plan and fight every major battle and campaign of the war.

Gettysburg Multimedia Battle Simulation. Swifte International, P.O. Box 144586, Coral Gables, FL 33114-4506. This simulation gives you a view of the action from the perspective of a field commander. Background on the battle is available, including clips from the documentary film and Lincoln's Gettysburg Address.

A House Divided: The Lincoln-Douglas Debates and Teacher's Guide. Grafica Multimedia, Inc., 940 Emmett Avenue, Suite 11, Belmont, CA 94002. Weaves together video reenactments, photos, music, illustrations, and political cartoons.

ON THE INTERNET

The Letters of Captain Richard W. Burt. http://www.infinet.com/~1stevens/burt/. This collection of letters presents a view of life in the field with Burt's patriotic war songs and poems

The National Civil War Association. http://ncwa.org/. A northern California nonprofit organization committed to educating the public about the Civil War. The group publishes a schedule of events around the country for the upcoming year.

The United States Civil War Center. http://www.cwc.lsu.edu. The center was created to facilitate the construction of archival databases of Civil War material and to promote the study of the war using a multiperspective approach. The web site currently receives four thousand "hits" a day (internationally) and is linked to more than eight hundred Civil War–related sites.

VIDEOS

Addresses for video sources are as follows: Acorn Media, 7910 Woodmont Avenue, Suite 350, Bethesda, MD 20814. Mastervision, 969 Park Avenue, New York, NY 10028. PBS Video, 1320 Braddock Place, Alexandria, VA 22314.

The Civil War. Florentine Films (see PBS), Walpole, New Hampshire, and WETA, Washington, D.C., 1990. This nine-part series by Ken Burns chronicles the war. Includes teacher's guide.

Civil War: The Fiery Trial. Acorn, 1988.

The Civil War Educator's Enhanced PBS Video Disc. PBS, 1994. A fully integrated teaching tool that includes a teacher's planning book, lesson plans, and a shortened version of Ken Burns's film *The Civil War* on videocassette.

Frederick Douglass: When the Lion Wrote History. PBS, 1994. An in-depth look at the life of one of America's most influential men.

Ironclads: The Monitor and the Merrimac. Acorn, 1988.

The Massachusetts 54th Colored Infantry. PBS, 1991. Relive the story of this African American regiment. Includes teacher's guide.

One Woman, One Vote. PBS, 1995. Follow the woman suffrage movement from the Seneca Falls convention in 1848 to the passage of the Nineteenth Amendment in 1920. Includes teacher's guide.

Robert E. Lee: Civil War Generals. Acorn, 1989.

Roots of Resistance — A Story of the Underground Railroad. PBS, 1989. Travel the secret Underground Railroad used by escaped slaves in the mid-1800s. Includes teacher's guide.

Smithsonian's Great Battles of the Civil War. Mastervision, 1994. This seven-volume video series puts you on the battlefield for a look at the military, political, and social history of the Civil War.

Ulysses S. Grant: Civil War Generals. Acorn, 1989.

PLACES TO VISIT

The Abraham Lincoln Museum, Lincoln Memorial University, Harrogate, Tennessee. This museum has one of the largest collections of Lincoln memorabilia, manuscripts, and books.

Appomattox Court House National Historical Park, Virginia. Restored village where Generals Lee and Grant met on April 9, 1865. Highlights include the reconstructed McLean House, where the generals signed the surrender papers, and Surrender Triangle, where the Confederates stacked their arms three days later.

Arlington House, The Robert E. Lee Memorial, Arlington National Cemetery, Arlington, Virginia. The home of General Robert E. Lee has been restored to its appearance in 1861.

Black History Museum and Cultural Center of Virginia, Richmond, Virginia. Virginia's African American history and culture are documented with artifacts, limited editions, prints, artwork, and photographs.

Chickamauga and Chattanooga National Military Park, Fort Oglethorpe, Georgia; *Lookout Mountain*, Lookout Mountain, Tennessee. The nation's first and largest national military park commemorates the Civil War battles that were fought in the Chattanooga area during the fall of 1863.

Confederate Museum, New Orleans, Louisiana. A military museum housed in Memorial Hall includes some of the personal effects of Jefferson Davis, Robert E. Lee, and other Civil War leaders.

Ford's Theatre, Washington, D.C. An extensive collection of items relating to Abraham Lincoln's life and death is on display.

Fort Sumter National Monument, Sullivan's Island, South Carolina. Visit the ruins of the fort and a museum that includes a model of the fort as it looked in 1861.

General Grant National Memorial, New York, New York. Also known as Grant's Tomb, this is the burial site of Ulysses and Julia Grant. The memorial houses Grant memorabilia, exhibit rooms, and a library.

Gettysburg National Military Park, Gettysburg, Pennsylvania. Preserved site of the war's most famous battle.

Harpers Ferry National Historic Park, Harpers Ferry, West Virginia. The park includes John Brown's "fort," a reconstructed village, and the Robert Harper home.

Hollywood Cemetery, Richmond, Virginia. Burial site of famous historical figures such as Presidents James Monroe and John Tyler, Jefferson Davis, and J.E.B. Stuart. Eighteen thousand Confederate soldiers are buried here.

Lee's Retreat: From Petersburg to Appomattox, The Final Days of the Civil War, Petersburg to Appomattox, Virginia. This twenty-stop driving tour through six counties follows the route of General Lee's retreat at the end of the Civil War.

Lincoln Home, Springfield, Illinois. The only home America's sixteenth president ever owned. Other Lincoln sites to visit in Springfield include *Lincoln Tomb*, Oak Ridge Cemetery; *Lincoln's New Salem*, a reconstructed historic village in the town where Lincoln lived from 1831 to 1837; and *Old State Capitol*, Downtown Mall, where an original copy of the Gettysburg Address is on display.

Lincoln Museum, Fort Wayne, Indiana. This museum displays one of the world's largest collections of Lincoln memorabilia, including thousands of books, documents, and photographs.

Museum of the Confederacy, Richmond, Virginia. An extensive collection of Confederate memorabilia, including the uniform and sword worn by Robert E. Lee for his surrender at Appomattox Court House. Contact the museum for information about Civil War Day Camps.

Petersburg National Battlefield, Petersburg, Virginia. Includes driving tours of the siege lines, walking tours at significant locations, and a visitors center.

Richmond National Battlefield Park, Richmond, Virginia. The National Park Service commemorates several Civil War battles of the 1862 Peninsular Campaign and the 1864 Richmond-Petersburg Campaign.

Shiloh National Military Park and Cemetery, Shiloh, Tennessee. The best-preserved Civil War battlefield includes a museum, two hundred artillery pieces, and one hundred fifty monuments of the Battle of Shiloh.

The United States Civil War Center, Louisiana State University, Baton Rouge, Louisiana. The center houses a number of original Edwin Forbes etchings from his *Life of the Great Army*, as well as a library focusing on unique works of the Civil War, including subjects such as medicine, sports, and religion explored through poetry, drama, children's fiction, and other sources.

U.S. Grant Home State Historic Site, Galena, Illinois. This memorial to Grant has been restored to its appearance in the 1870s.

Vicksburg National Military Park, Vicksburg, Mississippi. This park has a sixteen-mile tour road through Union and Confederate battle lines and the largest Civil War cemetery in existence.

Virginia Historical Society, Richmond, Virginia. Dramatic Civil War murals and a comprehensive collection of Virginia history.

The White House of the Confederacy, Richmond, Virginia. Home to Confederate president Jefferson Davis.